DRAMA AND THE DEATH OF GOD

DRAMA AND THE DEATH OF GOD

SECULARITY ON STAGE FROM ANTIQUITY TO SHAKESPEARE

JOHN PARKER

CORNELL UNIVERSITY PRESS
Ithaca and London

Copyright © 2025 by John Parker

All rights reserved. Except for brief quotations in a review, this book, or parts thereof, must not be reproduced in any form without permission in writing from the publisher. For information, address Cornell University Press, Sage House, 512 East State Street, Ithaca, New York 14850. Visit our website at cornellpress.cornell.edu.

First published 2025 by Cornell University Press

Library of Congress Cataloging-in-Publication Data

Names: Parker, John, 1972– author
Title: Drama and the death of God : secularity on stage from antiquity to Shakespeare / John Parker.
Description: Ithaca : Cornell University Press, 2025. | Includes bibliographical references and index.
Identifiers: LCCN 2025016453 (print) | LCCN 2025016454 (ebook) | ISBN 9781501785283 hardcover | ISBN 9781501785290 paperback | ISBN 9781501785306 pdf | ISBN 9781501785313 epub
Subjects: LCSH: Drama—History and criticism | Secularism in literature | Skepticism in literature | Religion and drama | LCGFT: Literary criticism
Classification: LCC PN1647 .P37 2025 (print) | LCC PN1647 (ebook) | DDC 809.2/984—dc23/eng/20250825
LC record available at https://lccn.loc.gov/2025016453
LC ebook record available at https://lccn.loc.gov/2025016454

And Cain said to his brother Abel, "There is no judgment, and there is no judge, and there is no other world, and there is no giving of a good reward to the just, and there is no retribution exacted from the wicked."

—*Targum Neofiti*, Genesis 4:8 (first century CE)

It is a miserable story: man seeks a principle through which he can despise men—he invents a world so as to be able to slander and bespatter this world: in reality, he reaches every time for nothingness and construes nothingness as "God," as "truth," and in any case as judge and condemner of *this* state of being.

—Friedrich Nietzsche, *The Will to Power* (1906)

The skeptical point of view has been common to the intellectual strata of every period.

—Max Weber, *Economy and Society* (1922)

Contents

Note on Texts and Translations   ix

Abbreviations   x

Introduction: Unbelief, Secularity,
Secularization   1

1. The Birth of Unbelief   21

2. Egypt and the Invention of the *Saeculum*   40
   Unbelief and the World—Enlightenment
   and the Flight from Egypt—The Flight to
   Egypt and the Destruction of Idols—*Ludus
   de Rege Aegypti*—Egypt in *Antony and
   Cleopatra*

3. The Secularization of the Liturgy   94
   Peter of Blois and the Music of
   Egypt—The Birth of Liturgy from the
   Spirit of Music—The *Ave Maria* as
   Ludus—The Doubts of Archisynagogus
   and the Devil

4. The Disenchantment of Astrology   143
   Yahweh Versus the Sky Gods—The
   Magi in the *Carmina Burana*—Medieval
   Optics and the Annunciation In
   Vitro—The Secularization of
   Benediktbeuern Abbey

5. *King Lear* and the Copernican Revolution   182
   The Disenchantment of the World—Theater, Astronomy, and Magic—Kepler and the King's Men—The Maidenliest Star in the Firmament

6. Medicine and the Secularization of Miracles   226
   The War Against Miracles—The Birth of an Asylum—Hippocratic Medicine and the Madness of Jesus—Medicine and the Process of Canonization—Hysteria and the Madness of Kings—Miracles and the Theater of Mind

   Epilogue: Secularization After Shakespeare   269

   Acknowledgments   *289*
   Index   *291*

Note on Texts and Translations

In all quotations I have regularized u/v, vv, and i/j, shortened the long s, expanded abbreviations, and eliminated superfluous italics. Spelling and capitalization have been standardized with the exception of early modern book titles, medieval Latin, Middle English, and Middle German. When dealing with non-English texts I cite the original first and then an available translation whenever possible, noting only the most significant modifications. Translations of the *Carmina Burana* are my own, but I have benefited from—and in places echoed—the work of Stephen Wright, P. G. Walsh, E. D. Blodgett, Roy Arthur Swanson, Konrad Vollman, David Bevington, Peter Dronke, and David Traill. Poems and plays copied into the manuscript by later hands—in some cases on pages that became detached—are cited with the customary asterisk (CB*). Except where noted, all translations of scripture are taken from the NRSV with reference to the *Biblia Hebraica Stuttgartensia* and the twenty-eighth edition of the Nestle-Aland *Novum Testamentum Graece*. I have reproduced the numbering of the Psalms according to the cited translation. I transliterate Greek in the main text but not in the notes if it would make tracing a reference more difficult. All quotations of Shakespeare are taken from individual volumes in the third series of the Arden Shakespeare. I specify the quarto (Q) and folio (F) texts of *King Lear* only when the wording differs.

ABBREVIATIONS

ANF	*Ante-Nicene Fathers*, 10 vols. (Grand Rapids, MI: Eerdmans, 1950–53).
CB	*Carmina Burana: Mit Benutzung der vorarbeiten Wilhelm Meyers*, ed. Alfons Hilka and Otto Schumann, 2 vols. in 4 parts (Heidelberg: Carl Winter, 1930– 1970).
CCCM	Corpus Christianorum, Continuatio Mediaevalis (Turnhout: Brepols, 1971–)
CCSL	Corpus Christianorum, Series Latina (Turnhout: Brepols, 1953–).
CSEL	Corpus Scriptorum Ecclesiasticorum Latinorum (Vienna, 1866–).
DR	*The New Testament of Jesus Christ, Translated Faithfully into English out of the Authentical Latin* (Rheims, 1582); *The Holie Bible Faithfully Translated into English, out of the Authentical Latin* (Douai, 1609).
DR 1914	*The Holy Bible Translated from the Latin Vulgate* (Baltimore, MD: John Murphy, 1914).
KGW	Johannes Kepler, *Gesammelte Werke*, ed. Walther von Dyck and Max Caspar, 26 vols. (Munich: C. H. Beck, 1937–2017).
KL	*King Lear*, ed. R. A. Foakes (London: Arden Shakespeare, 2001).
LCL	Loeb Classical Library.
LXX	*Septuaginta: Id est Vetus Testamentum graece iuxta LXX interpretes*, ed. Alfred Rahlfs, rev. Robert Hanhart (Stuttgart: Deutsche Bibelgesellschaft, 2006). English points of reference in *The Septuagint Version of the Old Testament with an English Translation* (London, 1879).
MWG	Max Weber, *Gesamtausgabe*, ed. Horst Baier et al. (Tübingen: Mohr, 1984–).
NKGW	Friedrich Nietzsche, *Werke: Kritische Gesamtausgabe*, ed. Giorgio Colli and Mazzino Montinari (Berlin: de Gruyter, 1967–).

PG	Patrologia cursus completus, Series Graeca, 161 vols. (Paris, 1857–66).
PL	Patrologia cursus completus, Series Latina, 221 vols. (Paris, 1844–64).
Vetus Latina	*Vetus Latina: Die Reste der altlateinischen Bibel nach Petrus Sabatier neu gesammelt und herausgegeben von Erzabtei Beuron* (Freiburg: Herder, 1949–).
Vulg.	*Biblia sacra iuxta vulgatam versionem*, ed. Robert Weber et al. (Stuttgart: Deutsche Bibelgesellschaft, 1994).
WSA	*Works of Saint Augustine: A Translation for the 21st Century*, ed. John E. Rotelle et al. (Hyde Park, NY: New City Press, 1990–).
Wycliffite	*The Holy Bible, Containing the Old and New Testaments: With the Apocryphal Books, in the earliest English Versions*, 4 vols. (Oxford, 1850).
York	*The York Plays: A Critical Edition of the York Corpus Christi Play as Recorded in British Library Additional MS 35290*, ed. Richard Beadle, 2 vols. (Oxford: Published for the Early English Text Society by the Oxford University Press, 2009–2013).
Young	Karl Young, *The Drama of the Medieval Church*, 2 vols. (Oxford: Clarendon, 1933).

DRAMA AND THE DEATH OF GOD

Introduction
Unbelief, Secularity, Secularization

One argument about secularization prevalent in studies of post-Reformation theater says that the difficulty of believing in a transcendent god becomes acute around the time of *King Lear*. This monumental shift, we're told, explains the play's exceptional, tragic power. Another argument says that *Lear* promotes a Christian worldview as yet untroubled by secular challenges to faith. We virtually never hear that doubting the existence of a transcendent god is as old as the Bible, or that medieval Christians transmitted to Shakespeare an ancient fascination with unbelief and secularity, but those are the claims I am going to make here.

The word *unbelief* first enters the English language in the mid-twelfth century and is used in the Old English and Wycliffite Bibles to translate *incredulitas*. According to scripture, "the sones of unbileve" disregard God while devoting themselves entirely to their appetites—"fornycacioun, unclennesse, leccherie, yvel covetyse, and avarice"—thereby inviting God's "wraththe" (Col 3:6, Wycliffite). By the time of the earliest English drama, a millennium of exegesis had made these *increduli* more or less synonymous with *infideles*: pagans, Jews, heretics, Muslims, or anyone else who lived without a feel for the real divinity. On account of their obliviousness, these people had no way to escape from a godless, secular world. Nor did they want to.

The words *secular* and *secularity* enter the language in the late thirteenth and fourteenth centuries, respectively, and also take their definition from the

Latin Bible. The root term, *saeculum*, likely derives from an Indo-European verb meaning *to sow* and includes *semen* and *seed* among its cognates.¹ Before Christianity, *saeculum* denotes a species, a breed, or a unit of time linked to sexual reproduction, as when Lucretius speaks of the "mortal generations" (*mortalia saecla*) that come and go in regular succession without fail.² Secular things are fleeting, if also cyclical: hence, for example, the "secular games" (*saeculares ludi*), which occurred at an interval of one hundred years.³ When multiplied ad infinitum, this form of measurement appears in the Old Latin Bible and Vulgate as an expression for eternity—"*in saecula saeculorum*"—but continues to signify mortal finitude when applied to the "worldes [*saecula*]" (Heb 1:2, DR) that God created from nothing at the onset of time and destined for annihilation at the *consummatio saeculi* (Mt 13:39–40, Vulg.). When used interchangeably with *mundus* to describe the sublunar world of strife and enjoyment, *saeculum* means an unsanctified sphere opposed to religion: "For all that is in the world [*in saeculo*]—the desire of the flesh and the desire of the eyes and worldly ambition [*ambitio saeculi*]—comes not from the Father but from the world. And the world is passing away" (1 Jn 2:16–17a, Vetus Latina). Corrupted and corrupting, the *saeculum* stands for everything that the gospel asks you to transcend.

Few threats to the faith have loomed larger over the course of the last two millennia than the temptation to find in secular pursuits the ultimate source of value: "For the cares of the world [*saeculi*]," Jesus warns, "and the deceitfulness of riches, and the lusts after other things entering in choke the Word, and it is made fruitless" (Mk 4:19, DR 1914). The seeds of secularity perpetually threaten to outgrow and stifle the seed of the gospel. Even Christians who outwardly accept the Word can find themselves "loving this world [*diligens hoc saeculum*]" (2 Tim 4:9, DR) so intensely that they turn their backs on Christ and come to live as they had before converting: "without God in this world [*in hoc mundo*]" (Eph 2:12, DR). Because they lack true religion, that is, people outside the church are considered secularists and "atheists" (*atheoi*)—the Greek term in Ephesians translated here "without God." The faithful, by contrast, are supposed to avoid unbelief alongside "impiety and worldly desires [*saecularia desideria*]" in order to "live soberly and justly and

---

1. Charleton Lewis, *An Elementary Latin Dictionary* (Oxford: Oxford University Press, 1993; originally published in 1891), 744–5, 948. Further citations and discussion in William N. West, "Titus's Infinite Jest," in *Sacred and Secular Transactions in the Age of Shakespeare*, ed. Katherine Steele Brokaw and Jay Zysk (Evanston, IL: Northwestern University Press, 2019), 27–47, esp. 33.
2. Lucretius, *De rerum natura* 5.791, 805, 1238 (LCL).
3. Suetonius, *De vita Caesarum*, Vitellius 7.2 and index, under *saeculares ludi* (LCL).

godly in this world [*in hoc saeculo*]" (Titus 2:12, DR). The key to their spiritual life is to be in the *saeculum*, but not of it. "It does not matter where you are in the world," writes Tertullian. "You, who are beyond the world!"[4]

Scripture abounds with condemnations of people who so love the world that they find in it a substitute for God. Their idols have to be denounced as mere "human precepts" (Is 29:13; Mk 7:7), "works of the hand" (Ps 135:15; Ws 14:8; Acts 7:41), and "beings that are not gods" (Gal 4:8), such as "the sun, the moon, and the stars" (Dt 4:19), or exaggerated memories of the dead (Ws 14:15). Only by dissolving the objects of others' devotion into the void of secular ephemera through literal and figurative acts of desacralization can a certain type of Christian take the first step toward salvation. The next step is to let the world pass or even hasten it on its way by means of a process that Rudolf Bultmann calls "desecularization" (*Entweltlichung*).[5] You have to let go of the fleshly attachments, the immanent valuations—the mere appearances and transient fictions—so as to stand for once on ground that is hallowed, save for the surrounding adversaries whose fleshly attachments and immanent valuations make your negative, transcendent vision look like the greater vanity. These atheists must be kept in the forefront of your mind as a warning. They are devoted to the gratification inherent in power, money, sex, food, drink, rhetorical language, music, art, natural philosophy—every conceivable form of secular self-enrichment. Their commitment to the world is so resolute as to form a rival school of wisdom, an indictment of everything Christian, and a sore temptation. They routinely appear in Christian dialogues and in dramas related to the liturgy, where medieval believers long scripted and performed the unbelief that was needed to make their faith live.

Christianity came to depend so heavily on unbelief in part because the infidel indifference to God allowed for the development of unsurpassed ways "to evaluate the world [*aestimare saeculum*]" (Ws 13:9, Vulg.). The clergy's investigative branches—the monasteries, the universities, and the awesome inquisitorial apparatus formally centralized in the Papacy by the Fourth Lateran Council (1215)—all relied on natural philosophy to isolate events that might transcend physical law and therefore bear witness to the immediate presence of God. There was no way to prove the occurrence of a miracle,

---

4. *Ad mart.* 2.5 (CCSL 1:4; ANF 3:694): "*in saeculo . . . extra saeculum.*"

5. Rudolf Bultmann, *Theologie des Neuen Testaments* (Tübingen: Mohr, 1953), 422–23, 514; Bultmann, *Theological Dictionary of the New Testament*, ed. Gerhard Friedrich, trans. and ed. Geoffrey W. Bromiley (Grand Rapids, MI: Eerdmans, 1968), 6:224–25.

much less to define the supernatural, without an intimate understanding of the *saeculares litterae* or secular literatures that described the natural world in arithmetical, astronomical, and medical terms. These discourses were cultivated from late antiquity onward, while a much greater portion of Greek learning became the subject of intense focus in Latin Christendom once Arabic texts and translations flooded in from North Africa, Iberia, and the Middle East at the time of the Crusades. By the twelfth century many scholastics were dedicated to the premise that Aristotelian logic and "secular knowledge" (*scientia saecularis*) provided a language of argument and proof that had to be fully integrated into the language of faith, if the faith was going to persuade unbelievers to look beyond the here-and-now world.[6] True objects of veneration had to be established through a highly rationalized, inquisitorial process of evidence gathering and examination whose purpose was to falsify the appearance of supernatural intervention to the furthest possible degree, so that whatever escaped elimination might have an irrefragable claim to legitimacy. True sanctity required a thorough debunking of error, illusion, and mere theatrics.

Christians also required theatrics, however. Beginning with the Fathers, the term *theatrum* exemplified more than any other aspect of ancient religion the infidel talent for finding momentary fulfillment in *manufacta*, fiction, magic, and fantasy. Such transient satisfaction was precisely what Christians were supposed to reject, and yet there was nothing on which the church depended more than the artificial enchantments of scripted performance. From Augustine onward the concern periodically arose that certain liturgical performances could not encourage anyone to move beyond the *saeculum* because they played primarily to the human appetite for audiovisual stimulants. Augustine himself allowed a cappella music only on the grounds that sensual accommodations had to be made for the weakest members of the assembly if the faith was to thrive—a major concession that would later authorize far more ornate embellishments. After the tenth century, when the liturgy of the high holidays first metastasized into full-blown playacting, the church was frequently transformed into a Dionysian laboratory for investigating the proximity between faith in miracles and a love of theatrical fiction. Such plays were not just a public expression of doubt. They were, in practice, an exploration of the extent to which miracles could be *staged*, and yet,

---

6. Thomas Aquinas, *Expositio super librum Boethii De Trinitate*, ed. Bruno Decker (Leiden: Brill, 1965), 90–97 (Pars 1, q. 2, a. 3); trans. Rose Emmanuella Brennan, *The Trinity and the Unicity of the Intellect* (St. Louis, MO: Herder, 1946), 56–62.

for all their artificiality, still valued. In these performances (to use a Nietzschean terminology) lies were sanctified and illusions affirmed as a needed corrective to the will to truth otherwise rampaging within the church. The puritanical voices critical of such theatrics might well have brought liturgical drama to an early end if their religious virtuosity had not been held in check by scholastic apologies for the restorative pleasure of play (*ludus*). Aquinas and Bonaventure in particular hoped to counterbalance the ethical and conceptual demands of the faith with moments of secular respite, but their fragile compromise lasted only until the outbreak of the Reformation. At that point Protestant animosity to the theatricalization of the liturgy and the performance of miracles reshaped the landscape of Europe—particularly in England, where the dissolution of vast amounts of church property, the insistence that all miracles had ceased, the suppression of the Latin liturgy and of traditional biblical drama enabled the emergence of custom-built, commercial theaters on the secularized grounds of former monastic estates.

Ever since the nineteenth century, the concept of secularization has been central to Western theater history, and to Shakespeare's "iconic role" in it, thanks primarily to German intellectuals.[7] "The more art is secularized [*sich verweltlicht*]," says G. W. F. Hegel, "the more it makes itself at home in the finite things of the world, is satisfied with them, and grants them complete validity, and the artist does well when he portrays them as they are"—a process of secularization epitomized "in Shakespeare's plays."[8] Hegel and his contemporaries were highly sensitized to the topic of secularization on account of having to live, as Shakespeare had, in the aftermath of a massive repurposing of church property. In 1803 religious houses across Bavaria were forcibly converted to profane use through an act of dissolution (*Aufhebung*) that for Hegel was emblematic of how the spirit animating history from the earliest scriptures to the French Revolution discredited every conventional understanding of the sacred.[9] The conversion of the Middle East, North Africa, and Europe had after all similarly required a violent, iconoclastic debunking of accepted pieties. Sacred groves fell, nature was "shorn of gods," magic was demonized; idols were burnt and exposed as godless

---

7. Brian Cummings, *Mortal Thoughts: Religion, Secularity, and Identity in Shakespeare and Early Modern Culture* (Oxford: Oxford University Press, 2013), 8.
8. G. W. F Hegel, *Werke*, ed. Eva Moldenhauer and Karl Markus Michel (Frankfurt am Main: Suhrkamp, 1969), 14:221; English in *Hegel's Aesthetics: Lectures on Fine Art*, trans. T. M. Knox (Oxford: Clarendon, 1975), 1:594 (modified).
9. Karl Löwith, "Hegels Aufhebung der christlichen Religion," in *Hegel und die Aufhebung der Philosophie im 19. Jahrhundert—Max Weber* (Stuttgart: J. B. Metzler, 1988), 116–66.

artworks.¹⁰ From the ashes arose a new "romantic" literature that accentuated "absolute inwardness" and its associated travails, as belatedly captured in Hamlet's "withdrawn inner life."¹¹ Secularization, for Hegel, is inherent to spirit's historical self-estrangement and subsequent self-reconciliation within human consciousness. Christianity functions on this model as "the paradigmatic modern religion" because it pushes humanity away from the immature thinking of traditional reverence into the deeply negative, critical reasoning appropriate to an adult philosophy.¹² If "what makes Hegel modern is his turn to the medieval," that is because for him, as for all of the Jena Romantics, modernity begins with the process of Christianization.¹³

Nineteenth-century German Shakespeareans extended to theater history more generally the secularization thesis first pioneered in Jena: "The Church," writes Hermann Ulrici, "was the birth place of the modern drama."¹⁴ Only artworks touched by "the Christian mind" (x) can reveal the divinity's rational self-realization within the material particulars of human life. Mixing biblical with worldly content in vernacular English, the mystery plays, for example, were "secularized" insofar as they descended "from the supernatural and semi-celestial sphere of the sacred past into the domain of a more earthly humanity" (5, 8). Morality plays underwent the same process by making "plentiful provision for fun and merriment" (6), notwithstanding their outward commitment to the value of sacraments. It is difficult, Ulrici admits, to recognize in these crude early materials "an indispensible step in the progressive development of art [*Kunstentwickelung*]" (8), but recognize them we must if we are to have any hope of understanding the roots of the London commercial stage. Secularization in his account is the achievement of an evolving Christian culture that reaches its apex in the Reformation, with the fully "awakened consciousness of the Christian mind" (16). Enter Shakespeare.

Shakespeare's first scholarly biographer in German, Karl Elze, adopted a similar framework while writing after the earliest German translators of Darwin had used the same word for biological "evolution" (*Entwickelung*) that Ulrici employed for the "development" of art. The theological implica-

---

10. Hegel, *Werke*, 14:137; trans. Knox, 1:524.
11. Hegel, *Werke* 14:129, 208; trans. Knox, 1:519, 584, respectively; see also Margreta de Grazia, *Hamlet Without Hamlet* (Cambridge: Cambridge University Press, 2007).
12. Terry Pinkard, *Hegel: A Biography* (Cambridge: Cambridge University Press, 2000), 293.
13. Andrew Cole, *The Birth of Theory* (Chicago: University of Chicago Press, 2014), 36.
14. Hermann Ulrici, *Shakspeare's Dramatic Art: And His Relation to Calderon and Goethe* (London, 1841; German published in 1839), 1.

tions of natural selection had yet to be settled, according to Elze, but pre-Darwinian models of cultural evolution were without question correct: "Darwinism in the history of creation may still present doubts, but the history of the world and of civilization acknowledges no other than the law of gradual development [*Entwickelung*]."¹⁵ Humans may or may not have been created by God, but theater history in Elze's view clearly shows a "Darwinian" advancement from lower to higher, with the secular London stage serving as drama's ultimate telos: "The dramatic performances [of the mystery plays] were thus step by step thrust back into the streets and on to the market-places, where they became completely secularized, both as regards performers as well as subject" (200). Lay people displaced the clergy in the enactment of biblical, sacramental, and saint plays, while mundane subjects with popular appeal crowded out narrow devotional aims. The Tudor interlude especially contributed to "the secularization of drama" (207), with the end result that Shakespeare no longer felt compelled to condemn the *saeculum* and was able to justify the things that exist "by reason of their very existence"—a position, Elze says, akin to Hegel's (468).

So the story went until 1893, when Wilhelm M. A. Creizenach published the first volume of his monumental *Geschichte des neuen Dramas* (*History of Modern Drama*). Creizenach excludes all mention of Hegel and Darwin while still attempting to explain how Shakespearean drama emerges from a centuries-long process of "evolution" or "development" (*Entwicklung*) whose defining feature is "secularization" (*Verweltlichung*). Creizenach is the first German theater scholar to include in his history the plays of the *Carmina Burana*—a wildly profane manuscript containing materials from the eleventh to thirteenth centuries that was taken from the Benediktbeuern Abbey at the time of its secularization in 1803 and brought to print under that title by its first editor, Johann Andreas Schmeller, in 1847.¹⁶ As a result of reading Schmeller's edition, Creizenach has to move drama's secularization back in

---

15. Karl Elze, *William Shakespeare: A Literary Biography*, trans. L. Dora Schmitz (London, 1888; German published in 1876), 197.
16. Printed in *Bibliothek des Literarischen Vereins in Stuttgart* XVI (Stuttgart, 1847). Tristan E. Franklinos and Henry Hope, the editors of *Revisiting the Codex Buranus: Contents, Contexts, Compositions* (Woodbridge, UK: Boydell & Brewer, 2020), make the puzzling claim that "the manuscript is frequently and erroneously called the *Carmina Burana* ("songs from Benediktbeuern"), a term which properly denotes the lyric contents, not the codex itself" (1). In fact Schmeller's title—which has been retained by every subsequent print edition—means "Bavarian songs" and is a fairly apt description of the codex itself, given its preservation in Bavaria and the way that its layout was designed to accommodate the musical notation appearing in the plays and a great many of the lyrics, as demonstrated by Heike Sigrid Lammers-Harlander in her excellent contribution to this collection (see esp. 252).

time by hundreds of years, into the heart of the twelfth-century liturgy. He notes that the secularity associated with wandering minstrels, for example, is fully incorporated into the Passion and Nativity plays: Mary Magdalene's encomium to the world in advance of conversion, the unbelief of Archisynagogus, and above all the dramatization of the Flight to Egypt, which opens with an "ode to spring in the fresh, world-loving tone of the Vagantes' poetry."[17] In an astonishing reversal of the Exodus narrative—long interpreted by exegetes as a model for renouncing worldly gratification—the Holy Family here flees from the Promised Land into the *saeculum*. Ostensibly a demonstration of Christ's power to destroy what humans idolize—our sensuous abandon, our reverence for secular letters—this episode also licenses clerics to impersonate pagans in church, to erect statues of the gods, to sing erotic lyrics, to praise ancient philosophy (Pythagoras, Socrates, Plato, and Aristotle are all mentioned by name), and to mock Christians: "They are fools," intone the Egyptians, "who say there is one god" (CB 228.V.3). In Christ's conflict with the world, clerics found an excuse to bring secular pageantry and a critique of Christianity into the church.

For much of the twentieth century, Anglophone scholars came to Creizenach's account by way of E. K. Chambers. His attempt at "a little book . . . about Shakespeare" produced two volumes on medieval drama that position secularization as the driving force in drama's evolution while rejecting *tout court* the unilinear, teleological gradualism of Shakespeareans like Ulrici and Elze:

> It must not be supposed that either the tendency to expansion [of the Mass] or the tendency to secularization acted universally and uniformly. The truth is quite otherwise. To the end of the history of the religious drama, the older types, which it threw out as it evolved, coexisted with the newer ones. The Latin tropes and liturgical dramas held their place in church services. And in the vernaculars, side by side with the growing Nativities and Passions, there continued to be acted independent plays of more than one sort . . . numerous plays drawn from hagiological legends . . . never came into connection with the cycles at all. . . . performances continued to be given or superintended by the clergy and their scholars. Priests and monks supplied texts and lent vestments for the lay plays. To the last, the church served from time to time as a theatre.[18]

---

17. Wilhelm M. A. Creizenach, *Geschichte des neueren Dramas* (Halle, 1893), 1:99.
18. E. K. Chambers, *The Mediaeval Stage* (Oxford: Clarendon, 1903), 1:v, 2:96–97, respectively.

What Chambers means by "secularization" is not the disappearance of religious content but rather the infiltration into the church of performance techniques whose shameless appeal to the human appetite for audiovisual stimulation ought to have remained in the *saeculum* according to medieval purists. Chambers has been criticized for giving these moral rigorists too much emphasis, but their voices speak to an ineradicable tension in the liturgy between its transcendental pretensions and material enactment.[19] The introduction of flamboyant histrionics into sacred ritual clearly blurred the boundary between the pagan *theatrum* and the Christian liturgy—to the point that "you would think" (says one shocked observer of participants in a liturgical Nativity staged at Christmas in 1141) "they had come not to prayer but to a theater."[20] Twelfth-century ecclesiastical performances could involve cross-dressing, blackface, and the musical instrumentation whose exclusion was elsewhere required to differentiate the a cappella liturgy from the superficial wonders of secular music drama. Try as authorities might to ban the *ludi theatrales* that threatened to convert Christian worship into a raucous form of play, clerical enthusiasm for embellishing the liturgy was both intense and widespread (*Mediaeval Stage*, 1:341–43).

Shortly after *The Mediaeval Stage* appeared, Max Weber presented in *The Protestant Ethic and the Spirit of Capitalism* (1904/5; revised 1920), a secularization thesis that shares with Chambers's any number of sociological presuppositions and has since become a ubiquitous point of reference in studies of Shakespeare. Chambers and Weber both have a Darwinian outlook insofar as they accept that humans are a type of primate whose evolution can be traced. For both it goes without saying that the biblical account of creation, along with any estimate of the world's age based on Genesis, cannot be supported by credible evidence. In reality, the creator god of the Hebrew Bible came into being at a fairly recent stage of human development and had to overcome alternate ways of accounting for our place in the cosmos—above all the ancient belief that the world is eternal or, if subject to periodic destruction, eternally recurring. Both Chambers and Weber were readers of Nietzsche and therefore had to contend with the further proposition that Abrahamic monotheism has been unusually effective at

---

19. Max Harris, *Sacred Folly: A New History of the Feast of Fools* (Ithaca, NY: Cornell University Press, 2011), 3–5.
20. Chambers, *Mediaeval Stage*, 1:31n7; English in Aelred of Rievaulx, *The Mirror of Charity*, trans. Elizabeth Connor (Kalamazoo, MI: Cistercian Publications, 1990), 211.

training and redirecting our primeval instincts.[21] According to all three, Christianity has had a measurable effect on the human psyche by targeting for reform what Weber calls "the average *habitus* of the human body"[22]— which is to say (in scriptural terminology) our propensity for fornication, idolatry, and greed, among the other vices epitomized by our keenness to eat, drink, and rise up "to play [*ludere*]" (Ex 32:6; 1 Cor 10:7, DR).

Chambers, for his part, focuses exclusively on the "instinct of play" and the "mimetic instinct" while trying to explain how a church opposed to theater on ascetic grounds could come to harbor extravagant performances "in the very bosom" of its rituals.[23] This development, he says, can be interpreted "either as an audacious, and at least partly successful, attempt to wrest the pomps of the devil to a spiritual service, or as an inevitable and ironical recoil of a barred human instinct within the hearts of its gaolers themselves" (ibid., 2:3). Neither of these explanations would have been foreign to the clerical authors studied by Chambers. Most accepted as a matter of course that an intense inner struggle was necessary to reroute the body's animalistic impulses toward morally approved ends. Believers were often asked to make of themselves the staging ground for a lifelong *psychomachia* between Christian virtue and the vices of the flesh, the devil, and the world. That the recommended courses of self-flagellation met with "inevitable and ironical" resistance is attested throughout medieval culture—by the Feast of Fools, the songs and plays of the *Carmina Burana*, the *gaya scienza* of the troubadours, the minstrelsy of Franciscans, and the belly cheer of monks, among many other equally colorful, carnivalesque extravagances.[24] All of these side with the appetites against the taxing requirements that seek to shape believers' passions through ever deepening self-surveillance and internalized controls. For Chambers, any moral regime in the Middle Ages that aimed to curtail the drive to play had to find an approved outlet or risk inciting an unfettered revolt. Either way it contributed to the secularization of the liturgy.

---

21. John Parker, "Who's Afraid of Darwin? Revisiting Chambers and Hardison . . . and Nietzsche," *Journal of Medieval and Early Modern Studies* 40, no. 1 (2010): 7–35; on Weber's debt to Nietzsche, see Wilhelm Hennis, *Max Webers Fragestellung: Studien Zur Biographie des Werkes* (Tübingen: Mohr, 1987), 167–91. For Weber's repeated insistence that biological models based on Darwin cannot replace cultural and social explanations for historical developments of recent millennia, see MWG 1/6:101, 247, 251, and Wolfgang J. Mommsen, *Max Weber and German Politics 1890–1920*, trans. Michael S. Steinberg (Chicago: University of Chicago Press, 1984), 41.

22. MWG 1/22.2:314; English in *Economy and Society: An Outline of Interpretive Sociology*, ed. Guenther Roth and Claus Wittich (Berkeley: University of California Press, 1978), 1:536.

23. Chambers, *Mediaeval Stage*, 1:147, vi; 2:2, respectively.

24. See Noah D. Guynn, *Pure Filth: Ethics, Politics, and Religion in Early French Farce* (Philadelphia: University of Pennsylvania Press, 2020).

Weber is not particularly concerned with the history of theater and drama, but those who are have had reason to consult his work and have often come away with the impression that secularization as a world-historical force is bound up with the rise of capitalism and therefore cannot begin in earnest until after the Reformation. Weber's view is in fact very different. Secularization in the narrow sense of a ruler or military force taking property from a temple, church, or priesthood is found often enough throughout history—as is the ruthless pursuit of profit: "Capitalism and capitalistic enterprises, even with a considerable rationalization of capitalistic calculation, have existed in all civilized countries of the earth so far as economic documents permit us to judge."[25] Weber wrote that sentence after years of scholarly debate between those who refused to call ancient and medieval economies "capitalist" (the so-called primitivist position, advocated most consequentially by Karl Marx) and those who saw abundant evidence of capitalism from antiquity onward (the so-called modernizing position, advocated for example by Eduard Meyer). The through line of Weber's corpus is that capitalism—like secularity—has existed at one time or another in a variety of forms over the course of recorded history, but the forms are not invariably identical. Some elements are unique to antiquity, some to the Middle Ages, some to modernity, and some elements—a money economy, credit, the production and exchange of commodities, tax-farming—are shared. The most ancient Hebrew legislation presupposes each of these, as does Jesus when he acknowledges the power of the *saeculum* to nullify the gospel.[26] "The love of money is the root of all evil" (1 Tim 6:10, AV) because it subjects humans to capitalist predation and—more worrisome still—convinces the faithful to pursue human flourishing in the here-and-now world. "Continued attachment to Mammon," Weber writes in summary of this scriptural truism, "constitutes one of the most difficult impediments to salvation into the Kingdom of God—for attachment to Mammon diverts the individual from religious salvation, the most important thing in the world" (MWG 1/22.2:445; *Economy and Society*, 1:632). Would-be, heretical, and fully lapsed Christians have been forever accused of promoting human economics at the expense of the

---

25. MWG 1/18:108; English in *The Protestant Ethic and the Spirit of Capitalism*, trans. Talcott Parsons (London: Routledge, 1992), 19; cf. MWG 1/23:379–82; *Economy and Society*, 1:164–66; John R. Love, *Antiquity and Capitalism: Max Weber and the Sociological Foundations of Roman Civilization* (London: Routledge, 2005). For ancient secularizations, see MWG 1/6:373, 420, 430, 435, 459; English in *The Agrarian Sociology of Ancient Civilizations*, trans. R. I. Frank (London: Verso, 1998), 79, 119, 126, 130, 223.

26. See *The Bible and Money: Economy and Socioeconomic Ethics in the Bible*, ed. Markus Zehnder and Hallvard Hagelia (Sheffield, UK: Sheffield Phoenix, 2020).

divine *oikonomia*. In fact the ascetic enterprise as formulated by scripture and its earliest Christian exegetes is almost always defined against an unsanctified sphere of economic activity; that is why "the whole history of monasticism is in a certain sense the history of a continual struggle with the problem of the secularizing [*säkularisierenden*] influence of wealth" (MWG 1/18:472; *Protestant Ethic*, 174). Without the antipode of money and the fungible pleasures on offer in the secular market, the ascetic ideal of renouncing the world in pursuit of transcendence has little meaning.

Weber's challenge in *The Protestant Ethic* is to explain how an ascetic religion opposed in principle to secular pursuits could produce so many and such enthusiastic accumulators of wealth. Could it be possible that Christianity's long struggle against Mammon somehow *aided* the development of modern capitalism? That here, too—as in the history of theater—there was an inevitable and ironical recoil to the demands of Christian morality? In the background of this inquiry stands Weber's earlier research into ancient economics, particularly an essay from 1896 on the decline of Roman civilization. The ancient economy began to collapse, he argues, once the imperial army reached the outermost limits of the peoples it could colonize, enslave, and send to inland plantations for the production of luxury goods.[27] This form of capitalism, like its British and American equivalents, asks little of Weber in the way of explanatory analysis. There is nothing peculiar about an institution that maximizes profit by burning through hundreds of millions in "speaking tools"—the ancient term for human chattel—"the way a modern blast furnace consumes coal."[28] Since the legal foundation for New World slavery was already laid in toto by Roman law, what needs explaining, for Weber, is how *unenslaved* humans over the course of intervening millennia could be acculturated to consider manual labor an ethical virtue, rather than a degrading enterprise best accomplished through the violent compulsion of others.[29] Before Christianity, almost no Roman of means thought that work was a path to moral betterment: "All hired workmen whom we pay for mere

---

[27]. MWG 1/6:99-127; trans. Frank, "The Social Causes of the Decline of Ancient Civilization," in *Agrarian Sociology*, 387–411. For a critique of this so-called conquest thesis, see Moses I. Finley, who otherwise adopts many of Weber's insights: *Ancient Slavery and Modern Ideology*, ed. Brent D. Shaw (Princeton, NJ: Markus Wiener, 1998), 191–217.

[28]. MWG 1/6:111; trans. Frank, *Agrarian Sociology*, 398. For the number of enslaved people in the Roman Empire, see Walter Seidel, "Slavery," in *The Cambridge Companion to the Roman Economy*, ed. Seidel (Cambridge: Cambridge University Press, 2012), 89–113.

[29]. See Finley, *Ancient Slavery and Modern Ideology*, 87 (on the ancient legal basis of modern slavery) and 299: "In the context of universal history, free labour, wage labour, not slavery, is *the* peculiar institution."

manual labour," writes Cicero, receive in their pay "a pledge of their slavery" (*De officiis* 1.42, LCL). In antiquity, the difference between those who were legally enslaved and those who were free from all but the pinch of necessity was that formally free workers had no hope of escape or manumission.

Only with the spread of Christianity do legally free people begin to feel that they, too, might be able to work toward "salvation" through "redemption"—ancient terms for the deliverance of war captives from enslavement through the payment of ransom.[30] With Christianity, that is, the conviction becomes widespread that everyone is by nature enslaved to something. There is no point in trying to revolt (Eph 6:5–8); instead, if you want the lightest possible yoke, you should endeavor to become a "slave of Christ" (*doulos*, Rom 1:1, 18; Gal 1:10; Col 4:12). This so-called slave revolt in morality entails not only the ethical triumph of the lowest classes over the values of their masters but the conversion of enslaved and legally free artisans into proselytes for a form of liberty that promotes work as a pathway to virtue and presses incessantly for internalized forms of pacification.[31]

It is in no way lost on Weber that the Benedictine Rule makes labor central to well-regulated, ethical behavior. Here he finds an early example of the Christian propensity to transform veneration of a transcendent deity into organized, rational, worldly activity. In fact Christian asceticism as a whole

> has had a definitely rational character in its highest Occidental forms as early as the Middle Ages, and in several forms even in antiquity. . . . In the rules of St. Benedict, still more with the monks of Cluny, again with the Cistercians, and most strongly the Jesuits, it has become emancipated from planless otherworldliness and irrational self-torture. It had developed a systematic method of rational conduct with the purpose of overcoming the *status naturae*, to free man from the power of irrational impulses and his dependence on the world and on nature. It attempted to subject man to the supremacy of a purposeful will, to bring his actions under constant self-control with a careful consideration of their ethical consequences. . . . This active self-control, which formed the end of the *exercitia* of St. Ignatius and of the rational

---

30. Diodorus Siculus 20.86.6; 23.18.5 (LCL); Polybius 2.6.6 and 10.17.6–15 (LCL); Mk 10:45; Rom 1:6; Eph 1:7 (and elsewhere in the New Testament); Henry George Liddell and Robert Scott, *A Greek-English Lexicon*, ed. Henry Stuart Jones (Oxford: Clarendon, 1940), under ἀπολύτρωσις, λύτρον, and σωτηρία.
31. MWG I/22.2:244 (on Paul and slavery), 257–65 (Nietzsche and *ressentiment*), 388 (the slave revolt in morality); *Economy and Society*, 1:485, 494–99, 592.

monastic virtues everywhere, was also the most important practical ideal of Puritans.[32]

What makes the Protestant ideal particularly amenable to capitalist accumulation is the denial of sacramental efficacy and free will, in combination with the Lutheran insistence that everyone, damned or saved, must have a calling. Believers can now work tirelessly toward certain knowledge of their election by directing the whole of their mental and physical discipline to amassing riches, on the understanding that "success in rationalized activity demonstrates God's blessing" (MWG 1/22.2:366; *Economy and Society*, 1:575). As this mentality penetrates ever more deeply into continental Europe and Anglo-American culture, the original motive for seeking worldly indicators of salvation is forgotten. The Protestant Reformation thus brings to fruition "the characteristic process of 'secularization' ["*Säkularisations*"*-Prozesse*], to which in modern times all phenomena that originated in religious conceptions succumb."[33] If you are good at knowing—in the manner of a medieval abbot or a Protestant entrepreneur—how to harness the labor of people who work as though their very souls were hanging in the balance, you can find your way to significant wealth and to all manner of technological advancement. For instance (as we'll see in chapter 4), when the abbot of Benediktbeuern, Karl Klocker, was forced off the premises in 1803, the group of entrepreneurial engineers that took his place retained the brothers with a knowledge of optics so that the monastery could be converted into a factory for the production of lenses. The buildings and surrounding estate provided a ready-made architectural layout, forests for firing kilns, a centuries-old culture of glass making, a habit of keeping trade secrets, and a predisposition to labor.

In order to describe how modern factory work capitalizes on Christian self-discipline, Weber introduces a term in *The Protestant Ethic* that has become almost synonymous with the process of secularization—namely, "disenchantment." Despite the ancient and medieval genealogy that Weber provides for this phenomenon, it's often taken by literary scholars to express his conviction that "the medieval world was limited or enchanted" because the Middle Ages had yet to experience "the rise in scientific bureaucratic rationality, by which natural phenomena are explained by science . . . thus mov-

---

32. MWG 1/18:324–26; *Protestant Ethic*, 118–19 (modified); cf. MWG 1/22.2:338; *Economy and Society*, 1:555–56.
33. MWG 1/18:501; English in *"The Protestant Ethic and the Spirit of Capitalism" with Other Writings on the Rise of the West*, trans. Stephen Kalberg, 4th ed. (Oxford: Oxford University Press, 2009), 189; on Weber's tendency to put this type of secularization in scare quotes, see Peter Ghosh, *Max Weber and "The Protestant Ethic": Twin Histories* (Oxford: Oxford University Press, 2014), 270.

ing religion from an inescapable epistemology and public reality to a more personal and optional way of understanding the world."[34] In fact Weber—a trained medievalist—counts "the Roman church" as one of "the two greatest powers of religious rationalism in history" (MWG 1/22.2:315; *Economy and Society*, 1:537). (Confucianism is the other.) He thinks that bureaucracies, along with science, were widespread in the Middle Ages after a period of recovery immediately following the collapse of the Roman Empire. He fully grasps the sophistication of the universities, of the imperial and Papal courts, and of medieval law—particularly the laws governing commercial contracts, on which he wrote his dissertation and to which he returned in his subsequent work to show how the legal foundations of modern capitalism were laid by medieval lawyers.[35] Like Nietzsche, he savors above all the contributions of the monasteries: "It was the monks or groups oriented toward monasticism, who, besides the priests or in their stead, concerned themselves with and wrote in all the areas of theological and ethical thought, as well as in metaphysics and considerable segments of science. In addition, they also occupied themselves with the production of artistic literature."[36] Indeed, for Weber, the Reformation arises in some measure from the conflict between ethical thought and the production of art. In scripture, works of the human hand are supposed to promise only an illusory salvation, even as the church has invariably relied on human fabrications to produce the effect of divinity. "Mass religion in particular," he writes, "is frequently and directly dependent on artistic devices for the required potency of its effects, and it is inclined to make concessions to the needs of the masses, which everywhere tend toward magic and idolatry" (MWG 1/22.2:412; *Economy and Society*, 1:609). There is consequently a permanent, constitutive tension between the transcendent divinity of Christian metaphysics and that divinity's alleged presence within churches ("the greatest of artistic productions") by way of the sacraments, icons, and ritual performance. The periodic outbreaks of iconoclastic vitriol—whether against pagan worship (as in the fourth to sixth centuries), Christian icons (as in the eighth century), heathen idols (as in the

---

34. Michelle Karnes, *Medieval Marvels and Fictions in the Latin West and Islamic World* (Chicago: University of Chicago Press, 2022), 25, and Katherine Steele Brokaw and Jay Zysk, "Introduction," in *Sacred and Secular Transactions*, 11, respectively.
35. MWG 1/1; English in Max Weber, *The History of Commercial Partnerships in the Middle Ages*, trans. Luz Kaelber (Lanham, MA: Rowman & Littlefield, 2003). See also MWG 1/22.1:152; *Economy and Society*, 1:379.
36. MWG 1/22.2:266; *Economy and Society*, 1:501; cf. Nietzsche, *Selected Letters of Friedrich Nietzsche*, ed. and trans. Christopher Middleton (Indianapolis, IN: Hackett, 1996), 67 ("We shall need monasteries again"), 204, 261.

northern Crusades), or liturgical plays (starting in the twelfth century)—are all moments in a long-standing process of disenchantment that for Weber culminates in the Reformation: "That great historic process in the development of religions, the disenchantment of the world [*Entzauberung der Welt*], which had begun with the Hebrew prophets and, in conjunction with Hellenistic scientific thought, had repudiated all magical means to salvation as superstition and sin, came here to its logical conclusion."[37] The Reformation marks a fresh beginning only insofar as it pushes an old polemic to a new extreme.

Of all the ancient developments that set the twin processes of secularization and disenchantment into motion, the most crucial for Weber is the scriptural doctrine of creation. Before the arrival of Yahweh, it was axiomatic in both Asiatic and Occidental religions that the world is eternal.[38] This could be proven ontologically, so to speak, with the maxim that "nothing can come of nothing" (KL 1.1.90, Q). Only in Abrahamic monotheism is the world transformed into a finite entity moving *ex nihilo, in nihilum*, whose ultimate meaning ought to come from on high but inevitably threatens to arise from within: "The world is full of temptations, not only because it is the site of sensual pleasures which are ethically irrational and completely diverting to things divine, but even more because it fosters in the religiously average person complacent self-sufficiency and self-righteousness in the fulfillment of common obligations, at the expense of the uniquely necessary concentration on active achievements leading to salvation" (MWG 1/22.2:320; *Economy and Society*, 1:542). As priestly intellectuals circulated their gospel of a transcendent creator across the Middle East, North Africa, and Europe, they deliberately stripped the world of its sacred aura in the hope of preventing its continued rivalry with their god as an alternate source of value. Earlier religions were discredited as magic, and the resulting vacuum was filled by a new set of ethical imperatives: "It is the intellectual who conceives of the 'world' as a problem of meaning. As intellectualism suppresses belief in magic, the world's processes become disenchanted, lose their magical significance, and henceforth simply 'are' and 'happen' but no longer signify anything. As a consequence, there is a growing demand that the world and the total pattern of life be subject to an order that is significant and meaningful" (MWG 1/22.2:273; *Economy and Society*, 1:506). The search for meaning now takes myriad forms, all of them prompted by the construction of a secular

---

37. MWG 1/18:280; *Protestant Ethic*, 105 (modified). *Entzauberung* is rendered by Parsons throughout as "the elimination of magic" rather than "disenchantment."

38. MWG 1/22.2:334, 342, 362; *Economy and Society*, 1:552, 558, 572.

sphere without inherent significance when compared to a divinity whose defining feature is jealousy over his followers' attachment to the world. To the extent that a systematic, disciplined inquiry into the meaning of life happens in the West outside the church or without regard for the pursuit of profit, it happens with special intensity in the university system. That system was founded in the Middle Ages, needless to say, and by the late nineteenth century had produced among some German academics a tremendous sense of disillusionment.[39] "We have become hard-boiled, cold, and tough," writes professor emeritus Nietzsche, "in the realization that the way of the world is not at all divine."[40]

There is nothing particularly modern about that realization. It is the product of a curriculum that required study of the Bible and therefore invited the observation that the prophets were "the first to use the word 'world' as an opprobrium."[41] Nor is there anything particularly modern about Weber's concept of disenchantment. This too was gleaned from a scrupulous reading of scripture. Earlier exegetes could also plainly see that wherever the Abrahamic godhead chose to reveal itself, it tended to do so at the expense of magicians. Starting in the eleventh century, believers could witness the knock-on effects in real time by attending one of the public executions inspired by the Mosaic dictum, "enchanters thou shalt not suffer to live" (Ex 22:18, DR). These killings were merely an extreme type of the humiliation that had been ongoing since Moses first channeled the Almighty to defeat the sorcerers of Egypt, drown Pharaoh's army, and deliver the law. According to a rabbinic saying in circulation among sixteenth-century Protestants, the law's arrival effectively emptied the previous millennia of significance by providing humanity with an ethical code that did not condone false gods or the whoredom of idolatry—much less magic.[42] After Moses there was nothing left but Yahweh to worship, and Yahweh, like nothing, could not be remotely pictured. He was literally out of this world.

To medieval and early modern Christians, the Old Testament attack on the false sanctity of the world was but a small foreshadowing of the disen-

---

39. See MWG I/17:71–111; English in Max Weber, *The Vocation Lectures*, ed. David Owen and Tracy B. Strong, trans. Rodney Livingstone (Indianapolis, IN: Hackett, 2004), 1–31; cf. Nietzsche, *Selected Letters*, 256n75.
40. NKGW 5/2:262; English in *The Gay Science: With a Prelude in German Rhymes and an Appendix of Songs*, ed. Bernard Williams, trans. Josefine Nauckhoff (Cambridge: Cambridge University Press, 2001), §346.
41. NKGW VI/2:119; English in *Beyond Good and Evil: Prelude to a Philosophy of the Future*, trans. Walter Kaufmann (New York: Vintage, 1989), §195.
42. On the *milia inane* preceding the law, see Margreta de Grazia, *Four Shakespearean Period Pieces* (Chicago: University of Chicago Press, 2021), 149.

chantment brought about by the BC/AD divide, which had been anticipated, on the one hand, by the Mosaic law and, on the other, by the ethical precepts of the prophets. According to Geoffrey of Monmouth, for example, Leir's father, Bladud, was a cunning man who taught necromancy throughout Britain and worked all manner of pseudo-miracles (*praestigia*) until he attempted to fly and crashed headlong into a temple of Apollo at the very moment when Elijah, halfway across the world, overcame the priests of Baal by praying for global drought.[43] Raphael Holinshed describes Leir's father in the same manner—a wizard who took pleasure "in artificial practices and magic" before being dashed to the ground "at what time Joas reigned in Juda."[44] Leir's rule, in other words, began with the desacralizaton of pagan worship, the discrediting of priests as mere magicians, the destruction of shrines, and the transformation of the cosmos into a natural rather than a supernatural matter through the violent imposition of the Mosaic code on rival cultic practices: "And he [Joas] destroyed the soothsayers, whom the kings of Juda had appointed to sacrifice in the high places in the cities of Juda, and round about Jerusalem: them also that burnt incense to Baal, and to the sun, and to the moon, and to the twelve signs, and to all the host of heaven" (4 Kgs 23:5, DR 1914; cf. 11:18). Thereafter pagan worship—above all worship of the stars—could amount to nothing more than the foppery of the world.

The fall of Leir's father is modeled on the demise of Simon Magus in the *Acts of Peter* and clearly functions in both Monmouth and Holinshed as a typological precursor to the disenchanting effects of Christ on the Magi. At the appearance of a new star over Bethlehem, claim several Fathers, "all magic and every kind of spell were destroyed."[45] Christ's apostles would subsequently have the same effect on a variety of magicians (Simon, Barjesus, the enslaved diviner), such that everything previously held sacred began to be drained of holiness by a debunking mentality whose momentum and force increased exponentially over coming millennia. After the Virgin Birth, the marvels of the world were nothing compared to divine intervention, which, as often as not, could also be explained away in terms of natural causation.

---

43. Geoffrey of Monmouth, *The History of the Kings of Britain: An Edition and Translation of "De gestis Britonum,"* ed. Michael D. Reeve, trans. Neil Wright (Woodbridge, UK: Boydell Press, 2007), 36–37; 3 Kgs 17:1, 18:27.
44. Raphael Holinshed, *Holinshed's Chronicles: England, Scotland and Ireland*, introduction by Vernon F. Snow (New York: AMS, 1976; reprint of the 1807 edition), 1:446.
45. Ignatius of Antioch, *Letter to the Ephesians* 19.3, in *The Apostolic Fathers: Greek Texts and English Translations*, ed. Michael W. Holmes (Grand Rapids, MI: Baker Books, 1999), 148–49; further citations in chapter 4.

The world that arises from this process of disenchantment is secular because it is finite and without inherent sanctity. It holds little value to believers trying to conform to the ascetic, anti-magical ideals laid out in scripture except as a system of imperfect correspondences to the transcendent godhead or, in the Protestant case, as a metaphor for the likelihood of one's salvation—a sign, in other words, that must not be mistaken for the signified lest the believer fall into idolatry. Unbelievers, by contrast, are supposed to find the *saeculum* worthy of veneration despite its specious magic, its evanescent joys, its lengthy torments, and its tragic lack of transcendent significance. They see the meaning in human affairs irrespective of eternal rewards or punishments.

Any book of this scope is going to challenge conventional period boundaries. I have employed the received terminology—antiquity, the Middle Ages, Renaissance, Enlightenment, modernity—to help orient readers within a familiar range of centuries, but have modeled my account of secularization on the so-called Axial genealogy.[46] Elaborated in various ways by Robert Bellah, Jan Assmann, Aleida Assmann, Marcel Gauchet, and Bruno Latour (among others), the Axial Period is a term first coined by Karl Jaspers in an attempt to take stock of the global sociology offered by Weber, a friend and colleague at the University of Heidelberg, "with his clear and multi-dimensional conceptuality in this widest of all the horizons of historical interpretation."[47] The underlying idea, which follows from the discovery of deep geological time and the pace of natural selection, is that the human animal has evolved too slowly for our usual periodic schemas to capture anything but comparatively superficial changes in the life of the species. The pivotal exception occurs in the middle of the first millennium BCE, when (to simplify a complicated story) the acquisition of language and the subsequent invention of writing belatedly register their effects on human cognition: hence the intellectual movements appearing across the planet within a handful of centuries—Hinduism, Judaism, Greek philosophy and drama, Zoroastrianism, Taoism, Confucianism, Buddhism. The great leap occurs with the thought of transcendence—a beyond so utterly remote and unlike anything we see around us that the world becomes subject to critical scrutiny

---

46. For an overview see Laurens ten Kate, "To World or Not to World: An Axial Genealogy of Secular Life," in *Radical Secularization? An Inquiry into the Religious Roots of Secular Culture*, ed. Stijn Latré et al. (New York: Bloomsbury Academic, 2015), 207–30.
47. Karl Jaspers, *The Origin and Goal of History* (London: Routledge & Kegan Paul, 1953), 266–67; cf. 277n1.

from a radically new viewpoint. Whatever historical periods might be said to follow are echoes of this cataclysmic shock. Unlike Weber—the most consequential forerunner to our current vogue for global perspectives—I have restricted myself to a comparatively narrow range of texts from Asia Minor, North Africa, and Europe in order to prioritize materials that might have some bearing on issues of unbelief, secularity, and secularization in the history of theater and drama.

CHAPTER 1

The Birth of Unbelief

How far back in time is it possible to push the history of atheism and unbelief? According to Charles Taylor, not very far. Only in the last three to four hundred years, he argues, has there emerged a "new context" for religious faith that "puts an end to the naïve acknowledgment of the transcendent.... Naïveté is now unavailable to anyone, believer or unbeliever alike."[1] The shift from the Middle Ages to modernity "consists, among other things, of a move from a society where belief in God is unchallenged and indeed, unproblematic, to one in which it is understood to be one option among others, and frequently not the easiest to embrace" (3). Atheism formerly came "close to being inconceivable" (26). But now "for more and more people unbelieving construals seem at first blush the only plausible ones" (12). The change happened abruptly enough and so outstripped its earlier foreshadowing in the Axial Age (151–58) and the Reformation (77–88, 263–69) as to appear like a "super-nova" compared to those previous novelties (300). Given the modern, "fractured culture of the nova" (299), today you can believe or not believe. There are however seemingly stronger reasons *not* to believe, so much so that maintaining your faith in a transcendent god is now as never before "challenged by others" (15). The "new conditions

---

1. Charles Taylor, *A Secular Age* (Cambridge, MA: Belknap Press, 2007), 21.

of belief" (20), unlike the old, burden faith with the ever-beckoning alternative of unbelief.

What Taylor considers a new condition is depicted everywhere in the New Testament. A nova appears above Bethlehem and thereafter everyone who wants to have faith struggles with its lack: "I believe; help my unbelief [*apistiai*]" (Mk 9:24). Any attempt at faith must overcome the argument that Jesus, far from being the Messiah, is a bastard (Lk 3:23; Jn 6:3), a friend of no-counts (Lk 7:34), a madman (Mk 3:21), a demoniac magician (Mt 12:24; Jn 10:20), or a straight-up fraud who, by his own admission, cannot perform miracles before "an unbelieving [*apistos*] and perverse generation."[2] Facing a crowd of incredulous onlookers, Christ is "amazed at their unbelief [*apistian*]" (Mk 6:6), and then later he is killed, which does not at first blush much help his case. The rumors that he rose from the grave strain whatever credulity might have been left: "These words seemed to them an idle tale" (or, in the Wycliffite rendering, like "madness [*deliramentum*]"), and those with ears to hear "did not believe them [*ēpistoun*]" (Lk 24:11). When he appears posthumously before his disciples—giving them, one might think, the proof that they crave—he upbraids them for their "unbelief [*apistian*]" (Mk 16:14, RSV), just as he always had, but now adds a terrible threat: "The one who does not believe [*apistēsas*] will be condemned" (Mk 16:16; cf. Rev 21:8). Some stare at his resurrected form with joy while still "disbelieving [*apistountōn*]" (Lk 24:41) and have to be given the redundant imperative of a faith whose definition evidently lies in its opposite: "Do not be an unbeliever [*apistos*] but a believer [*pistos*]!" (Jn 20:27, my trans.). When the disciples obey and start spreading the news, many find it "incredible [*apiston*]" (Acts 26:8) and "refuse to believe [*ēpistoun*]" (Acts 28:24). Meanwhile the converted must constantly examine the status of their own faith for fear of believing false prophecies (Mt 7:15–23) or falling victim to the Antichrist, whose minions are in the world and from the world, "and the world listens to them" (1 Jn 4:5).

Ever since Lucien Febvre's magnum opus on Rabelais, we have been told that the unbelief saturating scripture exists in the premodern world only as an accusation. The most fervent believers incessantly hurl the words "unbeliever" and "infidel" at other, equally fervent believers. So while the word *atheist* may carry us as far back as the fifth century BCE, once there we should conclude, according to Febvre, that "it did not have a strictly defined

---

2. Mt 17:17, Mk 9:19, Lk 9:41; cf. Mt 6:30, 8:26, 14:31, 16:8, 17:20: "You of little faith [*oligopistoi*]" and Mk 4:40: "Have you still no faith [*oupō exete pistin*]?"

meaning. It was used in whatever sense one wanted to give it."[3] It could not have its modern meaning because all eras prior to our own were "not times of a critical spirit" but, instead, "times of credulity—and fear" (407). They lacked "the only touchstone" that allows for the real differentiation between truth and error, the only "right scale on which to weigh opinions: a strong scientific method" (462). So while we may occasionally see phantom images of our own *esprit critique* in past thinking, we should no more take those chimaeras as "the starting point for our own ideas" than we should count "a savage who makes fire by energetically twirling a stick . . . as one of the inventors of the electric stove" (461). The premodern world, from this viewpoint, was a benighted, primitive place. It knew nothing of our epistemological struggles and contributed nothing to our accomplishments.

Very little of Febvre's perspective survives among current historians of science.[4] For them, the history of any scientific method (modern or otherwise) begins with the ability to record observations through the invention of writing: first in Egypt, where the length of the solar year was approximated at 365 days and the days divided into 24 hours; then in Babylonia, which was the envy of surrounding cultures on account of its achievements in computational astronomy—hence the Magi's arrival "from the East" (Mt 2:1) in pursuit of the nova over Bethlehem. The ancient Greeks inherited these systems of knowledge and further developed them alongside the geometry, physics, philosophy, and medicine that Alexander's conquests would spread throughout the wider Mediterranean by means of a supple, alphabetic form of writing. "This had the revolutionary effect," writes David Lindberg, "of opening knowledge claims to the possibility of inspection, comparison, and criticism."[5] We see in the middle of the first millennium BCE, that is, the emergence of a highly literate and therefore highly critical culture, one guided by an unusual intolerance for error. Thanks to the invention of written Hebrew, there came into existence at roughly the same time the other essential component of Christianity: the counterreligion we have come to call Abrahamic monotheism. This too was founded on a deep intolerance for error, plus a distinction between "belief and unbelief" that

---

3. Lucien Febvre, *The Problem of Unbelief in the Sixteenth Century: The Religion of Rabelais*, trans. Beatrice Gottlieb (Cambridge, MA: Harvard University Press, 1982), 132.
4. On the false opposition between science and religion specifically, see Brad S. Gregory, *The Unintended Reformation: How a Religious Revolution Secularized Society* (Cambridge, MA: Belknap Press, 2012), esp. chaps. 1 and 6.
5. David C. Lindberg, *The Beginnings of Western Science: The European Scientific Tradition in Philosophical, Religious, and Institutional Context, Prehistory to A.D. 1450*, 2nd ed. (Chicago: University of Chicago Press, 2007), 10.

secured for its creator god a sublime otherworldliness.⁶ In the amalgamation of Hebrew and Greek that is the New Testament, incredulity alone guarantees faith its transcendental object by providing testimony that God is "not of this world" (Jn 8:23) and that what he accomplishes is "impossible" for anyone but him (Lk 1:37). Christ *must* inspire disbelief. He requires the infidel. If atheism had not existed, Christianity would have had to invent it.⁷

And yet Christianity did not invent it. For the Lord had already looked down from heaven upon the children of men to see if any were seeking God and found a world of deeply internalized doubt: "The fool [*aphron*] has said in his heart, there is no God."⁸ This particular psalm is conventionally dated to the sixth century BCE and was translated about three hundred years later into the Greek version that Paul quotes: "There is no one who seeks God" (Rom 3:11b; Ps 13:1c–2, LXX). Readers of Greek could perhaps keep the bad fool of the Psalms—an *aphron* or "thoughtless person"—separate from the *moron* for Christ that Paul urged them to become in order to mock the "wisdom of the world" (1 Cor 3:18). But things were not so easy for readers of the Vulgate. Its translation of both the atheist and holy fool with the word *stultus* helped inspire an unrestrained, festive irreverence in the Middle Ages. Here God chooses the foolish things of the world (*stulta mundi*) in order to confound the wise (1 Cor 1:27, Vulg.), as though there were a hidden value in embracing reversals of hierarchy and entertaining forbidden doubts. In fact the most radical reversal of all was the Incarnation, such that God became one with humanity to the point of dying. The early criticism that Christ's advent had shattered traditional religion and raised in its place a form of atheism was preserved in the medieval commentary tradition, as V. A. Kolve has shown, where "the Jews bring Christ to trial explicitly as a God-denyer."⁹

---

6. Jan Assmann, *The Price of Monotheism*, trans. Robert Savage (Stanford: Stanford University Press, 2010), 2.
7. Stephen Greenblatt, *Shakespearean Negotiations: The Circulation of Social Energy in Renaissance England* (Berkeley: University of California Press, 1988), 23.
8. Ps 13:1 (LXX); repeated in Ps 52.
9. V. A. Kolve, "God-Denying Fools and the Medieval 'Religion of Love,'" *Studies in the Age of Chaucer* 19 (1997): 3–59 at 26. For the earliest accusations against Christians for being atheists, see Adolph Harnack, *Der Vorwurf des Atheismus in den drei ersten Jahrhunderten* (Leipzig: J. C. Hinrichs, 1905); E. Fascher, "Der Vorwurf der Gottlosigkeit in der Auseinandersetzung bei Juden, Griechen und Christen," in *Abraham unser Vater: Juden und Christen im Gespräch über die Bibel*, ed. O. Betz et al. (Leiden: Brill, 1963), 78–105; N. Brox, "Zum Vorwurf des Atheismus gegen die Alte Kirche," *Trierer Theologische Zeitschrift* 75 (1966): 274–82; P. F. Beatrice, "L'accusation d'athéisme contre les chrétiens," in *Hellénisme et christianisme*, ed. M. Narcy and É. Rebillard (Villeneuve d'Ascq: Presses universitaires du Septentrion, 2004), 133–52; Jan N. Bremmer, "Atheism in Antiquity," in *The Cambridge Companion to Atheism*, ed. Michael Martin (Cambridge: Cambridge University Press, 2007), 11–26.

There are marked similarities, Kolve claims, in the Western iconographical tradition between the atheist in illuminated psalters and the psalm-quoting, godforsaken blasphemer depicted on the cross (Mk 15:34; Ps 22:1). "Monastic communities *in their own voices* chanted the words of the fool aloud twice weekly across the medieval centuries," Kolve writes. "The text denying divinity—*non est deus*—could not itself be denied or suppressed."[10] Atheism was a necessary, ineradicable component of medieval Christianity.

A stronger alternative to Taylor's claim that atheism before the modern era was virtually inconceivable is Stephen Greenblatt's proposition that it was perfectly thinkable but "only as the thought of another."[11] Augustine notes, for example, the conspicuous absence of self-professed atheists despite their presumed ubiquity and interprets the discrepancy as a strategy to avoid scandal. There are plenty of people who "love the *saeculum* and do not love God," but they are too afraid of public censure to express their faithlessness out loud; they take care to say only *in their hearts*, "there is no God."[12] Secular sacrilege especially abounds in the secret thoughts of philosophers: Cicero, for example, advocated for the wisdom of atheism but was careful not to say so "in his own person [*ex sua persona*], for he saw how odious and offensive such an opinion would be" (*De civ. Dei* 5.9.1, LCL). He therefore assigned the denial of all divinity to a persona with the speech prefix "Cotta."[13]

Atheism would be similarly outsourced to philosophers in medieval literature—as when one of them declares in the *Gesta romanorum* that "God is dead"[14]—but before we agree with Febvre and Taylor that unbelief in this form is imaginary and therefore of little consequence for the development of "real" atheism, we should consider the impact on Western culture of other ideas that were also enabled by a speech prefix. Platonism in its entirety was originally thinkable only as the thought of another: "There is no writing by Plato and never will be," wrote someone purporting to be Plato (it may have even been Plato, whoever that was). "Those ascribed to him [i.e., "Plato"] belong to a Socrates made beautiful and new."[15] If we persist in granting

---

10. Kolve, "God-Denying Fools," 20.
11. Greenblatt, *Shakespearean Negotiations*, 22.
12. Augustine, *En. in Ps.* 13.2 (CCSL 38:86; WSA III/15:175).
13. See Cicero, *De divinatione* 2.42–47 (LCL).
14. *Gesta Romanorum*, ed. Hermann Oesterley (Berlin, 1871), 500, 503; English in *Gesta Romanorum: A New Translation*, trans. Christopher Stace (Manchester: Manchester University Press, 2016), 361, 365.
15. Plato, *Epistles* 2.314c (LCL, modified). Cf. *Ep.* 7.341c; for arguments against this letter's authenticity, see *Plato's Epistles*, trans. Glenn R. Morrow, rev. ed. (Indianapolis, IN: Bobbs-Merrill, 1962), 3–16. Cf. Augustine, *De consensu* 1.12: Plato "tried to embellish the thoughts of another rather than his own."

Platonic ideas a historical reality despite Plato's unwillingness or inability to speak for himself, what is it that makes the heartfelt atheism articulated by the fool, Cotta, or literary infidels any less significant? Many inordinately consequential writers never wrote *in propria persona*: not the Psalmist writing as David (writing as the fool); not Plato in his polyphonic dialogues; and least of all playwrights, whose contributions to Western culture are hard to overestimate if only because drama thrives on thinking and saying what has to be thought and said by others if it is to be said publicly in front of a crowd.

A Platonic persona articulates the two ways of looking at the world on which our narratives of secularization have largely come to depend—"the divine [*theiou*], which is most blessed, and the godless [*atheou*], which is most wretched" (*Theaetetus* 176e, LCL). The Socrates speaking these lines was likely designed to defend his historical namesake from the accusations of atheism first lodged against him when another character named Socrates convinced an acolyte on stage that there are no gods: "What foolishness [*mōrias*] to think that Zeus exists [*ton Dia nomizein onta*]!"[16] The verb "to think" (*nomizein*) in this passage could be translated "to believe," but I have avoided that rendering for the moment in order to differentiate pre-Christian reverence for Zeus from the act of believing (*pisteuein*) that requires the virtue of faith (*pistis*) according to the New Testament. *Nomizein* is at the center of ancient Greek religion, just as *pisteuein* is at the center of Christianity, and the difference between the two words captures in a nutshell a major transition. The older terminology focused on whether a person conformed to custom or law (*nomos*). Before the fifth century, the question had never been whether you "believed in" the gods; the question was whether you recognized, honored, and observed them correctly through active participation in the cult. The key moment of true commitment came when you took part in animal sacrifice, as the martyrs, who refused and were killed, would eventually witness. For many Christians it was de rigueur to interpret such deaths as "a testimony to those who do not believe [*non credentibus*] and a boon to those who do," lest "the weakness or hopelessness of faith" lead believers to join their adversaries.[17] The hope, in other words, was that martyrs could offer proof that their cause was truly divine, such that unbelievers might convert and believers might feel less inclined to abandon their otherwise precarious faith. This specific type of believer—the *pistos* or *fidelis* plagued by doubt and verging on faithlessness, as in Taylor's *Secular Age* and a great deal

---

16. Aristophanes, *Clouds* 818–19 (LCL).
17. *Passio sanctarum martyrum Perpetuae et Felicitatis*, Praef. (PL 3:16A; ANF 3:699).

of related Christian literature—appears for the first time once the existence of divinity as such has become subject to debate. Which is to say, this type of believer first appears once it becomes not only plausible but in some cases *necessary* to imagine that someone, somewhere, has no faith whatsoever; worse still, that this someone could be you. The New Testament is new to the extent that it is the basis for a religion whose specific formulation for faith (*pistis*) "always presupposes the possibility of 'unbelief.'"[18]

The innovations of the Christian Bible were made possible through the earlier arrival of a Greek word for atheism. "Here a wound was opened in practical religion," Walter Burkert writes, "which would never close again."[19] The earliest origins of the trauma have come down to us only in fragments, but we can nonetheless get a fairly detailed picture by juxtaposing those fragments with the two portraits of unbelief that survive intact thanks to medieval copyists of Aristophanes and Plato.[20] These represent Socrates in diametrically opposed ways but agree on the underlying catastrophe. Once people started paying sophists for an education in how to deconstruct any argument, "atheism" (*atheotēta*) became the coin of the realm.[21] The disagreement between Aristophanes and Plato is whether Socrates was sophistry's epitome or critic; whether he shrewdly capitalized on the new market or selflessly dispensed wisdom in the agora; whether he was an atheist or observed the gods in all his doings; whether he had the weaker argument defeat the stronger by stating the weaker in "new words" (*Clouds* 1397, LCL) or systematically championed the stronger argument because the stronger was rooted in eternal, transcendent values.

Aristophanes did not take the charitable view, and his was the one eventually adopted by the members of the Athenian assembly when they tried and then executed Socrates for peddling godlessness to fools—even to *older* people, like Euripides, who after listening to Socrates "chatter" began "working in tragedy"

---

18. Wilhelm Fahr, Θεους Νομιζειν: *Zur Problem der Anfänge des Atheismus bei den Griechen* (Hildesheim: Georg Olms, 1969), 5.
19. Walter Burkert, *Greek Religion: Archaic and Classical*, trans. John Raffan (Oxford: Blackwell, 1991), 311.
20. The earliest intact witness of Aristophanes is MS Ravenna, Biblioteca Classense 429 (tenth century); the earliest witness of Plato is Bodleian Library MS. E. D. Clarke 39 (ninth century, purchased from the monastery of St. John the Theologian on Patmos). On the relation between the two authors, see Charles Platter, "Plato's Aristophanes," in *Ancient Comedy and Reception: Essays in Honor of Jeffrey Henderson*, ed. Olson S. Douglas (Boston: de Gruyter, 2013), 132-65.
21. Scholium on *Clouds* 627 in Aristophanes, *Fragments*, #30 (LCL). Socrates explicitly defends himself against this term (*Apology* 26d); the Athenian Stranger, as we'll see below, defends astronomers against the same word (*Laws* 967a).

so as to persuade his audience "that the gods do not exist."[22] The chorus leader in *Clouds* compares Socrates's teachings to those of Prodicus, a champion of the doctrine "that the gods honored by custom do not exist . . . but that archaic man . . . [deified] the fruits of the earth and virtually everything that contributed to his subsistence."[23] (Jews and Christians who wanted to discredit pagan theology were quick to adopt this theory as they found it in Prodicus's most successful pupil, Euhemerus.) Socrates teaches on stage that a "cosmic whirl" (*Clouds* 379, LCL) governs the universe rather than Zeus, thus repeating the centerpiece of Democritus's atomic theory. Strepsiades, Socrates's less than bright pupil, applauds this innovative thesis by calling his teacher "the Milean" (*Clouds* 830, LCL), apparently confusing him with Diagoras of Melos, the reputed atheist who made fun of the Eleusinian mysteries at a time when the mysteries were being desecrated and the desecrators brought to heel.[24] Socrates's boast from his floating basket that he walks on air and "scrutinize[s] the sun" (*Clouds* 225, LCL) recalls the teachings of Anaxagoras that the sun is no god at all but "a red-hot mass of metal" and that the moon, equally inanimate, merely reflects its light[25]—doctrines for which he appears to have been hounded from the city along with all the others who did "not recognize the gods."[26]

Plato spent the whole of his career defending Socrates from this bad company before excluding him from *Laws*—the longest and latest of the dialogues. All three of its speakers readily concede that the culture of unbelief had become rampant on account of "the novel views of our modern scientists."[27] Things were just as Aristophanes had alleged. Here a new speech

---

22. *Frogs* 1493 (LCL) and *Women at the Thesmophoria* 450–51 (LCL), respectively. See also Mary R. Lefkowitz, *Euripides and the Gods* (New York: Oxford University Press, 2016).
23. PHerc 1428 fr. 19, ed. and trans. Albert Henrichs, "Two Doxographical Notes: Democritus and Prodicus on Religion," *Harvard Studies in Classical Philology* 79 (1975): 93–123 at 107–8 (trans. modified). Prodicus is mentioned in *Clouds* 361 (LCL).
24. Christoph Auffarth, "Aufnahme und Zurückweisung 'Neuer Götter' im spätklassischen Athen: Religion gegen die Krise, Religion in der Krise?" in *Die athenische Demokratie im 4. Jahrhundert v. Chr.*, ed. Walter Eder (Stuttgart: Franz Steiner, 1995), 337–65, esp. 339–41.
25. Diogenes Laertius 2.3.8 (LCL); Bremmer, "Atheism in Antiquity," 13–14; Robert Parker, *Athenian Religion: A History* (Oxford: Clarendon, 1996), 209.
26. Plutarch, *Pericles* 32 (LCL, modified); cf. Diodorus Siculus 12.39.2 (LCL); F. E. Romer, "Atheism, Impiety and the Limos Melios in Aristophanes's *Birds*," *American Journal of Philology* 115, no. 3 (1994): 351–65, esp. 352–53.
27. *Laws* 886d (LCL). Robert Mayhew renders the same phrase more literally as "our modern wise men" and identifies these thinkers with "materialists such as Archelaus and his followers," in Plato, *Laws 10*, trans. with a commentary by Robert Mayhew (Oxford: Clarendon, 2008), 303n2. See also E. B. England, *The Laws of Plato* (Manchester: Manchester University Press, 1921), 2:453; and Gregory Vlastos, *The Presocratics*, ed. Daniel W. Graham (Princeton: Princeton University Press, 1995), 1:86n177: "all those who sowed the materialist wind must be held responsible for the whirlwind."

prefix, the Athenian Stranger, reverses Socrates's earlier banishment of all poetry and drama from the ideal republic, arguing instead for strict regulation by the state, as though Plato had come to the belated realization that poetry and drama can at least "teach the *existence* of the gods whose *conduct* they so often and so sadly libel."[28] For these three conversationalists—whiling away their time on a pilgrimage to the mountain cave where Zeus was supposed to have handed down the laws of Crete to Minos—Socrates's seminal critique of mythology has implicitly joined the relativism of the sophists and the materialism of natural philosophy (*Laws*' explicit targets) to convince people to deny the existence of the gods. All three interlocutors want to grant the premise that every just law descends from the gods, yet they cannot help but question the myth that Crete's legal code came from Zeus since its legal code obviously lacks wisdom and foresight (*Laws* 630d, LCL). It is not hard to hear in their criticisms an echo of the ancient dictum that all Cretans are liars—a reputation apparently earned by the Cretans' insistence that Zeus had not only been born on the island and dictated its laws but had died there, too, and was buried in the very cave to which Plato's speakers are headed.[29]

"The death of the god," Martin Nilsson writes of this legend, "conflicts with all Greek ideas."[30] According to Plato's *Laws*, the conflict had recently reached an unprecedented fervor as people became convinced, on the basis of the latest investigations, that the gods were nonentities, the universe was soulless, and the world lacked any meaning beyond the compulsion of physical law:

> For they imagine that those who study these objects [i.e., stars] in astronomy and the other necessary allied arts become atheists [*atheous*] through observing, as they suppose, that all things come into being by necessary forces . . . for as regards the visible objects of sight, all that moves in the heavens appeared to them to be full of stones, earth and many other soulless bodies which dispense the causes of the whole cosmos. These were the views which, at that time, caused these thinkers to incur many charges of atheism [*atheotētas*] and much odium. (*Laws* 967a–c, LCL)

---

28. J. Tate, "Plato, Socrates and the Myths," *Classical Quarterly* 30, nos. 3–4 (1936): 142–45 at 143.
29. Callimachus, *Hymn* 1.8–9 (LCL); Titus 1:12; Minos Kokolakis, "Zeus' Tomb: An Object of Pride and Reproach," *Kernos* 8 (1995): 123–38; H. Verbruggen, *Le Zeus Crétois* (Paris: Les Belles Lettres, 1981), esp. 67–70; S. Spyridakis, "Zeus Is Dead: Euhemerus and Crete," *Classical Journal* 63, no. 8 (1968): 337–40.
30. Martin P. Nilsson, *Geschichte der Griechischen Religion*, 2nd ed. (Munich: C. H. Beck, 1955), 1:322.

According to the Stranger, this particular cause of atheism is paradoxically also its cure, insofar as a more careful observation of the heavens teaches that the planets do not wander (*planesthai*) at all but follow predictable orbits (*Laws* 822a, LCL). A deep contemplation of the heavens—one that goes beyond mere observation to inquire into the unseen structure that can be grasped exclusively through numbers—ought to be enough to disprove atheism by disclosing the hard evidence that leads "to faith in the gods [*peri theōn agonte eis pistin*]" (*Laws* 966d, LCL).

That last phrase contains the solitary instance in Plato of the word *pistis* meaning "belief" in the existence of divinity—a new usage, which will come to dominate the New Testament. Although it played little to no role in Greek religion, *pistis* had long been central to the Greek culture of disputation, as it was linked etymologically, conceptually, and practically to the art of persuasion.[31] At the end of the *Eumenides*, for example, Athena expresses relief that "the eyes of Peitho" (970, LCL), the goddess of persuasion, have witnessed her speech and allowed her to overcome the opposition through argument. In Athens especially any technique flourished that might convince interlocutors to abandon their convictions and adopt instead whatever beliefs were most advantageous to the speaker. Debate was the only way to know which propositions were most "persuasive" (*pithanos*, *peistikos*, or *pistikos*), hence most "convincing" and "credible" (*pistos*), thus worthy of "faith" (*pistis*)—a term that could be extended to whatever "proofs" (*pisteis*) inspired the most confidence.[32] Since assent was often cajoled through elaborate rhetorical means, there was always a potentially crippling overlap between rational argument and a confidence game. In fact Plato seems to have thought for much of his career that every belief (*pistis*) resulting from persuasion (*peitho*) was effectively the opposite of knowledge (*episteme*) because it concerned only the ephemeral world of becoming—the world of opinion—without any corre-

---

31. *Griechisches Etymologisches Wörterbuch*, ed. Hjalmar Frisk (Heidelberg: C. Winter, 1970), 2:487–88, under πείθομαι; Henry George Liddell and Robert Scott, *A Greek-English Lexicon*, ed. Henry Stuart Jones (Oxford: Clarendon, 1940), under πιστός (B), esp. A.2.2 and C.2; πιστικός (B), πειστικός, πιθανός; A. Oguse, "À propos de la Syntaxe de πείθω et de πιστεύω," *Revue des études grecques* 78 (1965), 513–41; Alexander Mourelatos, *The Route of Parmenides: A Study of Word, Image and Argument in the Fragments* (New Haven, CT: Yale University Press, 1970), 136–63; Laela Zwollo, *St. Augustine and Plotinus: The Human Mind as Image of the Divine* (Leiden: Brill, 2019), 339–40, esp. n73; cf. J. H. Sleeman and Gilbert Pollet, *Lexiconon Plotinianum* (Leiden: Brill, 1980) under πιστικός, πίστις ("assurance, belief, means of persuasion") and πιστός ("trustworthy, convincing"); E. Benveniste, *Le vocabulaire des institutions indo-européennes* (Paris: Éditions de Minuit, 1969), 1:115–16.

32. For *pistis* used as "proof" of the gods' existence see *Laws* 966c–d; for its use as argumentative proof more generally, Aristotle, *Rhetoric* 1356a; Plotinus, *Enneads* II.3.1; VI.9.10.

spondence to the truth of Being. That is why Socrates attacks the kind of speaking required in law and politics; their business is not to teach wisdom, much less the difference between right and wrong, but to create "belief without knowledge [*to pisteuein aneu tou eidenai*]."[33] Philosophical argument was supposed to transcend mere rhetoric through sheer force of reason, despite there being throughout the dialogues no end of rhetorical dissimulation—as in the "noble lies" permitted to the philosopher king.[34] Indeed some scholars have found in the tortured grammar and "cynical levity" of *Laws* a Plato—or perhaps one of his imitators—at last outwitted by discourse, increasingly at one with the historical Socrates in having become radically self-effacing and self-critical, unsure on principle that anybody knows anything, least of all about the gods, except on the basis of a debate-tested and therefore credible belief system.[35] If the course of study at Plato's theistic Academy was intended to convert the student from an untested faith to a faith that had been tried to its core, how different was the curriculum from that of the atheistic Socratic Thinkery in Aristophanes? "There are quite a number of men," says one of Plato's epistles, "who . . . now declare that the doctrines that they once held to be most incredible [*apistotata*] appear to them now the most credible [*pistotata*], and what they then held most credible [*pistotata*] now appears the opposite" (*Epistles* 2.314b, LCL).

The conversion technique that makes Plato's dialogues seem almost postmodern—particularly when Derrida reads them—is the relentless interrogation first perfected by sophists: "cross-examination [*elenchos*] of the foolish conceit of wisdom," says the Elean Stranger, "is the true-born art of sophistry."[36] The danger here is that after hearing cross-examinations of every conceivable opinion, you might no longer know *what* to believe. There is a risk in other words that the proliferating techniques of persuasion and counterargument will lead every belief into the *aporia* of universal doubt. The interlocu-

---

33. *Gorgias* 454e (LCL). Cf. Aristophanes, *Frogs* 1398: "persuasion is empty and mindless" (LCL, modified).
34. *Republic* 382c-d, 389b-d, 414b, 459d (LCL). Cf. Jody Enders, *Rhetoric and the Origins of Medieval Drama* (Ithaca, NY: Cornell University Press, 1992).
35. *The Dialogues of Plato*, trans. B. Jowett (Oxford, 1871), 4:4; Emilio Di Somma, *Fides and Secularity: Beyond Charles Taylor's Open Faith* (Eugene, OR: Pickwick Publications, 2018), 31–42.
36. Plato, *Sophist* 231b (LCL, modified); see Charles M. Young, "The Socratic Elenchus," in *A Companion to Plato*, ed. Hugh H. Benson (Oxford: Blackwell, 2006), 55-69; Gregory Vlastos, *Socrates: Ironist and Moral Philosopher* (Ithaca, NY: Cornell University Press, 1991), esp. 132; David D. Corey, *The Sophists in Plato's Dialogues* (Albany: State University of New York Press, 2015); Jacques Derrida, "Plato's Pharmacy," in *Dissemination*, trans. Barbara Johnson (Chicago: University of Chicago Press, 1981), 61–171.

tors in Plato's *Laws* are deeply concerned that their arguments for believing in the existence of the gods merely extend a culture of disputation without end. Every strategy of argumentation, as strategy, is already suspect. How do they defend the gods' existence when the people they're trying to convince are "unpersuaded [*ou peithomenoi*] by the myths, which they heard as infants" (*Laws* 887d, LCL)? The same people now look on philosophical noodling about unseen realities as equally childish and fictive. How is it possible to convince unbelievers that proofs of the divine are more than a rhetorical dodge, "tricked out with words to make them persuasive [*pithanon*]" (*Laws* 886e, LCL)?

The only solution, it would seem, is to promise "adequate proofs that gods exist" by mustering every "power of persuasion" (*Laws* 885d, 887c, LCL) and then to pray. "Let the gods be invoked with all zeal to aid in the demonstration [*apodeixin*] of their own existence" (*Laws* 893b, LCL). Perhaps it is merely a "benign circularity" for the speakers to call on the gods rather than to trust their own ability to counter with reason the arguments of atheists.[37] But it is quite another thing, after the prayer, for them to assume—along with the atheists—that the gods are not going to help. Laws, they decide, must be devised to punish the hardened unbelievers whom nothing can persuade (*Laws* 908, LCL). Less hardened, more "honest" and therefore corrigible atheists will be sent to a reeducation camp that the Stranger names the Sound-Mind Center (*sōphronistērion*) in a comical and grim recollection of the atheistic Thinkery (*phronistērion*) in *Clouds*.[38] (Nietzsche recalls with amusement the story that when Plato died there was discovered under his pillow "no 'Bible,' nor anything Egyptian, Pythagorean, nor Platonic—but a volume of Aristophanes.")[39] At the Sound-Mind Center people would presumably learn, if nothing else, the cosmological proof for the existence of god, which enters history for the first time in *Laws* and serves mainly to demonstrate that the burden of proof is on believers. It has been on them for millennia.

"This particular philosophical text," writes Russell Gmirkin of Plato's *Laws*, "exerted a profound influence on the political thinking, educational philosophy and literary activities of the biblical authors."[40] Gmirkin's late date for

---

37. John J. Cleary, "The Role of Theology in Plato's *Laws*," in *Plato's Laws and Its Historical Significance*, ed. Francisco L. Lisi (Sankt Augustin: Academia, 2001), 125–140 at 130.
38. *Clouds* 142 (LCL); the parallel is noted by Mayhew in Plato, *Laws 10*, 196, whose translation of *sōphronistērion* I give here.
39. NKGW VI/2:43; English in *Beyond Good and Evil: Prelude to a Philosophy of the Future*, trans. Walter Kaufmann (New York: Vintage, 1989), §28.
40. Russell E. Gmirkin, *Plato and the Creation of the Hebrew Bible* (London: Routledge, 2017), 250; see esp. 129–36 comparing the laws regulating impiety in Athens, Plato, and Deuteronomy.

significant portions of the Hebrew Bible may or may not be correct, though much of what he says about the Bible's indebtedness to Plato applies to various moments in the Septuagint and, even more so, to the New Testament, where the Hellenic element goes well beyond Platonism: "Just as there was a Koine Greek language which was adopted by Hellenistic Jews," write Henry Cadbury and Kirsopp Lake, "so there was a Koine Greek philosophy."[41] This common language and common philosophy could be one and the same, insofar as Greek contained a specific and novel vocabulary for persuasion and belief, disputation and doubt, including a new usage of the verb "to be" unattested before Protagoras's confession of his inability, concerning the gods, to determine "whether or not *they are*."[42] We find the same verb commonly used thereafter without any predicate to signify existence, just as we will find it later in two monuments of modern skepticism: *to be or not to be; I think therefore I am*. According to Charles Kahn, the new usage (classified by him as type VI) "appears in Greek literature only with the rise of theological skepticism in the age of the Sophists. . . . [and] presupposed a climate of theoretical speculation and an attitude of doubt concerning traditional belief (like the doubt expressed in the biblical verse, "The fool hath said in his heart, 'There is no God'"). Type VI provides an ancient precedent for the kind of existential statements that are characteristic of post-Cartesian philosophy."[43] Kahn's parenthetical reference to the Bible is more historically significant than he lets on. At the same time as Greeks were reexamining their mythology, so too were Jews attacking the gods by placing Yahweh, in the words of Robert Bellah, "finally outside society and the world" so that he might provide "the point of reference from which all existing presuppositions can be questioned."[44] The fool of the Psalms is a symptom and an extension of this questioning. Translated into Greek at some point in third-century Egypt, he was given full access to the syntax of axial-age, philosophical atheism.

As was God. Yahweh's unusual loathing of his fellow deities, when rendered into Greek, found an argument against their very being—and an argu-

---

41. F. J. Foakes-Jackson and Kirsopp Lake, eds., *The Beginnings of Christianity: Part 1: The Acts of the Apostles* (London: Macmillan, 1933), 4:209; for Platonic influence on the Septuagint, see Morton Smith, "The Image of God," *Bulletin of the John Rhylands Library* 40 (1958): 473–512.
42. Protagoras B4 in Hermann Diels, *Die Fragmente der Vorsokratiker: Griechisch und Deutsch*, ed. Walter Kranz, 8th ed. (Berlin: Wiedmann, 1956), 2:265: "περὶ μὲν θεῶν οὐκ ἔχω εἰδέναι, οὔθ' ὡς εἰσὶν οὔθ' ὡς οὐκ εἰσίν."
43. Charles H. Kahn, *The Verb "Be" in Ancient Greek: With a New Introductory Essay* (Indianapolis, IN: Hackett, 2003), xxiv–xxv; also 228–330.
44. Robert Bellah, *Religion in Human Evolution: From the Paleolithic to the Axial Age* (Cambridge, MA: Belknap Press, 2011), 322.

ment for his being Being's very definition. Anyone who put his existence on trial alongside nonentities like Zeus would soon learn that he was his own best witness; also that he had other witnesses, too, "so that you may know and believe [*pisteusēte*] and understand that I exist [*ego eimi*]" (Is 43:10, LXX). The enigma of the Tetragrammaton, to which this passage alludes, thus came to mean something rather more specific than the traditional tautology, *I am who I am* (Ex 3:14). When translated into Greek, God's unspeakable name makes the more polemical claim *I am the one that exists*—in contradistinction to all the others.[45] With respect to all other gods, simply put, Yahweh is an atheist. The denial of their existence is how he asserts his own reality, which, thanks to his radical transcendence of anything resembling *our* reality, sometimes resembles the gods' vacuity. The God of Job and Ecclesiastes is for this reason "very general, impersonal," and—in the words of Martin Hengel—"maintained only with difficulty."[46] Pagans frequently imagined a similar power above and beyond all things, but in comparison with the old myths, this abstract and implacable "fate" or *tuchē*—more or less synonymous with chance—"often had a fully secularized sense and simply meant the established course of events" (ibid., 125). Here we see a conception of the cosmos intimately bound up with the atheist teaching that "all things which are coming into existence, or have or will come into existence, do so partly by nature, partly by art, and partly owing to chance [*tuchēi*]" (*Laws* 888e, LCL). From the late Hellenistic period onward beleaguered believers—whether Platonic, Jewish, or Christian—had to find ways to make arguments for faith in the existence of their divinity responsive to the difficulty of accepting any god beyond the ordinary course of nature, fabricated images, or sheer luck.

It is against this "fully secularized" understanding of the world that Paul instructs his readers to train whatever willpower they have. Essential to his argument is the proposition that the cosmos, far from being eternal, has a distinct beginning and is destined to end: "The appointed time has grown short," he tells the Corinthians. The great historical pivot—for all practical purposes the end of the world—has been realized in principle with Christ's advent and merely requires for its full actualization an interval of expectant detachment: "From now on let even those who have wives be as though

---

45. ἐγώ εἰμι ὁ ὤν; on this construction see Kahn, *The Verb "Be,"* 453–57; Ws 13:1; 4 Mc 5:24: "we worship only the god who exists [μόνον τὸν ὄντα θεόν]." Cf. Philo, *On Creation* 61 (170); *That the Worse is Wont to Attack the Better*, 89–90; and Heb 6:1, 11:5; see also Jan Assmann, *The Invention of Religion: Faith and Covenant in the Book of Exodus* (Princeton, NJ: Princeton University Press, 2018), 132–33.

46. Martin Hengel, *Judaism and Hellenism: Studies in their Encounter in Palestine during the Early Hellenistic Period*, trans. John Bowden (London: SCM Press, 1974), 1:124.

they had none, and those who mourn as though they were not mourning, and those who rejoice as though they were not rejoicing, and those who buy as though they had no possessions, and those who deal with the world as though they had no dealings with it. For the present form of this world is passing away" (1 Cor 7:29–31). Faith here leads to a counterfactual, almost fictive way of living in the secular world "as though not." It goes without saying that the wives, the mourning, the rejoicing, and the purchasing—all the dealings with the world—continue on in any case; indeed the present form of the world *must* continue on as an all-too-present touchstone, without which the counterfactual life of faith would have nothing to transcend. "The essence of [Paul's] charge against the Corinthians," writes Bruce Winter, "is that they behave in a secular fashion, that is, they measure their instructors by the same canon as do the secular Corinthians."[47] Only once that charge is laid against them can Paul articulate his vision of the sacred as a form of desecularization.

It is imperative for Paul that the object of his faith and the subject of his preaching appear as "a scandal to Jews and foolishness to Gentiles" (1 Cor 1:23)—"unworthy of credence," in Rudolf Bultmann's summary, "from the standpoint of worldly understanding."[48] That is how Paul's listeners are supposed to know that his teaching utterly surpasses the world: "My speech and my proclamation," he writes to the Corinthians, "were not with persuasive [*peithois*] words of wisdom, but with a demonstration [*apodeixei*] of spirit and of power, so that your faith [*pistis*] might rest not on human wisdom but on the power of God" (1 Cor 2:4–5). Paul goes out of his way to differentiate the proper use of language from the rhetorical techniques of classically trained sophists, but he can only do so by parroting and adopting their terminology. He may disavow persuasive words of wisdom, that is, but he too aims to win his listeners' faith (*pistis*) by means of a demonstration (*apodeixis*).[49] No one knows what sort of rhetoric-transcending performance Paul put on for the Corinthians, but we can guess that it involved something hard to comprehend and that it inspired as much doubt as it quelled—hence the need for him to follow up with a letter explaining in clearer words that what the

---

47. Bruce W. Winter, *Philo and Paul Among the Sophists: Alexandrian and Corinthian Responses to a Julio-Claudian Movement*, 2nd ed. (Grand Rapids, MI: Eerdmans, 2002), 175.
48. *Theological Dictionary of the New Testament*, ed. Gerhard Friedrich, trans. and ed. Geoffrey W. Bromiley (Grand Rapids, MI: Eerdmans, 1968), 6:225.
49. See Aristotle, *Rhetoric* 1356a (LCL). Cf. Plato, *Laws* 887a, and Quintilian, *The Orator's Education* 5.10.7: "'Ἀπόδειξις est evidens probatio [*Apodeixis* is clear proof]" (LCL); for analysis, see Winter, *Philo and Paul Among the Sophists*, 149–50, 159–64.

Corinthians had witnessed was a demonstration of God's power, in the event that any of them had perceived something less grand. Like the teachings of Socrates—to whom Paul is implicitly compared in Acts 17—Paul's doctrines open him to the charge of having invented a dangerous sophistry that promotes a godless perspective.[50] Paul, too, insists that the idols worshipped as gods are "nothing in the world" (1 Cor 8:4, AV) because, in point of fact, "there is no god [*oudeis theos*]" (1 Cor 8:4).

Or at any rate, no god "but one [*ei mē eis*]" (1 Cor 8:4). I will return in future chapters to Paul's belief in the existence of "so-called gods" (aka demons) but want to linger for a moment over his integration of the fool's atheism into his definition of monotheism. I take it as a model for how the Pauline corpus more generally coopts the ancient skepticism whose presence has been all but erased by scholars writing in the wake of Febvre. The erasure often prides itself on a unique ability to read the texts of the past without anachronism, "from within" the communities of meaning that produced them. Those communities become in this way the safeguard of a peculiarly modern, pious fantasy that the writers of scripture lived at a time when faith was so unquestioned its absence could not be imagined. If scripture literally contradicts this fantasy, then the literal meaning must be set aside in favor of a complex hermeneutical framework, so that the fantasy may survive. Consider for example this paradigmatic statement from the letter to Hebrews: "Without faith [*pisteōs*], it is impossible to please God, for whoever would approach him *must believe that he exists* [*pisteusai . . . oti estin*]" (Heb 11:6a, my emphasis). We can see with great clarity the tendency of *l'histoire des mentalités* to blind itself to anything in the past that might threaten modernity's unique, scientific ability to conceive of God's nonexistence in Teresa Morgan's difficulty with this verse: "It cannot be right," she insists, "that this passage and 6.1 refer to belief in the existence of God." Her argument takes place on the circular grounds that the Greek verb "to be" is exceedingly unlikely to mean "exists" because Greeks at the time (not to mention Romans) "believed—or simply assumed—that the gods existed."[51] In fact they knew many atheists by name (Epicurus, Prodicus,

---

50. See Mark D. Given, *Paul's True Rhetoric: Ambiguity, Cunning, and Deception in Greece and Rome* (Harrisburg, PA: Trinity Press International, 2001), 3. On the Socrates–Paul parallels, see Foakes-Jackson and Lake, *Beginnings of Christianity*, 4:212; Hans Dieter Betz, *Der Apostel Paulus und die sokratische Tradition: Eine exegetische Untersuchung zu seiner "Apologie" 2 Korinther 10–13* (Tübingen: Mohr, 1972); Betz, "The Problem of Rhetoric and Theology According to the Apostle Paul," in *L'Apôtre Paul: Personnalité, Style et Conception du Ministère*, ed. A. Vanhoye (Leuven: Leuven University Press, 1986), 16-48.

51. Teresa Morgan, *Roman Faith and Christian Faith: "Pistis" and "Fides" in the Early Roman Empire and Early Churches* (Oxford: Oxford University Press, 2015), 334 and 126, respectively, contradicting William L. Lane, *Hebrews 9–13* (Dallas, TX: World Books, 1991), 338, who presents a wealth of counterevidence.

Euhemerus, Diagoras, Critias, Socrates, among others) and assumed that the existence of the gods was subject to intense debate: "No one has been prolific in finding convincing demonstrations for the existence of the gods," writes Philodemus sometime in the first century BCE.[52] The use of *estin* as an existential predicate with respect to the gods is well attested before, during, and after the composition of the New Testament. It appears, for example, in the discussion of atheism by Plutarch—an exact contemporary of the letter to Hebrews and, like it, one of the more consequential representatives of Middle Platonism.[53] It seems highly probable that the letter to Hebrews follows Plato in positing as real, reacting against, and so incorporating the atheist's unbelief. Whether *we* think atheism was real at the time is almost beside the point. The letter needs unbelief—together with the potential nonexistence of God—so that it can articulate the meaning of "faith."

Faith in that case does not mean overcoming doubts so much as redeploying them strategically against whatever one's severest critics hold sacred. Jews, according to this letter, must learn *not to believe* that their rituals in any way suffice to bring them closer to the divine. They must learn to view their priests as the equivalent of cave dwellers offering worship "in a sanctuary that is a sketch and a shadow of the heavenly one" (Heb 8:5). They must come to accept that the law itself is an empty "shadow of the good things to come and not the true form of these realities" (Heb 10:1). The old covenant—"subject to corruption, and therefore imperfect" (Heb 8:13n8, Geneva 1587)—calls out for replacement with a "new testament" (Heb 8:8, Geneva 1587), and by "new" the epistle unambiguously means more advanced and "better" (Heb 8:6). For "in speaking of 'a new covenant,' he [the Lord] has made the first one obsolete. And what is obsolete and growing old will soon disappear" (Heb 8:13). To accept the new testament, in this telling, requires a skeptical condemnation of traditional belief as an outmoded superstition.

Here is the new regime, the rupture, the "revolution in time" that descriptions of modernity so often replicate.[54] The past is now a primitive place whose obsolescence must nonetheless be maniacally preserved in order to provide the

---

52. Philodemus, *On Piety*, ed. Dirk Obbink, part 1 (Oxford: Clarendon, 1996), 151 (§23); cf. 1–23, 143, 377.
53. Plutarch, *Superstition* §2 (LCL). For Hebrews' Platonism, see Luke Timothy Johnson, *Hebrews: A Commentary* (Louisville, KY: Westminster John Knox Press, 2006), and Ronald Cox, *By the Same Word: Creation and Salvation in Hellenistic Judaism and Early Christianity* (Berlin: de Gruyter, 2007). Pace Morgan, *Roman Faith*, 151–57.
54. Bruno Latour, *We Have Never Been Modern*, trans. Catherine Porter (Cambridge, MA: Harvard University Press, 1993), 10.

most recently enlightened with grounds to insist on their novelty (ibid., 69; cf. 114). The decision to retain the Hebrew Bible, rechristened by the early Fathers as the "Old Testament" and expanded to include a greater range of uniquely Greek elements, sowed the seeds of the (post)modern condition—one haunted by a past whose inadequacy cannot be abjured, ill at ease in a present whose fulfillment proves day by day equally empty and deferred. After all, the defining feature of the gospel's good news, according to Hebrews, is that the *really* new thing has not even happened yet: "so Christ, having been offered once to bear the sins of many, will appear a second time, not to deal with sin, but to save those who are eagerly waiting for him"—eagerly and, some manuscripts add, "through faith" (*dia [tes] pisteos*) (Heb 9:28). They could not help but feel eager, these forward-looking Christians, as they found themselves stuck for the time being in a disenchanted shadow-world of their own making. The law no longer applied, the old gods had been discredited, the new god had died, and his corpse had disappeared. "Where is the promise of his coming?" Christians began asking. "All things continue as they were from the beginning of creation" (2 Pet 3:4). Until Christ came back believers were left "in this middle age [*in hoc interim saeculo*]," filled with trials and secular temptations, with disappointment and dissention, and with the constant concern that their faith might be no faith at all.[55] Meanwhile the seductions of the world were still capable of offering, to believers and unbelievers alike, no small consolation. In advance of the second coming, everything would continue just as it had before the Flood and the destruction of Sodom: "They did eat and drink, they married wives and were given in marriage. . . . Likewise as it came to pass in the days of Lot. They did eat and drink, they bought and sold, they planted and built" (Lk 17:27–28, DR). This middle age and interim *saeculum* is the real beginning of the secular age.

"Seen things are a delight," writes Hermes Trismegistus—an alleged Egyptian mystic of great use to neo-Platonic Christians. "But unseen things inspire disbelief [*dyspistian*]."[56] Hermes means that people take too much pleasure in their senses to believe in what they cannot perceive. An ingrained skepticism therefore arises from our sensuous orientation to the world: "It is sense-perception," Plotinus concurs, "that does not believe [*apistoun*]."[57] Unbelief

---

55. Augustine, *De civ. Dei* 11.1 (LCL, modified). I have followed the translation proposed by George Gordon, "*Medium Aevum* and the Middle Age," *S.P.E. Tract* No. 19 (London: Clarendon, 1925), 1–25 at 6.
56. *Corpus Hermeticum* 4.9, in *Hermetica: The Ancient Greek and Latin Writings Which Contain Religious or Philosophical Teachings Ascribed to Hermes Trismegistus*, ed. and trans. Walter Scott (Oxford: Clarendon, 1924), 1:154–55 (modified); δυσπιστίαν is Scott's emendation for δυσπιστεῖν. See Peter Dronke, *Hermes and the Sybils: Continuations and Creations* (Cambridge: Cambridge University Press, 1990).
57. Plotinus, *Enneads* V.8.11 (LCL): "τὸ οὖν ἀπιστοῦν ἡ αἴσθησίς ἐστιν."

according to this viewpoint is a choice grounded in the widespread preference for "the good things that are" (Ws 2:6, DR) such as marriage, trade, gardening, and building—things whose existence can be confirmed over and against an unverifiable godhead and its promise of eternal rewards: "After this, we shall be as if we had not been," declare the unbelievers (Ws 2:2, DR). Christians have never known a time when the pursuit of human flouring and "the Epicures life," which proceeds from "infidelity" (Ws 2:6, DR marginal gloss), could not offer humans a pathway to temporary but immediate fulfillment: "Everywhere let us leave signs of joy: because this is our portion, and this our lot" (Ws 2:9, DR). Nor were ancient materialists, in the eyes of the church, the only people committed to unbelief. "Be he Jew, pagan, or heretic," write the commentators of the Douai-Rheims, "the infidel . . . is already (if he die in his incredulity) by his own profession and sentence condemned" (Jn 3:18, DR annotation). What Jews, pagans, heretics, and, eventually, Muslims *thought* they believed was of no consequence. Their perspectives had to be overwritten as a radical absence of faith if true belief was going to be the exclusive provenance of whatever Christian faction called itself orthodox. The church created in this way a world overwhelmed by atheists, infidels, and idol worshippers, against which true believers had constantly to defend themselves so as not to fall prey to temptation and enter a secular abyss of their own making.

Chapter 2

Egypt and the Invention of the *Saeculum*

Unbelief and the World

When Augustine read that God had been in the world, "but the world did not know him" (Jn 1:10), "the world," he inferred, must function in scripture as code for "unbelievers."[1] Of these there were several types. Jews were the most abject, variously described by him (and by later schoolmen) as *infideles* or *increduli* because they "did not know how to rejoice in the hope of things unseen" and were content to sell "their birthright for the pleasures of the flesh."[2] Another type felt the same pull toward immediate gratification without sharing the same depth of guilt, having been born beyond scripture's reach, "'without hope and without God in this world,' where no prophet, no preacher of God's word, [and] as it were, no human had dwelt."[3] Unbelievers such as these loved the world because, so far as they knew, there was nothing greater to love. Still others had access to the gospel and consulted it gladly but found themselves inspired by their reading to

---

1. *Serm.* 121.1 (PL 38:678; WSA III/4:234): "*homines infideles.*"
2. *En. in Ps.* 105.37 (CCSL 40:1568; WSA III/19:221); *En. in Ps.* 113.2 (sermo 1) (CCSL 40:1636; WSA III/19:306). Cf. *Serm.* 77.15 (PL 38:490; WSA III/3:325): "*Judaei increduli*" and *Ep.* 137.16 (CCSL 31B:271; WSA II/2:222): "*Reproba per infidelitatem gens ipsa Judaeorum.*"
3. *En. in Ps.* 28.8 (CCSL 38:170–1; WSA III/15:295). Quoting Eph 2:12.

doubt. They acted like evangelists in reverse, seeking people out and posing difficult questions, "either to hold some back from the faith, lest they come to believe, or to trouble as much as possible those who already believe by harassing them."[4] This type comprised well-informed pagans and Jews together with the self-professed Christians that other Christians called *heretici*. As a result of the overall dissention even those "with a healthy faith," according to Augustine, were in the habit of voicing great skepticism under color of wanting "to advance their own knowledge or to refute the vain utterances of others" (ibid.). And in either case, whether it was to redress their own ignorance or to win a dispute with godless men, they wanted to know above all how to counter the impression "that the evangelists themselves contradict one another" (ibid.) and that scripture was therefore itself to blame for the rampant unbelief everywhere surrounding the one true faith.

"O church," preaches Augustine, "your enemy is the pagan, the Jew, the heretic—it is the earth!"[5] Throughout the Middle Ages each of these figures was repeatedly made to signify the sort of person who refused to believe. By targeting them for critique, Augustine and the Fathers created not only a series of phantasmatic enemies but a church whose experience of transcendence was bounded by the lure of immanent valuation; a church consequently defined as much by its faith in Christ as by its rivalry with the *infideles, increduli*—even straight-up *atheoi*—who mistook "the earth" for a legitimate source of value and then compensated for its obvious limitations with imaginative fabrications so enticing that mere aesthetics readily stood in, among these people, for the promise of further deliverance. Their unbelief was intimately connected to the time-bound world (whether figured as *terra, mundus*, or *saeculum*) and to the pleasures of the flesh, which medieval Christians usually took to mean the pursuit of human fulfillment—through sex, for example, power, money, or the cultivation of art, "for whiche thingis," says the Wycliffite Paul, "the wraththe of God cam upon the sones of unbileve."[6] That last phrase translates *filios incredulitatis*, the Vulgate's rendering

---

4. *De consensu* 1.7.10 (CSEL 43:11; WSA I/15/16:144).
5. *Serm.* 56.14 (PL 38:384; WSA III/3:103). Cf. Ethan H. Shagan, "Periodization and the Secular," in *Early Modern Histories of Time: The Periodizations of Sixteenth- and Seventeenth-Century England*, ed. Kristen Poole and Owen Williams (Philadelphia: University of Pennsylvania Press in cooperation with Folger Shakespeare Library, 2019), 72–87, esp. 73: "Medieval Christians always already imagined that they were living in a secular time, a world so corrupted that religion could subsist there only as a pale shadow."
6. Col 3:6, early Wycliffite. Cf. Augustine, *De sermone Domini in monte* 1.16.46 (CCSL 35:52; WSA I 15/16:48) equating unbelief (*infidelitas*) with fornication, avarice, and idolatry.

of *hious tēs apeitheias* and one that stays true, where modern Bibles generally no longer do, to the etymological root of *apeitheias*: literally "unconvinced" by the "proofs" (*pisteis*) marshaled in support of "faith" (*pistis*)—all words that derive from Peitho, the Greek goddess of persuasion, mother of tragedy, and, in my reading, the patron saint of medieval drama.

Tragedy and philosophy from antiquity forward, Russ Leo has shown, both operate as venues for debate, the staging of contradiction, and the exploration of whatever it is that might count as credible proof, worthy of belief.[7] Both are bound up with the prospect that every god is merely *ex machina*—a fiction or gimmick papering over the fact (as Jason will say of Medea's heaven-sent chariot) that "there are no gods."[8] Atheistic statements of this kind were in Seneca's day already centuries old. And they would be cultivated further by the process of Christianization because Christians openly avowed them, even while insisting that "the one who exists" (Ex 3:14, LXX) had taken on mortal form with the Virgin Birth and then was crucified. The skeptical and secularizing elements that Leo and others have found in the *Herodes Infanticida*—a play written at roughly the same time as *Lear* in the Dutch Republic by Daniel Heinsius, a leading scholar and commentator on Aristotle's poetics in the tradition of Hermannus and Averroes—are also present in earlier dramatizations of the Nativity, above all the one in the *Carmina Burana*.[9] Well before the seventeenth century it was possible for such plays to represent a debate about the status of the nova over Bethlehem, to explore its catastrophic results in the Slaughter of the Innocents and the Flight to Egypt, and to stage "a scene of interpretation," in Leo's fine phrase, "based on limited information, in the absence of faith."[10] The very idea that faith might *be* absent—such that Herod, for example, could set God aside to focus instead on maximizing his temporal power—is both a commonplace of Christian theology and the result of its spread.

Before Heinsius's circle in Leiden or Shakespeare's in London could present events in Egypt as a secular antipode to Christianity, that is, earlier Christians first had to establish that the *saeculum* as such has no transcendent meaning, that people enjoy its transient rewards out of sheer animal instinct, and (most importantly) that the apparitions of a finite, material existence are an all too tempting stand-in for God because God is virtually impossible to

---

7. Russ Leo, *Tragedy as Philosophy in the Reformation World* (Oxford: Oxford University Press, 2019).
8. Seneca, *Medea* 1027 (LCL); see Jeff Jay, *The Tragic in Mark: A Literary-Historical Interpretation* (Tübingen: Mohr Siebeck, 2014), 100–5, 198–204, and Leo, *Tragedy as Philosophy*, 105–6, 111, 115–16, 246.
9. See also Mark Somos, *Secularisation and the Leiden Circle* (Leiden: Brill, 2011).
10. Leo, *Tragedy as Philosophy*, 201.

grasp whereas money, sex, power, knowledge, food, drink, and art are easy to exalt—so much so that it remains a permanently open question whether any god you might manage to love, including Christ, is anything other than an extension of this all too seductive, fascinating world: "You do not worship Christ but something else under the name of Christ, which you have made up by lying to yourselves," Augustine tells Faustus. "And the gods you serve are either the bodies visible in the heavens or hosts of your own contrivance; to these creatures of your imagination you have not built shrines, as if for vain and inane simulacra, but rather you have made your hearts their temple."[11] The splendors of the heavens, around which Mani constructed an astrological theology of light, are not gods but *vanitas poetica*, Augustine elsewhere explains.[12] Faustus can profess his devotion to heavenly matters till he is blue in the face, for all Augustine cares; in reality he and every other Manichean are "defiled with unbelief [*infidelitatis*] and error" by virtue of their false piety—in particular their worship of "things that have no existence at all but are fabricated, rather, by the vanity of your deceptive fables."[13]

Augustine wants to see such inanities destroyed and the "dead souls" that linger over the ruins taught to understand that the physical cosmos as a whole will be returned to the void from which it has been momentarily called *ex nihilo*.[14] They will then learn that what they had mistaken for substantive being is nothing but show—mere appearance, the flickering shadow world of *aisthēsis*, as explained in the previous millennium by Plato and the prophets: "Their work is of nothing," Isaiah says of every other religion. "Their images are wind and confusion" (Is 41:29, Geneva 1587). While awaiting the final conflagration Augustine is glad to find himself living through a period of iconoclasm sufficiently violent to justify his claim that Christians have a better grasp of the truth than infidels: "If they refuse to believe that Christ taught such things, let them read the prophets, who not only enjoined the destruction of the superstitions of idols, but also predicted that this destruction would come to pass in Christian times. And if they were mistaken, why is there so clear a demonstration?"[15] Augustine feels great vindication in witnessing the manifest fulfillment of the prophets' demand

---

11. *Contra Faust.* 16.10 (CSEL 25:449; WSA I/20:204–5).
12. *De consensu* 1.23.32 (CSEL 43:30; WSA I/15/16:154).
13. *Contra Faust.* 6.3, 20.5 (CSEL 25:287, 539; WSA I/20:94, 284), respectively.
14. Ps(?)-Augustine, *Exp. in Apocal. Joh.*, Hom. 3 (PL 35:2421); Augustine, *Serm.* 65.6.7 (PL 38:430; WSA III/3:196): "Every man without God has a dead soul . . . You bewail the dead . . . bewail instead the infidel [*infidelem*]"; similarly *Serm.* 62.2 (PL 38:415; WSA III/3:157).
15. *De consensu* 1.16.24 (CSEL 43:22–23; WSA I/15/16:150).

that all prior representations of the sacred be exposed as mere things of the world and forcibly stripped of their fraudulent holiness; that they be, in a word, secularized. Often enough Augustine's most fervent hope (whether he's channeling at any given moment the prophets, Plato, Euhemerus, or Paul) is to show that the infidels who do not share his beliefs believe in *nothing*; that they have placed their trust in little more than the ephemera of a passing world. Augustine delights in exposing the vacuity of charms that once counted as sacred but, when broken, hold no further enchantment. Everywhere he looks he sees with satisfaction "this destruction of temples and condemnation of sacrifices and smashing of images" in conformity with the Decalogue's ban, which he thinks has proven not only the existence but the supremacy of his god, "who thus betrays, and thus extinguishes, all their sacred rites."[16]

Augustine stands at roughly the midway point between the originators of the "Yahwistic puritan tradition" and the Protestants who turned its ancient iconoclasm against the Catholic Church.[17] As central to medieval theology as to Protestantism, he translates into the skeptical language of Greco-Roman philosophy what Aleida Assmann has called "the big bang of modernization"—namely, the introduction of "a clear distinction between the creator and his work. The Jewish monotheistic God no longer resides in the world but has withdrawn from it into new and abstract spheres . . . In the course of this withdrawal, the world was suddenly reduced to the profane, the disenchanted, the objectified, the materialized, and the site of human responsibility."[18] If we want to find the moment, in the words of Regina Schwartz, "when God left the world," we cannot start with the Renaissance or the Reformation—much less Shakespeare—because these supposedly decisive phenomena come late to a landscape emptied of divinity.[19]

The evacuations of the sacred, secularizations, and attacks on magic that many scholars of English literature have placed in the sixteenth century depend on a much earlier invention—the *saeculum*. Its construction is accomplished conceptually through biblical exegesis and materially through

---

16. *De consensu* 1.16.24, 1.21.29 (CSEL 43:22–23, 28; WSA I/15/16:150, 153), respectively.
17. MWG 1/19:535; English in Max Weber, *Ancient Judaism*, trans. and ed. Hans H. Gerth and Don Martindale (Glencoe, IL: Free Press, 1952), 210.
18. Aleida Assmann, *Is Time Out of Joint? On the Rise and Fall of the Modern Time Regime* (Ithaca, NY: Cornell University Press, 2020), 65–66.
19. Regina Schwartz, *Sacramental Poetics at the Dawn of Secularism: When God Left the World* (Stanford: Stanford University Press, 2008). For a model of periodization closer to my own, see Schwartz, *The Curse of Cain: The Violent Legacy of Monotheism* (Chicago: Chicago University Press, 1997).

the evangelical conquest of Asia Minor, North Africa, and Europe from the fourth to the twelfth centuries. Egypt is central to the process because it stands for the paradigmatic, godless domain from which Moses first opened an avenue of escape and to which Christ returned to destroy any residual vestige of sanctity. Egypt in other words represents the place where infidels from time immemorial have pursued nothing beyond their own flourishing. I am going to spend this chapter describing the exegetical and cultural histories that inspired dramatizations of the Exodus and Flight to Egypt in the millennia before Shakespeare's *Antony and Cleopatra*, giving pride of place to the destruction of Egyptian idols that concludes the *Carmina Burana* in its earliest reconstructible form. This scene of ruination memorializes the process of Christianization from the fourth to the sixth centuries while at the same time speaking to contemporaneous conflicts with the infidel in Egypt, the Holy Land, and the northern frontier at the time of the Crusades. After Christ's legendary iconoclasm had been exported across the greater Mediterranean and into the far north—toward the end of securing the transcendence of the godhead in contrast to the secular world—late antique and medieval Christians seem to have found that the secular world could also lay claim to their own cultic practices. If other peoples' religious undertakings were easy to expose as a vacuous devotion to human appetites, what about the Christian liturgy? Was it not an idol before which any believer risked reveling out of sheer worldly joy? And if so, was it not possible to find in the pure theater of it all a certain, ironic satisfaction? Evidently the secularization of others' sacred objects was at once a means of desacralization and, in the medieval performance of Egyptian devotion, a strategy for keeping unbelief and the delights of idolatry in play, notwithstanding the official animus of the church against them.[20]

Enlightenment and the Flight from Egypt

A more conventional narrative of secularization would have us believe that before the Enlightenment "western civilization was based on a largely shared core of faith, tradition and authority."[21] According to this viewpoint—which has already come in for plenty of criticism—questions about the value of secular existence were not asked in the Middle Ages, and various answers we now take

---

20. Joe Moshenska, *Iconoclasm as Child's Play* (Stanford: Stanford University Press, 2019), esp. xi and 7.
21. Jonathan Israel, *Radical Enlightenment: Philosophy and the Making of Modernity 1650–1750* (Oxford: Oxford University Press, 2001), 3.

for granted were never uttered.²² Since every spiritual conflict could be resolved with reference to faith, tradition, and authority, "the commonly accepted medieval system of values was not subject," D. W. Robertson explains, "to the kind of initial fragmentation necessary to produce an Hegelian tragic situation."²³ Cracks within this monolithic consensus first appeared with the quattrocento recovery of antiquity, the invention of printing, the discovery of the New World, the Reformation, the Copernican revolution, and the rise of empirical science, among other destabilizing factors—all of which contributed to the development of an enlightened outlook wholly at odds with the previous millennium. Modernity is thus removed from the Middle Ages not only by a certain number of centuries but by "epistemological breaks, epistemic ruptures so radical that nothing of that past survives in them."²⁴ Shakespearean tragedy counts among the most powerful signs of modernity's onset because it dramatizes in full our present, unprecedented dilemma. Behold unaccommodated man, deprived of illusion, newly awakened, staggered by the antinomies of reason.

And yet if we take at face value Kant's famous one-sentence definition of enlightenment as "humanity's exodus [*Ausgang*] from its self-incurred immaturity," the modern divide appears as little more than the latest version of the differentiation in scripture between idolators and monotheists.²⁵ *Ausgang* is the term Luther had used to translate *lə-ṣêt*, or what readers of the English Bible know from the Greek rendering—literally "road out" or "exit" (Ex 19:1). *Exodus* became a standard title for the second book of Moses in the Vulgate (originally *Shemōt* or *Names*), just as Greek words eclipsed other Hebrew titles in the so-called Pentateuch (Greek for "five scrolls"). Such rechristening was part and parcel of a broader process of Hellenization, one that looked on the story of Moses as a Neoplatonic allegory for the liberation of "all souls," in Philo's telling, "from the objects of sense-perception, doomed to die."²⁶ The foundation was thus laid for the flight from Egypt to function as a model for the global adoption of a transcendental or

---

22. See Margreta de Grazia, "The Modern Divide: From Either Side," *Journal of Medieval and Early Modern Studies* 37, no. 3 (2007): 453–67; Bruno Latour, *We Have Never Been Modern*, trans. Catherine Porter (Cambridge, MA: Harvard University Press, 1993); Leszek Kolakowski, *Modernity on Endless Trial* (Chicago: University of Chicago Press, 1990), esp. 5: "Modernity itself is not modern."
23. D. W. Robertson, *A Preface to Chaucer: Studies in Medieval Perspectives* (Princeton, NJ: Princeton University Press, 1962), 43.
24. Latour, *We Have Never Been Modern*, 68.
25. Immanuel Kant, "Beantwortung der Frage: Was ist Aufklärung?" in *Kant's Gesammelte Schriften*, ed. Königlich Preussischen Akademie der Wissenschaften, Part 1 (Berlin: de Gruyter, 1923), 8:35: "*Aufklärung ist der Ausgang des Menschen aus seiner selbstverschuldeten Unmündigkeit.*"
26. Philo, *On the Migration of Abraham* 3.14 (LCL).

critical philosophy able to posit regulative principles beyond the immediate, ephemeral world of *aisthēsis* through the use of pure reason. Christian writers were thereafter empowered to reinterpret Moses as a typological variant of the *Logos*, usually translated as "the Word" (Jn 1:1) but intimately bound up in Greek with questions of logic, mind, and the principle of rationality that moral philosophers from antiquity to now have hoped might function as an internal legislator between right and wrong.[27]

For Kant the long struggle of *Kritik* had always been to set philosophy's synthetic a priori cognition on par with mathematics, which was "left groping about for a long time (chiefly among the Egyptians)" before a "mindset revolution" produced Thales's geometrical proof, Pythagoras's attempt "to purge religion of popular delusion," and Plato's demythologized vision of an ethical commonweal that could maximize "the greatest human freedom according to laws."[28] Schopenhauer noted early on that Kant's fondness for liberation through legislation drew inspiration from a set of prohibitions that were "foreign to philosophy" insofar as they had been revealed by divine fiat in "the Mosaic Decalogue."[29] In fact Kant's overall critical project takes as its primary point of departure the ban on images: hence the unbridgeable disconnect, at the heart of all three *Critiques*, between any representation—aesthetic or conceptual—and the thing-in-itself.[30] God, immortality, and the freedom necessary for moral accountability are not to be found anywhere in the world of sensory perception but can still be inferred as reasonable postulates, provided that reason is willing to follow Kant's exodus on "this path, the only one left" leading from empty speculation to the promised land of all future metaphysics.[31] "When Kant imputes 'idleness and cowardice' to those who

---

27. On Moses as a type of Christ see Wayne Meeks, *The Prophet King: Moses Traditions and Johannine Christology* (Leiden: Brill, 1967), esp. 119–20 on the Logos; also, Ronald Cox, *By the Same Word: Creation and Salvation in Hellenistic Judaism and Early Christianity* (Berlin: de Gruyter, 2007).
28. Immanuel Kant, *Kritik der reinen Vernunft* (Frankfurt am Main: Suhrkamp, 1974), 1:22, 323–24; English in *Critique of Pure Reason*, trans. and ed. Paul Guyer and Allen W. Wood (Cambridge: Cambridge University Press, 1998), 107, 108, 397. The remark about Pythagoras occurs in Kant's lectures: see *Immanuel Kant's Sämmtliche Werke*, ed. G. Hartenstein (Leipzig, 1868), 8:29.
29. Arthur Schopenhauer, *The Two Fundamental Problems of Ethics*, trans. David Cartwright and Edward E. Erdmann (New York: Oxford University Press, 2010), 138, cf. 140, 149.
30. See esp. Immanuel Kant, *Critique of Judgment*, trans. Werner S. Pluhar (Indianapolis, IN: Hackett, 1987), 135; Theodor W. Adorno, *Negative Dialectics*, trans. E. B. Ashton (New York: Continuum, 1997), 207, 298; Thomas Rentsch, *Transzendenz und Negativität: Religionsphilosophische und ästhetische Studien* (Berlin: de Gruyter, 2010): "Socratic not-knowing, ethical monotheism's ban on images, and the negative theology of Neoplatonism are the founding endowments of the European history of reason" (217).
31. Kant, *Kritik der reinen Vernunft*, 1:12; trans. Guyer and Wood, 101.

remain unenlightened and scolds their laziness," writes Albrecht Koschorke, "he sounds like Moses, who wanted to free the people of Israel from Egyptian servitude. In a subtle way, he sets up a parallel between himself and the founder of the Jewish religion and redirects some of the mythic force of the biblical narrative to the narrative of the secular project of Enlightenment."[32]

The secular Enlightenment—such as it was—found any number of similar ways to reconstitute and appropriate for itself the authority of biblical narrative.[33] Kant is explicit in making the traditional argument that scripture, when correctly interpreted, is not only compatible with reason but amounts to "the worthiest and, now in the most enlightened [*aufgeklärtesten*] part of the world, the only instrument for the unification of all humanity in one church."[34] For him, as for the Fathers and schoolmen, Christian evangelism does not evaporate in the presence of reasoned criticism. On the contrary, reasoned criticism is its premise. In fact unbelievers' misapprehension of what constitutes reason is a primary target of Kant's first *Critique*, which he hopes might sever at last "the roots of materialism, fatalism, atheism . . . [and] free-spirited unbelief," among other aberrations, including "enthusiasm and superstition," together with "idealism and skepticism."[35] For Kant—as, again, for the Fathers and schoolmen (to say nothing of Luther)—scripture is if anything more suited than philosophy to the task of universal enlightenment because scripture contains in widely digestible form "the purest moral doctrine of religion" that can be harmonized with legal statutes.[36] Once reason has independently confirmed biblical teachings, "the universal church starts to form itself into an ethical state of God and to advance, according to an established principle that is one and the same for all human beings and for all times, toward this state's completion."[37] The *civitas Dei* is just over horizon.

The scriptural origin for such universality, as Kant well knew, appears in the first book of Moses and contains in germinal form the problem inherent to every monotheism—namely, its exclusions. How is it reasonable for the one

---

32. Albrecht Koschorke, *Fact and Fiction: Elements of a General Theory of Narrative*, trans. Joel Golb (Berlin: de Gruyter, 2018), 222.
33. Jonathan Sheehan, *The Enlightenment Bible: Translation, Scholarship, Culture* (Princeton, NJ: Princeton University Press, 2005).
34. Immanuel Kant, *Die Religion innerhalb der Grenzen der blossen Vernunft*, in *Kant's Gesammelte Schriften*, ed. Königlich Preussischen Akademie der Wissenschaften, Part 1, (Berlin: Georg Reimer, 1907), 6:112; English in *Religion within the Bounds of Bare Reason*, trans. Werner S. Pluhar (Indianapolis, IN: Hackett, 2009), 124.
35. Kant, *Kritik der reinen Vernunft*, 1:35; trans. Guyer and Wood, 119.
36. Kant, *Religion innerhalb der Grenzen*, in *Gesammelte Schriften*, 6:107; trans. Pluhar, 117.
37. Kant, *Religion innerhalb der Grenzen*, in *Gesammelte Schriften*, 6:124; trans. Pluhar, 138.

and only God of all to announce his absolute sovereignty to—and distribute his blessings through—only one people? Each of the three Abrahamic religions has offered a different response to this "scandal of particularity" (in the words of Emile Fackenheim), but one traditional answer from Philo onward has involved positioning Judaism as a philosophical movement illuminating the way, in the manner of Moses, for the rest of humanity.[38] "By your offspring," God promises Abraham, "shall all the nations of the earth gain blessing for themselves" (Gen 22:18). Jews may well be the "guardians of a truth that concerns everyone," Jan Assmann explains, but that truth has been "entrusted to them for the time being as a kind of spiritual avant-garde" and, in advance of the Messiah's arrival, does not need to be preached to—or imposed on—anyone other than themselves.[39] Even so, the promise of deliverance in Exodus is inextricable from the threat of violent ingress, and scripture is clear about the consequences for the indigenous: "I will drive out before you the Amorites, the Canaanites, the Hittites, the Perizzites, the Hivites, and the Jebusites," the Lord tells Moses. "You shall tear down their altars, break their pillars, and cut down their sacred poles" (Ex 34:11, 13). Medieval Christian theologians took it for granted—on the authority of pagan, patristic, and rabbinic sources—that the Jews had done the same thing to their oppressors on the way out of Egypt in an attempt to evacuate the old religion of every last hint of the sacred. When Moses expresses a fear of performing animal sacrifice, lest he and his followers offend animal-worshipping Egyptians, a rabbinic gloss has God explain that the Jews "will not depart from here before they slaughter the gods of Egypt before [the Egyptians'] eyes, that I may teach them that their gods are really nothing at all."[40] The laws enjoining Jews to sacrifice animals and to keep the meat kosher by draining the blood were expressly designed, according to this reading, to desecrate the beings that were worshipped in Egypt.[41]

---

38. Emil L. Fackenheim, *Encounters Between Judaism and Modern Philosophy: A Preface to Future Jewish Thought* (New York: Schocken, 1980), 18.
39. Jan Assmann, *The Price of Monotheism*, trans. Robert Savage (Stanford: Stanford University Press 2010), 17.
40. Midrash Exodus Rabbah XVI.3, in *Midrash Rabbah*, trans. H. Freedman and Maurice Simon, vol. 3: *Exodus*, trans. S. M. Lehrman (London: Soncino Press, 1939), 209; cf. Midrash Exodus Rabbah XVI.2 (*Midrash Rabbah*, 207–208); *Targum du Pentateuque: traduction des deux recensions palestiniennes complètes avec introduction, parallèles, notes et index*, trans. Roger le Déaut with Jacques Robert (Paris: Éditions du Cerf, 1978–81), 1:392–93, 2:62–65; Louis Ginzberg, *The Legends of the Jews*, trans. Henrietta Szold (Philadelphia: the Jewish Publications Society of America, 1910), 2:367; K. A. D. Smelik and E. A. Hemelrijk, "Who Knows Not What Monsters Demented Egypt Worships? Opinions on Egyptian Animal Worship in Antiquity as Part of the Ancient Conception of Egypt," in *Aufstieg und Niedergang der römischen Welt* II, vol. 17, part 4, ed. Wolfgang Haase (Berlin: de Gruyter, 1984), 1852–2000.
41. Josephus, *Against Apion* 1.239, 249 (LCL); similarly in Tacitus, *Hist.* 5.4; for analysis see John G. Gager, *Moses in Greco-Roman Paganism* (Nashville, TN: Abington Press, 1972), esp. 83–84, 117.

Because the Jewish exodus had failed to carry out this iconoclastic program against "all the nations of the earth," Augustine thought, responsibility for the universal dispersal of God's blessings must have been transferred, along with Esau's birthright, from the synagogue to a second-born church. The ongoing destruction of paganism in his lifetime and the gradual conversion of the wider Mediterranean verified Christ's fulfillment of the Mosaic agenda while at the same time providing a much-needed rejoinder to Judaism's rejection of his messianic status. Jews henceforth appear in the normative Christian interpretation of the so-called Old Testament as the opposite of a philosophical, avant-garde people.[42] They are the paradigmatic unbelievers and a model for the unenlightened reactionaries who actively choose to remain "immature children . . . held in bondage to the elements of the world."[43]

That translation of Paul first appears in Johann Piscator's New Testament (1604), remains current in the eighteenth century, and is quoted in a sermon by Johann Joachim Spalding, a well-known *Aufklärungstheologe* for whom Kant expresses admiration.[44] Its echo in Kant's definition of enlightenment, alongside his likening of enlightenment to Exodus, is in other words a late example of the millennia-long, theological-theoretical project of "rewriting the Jewish textual and cultural heritage in a form usable for Gentiles," one that has traditionally transformed the Jews from progenitors and custodians of a totalizing historical narrative into the primary obstacle to its realization.[45] Their stiff-necked commitment to tribal identity and primitive ritual

---

42. J. S. Siker, *Disinheriting the Jews: Abraham in Early Christian Controversy* (Louisville, KY: Westminster/John Knox, 1991); Craig A. Evans and Donald A. Hagner, eds., *Anti-Semitism in Early Christianity: Issues of Polemic and Faith* (Minneapolis, MN: Fortress Press, 1993); Peter Richardson, ed., with David Granskou, *Anti-Judaism in Early Christianity*, 2 vols. (Waterloo, ON: Wilfrid Laurier University Press, 1986); Hershel Shanks, ed., *Partings: How Judaism and Christianity Became Two* (Washington, DC: Biblical Archaeology Society, 2013); John G. Gager, *The Origins of Anti-Semitism* (Oxford: Oxford University Press, 1983); on the particularly vexed case of Paul, see Daniel Boyarin, *A Radical Jew* (Berkeley: University of California Press, 1994) and Alan Badiou, *St. Paul: The Foundation of Universalism*, trans. Ray Brassier (Stanford: Stanford University Press, 2003).
43. Gal. 4.3, in *Biblia, das ist: Die Gantze Heilige Schrifft, Alten und Neuen Testaments* [etc.], trans. Johannes Piscator (Bern, 1736; originally published in 1604): "*unmündige Kinder . . . als Knechte gehalten unter den elementen der Welt*" (2:223).
44. Norbert Hinske, "Nachwort zur zweiten Auflage," in *Was ist Aufklärung? Beiträge aus der Berlinischen Monatsschrift*, ed. N. Hinske and M. Albrecht (Darmstadt: Wissenschaftliche Buchgesellschaft, 1977), 545–47; Ursula Goldenbaum, "Understanding the Argument Through Then-Current Public Debates or My Detective Method of History of Philosophy," in *Philosophy and Its History: Aims and Methods in the Study of Early Modern Philosophy*, ed. Mogens Laerke et al. (Oxford: Oxford University Press, 2013), 71–90, esp. 78–79.
45. Fredric Jameson, *The Political Unconscious: Narrative as a Socially Symbolic Act* (Ithaca, NY: Cornell University Press, 1981), 29.

has been offered up time and again to demonstrate just how deeply they are "yoked, kept occupied and in awe, with innumerable fleshly, gross, and cumbersome offices" (Gal 4:3, DR annotation). Thanks especially to Luther, this commonplace of medieval theology had an extensive afterlife among the thinkers frequently cited today as representatives of the modern mindset—whether Kant, Hegel, Marx, or Wagner: "Ultimately, the belief that the Jews were possessed of an immoral national character in need of reform," writes Paul Lawrence Rose, "integrates Christian consciousness with that of the Enlightenment and its offspring, revolution."[46] Kant's Moses, in short, is not the Hebrew Moses but rather the patristic and medieval one, whose original *Ausgang* has to be repeated on a grander scale by Christ, because the Jews had "turned in heart back to Egypt . . . and rejoiced in the works of their hands" (Acts 7:39, 41). They had consequently left the liberation promised by Exodus, together with the meaning of the Hebrew Bible as a whole, to be fulfilled by the Christian Church. In order to become a member, it is essential to be baptized, which from the patristic era forward has been synonymous with becoming "enlightened [*illuminatus*]."[47] According to the typological substitution on which both medieval and modern Christianity depends, it is *Christ* who "enlightens [*illuminat*] the saints in the shadows of Egypt"—granted that Egypt "must be understood," in the standard patristic formulation, "as a figure of this world [*saeculi*]."[48]

We can see in scripture, in Augustine, and in Kant, that is, the shadow cast by every enlightenment over the Dark Ages, the primitive, the subaltern, the irrational, the impious, and all the other infidels who devote themselves to the groundless appreciation of a shadowy, transient world of immediate gratification; who are immature children, "deceived like foolish infants" (Ws 12:24) in treating the mundane, by virtue of its "beauty" (Ws 13:3, 14:20), *as though* it were divine. For the better part of postclassical Western history—including much of what we now call modernity—the disenchanted person who pierces the veil of illusion only to see a natural world bereft of transcendent, eternal meaning (all too full, however, of immanent,

---

46. Paul Lawrence Rose, *Revolutionary Anti-Semitism in Germany from Kant to Wagner* (Princeton, NJ: Princeton University Press, 1990), 17; cf. Michael Mack, *German Idealism and the Jew: The Inner Anti-Semitism of Philosophy and German Jewish Responses* (Chicago: University of Chicago Press, 2003); Arthur Hertzberg, *The French Enlightenment and the Jews* (New York: Columbia University Press, 1968).
47. Augustine, *Tract. in Joh.* 13.16 (CCSL 36:139; WSA III/12:256). Cf. Heb 6:4, 10:32.
48. *Biblia Latina cum Glossa Ordinaria: Facsimile Reprint of the Editio Princeps Adolph Rusch of Strassburg 1480/81*, ed. Karlfried Froehlich and Margaret T. Gibson (Turnhout: Brepols, 1992), 1:112, interlinear gloss on Ex 1:1, quoting Isidore of Seville, *Quaestiones in Vetus Testamentum*; Augustine, *En. in Ps.* 77.12 (CCSL 39:1078; WSA III/18:103): "*Terra itaque Aegypti in figura intelligenda est huius saeculi.*"

fleeting luxuriousness) has been the monotheist. Indeed we owe the widespread desanctification of the *saeculum* to the early medieval iconoclasms (Jewish, Christian, and Muslim) that successfully imposed on Asia Minor, North Africa, and Europe the Mosaic distinction between true and false religion—first, by denying the existence of the gods (or what amounts to the same thing, by celebrating exclusively "the one that exists" [Ex 3:14, LXX]) and, second, by projecting the most extreme forms of unbelief onto others and characterizing their so-called religions as "the atheism of the Egyptians."[49] The original opponents of Abrahamic monotheism could and did return the favor, accusing Jews, Christians, and Muslims of being the true atheists—with the result that not long after the birth of Christ, for the first time in Western history, virtually everyone with an education assumed that radical unbelief was a live option for somebody. Monotheism and atheism became thereafter inextricably intertwined in a millennia-long codependence neatly captured by an exchange between Saint Polycarp and those demanding his execution for destroying their gods: "Away with the atheists!" cheers the crowd. Polycarp is paraded into the stadium, groans, and looks to heaven: "Away with the atheists!" he says.[50]

In this radical questioning of what makes for a legitimate divinity we find the constitutive contradiction of biblical drama. It is especially well attuned "to conflict and to irreconcilable elements of life"—to borrow again from Russ Leo—if only because it is so closely tied to scripture, portions of which are indebted to ancient tragedy, both in their composition and subsequent exegesis.[51] Jan Assmann is not being entirely metaphorical when he (among many others) interprets the second book of Moses as a "monumental five-act drama of revelation," insofar as the word *exodos*, before being adopted as the title, was used to describe the outro that follows the last choral ode of a tragedy.[52] Whether or not that particular resonance motivated the transla-

---

49. Philo, *On the Posterity of Cain* 1.2 (LCL). See also *On Flight and Finding* 180 (LCL), where Moses brands "the Egyptian character as atheistical"; *Moses II*, 36.194 and 37.196 (LCL). On the Mosaic distinction, see Assmann, *Price of Monotheism*, 3.
50. *Martyrdom of Polycarp* 3.2, 9.2, in *Polycarp's Epistle to the Philippians and the Martyrdom of Polycarp: Introduction, Text, and Commentary*, ed. Paul Hartog (Oxford: Oxford University Press, 2013), 244–45, 252–53; cf. 12.2 ("destroyer of our gods").
51. Leo, *Tragedy as Philosophy*, 7.
52. Jan Assmann, *The Invention of Religion: Faith and Covenant in the Book of Exodus*, trans. Robert Savage (Princeton, NJ: Princeton University Press, 2018), 333; Aristotle, *Poetics* 1452b (LCL); Kevin J. Vanhoozer, *The Drama of Doctrine: A Canonical-Linguistic Approach to Christian Theology* (Louisville, KY: Westminster John Knox Press, 2005), 41; Peter Enns, *Exodus* (Grand Rapids, MI: Zondervan Publishing House, 2000), 172, 306, 363, and passim.

tors of the Septuagint and Vulgate, it was fairly routine among Christians to impose on scripture the conventions of Greek drama, either by composing the gospels on its model, by putting Dionysus in the mouth of the Lord (Acts 26:14; *Bacchae* 795), by alluding to *Medea* (Rom 7:15–20; *Medea* 1077–80) and to Menander (1 Cor 15:33), or by assigning speech prefixes to the books of the Old Testament so as to make their dramatic structure and their relation to the gospels more evident.[53] In the process, the birth of monotheism and the birth of tragedy—two originally independent developments from the Axial Age, each with a propensity "to call into question everything in heaven and on earth"—were conjoined to form the basis for a wildly conflict-ridden, medieval culture of performance.[54]

Vernacular stagings of the Exodus story find their earliest antecedent in a Greek play ascribed to Ezekiel the Tragedian, presumably a Hellenized Jew of second-century BCE Alexandria, sometimes identified with the Ezekiel named by Aristeas as one of the translators of the Septuagint.[55] The surviving fragments of his work are preserved mainly in Eusebius, though certain lines appear in Clement of Alexandria and Pseudo-Eustathius.[56] Once reassembled, they constitute the most extensive Hellenistic tragedy that we have and show a particular indebtedness to Aeschylus's *Persians*. The destruction of Xerxes's army while he tries to cross the Hellespont, for example, becomes in Ezekiel's play the destruction of Pharaoh and his army while they pursue the Jews across the Red Sea. This and several other

---

53. Robert Renehan, "Classical Greek Quotations in the New Testament," in *The Heritage of the Early Church*, ed. David Neiman and Margaret Schatkin (Rome: Pontificale Institutum Studiorum Orientalium, 1973), 17–46; George Mlakuzhyil, *The Christocentric Literary Structure of the Fourth Gospel* (Rome: Editrice Pontificio Istituto Biblico, 1987), 151; Jay, *Tragic in Mark*; John Parker, "Religion, Ritual and Myth," in *A Cultural History of Tragedy*, ed. Rebecca Bushnell, vol. 2: *In the Middle Ages*, ed. Jody Enders et al. (London: Bloomsbury, 2020), 81–98; and Parker, "Persona," in *Cultural Reformations: Medieval and Renaissance in Literary History*, ed. Brian Cummings and James Simpson (Oxford: Oxford University Press, 2010), 591–608. Cf. Leo, *Tragedy as Philosophy*, 50–51, 111, 211–15.
54. Robert Bellah, *Religion in Human Evolution: From the Paleolithic to the Axial Age* (Cambridge, MA: Belknap Press, 2011), 355.
55. Howard Jacobson, *The "Exagoge" of Ezekiel* (Cambridge: Cambridge University Press, 1983), 6–7; on the Aristeas letter, see John Parker, *The Aesthetics of Antichrist: From Christian Drama to Christopher Marlowe* (Ithaca, NY: Cornell University Press, 2007), 139–51.
56. Eusebius, *Praeparatio evangelica* 9.28–29, in *Eusebius Werke*, ed. Édouard des Places, 2nd ed. (Berlin: Akademie, 1982), 8.1:524–38; Eusebius, *Preparation for the Gospel*, trans. Edwin Hamilton Gifford (Oxford: Clarendon, 1903), 1:467–75; Clement of Alexandria, *Stromata* 1.23.155–56, in *Clemens Alexandrinus*, ed. Otto Stählin (Berlin: Akademie, 1985), 2:96–98; Ps-Eustathius, *Commentarius in Hexaemeron* (PG 18:729). The standard edition is B. Snell, ed., *Tragicorum Graecorum Fragmenta* (Göttingen: Vandenhoeck & Ruprecht, 1971), 1:288–301, but I have relied on the parallel Greek–English edition by Jacobson.

transpositions carry over a crucial ambiguity from the original. The defeat of Xerxes's army had occurred only a year before the first performance, but rather than playing to the Athenians' patriotism, Aeschylus's drama seems designed to generate "tragic compassion" for their enemies by making the Persians heroic but flawed and therefore doomed to be crushed in "recompense for their hubris and godless [*atheōn*] arrogance."[57] So too, in Ezekiel's tragedy, are the godless Egyptians killed by Yahweh. Their drowning stands out not merely as an ambiguous sign of Jewish triumph and a testimony to the tragic costs of monotheistic enlightenment but as an ominous warning of what now awaits any unbelieving Jew who strays from the faith. When, in scripture, the followers of Moses fashion a Golden Calf reminiscent of the Egyptian god Apis, they too are slaughtered, "as Moses commanded" (Ex 32:28). Even if the play ended before that fatal occurrence, it is foreshadowed in the death of Pharaoh and his army—as is the moment when, according to scripture, Moses fails to reach the Promised Land, dies in the desert, and is lost to an ocean of sand, such that "no one knows his burial place to this day" (Dt 34:6).

It is impossible to say exactly how the full text of Ezekiel's play might have handled the tragedy of Moses's life as reported by scripture, but the fragments we have are characteristic of tragedy in another respect—namely, the way they ask an audience "to think critically about what is possible, probable, and credible."[58] As we saw in the last chapter, a cluster of words emerged among Greek philosophers to define the credible (*pistos*) in conjunction with the persuasive (*pithanos*, *peistikos*, *pistikos*) laying out of proofs (*pisteis*) that give rise to faith (*pistis*); the same cluster produced in turn a nomenclature for the unbelievers (*apistoi*) who remain unpersuaded and rely on sense perception to generate their counterarguments. The Greek translation of the Exodus narrative foregrounds this terminology when Moses worries that his own people will "not believe [*mē pisteusōsi*]" that God has appeared to him (Ex 4:1, LXX). God must supply proof by way of miracles, which is to say, by way of signs (*sēmeia*) that have to be interpreted, like any other form of evidence. If the Jews "will not believe" the first sign, there will be a second (Ex 4:8, LXX); if they "will not believe" the second, there will be a third (Ex 4:9, LXX). At last "the people believed" (Ex 4:31, LXX), but not without foreshadowing the unbelief of Pharaoh in their initial refusal.

---

57. *Persians* 809 (LCL); for "tragic compassion" see Paul Ricœur, *The Symbolism of Evil* (Boston: Beacon Press, 1969), 218.
58. Leo, *Tragedy as Philosophy*, 5.

The official moral of the Exodus narrative may well be that Pharaoh's hardened heart exemplifies sin and deserves condemnation, but in Ezekiel's dramatic retelling, the story also illustrates the incomprehensible will of a god who darkens the eyes of incredulous mortals while empowering believers to terrorize them: "You shall work all manner of evil [*panta kaka*]," God tells Moses, as just comeuppance for "the hubris of evil men."[59] This is as good an example of "an Hegelian tragic situation" as any, and it happens in the earliest extant drama written by a monotheist; two equally valid moral imperatives stand in contradiction to one another, such that both "become wrongs."[60] Proponents of competing moral orders, equally convinced of their own righteousness, are equally capable of evil, and there is no rational way of knowing which is the correct view, only an unending series of investigations, falsifications, and highly fragile empirical confirmations that any given revelation stems directly from "the finger of God" (Ex 8:15).

In both Ezekiel's tragedy and later dramatizations of the flight from Egypt, these two competing orders—that of Pharaoh and that of Moses—are united by a shared skepticism. Moses's initial reaction to a divine miracle, same as Pharaoh's, is *not* to accept it but to look for more evidence out of sheer incredulity:

> What is this portent from the bush,
> Miraculous and incredible [*apistia*] to mortals?
> . . . I shall approach and examine this
> great miracle. For it does not produce belief [*pistin*] in men.[61]

I tried in my first chapter to show how the translators of the Septuagint and, subsequently, the writers of the New Testament incorporated into Judeo-Christian monotheism the language of (un)belief that originates in Greek philosophical debates over the existence of the gods. We can see here an especially consequential result of that incorporation; the ultimate apodeictic demonstration of the one true god's existence and power *must* be "incredible [*apistia*]," lest it be explainable as a natural phenomenon and therefore fail to indicate that its source transcends the laws of physics. Indeed Moses here confronts a problem that would become fundamental to the process of canonization and to the persecution of heretics and witches: "Doubt and controversy

---

59. Jacobson, *"Exagoge" of Ezekiel*, 58–59 (lines 132 and 148), modified.
60. Robertson, *Preface to Chaucer*, 43. Cf. Rebecca Comay, *Mourning Sickness: Hegel and the French Revolution* (Stanford: Stanford University Press, 2011): "The ultimate evil proves to be the beautiful morality that condemns evil" (151).
61. Jacobson, *"Exagoge" of Ezekiel*, 57 (lines 90–92, 94–95), modified. See Erkki Koskenniemi, *The Old Testament Miracle-Workers in Early Judaism* (Tübingen: Mohr Siebeck, 2005), 66–69.

not only attended miracles," Steven Justice has said of the Middle Ages, "but were actively cultivated in defining them."[62] Thinking critically about what was possible, probable, and credible meant adopting the posture of the skeptic, the atheist, the unbeliever, or infidel, whose incredulity belonged to faith as a necessary precondition and counterpart. The believer and unbeliever both recognized that any alleged miracle might be merely apparent—an illusion or misperception arising immanently from the world. The believer and unbeliever both understood that miraculous effects were cultivated by various magical techniques and theatrical reenactments in the hope of offering rewards independent of divine influence. If the necessary mark of supernatural intervention was that something incredible had happened—thus demonstrating that "nothing will be impossible with God" (Lk 1:37)—there was only a very short distance between genuine revelation, designed by God to provoke an enlightened faith, and the patent contrivances designed by jugglers to titillate the senses of those who did not believe but rather suspended their disbelief in service of an even greater, sensuous enjoyment.

If it was possible for devout Jews to turn "in heart back to Egypt" and to rejoice "in the works of their hands" (Acts 7:39, 41), it was possible for Christians. According to Ambrosiaster, the eating, drinking, and playing that went on before the Golden Calf symbolize "the extravagance in which unbelievers [*infideles*] in the things of God have always taken delight."[63] That is why, Ambrosiaster thinks, Paul refers to the Golden Calf when speaking *to Christians* about the dangers of idolatry. It is to warn us—us Christians—"lest we fall into this same doubt [*hanc diffidentiam*] by approving of indulgence in idols" (ibid.; citing 1 Cor 10:7 and Ex 32:6). The same line of thinking accounts for the objections to drama from Tertullian and Augustine through to the Fourth Lateran Council's declaration in canon 16 that "clerics should not practice callings or business of a secular nature [*officia vel commercia secularia*], especially those that are dishonorable. They should not watch mimes, jesters or actors."[64] Hence, as well, the late medieval attack on vernacular playacting, which likened theater to the "golden calf that the puple worschipid."[65] Losing faith and turning back in heart to the enslave-

---

62. Steven Justice, "Did the Middle Ages Believe in their Miracles?" *Representations* 103, no. 1 (2008): 1–29 at 6.
63. Ambrosiaster, *Comm. in 1 Cor* 10:6–7 (PL 17:234D).
64. *Decrees of the Ecumenical Councils*, ed. Norman P. Tanner (Washington, DC: Georgetown University Press, 1990), 2:243–44 (modified).
65. Clifford Davidson, ed., *A Tretise of Miraclis Pleyinge* (Kalamazoo, MI: Medieval Institute Publications, Western Michigan University Press, 1993), 112.

ment of sensory enjoyment is a constant risk to the pious. In some sense, that risk constitutes what it means to be Christian. Because "our hearts and our thoughts are not in our power," Ambrose explains, they inevitably call us back "to worldliness [*ad saecularia*], introduce earthly things, bring in pleasures, [and] interweave enticements."[66] If the Jews became infidels by fashioning an idol before which they rose up "to play" (*ludere*)—a word that would come to cover everything from sex, gambling, song, and dance to liturgical drama—what were the Christians who staged fake miracles while awaiting the as-yet-deferred end of all things?

That is a question formulated more or less openly by the York *Moses and Pharaoh*. Put on by the Hosiers and dating from the late fourteenth or early fifteenth century, the play tests the proximity between a divine miracle and the apotheosis of human fabrication. We can't say for sure how the players would have fashioned the burning bush, but presumably its wonder lay in the artificiality of the contrivance. When Moses moves closer to the flame to find out "if it be werke of worldly wight" (York 11.103), everyone could plainly see that it was an artisanal contraption, and many would have understood the term "worldly" to mean *secular*. Indeed "werke of worldly wight" is effectively a Middle English translation of the Greek term we find in scripture for "a work of the hand" (*cheiropoiēton*), or what the Vulgate had rendered as *manufactum*, *simulacrum*, and *idolum*. From the middle of the first millennium BCE onward the purpose of this terminology had always been to "empty the claims of a salvation from above," as Latour argues; to show, that is, "the hands of humans at work everywhere, so as to slaughter the sanctity of religion."[67] Part of the joke in York is that the artisan players, like icon makers everywhere, openly fabricate by hand through purely artificial means the sacred effects on which the church depends for its legitimacy.

The other part of the joke is that the disenchanting gestures of iconoclasts and ironic playwrights could only make human fabrication seem all the more divine: "The more humans there are, the more human-work is shown," writes Latour, "the better is their grasp of reality, of sanctity, of worship. The more images, mediations, intermediaries, and icons are multiplied and overtly fabricated—explicitly and publicly constructed—the more respect we have for their capacity to welcome, gather, and recollect truth and sanctity . . . Far from

---

66. Ambrose, *De fuga saeculi* 1.1 (CSEL 32.2:163); English in *Saint Ambrose, Seven Exegetical Works*, trans. Michael P. McHugh (Washington, DC: Catholic University of America Press, 1972), 281, noting Augustine's fondness for this passage (281n1).
67. Bruno Latour, *On the Modern Cult of the Factish Gods* (Durham, NC: Duke University Press, 2010), 71.

despoiling access to transcendent beings, the revelation of human toil, of the tricks, reinforce the quality of this access" (ibid., 71–72). Although Latour means to envision with these words a future form of art and commentary at last unburdened by the ancient critique of images, he inadvertently provides a good description of the revelation on display throughout medieval drama, which is often at pains to reveal the human toil and tricks that go into fabricating gods—including its own. Latour's description is especially apt at the end where he falls into the vortex that devours all iconophiles; despite their hope to disassociate their own position from "the critical mood" of iconoclasm, they have always had to presuppose and extend that mood. Otherwise they can offer no "revelation of human toil, of the tricks" that go into fabricating gods so as to reinforce the supreme value of that toil.

Such revelation, such *exposure*, is usually outsourced on the medieval stage to the unbeliever: "all thair gaudis [tricks]," says Pharaoh of the Jews, "sall noght tham gayne" (York 11.248). Given the thoroughness of Christianity's appropriation of the Exodus narrative and the widespread conviction that the church was the true Israel, many in the audience must have taken this phrase as the empty vaunt of a hard-hearted idolater about to get his just comeuppance by drowning at the end of the play, while Moses and the Jews—typological representatives of Christ and the church—sing a liturgical song in celebration of their escape from the *saeculum*.[68] At the same time, however, Pharaoh's skepticism about the long-term benefits that would accrue to the Jews, qua Jews, is no different from the view of Christians who thought that Jews could "gayne" nothing from their adherence to the Mosaic law. After all God had saved his chosen people only in show, as a sign of the future redemption reserved for a different, still more enlightened people. And because the true Israel was *also* still awaiting the Kingdom, Christians, too, were evidently able to imagine how the unbelieving Jews must have felt when they abandoned God for the *saeculum* and decided to revel in the work of their hands.

"Hefe uppe youre hartis ay to Mahownde," says the York Pharaoh at the moment of his drowning. "He will be nere us in oure nede" (York 11.401–2). The conflation of Egyptian religion with Islam is both a legacy of the Crusades and a function of the infidel's power as a category: pagans, Jews, Muslims, heretics—same difference. All were "sons of unbelief" who worshipped "mawmetes"

---

68. For evidence that the play ends with the *Canticum Moysi*, see Richard Rastall, *Music in Early English Religious Drama* (Rochester, NY: D. S. Brewer, 1996), 1:23–24. On the liturgical setting, DeVan Dumas Ard, "Opus Lyricus: Liturgical and Lyric Forms in Late-Medieval British Poetry (PhD diss., University of Virginia, 2020), 24–35.

(Col 3:5)—to quote the word that in the later Wycliffite Bible replaces "idol" due to the certainty that Muslim unbelievers worshipped statues of "Mahownde" in a manner parallel to the way Christians venerated images of Christ. For any number of people in York, the largely semantic difference between worship and veneration could easily have been lost, such that the idolatry of unbelievers and the devotion of Christians might appear all too similar. Anyone could have heard in Pharaoh's prayer to his idol, for example, a hair-raising echo of the liturgical words that marked the beginning of the Eucharist—"Lift up your hearts [*sursum corda*]"—which were spoken with the hope that the ritual reenactment of the Last Supper might make Christ "nere" or even present.[69] Such hope was necessary because Christians retained from the Fathers a disturbing sense that any reenactment might amount to mere theater, and theater more than anything marked God's absence. By the late fourteenth century, in fact, dissidents had taken to calling the Eucharist "the fake miracle [*fictum miraculum*] of the sacrament of bread," which, they claimed, led people "into idolatry."[70] These dissidents were of course condemned in turn for having strayed from the faith. The one thing on which they and their inquisitors could all agree was the ubiquity of unbelief.

The Flight to Egypt and the Destruction of Idols

The earliest extant witness to the full set of liturgical reproaches or *improperia* that Christ is made to take up against the Jews every Good Friday dates from the tenth century, though performances of the chant were much older and would go on to have a long and troubling modern afterlife.[71] The first complaint begins with some verses from Micah rebuking God's chosen people for backsliding after being led "from the land of Egypt" (Mi 6:4). The chant goes on to pair this complaint—and each subsequent grievance, drawn

---

69. Frank C. Senn, *The Eucharistic Body* (Minneapolis, MN: Fortress Press, 2017), 35; R. C. D. Jasper and G. J. Cuming, eds., *Prayers of the Eucharist: Early and Reformed*, 3rd ed. (Collegeville, MN: Liturgical Press, 1992), 120.

70. *Concilia Magnae Britanniae et Hiberniae ab Anno MCCCL ad Annum MDXLV*, ed. David Wilkens (London, 1737), 3:221.

71. On the textual history of the chant, see Johann Drumbl, "Die Improperien der lateinischen Liturgie," *Archiv für Liturgiewissenschaft* 15 (1973): 68–100; Eric Werner, "Melito of Sardis, the First Poet of Deicide," *Hebrew Union College Annual* 37 (1966): 191–210; Armin Karim, "'My People, What Have I Done to You?': The Good Friday *Popule Meus* Verses in Chant and Exegesis, c. 380–880" (PhD diss., Case Western Reserve University, 2014); on its place in medieval drama and poetry, see Ard, "Opus Lyricus" (PhD diss., University of Virginia, 2020), 21–57, and O. B. Hardison, Jr., *Christian Rite and Christian Drama in the Middle Ages: Essays in the Origin and Early History of Modern Drama* (Baltimore, MD: Johns Hopkins University Press, 1965), 131–33; for an early modern version, see Giovanni Pierluigi da Palestrina, *Opera Omnia*, ed. Fraz Xaver Haberl (Leipzig, 1892), 31:171–72.

from elsewhere in the Old Testament—with a reminder that the Jews are also Christ killers. "O my people!" two *presbyteri* sing in the persona of Christ, who for his part now speaks in the person of Yahweh:

> I led you out of Egypt, plunging Pharaoh into the Red Sea, and you delivered me to the chief priests . . . I opened the sea before you, and you opened my side with a lance . . . I went before you in the pillar of cloud, and you guided me to Pilate's court . . . I struck the Canaanite kings for your sake, and you struck my head with a reed . . . I granted you a royal scepter, and you granted my head a crown of thorns . . . I raised you up in great power, and you hung me on the gibbet of the cross.[72]

Medieval participants in this ritual had it on the authority of the gospels and Paul that it was "the Jews who killed both the Lord Jesus and the prophets" (1 Thes 2:14–15)—a sentiment amplified by Augustine, among many others—so it must have been no great strain to imagine that crucifixion could count as a Jewish means of execution, despite the contrary evidence provided by scripture.[73] What's remarkable is not just the ferocity of the participants' Jew-hatred but the ease with which they address *themselves* as though they, too, were suffering from the same lack of faith as their most malevolent and phantasmatic antagonists. The chant, in other words, is not merely an example of the antisemitism uniting the medieval and modern periods—though it is certainly that.[74] It is also an example of Christian believers acknowledging that they, too, are in danger of joining the unbelieving world, same as any Jew atheist. In reproaching the infidel, they reproach themselves—for their manifest indifference to the divine, their remorseless attachment to the flesh, their voluntary refusal to exit the *saeculum*. More remarkable still, they understand these failures in terms of deicide, as though unbelief and an excessive love of the world led directly to the death of God.

It has been easier for scholars to understand the "doubt, fear and mortification" expressed on Good Friday—and easier to imagine that the Easter celebration allayed the anxieties of earlier, more naïve Christians—than to grasp how Christmas might inspire the same existential panic.[75] And yet the

---

72. *The Liber usualis*, ed. the Benedictines of Solesmes (New York: Desclée, 1963), 737–41; cf. *Processionale ad usum insignis ac praeclarae ecclesiae Sarum*, ed. W. G. Henderson (Leeds, 1882), 69–70. Further scriptural passages alluded to or quoted here are Dt 8:2–7 and Is 5:4.
73. Augustine, *De consensu* 1.13.20 (CSEL 43:19; WSA I/15/16:148): *"impio furore Christum occiderunt."* Cf. *Tract. in Joh.* 51.9 (CCSL 36:442): *"mortificandum infidelitate Judaeorum"* (commenting on Jn 12:24).
74. Jules Isaac, *Genèse de l'antisémitisme* (Paris: Calmann-Lévy, 1956), 306–12.
75. Hardison, *Christian Rite*, 131.

Nativity was also the occasion for consternation insofar as the birth of God had joined unbelief as a cause of his death. That is why, after cycling through questions about the Crucifixion—"How can it be that God has died? How did God die? Can God die?"—Augustine's mind goes to the Incarnation: "It is not possible to die, except for flesh; it is not possible to die, except for the mortal body . . . Where did he clothe himself in [this] death? In the virginity of the mother."[76] The scandal of the cross was already present at Christ's conception, consignment to the manger and, from there, to the secular world of consumption and decay. It was present in the gift of myrrh, a key ingredient in the anointment of the dead, which he received "as a sign of his future burial. In the tiny children whom Herod slew he also showed what sort of people were going to die for his name; how innocent they would be, and how humble."[77] There was a whole theology devoted to recasting the Slaughter of the Innocents—celebrated three days after Christmas—as a form of self-sacrifice, akin to the death of Jesus and therefore worthy of eternal life, but that theology stumbled repeatedly on these particular martyrs, given their lack of volition and the absence of baptism. It stumbled further on the report that Christ had escaped the slaughter only by fleeing to the least appropriate of all possible sanctuaries, a land given over to the grossest sensuality and the most rank idolatry, where the inhabitants were "both avaricious and gluttonous, together with their other vices. For there were the flesh-pots . . . there," John Chrysostom says of Egypt, "the great tyranny of appetite."[78]

Here was a series of Christmas events, in short, to shatter the faith of even the most credulous. Scripture seemed to have raised the possibility that the Messiah's long-awaited advent had been a threefold calamity, resulting in the death of God, the slaughter of children, *and* a reversal of the Exodus narrative. "Why is it," asks Peter Chrysologus (bishop of Ravenna and the younger contemporary of Augustine and Chrysostom), "that a heavenly matter is treated in such a way that the human understanding is confounded, the mind tires, the intelligence is troubled, hearing is dulled, faith wavers, hope falters, and the very capacity for believing fails [*credulitas ipsa succumbat*]? . . . Why are these things committed to writing, why are they mentioned in books, why are they recited through the ages, why are they noted in the daily read-

---

76. *En. in Ps.* 148.8 (CCSL 40:2171; WSA III/20:482). The last question and answer—*Ubi se induit morte? In virginitate matris*—were incorporated into the Gloss at Rom 5:6.
77. Augustine, *Serm.* 202.2 (PL 38:1034; WSA III/6:92).
78. John Chrysostom, *Hom. in Matt.* 8.6 (PG 57:88); English in *A Select Library of the Nicene and Post-Nicene Fathers of the Christian Church*, ed. Philip Schaff (New York: Scribner's, 1908), 10:54.

ings, why are they revealed to every people?"[79] Chrysologus, like any other authority momentarily shaken by scripture, finds a path to solace by way of the usual exegetical gymnastics—arguing in this case that if Christ had refused to flee the massacre and stood his ground as God Almighty, the Holy Innocents would have lived to be a sore disappointment: "The synagogue would have them as sons, and the church would not have them as martyrs."[80] Apologetic maneuvers of this sort could not, however, wholly overcome the distress that inspired them. Whatever reassurance close readers of scripture managed to recoup from the Nativity came at the cost of a terrifying realization. God's ingress at birth "into the Egypt of this world," far from completing the Exodus at a higher, more spiritual level, suggested that he had become subject to the very *saecularia* he was supposed to transcend.[81]

Of all the plays that allude to or dramatize the events of the Nativity—from the Latin Epiphanies and *Ordo Rachelis* to the seventeenth-century *Herodes Infanticida* (whose first printing includes an extract from Chrysologus's sermon)—none surpasses in its depiction of unbelief what appears at the end of the *Carmina Burana*.[82] To understand this play's full ramifications for the history of secularization, I want to entertain at greater length Chrysologus's most basic question. Why *were* the worrisome stories attending Christ's birth ever committed to writing? The standard answer in New Testament studies is fairly straightforward; they're an attempt to stymie the pervasive conviction that "Jesus of Nazareth" (Mt 26:72; Lk 8:37; Mk 1:24; Jn 18:5) was not a credible claimant to the title *King of the Jews*, much less *Messiah*, and even less *God*. "Surely, the Messiah does not come from Galilee, does he? Has not the scripture said that the Messiah is descended from David and comes from Bethlehem, the village where David lived?"[83] The nativity narratives, in short, were inspired by this doubt. They were born to counter it.

Because Matthew and Luke arrived at mutually exclusive ways to show that the person everyone knew as "Jesus of Nazareth" was born in Bethlehem, their narratives came to occasion the same doubt that they were

---

79. *Serm.* 150.2–3 (PL 52:600A); English in *St. Peter Chrysologus: Selected Sermons*, trans. William B. Palardy (Washington, DC: Catholic University of America Press, 2005), 3:251–52.
80. Chrysologus, *Serm.* 153.3 (PL 52:608A); trans. Palardy, 3:263.
81. Jerome, *Comm. in Esaiam* VII.xix.2/4 (CCSL 73:278); English in *St. Jerome: Commentary on Isaiah*, trans. Thomas P. Scheck (New York: Newman, 2015), 347.
82. Daniel Heinsius, *Herodes Infanticida, Tragoedia* (Lvgd. Batavorvm, ex officinâ Elzeviriana, 1632), 70 (Chrysologus's sermon).
83. Jn 7:42; cf. Mi 5:2; 1 Sm 16:1–4; E. P. Sanders, *The Historical Figure of Jesus* (New York: Penguin, 1995), 80–91; see also Raymond Brown, *The Birth of the Messiah: A Commentary on the Infancy Narratives in the Gospels of Matthew and Luke* (New York: Doubleday, 1993).

meant to assuage. For example, Matthew's version begins with Mary and Joseph originally living in Bethlehem rather than traveling there to be enrolled in a census, taxed, or otherwise "registered" (Lk 2:1).[84] Matthew is not worried in the least about the subsequent flight to Egypt because it does not matter to him that Christ went *to* Egypt; it does not matter what happened there. What matters is that Christ *left*, in fulfillment of "what had been spoken by the Lord through the prophet, 'Out of Egypt I have called my son'" (Mt 2:15; Hos 11:1). Jesus's return to the Promised Land in turn fulfills yet another prophecy. Being warned in a dream not to go back to Bethlehem, Joseph "made his home in a town called Nazareth, so that what had been spoken through the prophets might be fulfilled, 'He will be called a Nazorean'" (Mt 2:23).

Each of the verses cited to prove the divine calling of Jesus would become in a matter of decades a threat to his legitimacy. None of the prophets had ever heard, much less used, the word "Nazorean" for the simple reason that Nazareth was settled in the second century BCE and therefore postdates the composition of the Hebrew Bible.[85] Nor was the absence of any such reference lost on the Fathers: "All churchmen seek and do not find," Jerome admits, "where it is written, 'He will be called a Nazorean.'"[86] There were ways around this and the other problems with the Nativity—"lest they similarly agitate and disturb the mind," as Augustine feared—but the manifestly defensive posture of the New Testament and of the Fathers tended to highlight for medieval Christians grounds for doubt.[87] The most notorious instance was Matthew's apology for the oxymoronic Virgin Birth by citing Isaiah 7:14 in the wording of the Septuagint. Any Latin scholar in the Middle Ages who cared to learn could learn from Jerome, among others, that the rendering of this verse had transformed the Hebrew word for "young girl" (*alma*) into the Greek word for "virgin" (*parthenos*) (Mt 1:23). "Let us fight toe to toe with the Jews," writes Jerome of the apparent error, "and in our tug-of-

---

84. Evidence weighs against the possibility that either a census or tax called the Holy Family to Bethlehem, given that Galilean Jews did not pay Roman tribute in Jesus's lifetime. See Fergus Millar, *The Roman Near East, 31 B.C.–A.D. 337* (Cambridge, MA: Harvard University Press, 1993), 46–47.
85. See Adrian M. Leske, "Jesus as Ναζωραῖος," in *Resourcing New Testament Studies: Literary, Historical, and Theological Essays in Honor of David L. Dungan*, ed. Allan J. McNicol et al. (New York: T&T Clark International, 2009), 69-81, esp. 70.
86. Jerome, *Comm. in Esaiam* IV.xi.1/3 (on Is 11:1–3a) (CCSL 73:147); trans. Scheck, 214. Cf. Bede, *In Matt. ev. exp.* 1.2 (PL 92:15B). If Matthew's reference misconstrues an extant passage, a likely candidate is the word "nazirite" in Jgs 13:5, 1 Sm 1:11, or Dt 33:16.
87. Augustine, *De consensu* 2.5.16 (CSEL 43:98; WSA I/15/16:177).

war let us offer them no occasion for laughter at our ignorance."[88] The barrage of pedantry he unleashes in defense of the very translation whose contamination of the *hebraica veritas* he was elsewhere at pains to excise could not stop Jews from laughing, any more than it could stop the laughter of future Christians who would impersonate these incredulous infidels toward the end of getting the whole church to laugh.[89] In the *Carmina Burana*, when Archisynagogus "with his Jews" (CB 227.44, rubric) interrupts a procession that begins with Isaiah's prediction of the Virgin Birth, the prophets appeal to Augustine to defend them from their unbelieving critics: "Whenever we talk of Christ, they laugh and offer / us reasons for their bravado" (CB 227.59–60). Stage-Jews were probably not the only ones laughing, not then and not during the darkly comic debate about whether the alleged miracle of the Virgin Birth is "a thing to be denied [*res neganda*]" (in the words of Archisynagogus) or "a thing to be marveled at [*res miranda*]" (in the words of Augustine) (CB 227.108–11). Laughter was one means for Christians to deny and to marvel all at once. By impersonating unbelievers, they found ways to express their unbelief and, at the same time, to enjoy what they suspected was untrue. The stage-Jew of Christendom—as later epitomized, for example, in Marlowe's Barabas and Shakespeare's Shylock—is at its earliest origins already a projection of Christianity's bad conscience, a figure for its internalized skepticism, and a manifestation of "the will to absolute play."[90]

Given Matthew's silence about what happened once Christ arrived in Egypt, the Fathers had to rely exclusively on the Old Testament to tell them. Several verses from Isaiah stood out, beginning with his prediction that "our Lord will ascend upon a swift cloud, and will enter into Egypt" (Is 19:1a, DR). The patristic conscription of this passage into various apologies, while motivated by a need to combat the argument that Jesus was in no way the Messiah predicted by the Hebrew Bible, also provided an opportunity to acknowledge that Christ's advent could leave the believer's vision permanently darkened, uncertain, and trapped in an ever-shifting world of perception. The cloud in Isaiah's prediction, Jerome explains, is "the human body, which Christ assumed from the Virgin"; it was akin to the clouds and darkness that obscure or abscond with the divine presence elsewhere in the

---

88. Jerome, *Comm. in Esaiam* III.vii.14 (CCSL 73:103); trans. Scheck, 169. For a vernacular staging of the tension between "young girl" and "virgin" in Isaiah, see Parker, *Aesthetics of Antichrist*, 178–82.
89. On the laughter that Mary's virginity inspires on the medieval stage, see Emma Maggie Solberg, *Virgin Whore* (Ithaca, NY: Cornell University Press, 2018).
90. Stephen Greenblatt, *Renaissance Self-Fashioning: From More to Shakespeare* (Chicago: University of Chicago Press, 1980), 193.

Hebrew Bible.[91] Perhaps the darkest of those clouds of unknowing throughout the Middle Ages was the one surrounding God's entombment in the flesh from birth to burial. "Hear that the flesh of the Lord was a shadow," preaches Ambrose, before turning to the key lines from Isaiah:

> "Behold, the Lord is seated on a light cloud and will come to Egypt" [Is 19:1] . . . For we saw him in a shadow when the faith first arose. Now that he enlightens [*inluminat*] the whole world, we nevertheless still see him through the shadow of his body, which is the church, not yet face to face, for our bodily eyes are not able to receive the brilliance of divinity. Everyday this shadow forms a protective covering over the whole globe of the earth. The blockade has truly been all to the good: "God enclosed all in unbelief [*in incredulitate*], that he might have mercy on all" [Rom 11:32].[92]

The equation of darkness with Christ's body, his body with the church, the church with a fortunate fall into global unbelief is difficult to follow unless you keep in mind that unbelievers and believers alike are *supposed* to find the revelation recorded in scripture totally incredible and fundamentally unknowable. Centuries later, when the *Golden Legend* came to enumerate the ungraspable miracles of the Nativity, it counted alongside the impossibility of a "virgin birth" and the absurdity of combining human flesh with divinity ("such vileness and such sublimity") the further miracle that such things "could be believed" at all, since they were completely unheard of "from the beginning of the world [*a saeculo*]."[93] A frequent assumption throughout the Middle Ages was that the gospel by itself, barring a miracle, could do nothing but inspire *incredulitatem*; it could not help but create infidels. And these infidels would always have grounds to accuse Christians of being unbelievers as well, since Christians themselves so often settled for sensuous confirmation in lieu of transcendence. They valued most what they understood, and "if you understand it," Augustine explains, "it is not God."[94]

---

91. Jerome, *Comm. in Esaiam* V.xix.1 (CCSL 73:192); trans. Scheck, 259; see also *Comm. in Esaiam* XII. xlv.14/17 (CCSL 73a:511); trans. Scheck, 593, on Is 45:15: "he is called a *hidden God* because of the mystery of the body he assumed." Cf. Denys Turner, "Apophaticism, Idolatry and the Claims of Reason," in *Silence and the Word: Negative Theology and Incarnation*, ed. Oliver Davies and Denys Turner (Cambridge: Cambridge University Press, 2002), 11–24 and Paul Rorem, "Negative Theologies and the Cross," *Harvard Theological Review* 101, nos. 3–4 (2008): 451–64. See also Pss 97:2, 104:3; Dan 7:13.
92. Ambrose, *Exp. Ps.* 118, 19.6 (CSEL 62:425).
93. Jacobi a Voragine, *Legenda Aurea: Vulgo Historia Lombardica Dicta*, ed. Th. Graesse (Leipzig, 1850), 42; English in Jacobus de Voragine, *The Golden Legend: Readings on the Saints*, trans. William Granger Ryan (Princeton, NJ: Princeton University Press, 1993), 1:39, quoting Bernard of Clairvaux and Jn 9:32.
94. Augustine, *Serm.* 117.3.5 (PL 38:663; WSA III/7:211): "*Si enim comprehendis, non est deus.*"

After Constantine and the council of Nicaea, the most winning patristic counterargument against the infidel menace was inspired as much by scripture as by the lived experience of witnessing scripture's fulfillment in the ongoing, violent destruction of the pagan world. The Fathers took the prophets to have said that one of Christ's primary missions, only just then coming to fruition, was to nullify every other god: "and the *simulacra* of Egypt shall be moved at his presence, and the heart of Egypt shall melt in the midst thereof . . . And the spirit of Egypt shall be broken in the bowels thereof" (Is 19:1b, 3, Vulg.). *Simulacra* is one of the Vulgate's ways of translating *ĕlîlîm*, a key term in the Yahwistic puritan tradition meaning "non-entities" or, in Paul's rendition, "nothing in the world."[95] For all the ambiguity surrounding the question of what it might signify that the *simulacra* would be "moved" (*movebuntur*), the literal meaning of the verb was obvious to the Fathers who had witnessed the Christianization of the ancient world and who in any case habitually cross-referenced Isaiah with other prophets: "Thus says the Lord God: I will also destroy the *simulacra*, and I will make an end of the *idola* of Memphis: and there shall no longer be a prince of the land of Egypt and I will cause a terror in the land of Egypt" (Ez 30:13, Vulg.). For the *simulacra* or *idola* of Egypt to be moved meant in the first instance that its statues would physically deteriorate in the way of all ancient ruins. They were doomed to fall down through a normal, historical process that the arrival of Christ would accelerate on a vast scale. True religion could then emerge from the debris: "The war trophies of the churches rise up," Jerome explains, "and throughout all of Egypt the idols have fallen down [*corruerunt*]."[96]

According to Eusebius, Constantine sent a delegation throughout the empire under orders to force local priests to "bring out their gods"—meaning their statues—and then to deprive them "of their fine appearance . . . [thus] revealing to every eye the ugliness that lay within the superficially applied beauty."[97] Here the main purpose of iconoclasm was to convert "atheists"

---

95. 1 Cor 8:4, AV; *Isaiah 1–39: A New Translation with Introduction and Commentary*, ed. Joseph Blenkinsopp (New York: Doubleday, 1964), 314–15.
96. Jerome, *Comm. in Esaiam* V.xix.8/10 (CCSL 73:195); trans. Scheck, 262 (modified). *Corruerunt* becomes the standard verb in the commentary tradition and replaces the scriptural *movebuntur* in medieval stage directions instructing the idols of Egypt to fall (discussed below).
97. Eusebius, *De vita Constantini* 3.54.6, in *Eusebius Werke*, ed. Friedhelm Winkelmann (Berlin: Akademie, 1975), 1.1:108; English in *Life of Constantine*, trans. Averil Cameron and Stuart G. Hall (Oxford: Clarendon, 1999), 144; see also John Curran, "Moving Statues in Late Antique Rome: Problems of Perspective," *Art History* 17 (1994), 46–58; Ramsey MacMullen, *Christianizing the Roman Empire (A.D. 100–400)* (New Haven, CT: Yale University Press, 1984), 97–101; Robin Lane Fox, *Pagans and Christians* (New York: Penguin, 1987), 671–72; Frank R. Trombley, "The Destruction of Pagan Statuary and Christianization (fourth–sixth century C.E.)," in *The Sculptural Environment of the Roman Near East: Reflections on Culture, Ideology and Power*, ed. Yaron Z. Eliav et al. (Leuven: Peeters, 2008), 143-64.

EGYPT AND THE INVENTION OF THE *SAECULUM*

(*atheoi*) of one sort—people who did not believe in Christ but claimed to believe in the gods depicted by pagan art—into Christians.[98] Failing that, the delegation was not unhappy to convert them into atheists of another sort: namely, people who did not believe in any god whatsoever. Radical unbelief was something Christians were perfectly capable of promoting as the next best thing to their peculiar brand of monotheism. Eusebius says, for example, that pagans "enforced the worship of gods who do not exist, forsaking the one that does—while he [Constantine], by proving in words and deeds the nonexistence of those who are not, urged recognition of the one who alone is. Next, they mocked the Christ of God with blasphemous words; but the very thing the atheists chiefly aimed their slanders at, he endorsed as his victorious protection, taking pride in the trophy of the Passion."[99] Eusebius's premise is that the existence of any given deity can be disproven through violence. The challenge is to explain why Christ is the solitary exception—a fully humanized god, subject to the utmost degradation, whose claim to everlasting divinity is somehow *proven* at the moment of his shameful annihilation. Eusebius expresses his hope that people who come to the realization that the gods are pure fiction will take "refuge in the saving Word."[100] Yet he openly acknowledges that certain unbelievers, having arrived at a wholehearted agreement with Christians about the gods' nonexistence, did *not* take refuge in the Word or convert to Christianity but nonetheless "still condemned the folly of their ancestors and laughed at and mocked what had been held by them from antiquity to be gods."[101] Eusebius is glad to encourage this mindset. If some pagans only get so far as the realization that the gods do not exist; if they mock Christ as much as they mock their own forsaken deities, so be it. The numberless ruined sanctuaries will forevermore speak of a terrifying but instructive absence: "There was no resident in their dark sanctuaries, no spirit, no oracle, no god, no prophet, as they had previously supposed, and not even a vague shadowy ghost."[102] Secularization and Christianization here go hand in hand.

The primary point of contact between the Christianization of the ancient world, the patristic exegesis of the flight to Egypt, the conversion of north-

---

98. See e.g. Eusebius, *De vita Constantini* 3.1.2, 3.1.8, 3.26.2, 3.63.1, in *Eusebius Werke*, 1.1:80–81, 95, 117; *Life of Constantine*, 120–21, 132, 151 (where γένος ἀθέων ἀνδρῶν—literally "race of godless men"—is translated "another kind of men").
99. Eusebius, *De vita Constantini* 3.1.2, in *Eusebius Werke*, 1.1:80; trans. Cameron and Hall, 120 (modified).
100. Eusebius, *De vita Constantini* 3.57.1, in *Eusebius Werke*, 1.1:110; trans. Cameron and Hall, 146.
101. Eusebius, *De vita Constantini* 3.57.1, ibid.
102. Eusebius, *De vita Constantini* 3.57.3, ibid.

68　　CHAPTER 2

ern Europe, the "performative exegesis" of the liturgy and liturgical drama is the Gospel of Pseudo-Matthew—a seventh- to eighth-century text supposedly written by Matthew in his native Hebrew and then translated into Latin shortly before the original was lost, as explained by a letter of authentication forged in Jerome's name and appended to the gospel as its preface.[103] Pseudo-Matthew effectively writes into the text of the medieval Bible a summary of the patristic interpretation of Christ's flight to Egypt:

> And it came to pass, when the most blessed Mary went into the temple with the little child, that all the idols were thrown down to the ground, so that all of them were lying on their faces shattered and broken to pieces and thus they plainly showed that they were nothing [*sic se nihil esse evidenter docuerunt*]. Then was fulfilled that which was said by the prophet Isaiah: Behold, the Lord will come upon a swift cloud, and will enter Egypt, and all the handiwork [*manufacta*] of the Egyptians shall be moved [*movebuntur*] at his presence.[104]

One of Pseudo-Matthew's additions to the gospel foregrounds an ancient scriptural idiom; the idols who "plainly showed that they were nothing" are the same nonentities derided by the prophets as *ĕlîlîm* (Is 19:1b) and by Paul as *nihil in mundo* (1 Cor 8:4, Vulg.). Calling those idols *manufacta* (literally "made by hand") recalls various denunciations scattered across the Latin Old Testament—"I do not worship," states Daniel, *"idola manufacta"* (Dan 14:4, Vulg.); "the *simulacra* of the Gentiles," intones the Psalmist, are "the works of men's hands [*opera manuum hominum*] (Ps 134:15, Vulg.)—all sayings that were repeated in the New Testament as part of its core mission to disgrace the unbelievers who "rejoiced in the works of their hands [*laetabantur in operibus manuum suarum*]."[105]

When Christians in later centuries encountered idolatry on their northern frontiers, they hastened to imitate Christ's attack on Egyptian worship. Take for example Otto of Bamberg's Christianization of the Slavs in 1127 as described by a twelfth-century monk named Ebbo:

> There was a delightful spectacle when idols of astonishing size and statues carved in an incredibly beautiful way [*simulacra mire magnitudi-*

---

103. Susan Boynton, "The Bible and the Liturgy," in *The Practice of the Bible in the Middle Ages: Production, Reception and Performance in Western Christianity*, ed. Susan Boynton and Diane Reilly (New York: Columbia University Press, 2011), 10-33 at 24; Parker, *Aesthetics of Antichrist*, 170–72 (on Ps-Mt) and 40–41 (on issues of forgery).
104. Ps-Mt 23, in *Evangelia Apocrypha*, ed. Constantinus de Tischendorf, 2nd ed. (Leipzig, 1876), 91; English in J. K. Elliott, *The Apocryphal New Testament* (Oxford: Clarendon, 1993), 96 (modified).
105. Acts 7:41, Vulg.; Cf. Mk 14:58, Acts 7:48, 17:24; Heb 9:11, 24.

nis et sculptoria arte incredibili pulchritudine], which many pairs of oxen could barely move, having had their hands and feet cut off, their eyes gouged out and noses lopped off, were dragged across a bridge to be burnt... while people shouted, "if the gods existed, they would be able to defend themselves, but since they themselves are silent and are not moved from their places unless dragged, let them be shown to lack all sensation or vital, inward spirit!"[106]

These objects were no gods but exquisitely worked pieces of sculpture with eyes that did not see, ears that did not hear, and "no breath in their mouths" (Ps 135:17)—now further reduced to formless material without eyes, ears, or noses, even. The closest they would ever get to spirit was the moment they went up in smoke. They lacked animation of any sort, unable to move or be moved unless physically dragged. If you believed otherwise, here was proof that they had no inner life. Such absence, at such "astonishing" scale, rendered in such an "incredibly beautiful way!" Those last words are almost too overdetermined to parse, though I suspect we're hearing, on the one hand, a sarcastic joke about the dedication of unbelievers to inanimate matter, their incessant habit of pulling from it an illusion of spirit until they are forced to abandon their admiration. On the other hand, we're also hearing an unexpected appreciation for artworks whose beauty is weirdly enhanced by a "delightful spectacle" dramatizing in full their want of spirit.

The Christians who destroyed such statues were not the first to "savour the radical desacralization involved in distributing the timber from pagan temples as firewood, in spitting on the gods," nor the first to feel an intimation of eternity in proving that works of the hand, no matter how beautiful, had no purchase on anything beyond transient appearance.[107] But they were the first to do it when Christian icon makers, inspired by the Crusades, thought it prudent to depict idols on stage more assiduously and graphically than ever before. When Christian soldiers journeyed to Egypt in the early thirteenth-century to fight the Ayyubids (more or less contemporaneously with the copying of the *Carmina Burana*), they encountered a landscape littered with desecrated temples: Chi-Rho's carved among the hieroglyphs, the occasional pagan statue with its nose broken off or forehead branded by the cross.[108]

---

106. *Ebonis vita Ottonis* 3.10, in *Monumenta Bambergensia, Bibliotheca rerum Germanicarum*, ed. Philip Jaffé (Berlin, 1869), 5:664.
107. Robert Bartlett, "The Conversion of a Pagan Society in the Middle Ages," *History* 70 (1985): 185-201 at 197–98.
108. Frank R. Trombley, "Destruction of Pagan Statuary," 143–64.

And lying not far from this evidence for the success of Christ's conquest were places where Muslims had damaged Christian icons.[109] By the time our earliest plays allude to Christ's entrance into Egypt "on a light cloud of flesh / as the idols of Egypt fall [*corruentibus*]" (Young 2:118) any number of the idols that had fallen were the ones held sacred by Christians—the real infidels according to Islam. When the *Carmina Burana* was being copied, learned Christians knew that Egypt had been repossessed by unbelievers, despite Christ's alleged triumph over the idols: thus the call for reconquest recorded in the manuscript alongside the hope that Egypt's "pagan king" might be destroyed (CB 51a, stanza 3). By then control of Jerusalem had exchanged hands more than once. When Saladin's armies took it back again in 1187, they were keen on "emptying the holy places of . . . Christian images" because Saladin's armies, like earlier Christians, were also trying to purge the world of its inveterate idolatry.[110]

If there was in fact a difference between an idol and an icon, the Middle Ages did not want for voices saying there was none. That was the accusation lodged against Christian iconography by every kind of infidel. We find it in rabbinic references to *avodah zarah* (foreign worship), in the Quran (5:17, 72), in the Hadith, and in Christian teachings that were declared heretical.[111] The eighth-century justifications that ultimately secured a central place for art within the church border on being "incoherent," Peter Brown writes, "precisely because they accept the terms of their opponents"[112]—which is to say, they coopt for themselves the negative, disenchanting energies that had been swirling around mimetic representation since the days of the prophets. Theodore the Studite, for example, defends icons from the charge that they subject God to comprehensible, secular limitations by insisting on a theology so negative it approximates atheism: "So far from

---

109. Patricia Crone, "Islam, Judeo-Christianity and Byzantine Iconoclasm," in *Arab-Byzantine Relations in Early Islamic Times*, ed. Michael Bonner (Burlington, VT: Ashgate, 2004), 361–400.
110. Michael Camille, *The Gothic Idol: Ideology and Image-Making in Medieval Art* (Cambridge: Cambridge University Press, 1989), 137.
111. See Philip S. Alexander, "'The Parting of the Ways' from the Perspective of Rabbinic Judaism," in *Jews and Christians: The Parting of the Ways A.D. 70 to 135*, ed. James D. G. Dunn (Tübingen: Mohr, 1992), 1–26; for the Hadith, Rudi Paret, "Textbelege zum islamischen Bilderverbot," in *Das Werk des Künstlers: Studien zur Ikonographie und Formgeschichte, Hubert Schrade zum 60. Geburtstage dargebracht von Kollegen und Schülern* (Stuttgart: W. Kohlhammer, 1960), 38–40, and Oleg Grabar, *The Formation of Islamic Art*, rev. ed. (New Haven, CT: Yale University Press 1987), esp. 83–84; I have benefited in particular from Crone, "Islam, Judeo-Christianity and Byzantine Iconoclasm."
112. Peter Brown, "A Dark-Age Crisis: Aspects of the Iconoclastic Controversy," *English Historical Review* 346 (1973): 1–34 at 6; cf. Latour, *On The Modern Cult of the Factish Gods*, 67–97; Latour and Peter Weibel, eds., *Iconoclash: Beyond the Image Wars in Science, Religion and Art* (Cambridge, MA: MIT Press, 2002); James Simpson, *Under the Hammer: Iconoclasm in the Anglo-American Tradition* (Oxford: Oxford University Press, 2009).

inventing some kind of circumscription or comprehension (perish the idea! for this was an invention of pagan thought), we do not know that the Godhead even exists!"[113] Another, less extreme tack is taken by an iconophile named Epiphanius: "How can Christians be charged with idolatry," he asks, "when the coming of Christ has destroyed idolatry, according to the prophecy of Zechariah, 'on that day the Lord will appear and will destroy the gods of the nations of the earth'?"[114] Christian images should not be subject to violence, in other words, because they are the *result* of violence directed against others. After Christ destroyed non-Christian cults, the church was free to venerate whatever images it liked. Or to put this another way, Christ's violence against images created a way of enjoying them without guilt, not so much because he had eliminated idolatry but because he had refined it to a higher plane of spiritual pleasure. The illicit worship of imaginary gods could then find something like its typological fulfillment in the iconography of the Trinity and saints. "God transformed these heathen pictures into holy ones," says Sergius the Stylite in an eighth-century dialogue. "Instead of the name of gods and goddesses being commemorated through the images of idols, behold, through the icons the name of holy men and women is commemorated . . . Entirely for this purpose Christ came—*that he might destroy the works of Satan* [1 Jn 3:8]."[115]

Appeals to Satan of this sort are ancient and can seem to provide the traditional historiography of secularization from Febvre to Taylor with a certain vindication. We have clearly moved away from a Euhemerist critique and the atheistic repudiation of gods that do not exist toward a discourse that demonizes idols as the inhuman work of an evil spirit. Is this not a spiritualizing rather than a secularizing outlook? After all, Paul himself appends to the monotheistic dictum, "an idol is nothing in the world and there is no god but

---

113. Theodore the Studite, *Antirrheticus* 1.2 (PG 99:329): "οὐδ' ὅτι ποτὲ ἔστιν ἴσμεν τὸ Θεῖον." English in *On the Holy Icons*, trans. Catharine P. Roth (Crestwood, NY: St. Vladimir's Seminary Press, 1981), 21.

114. *Sacrorum conciliorum nova, et amplissima collectio* [etc.], ed. Joannes Dominicus Mansi, (Florence, 1767), 13:446D; trans. in L. W. Barnard, *The Graeco-Roman and Oriental Background of the Iconoclastic Controversy* (Leiden: Brill, 1974), 47; see also John Travis, *In Defense of the Faith: The Theology of Patriarch Nicephorus of Constantinople* (Brookline, MA: Hellenic College Press, 1984), 138–43, and Kathleen Corrigan, *Visual Polemics in the Ninth-Century Byzantine Psalters* (Cambridge: Cambridge University Press, 1992), 37–38.

115. *The Disputation of Sergius the Stylite against a Jew* XVII.2–3, in *Corpus Scriptorum Christianorum Orientalium*, vol. 339, trans. A. P. Hayman (Louvain: Secretariat du CorpusSCO, 1973), 52. Cf. *Dialogue of the Jew Papiscus and Philo with a certain Monk*, ed. A. C. McGiffert (Marburg, 1889), 73–74, para. 13.

one," the seemingly contradictory assertion that "there are many gods" (1 Cor 8:4–5, DR)—by which he means "demons" (1 Cor 10:20–22). Up to now I have wanted to stress Christianity's emptying, secularizing discourse because it has received so little attention in the study of art and drama prior to the Reformation. My interest so far has centered on a specific version of the infidel—not the *worshippers* of gods but rather "the *makers* of gods," in the words of Clement of Alexandria; the people, that is, who serve "neither gods nor demons but mere earth and art [*gēn kai technēn*], for that is what images are."[116] And yet a view such as this, derived from the Yahwistic tradition by way of Greek atheism, is "not really consistent," Edwyn Bevan writes, "with the view that the images were animated by devils."[117] In fact it is possible to see the conflict between the desacralizing discourse of Yahwistic puritans and the demonizing discourse of their less pure brethren in one and the same biblical verse. Where the Masoretic text says that "all the gods of the nations are *ĕlîlîm*" (Ps 96:5)—that is, "non-entities," as in Isaiah 19:2—the Greek text, by contrast, transforms these airy nothings into "demons [*daimōnia*]" (Ps 95:5, LXX). The discrepancy is readily explained as the long-standing tension between monotheism proper (only one god exists to be worshipped) and monolatry or henotheism (many gods exist, but only one *ought* to be worshipped as the supreme being or unitary principle).[118] The first gives rise to infidels who are "without faith" because they believe in nothing; the second gives rise to infidels who have sensuous liaisons with the wrong gods (aka demons) and are therefore guilty of infidelity in the sense of adultery or "whoredom"—a word that often functions in scripture as a synonym for idolatry.[119]

Art historians as well as drama scholars (myself included) have generally supposed it was the latter, demonizing view of idolatry that made images a privileged domain for otherworldly experience. I am no longer so sure. It's worth remembering that a common way of preventing the devil from

---

116. Clement of Alexandria, *Exhortation to the Greeks* 4.51 (LCL), modified. Cf. Ez 20:32: "Let us be like the nations . . . and worship wood and stone."
117. Edwyn Robert Bevan, *Holy Images: An Inquiry Into Idolatry and Image-worship in Ancient Paganism and in Christianity* (London: G. Allen & Unwin, 1940), 90.
118. See M. L. West, "Toward Monotheism," in *Pagan Monotheism in Late Antiquity*, ed. Polymnia Athanassiadi and Michael Frede (Oxford: Clarendon, 1999), 21–40, esp. 24; Jan Assmann proposes an alternate terminology: "the monotheism of truth" vs. "the monotheism of loyalty" (*Invention of Religion*, 83–90).
119. See Catherine E. Winiarski, "Adultery, Idolatry, and the Subject of Monotheism," *Religion and Literature* 38, no. 3 (2006): 41–63; Raymond C. Ortlund, Jr., *Whoredom: God's Unfaithful Wife in Biblical Theology* (Grand Rapids, MI: Eerdmans, 1996); and John Parker, "Holy Adultery: Marriage in *The Comedy of Errors, The Merchant of Venice* and *The Merry Wives of Windsor*," in *The Oxford Handbook of Shakespearean Comedy*, ed. Heather Hirschfeld (Oxford: Oxford University Press, 2018), 489–503.

becoming a rival deity on par with Christ or Yahweh was to suppose that he ultimately had no positive substance and was therefore best thought of as a form of privation, nothingness, vanity, the *absence* of divinity. "Evil is nothing," explains Boethius's Lady Philosophy, "since God cannot do it and there is nothing he cannot do."[120] If the devil could nonetheless influence humans—and few doubted he could—his exertions had to happen through purely natural, fallen mechanisms in order for his vacuous agency to be differentiated from the impossibilities accomplished by God through miracles (if there is in fact nothing that God cannot do). For God to be God, the devil had to be restricted to the domain of worldly causation. Despite being a spirit, Satan became in the process a secular agent.

By the same logic, the demons who were said to animate and to that extent respiritualize or even "move" an image could readily become personifications of the degrading, hollow passions that drove humans to embrace the short-lived pleasures of the *saeculum*: "Devils are creatures totally given up to the illusions of desire," writes Michael Camille, summarizing Augustine's position, and, by extension, a normative view among Christian Platonists. According to this perspective, demons are "slaves of vice who delight in fiction, like 'the obscenities of the stage, which modesty detests.' The notion of a demon inhabiting a fictitious shell and making it speak and live reminded Augustine of the activities of mimes and masks in the ancient theater—a link between idolatry and theatrical representation that prevailed throughout the Middle Ages."[121] Although it is possible to take Camille to mean that the gothic idol, on stage and off, drew its power from the belief that images were a special locus for the sacred (whether in negative form as an idol or in positive form as an icon), I think we should see in the Christian fascination with idols something else—namely, an unrelenting obsession with the power of art and nature to become immanent sources of value in the absence of divinity.

Ludus de Rege Aegypti

Sometime in the second half of the twelfth century or the first decades of the thirteenth, a cleric now called the Third Vatican Mythographer sat down

---

120. Boethius, *Consolatio* 3.12.29 (CCSL 94.1:62). The idea finds frequent expression among Christian Neoplatonists: see e.g. Augustine, *Conf.* 7.12.18, 7.15.21; on the role of privation or *Carentia* in Calcidius, see Peter Dronke, *The Spell of Calcidius: Platonic Concepts and Images in the Medieval West* (Florence: SISMEL edizioni del Galluzzo, 2008), 28.
121. Camille, *Gothic Idol*, 61.

to compile everything known about the pagan gods. His professed goal was to refute "the errors of antiquity" and to "drive away the mists of ignorance with the scourge of mightier authorities," but he seems in places to have indulged a suspicion that the conventional critiques of pagan mythology could apply just as easily to Christianity.[122] His work begins with a classic of the debunking genre. Long ago a rich man in Egypt named Syrophanes, having suffered the untimely loss of his "only-begotten son [*filium unigenitum*], whom he loved beyond measure," commissioned a *simulacrum* of the boy to stand in his home as a sculpted memorial.[123] Soon the whole household began to pay its respects by surrounding the artwork with flowers, garlands, and incense: "Even the accused took refuge at the statue, obtained pardon from the master, and venerated that statue more from a feeling of fear than of love. Thus is said: 'Fear first made gods in the world.' After this the longstanding human error of worshipping pagan idols began to be diffused everywhere."[124] Although demons will appear later in the mythographer's account of magic, he does not find them in the least necessary or even desirable to mention here at the primal scene of idolatry. Instead he leads with a more damning argument, one grounded in *error humanus*, in the gods' nonexistence, in their purely aesthetic character, and in their Egyptian origin.

The parallel between Syrophanes's false worship and iconographical depictions of Christ—another *filium unigenitum* (Jn 3:16) to whom believers appealed for grants of mercy—could have been explained, to some extent, as a tragedy for pagans. They unwittingly aped genuine worship out of sheer terror and did not yet know the solace that Christians would find in representations of their mightier man-god. At the same time the parallel seems to have invited the inference that when Jesus died, he left in his absence an unending series of captivating *simulacra* and a sanc-

---

122. Latin in *Scriptores rerum mythicarum latini tres Romae nuper reperti*, ed. Georg Heinrich Bode (Celle, 1834), 3.proem (133); Ronald E. Pepin, trans., *The Vatican Mythographers* (New York: Fordham University Press, 2007), 209. The manuscripts variously identify the third mythographer as Alberic of London (active c. 1160) or Alexander Neckam (1157–1217).
123. *Scriptores rerum mythicarum* 3.proem, ed. Bode, 132; trans. Pepin, 209. The story comes from Fulgentius, a late fifth–, early sixth–century African grammarian; see *Fabii Planciadis Fulgentii V. C. opera*, ed. Rudolfus Helm (Leipzig, 1898), 15–17; trans. Leslie George Whitbread, *Fulgentius the Mythographer* (Columbus: Ohio State University Press, 1971), 48–49; for other medieval retellings, see Jane Chance, *Medieval Mythography*, vol. 2: *From the School of Chartres to the Court at Avignon, 1177–1350* (Gainesville: University Press of Florida, 2000), 287–93.
124. *Scriptores rerum mythicarum* 3.proem, ed. Bode, 132; trans. Pepin, 209. The quotation is attributed to Petronius by Fulgentius but is similar to Statius, *Theb.* 3.661 (LCL). See also Chaucer, *Troilus* 4.1408, in *The Riverside Chaucer*, ed. Larry D. Benson, 3rd ed. (Boston: Houghton Mifflin, 1987), 556: "Dred fond first goddes."

tuary produced entirely by artifice. The story of Syrophanes raises the possibility, in other words, that life among Christians might also be lived in unending pursuit of sensuous stimulation and of what the mythographer calls the *voluptaria vita*: "Among the ancients," he says, "only the Epicureans exhibited this way of life. Among us, a life of this sort is in the nature of things."[125] According to the mythographer, a cultivated reverence for secular pleasures—rather than being restricted to poets like "Lucretius, who followed only the Epicureans"—was close to universal among Christians.[126] Antipathy to the apotheosis of the flesh had somehow encouraged idolatry to live on in the fully sanctioned form of an incarnate, crucified god.

There are at least seven extant plays from the Middle Ages that dramatize Christ's arrival in Egypt and the fall of its idols.[127] All of them require pagan statues to be set up on stage so they can topple when Mary enters with her infant—also a statue or wooden doll, presumably crafted by the same artisans who supplied the church with icons and, in this case, fashioned the idols as well.[128] All of these plays draw an explicit link between the iconographical devotion pursued by Christians and the worship of art attributed to unbelieving pagans. In a late medieval French play, for example, a fool mocks the Egyptian priests for their impotence in the presence of the Christ icon—a new, *sauvage dieu*—by propping up in place of their fallen idols his own *marotte* or doll and lauding its transcendent rule.[129] Jelle Koopmans's speculation that this parody of icons, "among

---

125. *Scriptores rerum mythicarum* 3.11.22, ed. Bode, 241; trans. Pepin, 316.
126. *Scriptores rerum mythicarum* 3.9.9, ed. Bode, 218; trans. Pepin, 288. "No one lives a pure life," writes Walter of Châtillon, "Epicurus is praised" (CB 8.8). See also CB 5.11, CB 92.15–16, CB 211, and John Parker, "The Epicurean Middle Ages," *Exemplaria: A Journal of Theory in Medieval and Renaissance Studies* 25, no. 4 (2013): 324–29.
127. CB 228; Chester 10.281–88 + SD, in *The Chester Mystery Plays*, ed. R. M. Lumiansky and David Mills (London: Published for the Early English Text Society by the Oxford University Press, 1974), 1:195–96, 2:152, and *The Killing of the Children of Israel* 241–48 and 280 + SD, in *The Digby Plays*, ed. F. J. Furnivall (London: Published for the Early English Text Society by the Oxford University Press, 1967), 10–11; *Le mystère de la Passion: texte du manuscrit 697 de la bibliothèque d'Arras*, ed. Jules-Marie Richard (Arras, 1891), 56–57; *Le "Mystère de la Passion" d'Arnoul Gréban*, ed. O. Jodogne (Brussels: Palais des Académies, 1965), 1:102–3. Gréban's wording shows up more or less verbatim in the Nativity play contained in Paris, Bibl. Nat. Réserve VF 1604; see also *Le Mystère de la Passion de Troyes*, ed. J.-C. Bibolet (Geneva: Droz, 1987), 1:345–48.
128. Camille, *Gothic Idol*, 130; Lynette R. Muir, *The Biblical Drama of Medieval Europe* (Cambridge: Cambridge University Press, 1995), 110nn59–60; Young 2:26.
129. *Le Mystère de la Passion de Troyes*, 1:347, lines 7254 and 7256 + SD. On medieval French farce, see Noah Guynn, *Pure Filth: Ethics, Politics, and Religion in Early French Farce* (Philadelphia: University of Pennsylvania Press, 2019); on iconoclasm, puppets, and dolls, see Moshenska, *Iconoclasm as Child's Play*.

other such iconoclastic rituals in religious theater, may have influenced the iconoclastic rage of Protestants" raises a crucial series of questions for theater history.[130] Was it in some sense *inevitable* that those who witnessed and performed on stage the destruction of Egypt's idols—as preserved, for example, in the Digby *Massacre* and the Chester *Flight*—would contribute to (and in some cases perhaps even participate in) the destruction of Christian icons? Was it not to some degree predictable that an equally extravagant, commercial theater would then arise in place of the old imagery? "Why is it that all those destroyers of images," Latour asks, "have also generated such a fabulous population of new images, fresh icons, rejuvenated mediators, greater flows of media, more powerful ideas, stronger idols?"[131]

The answer, it would seem, is that destroyers of images cannot live without the idolatry they despise. The earliest surviving dramatization of Christ's destruction of the idols appears in the *Carmina Burana* and originally served as the conclusion to the Nativity play that immediately precedes it.[132] Both sections were copied by the same scribe (so-called h^1), who worked in close collaboration with a second hand (so-called h^2) to produce the earliest reconstructible version of the manuscript. Both the Nativity and the Flight were printed contiguously as a single play by their first editor, Johann Andreas Schmeller, whose edition also made visible the multiple connections between the drama and the "jovial Goliardic poetry" with which the manuscript as a whole has since become "synonymous."[133] In fact two of the profane *carmina* first transcribed by h^2—CB 80 and 161—were partially recopied by h^1 so that they could be sung on stage to mark the shift from Bethlehem to Egypt. After an angel warns Joseph to flee and Mary delivers her departing lines to the donkey (in all likelihood a wheeled mock-up)—"Now I will go; may you be my companion!" (CB 227.321)—there's a short gap in the manuscript followed by a rubric directing the King of Egypt and his retinue to enter singing the two lyrics embedded earlier in the manuscript among all the other notorious encomia to what the Third Vatican Mythographer calls *saecularibus deliciis*: "at the threshold of summer / Love greets us."[134] It is here, in the sensuous and warm abandon of Egypt, that h^1 brought the

---

130. Jelle Koopmans, *Le théâtre des exclus au Moyen Âge: Hérétiques, sorcières et marginaux* (Paris: Editions Imago, 1997), 173.
131. Latour, *On the Modern Cult of the Factish Gods*, 69.
132. Hansjürgen Linke, "Der Schluß des Mittellateinischen Weihnachtsspiels aus Benediktbeuern," *Zeitschrift für Deutsche Philologie* 94 Sonderheft (1975): 1–22.
133. Bernhard Bischoff, ed., *Carmina Burana* (Munich: Prestel, 1967), 1:5 (German), 1:19 (English).
134. CB 161.1–2 / CB 228.II.1.1–2; *Scriptores rerum mythicarum* 3.11.9, ed. Bode, 234; trans. Pepin, 306.

manuscript to an end.[135] In doing so, he provided Wilhelm Creizenach (the first German historian of theater to consider these plays) with evidence for what he called the "secularization" (*Verweltlichung*) of the liturgy—a term subsequently introduced into Anglophone scholarship by E. K. Chambers in 1903.

By the end of the twentieth century, medieval drama scholarship had largely severed all connection between the plays of the *Carmina Burana* and its secular content, along with the connection between the Nativity and the Flight to Egypt. The first step was taken by Karl Young in *The Drama of the Medieval Church*. This understandably reproduced the drama without the bacchanalian songs and satires that were copied by the same scribes into the same manuscript. Young then took the further, ill-judged step of separating the debauchery of the Flight to Egypt from the Nativity and relegating the Flight to an appendix "as a separate, though fragmentary, dramatic composition" with the title *Ludus de Rege Aegypti*, invented by him "for convenience" (Young 2:463). David Bevington followed Young's lead in his popular textbook, *Medieval Drama*, and omitted the Flight altogether, with the result that several generations of Anglophone readers have encountered an artificially atomized "Christmas Play (*Ludus de Nativitate*) from Benediktbeuern" without the goliardic poems and idolatry appended to its end.[136] Meanwhile readers who turn to translations of the erotic lyrics earlier in the manuscript are reassured that the "Spiritual Dramas" in which it culminates are "reverent and serious and not at all goliardic"[137]—this despite the fact that the Nativity quotes verbatim two of the erotic, goliardic lyrics, while the Passion Play (added later in the thirteenth century) includes Mary Magdalene's songs of shameless praise for "the world" (*werlt*) and "worldly pleasure" (*mundi delectatio*) over the course of her negotiations with a merchant for cosmetics (CB 16*.19, 47).

There is no getting around the dramas' connection to the secularity of the manuscript as a whole. Indeed the Nativity stages nothing less than the moment

---

135. The gap in the manuscript between the Nativity and the Flight to Egypt was subsequently filled by a later hand (so-called h[13]) with a topical poem (CB 6*) that gives us a *terminus ad quem* of 1230–1 for the earlier transcriptions; see Bischoff, *Carmina Burana*, 1:29. Because those earlier transcriptions include CB 211, stanza 6—the earliest extant copy of a poem by Walter von der Vogelweide, written sometime after 1221—we can safely date the work of h[1] and h[2] to the decade before 1230. The borrowings in the Flight to Egypt from the Tegernsee Antichrist play (1159–60) provide the *terminus ab quo* for the composition of the Nativity play as a whole.

136. David Bevington, ed., *Medieval Drama* (Boston: Houghton Mifflin, 1975), 178–201. *Ludus de Nativitate* is borrowed from Schmeller's 1847 edition of the *Carmina Burana* and does not appear in the manuscript.

137. *The Love Songs of the "Carmina Burana,"* trans. E. D. Blodgett and Roy Arthur Swanson (New York: Garland, 1987), xiv. Cf. *Selections from the Carmina Burana: A Verse Translation*, trans. David Parlett (New York: Viking Penguin, 1986).

when proponents of an ancient religion were supposed to have learned that their pleasurable objects of devotion were finite and without sacred content—the moment, in other words, when the world was secularized. "Love greets *us*" (CB 161.1.2, my emphasis) has to refer to the *vagantes clerici*, goliards, university students, *Minnesänger*, monks, friars and/or secular clergy who were notoriously devoted to profane lyrics of this sort. When sung in the performance of the Flight to Egypt (CB 228.II.1.2), the first-person plural refers to the Egyptians whose devotion to the here-and-now world had become central to the Christian understanding of the *saeculum*. Virtually everyone involved in staging the drama has to have understood that by playing Egyptians they were playing a version of themselves, or barring that a version of their co-religionists—the belly cheer, the laissez-faire, the craving for spectacle. It would have been obvious when the scene shifted from Bethlehem to Egypt that the Holy Family was being received—and to some extent absorbed—by a secular world that was more than happy to replace the celebration of Christ's Nativity and of Marian chastity with adulation for nature's unbound libido.

After the King of Egypt and his retinue conclude their erotic lyric, another lyric follows—possibly sung by a different group of pagans; this continues on in the same vein while ironically echoing the Christian liturgy:

Omnium principium	The beginning of everything
dies est vernalis.	is a day in springtime.
vere mundus celebrat	Truly the world then celebrates
diem sui natalis.	its birthday.
omnes huius temporis	All days of this season
dies festi Veneris.	are feast days of Venus.
regna Iovis omnia	Let the whole realm of Jove
hec agant sollemnia!	celebrate these sacred rites!

(CB 228.II.2/CB 161.2)

D. W. Robertson was not far from the truth when he wrote of a kindred moment earlier in the manuscript that "the passions of worldly concern, typified by Venus, lead to a 'sleep' from which all Christians are urged to awaken."[138] Christ's arrival in Egypt was supposed to have torn humanity

---

138. D. W. Robertson, Jr., "Two Poems from the *Carmina Burana*," *The American Benedictine Review* 27, no. 1 (1976): 36–59 at 44–45; see also Barbara Newman, *Medieval Crossover: Reading the Secular Against the Sacred* (Notre Dame, IN: University of Notre Dame Press, 2013), 9–10.

from its worldly somnambulism by bringing to full realization the prophets' animosity to images. And yet precisely this paradigmatic gesture of Christian iconoclasm gave rise to situations in which a person could be all the more "bound to the earth," in the words of Augustine (speaking of his former self), "sweetly pressed with the burden of the secular world [*sarcina saeculi*]" where thoughts of God were like the thoughts of "those who have willingly tried to awaken but, overcome with deep sleep, are re-submerged" (*Conf.* 8.5.11–12 [CCSL 27:120; WSA I/1:193]). Such people surrounded Christendom, defined its borders, and circulated widely within it. Because of the ongoing dispute between the church and the synagogue, between the church and the mosque, between the church and the fane, between the church and its heretics—in a word, between the church and unbelief—the church was forever in thrall to an overwhelmingly attractive, perishable world of its own making. Medieval Christian iconography and ritual performance were trapped in a rivalry with the purely aesthetic and vanishing pastimes to which an antichurch of unbelievers was said—and shown in performance—to be flamboyantly devoted. Rather than worshipping the "one God alone, the beginning of everything [*omnium principium*]," these sons of unbelief had found a way with their *simulacra* and mawmetes to worship material ephemera as though the most fleeting and inconsequential aspects of creation were themselves worthy of adoration; as though each passing spring day, for all its evanescent finitude, could be treated as the *omnium principium* by virtue of making incarnate the infinitely renewable energy of the cosmos.[139]

The Egyptian celebration of vernal rejuvenation concludes with an exhortation for "the whole realm of Jove" to join in the "sacred rites [*sollemnia*]" (CB 228.II.2.7–8 / CB 161.2.7–8). Such rites were closely associated with the musical form stipulated in the rubric (a *conductus*) and were understood at the time to serve purely secular rather than sacred ends: "When the world [*werlt*] rejoices in summer . . . we should be cheerful!" (CB 161a.1, 8). The Third Vatican Mythographer explains that some pagan "philosophers," when speaking of Jove, "accept him as a figure of this world [*huius mundi*] . . . because by enduring and renewing its cycles, it seems to bind itself to a certain form of eternity."[140] The

---

139. Augustine, *De vera religione* 55.112 (CCSL 31:259). The phrase *omnium principium* is common in medieval theological writings as a term for God. CB 161/228.II.2 is likely playing off the fact that March 25—the spring equinox on the Julian calendar—had been widely adopted by Christians as the date of creation.
140. *Scriptores rerum mythicarum latini* 3.3.9, ed. Bode, 164; trans. Pepin, 223.

80　　CHAPTER 2

philosophers in this case could be Epicureans, Stoics, or Peripatetics—virtually anyone who held to the dictum that nothing can come of nothing.[141] For them the cosmos could have neither beginning nor end, except insofar as it might be subject to eternal cycles of death and renewal. And pagan philosophers were far from alone. Medieval poets, university professors, and monastic scribes like h¹ and h² found all manner of ways to delight in the unbelievers' cosmos. It throbbed with desire, and the desire had only been augmented by the Christian proposal that one day even these seemingly endless cycles would vanish:

Saturni sidus lividum Mercurio micante	When Mercury shines, the clear star of Saturn
fugatur ab Apolline risum Iovis nudante;	is put to flight by Apollo who uncovers Jove's smile.
redit ab exilio ver coma rutilante.	Spring returns from exile with shining hair.
. . .	. . .
Mater Venus subditis amori	On those subdued by love, mother Venus
dulcia	delights in lavishing sweet
stipendia	tribute
copia	in rich
largiri delectatur uberiori.	abundance.
Dulcis aura Zephyri	Zephyr's sweet breeze
spirans ab occidente	blowing from the west
Iovis favet sideri	favors the star of Jove
alacriori mente,	with a livelier feeling,

---

141. See Parmenides, fragment B 8.5–11, in *The Presocratic Philosophers: A Critical History with a Selection of Texts* (Cambridge: Cambridge University Press, 1983), 249–50; the exact phrase "nothing from nothing" (οὐδὲν ἐξ οὐδενός) does not occur in Parmenides's extant fragments but has been attributed to his influence: see Leonardo Franchi, "Parmenide e l'origine della nozione di nulla," *Giornale critico della filosofia italiana* 97, no. 2 (2018): 247–74. See also Epicurus, "Letter to Herodotus," in *Diogenes Laertius* 10.39 (LCL); Lucretius 1.150–56 (LCL); Boethius, *Consolatio* 5.1.9 (CCSL 94:89); on the eternity of the world, Aristotle, *Physics* 252b5, 258b10 (LCL) and Ps-Aristotle, *On the Cosmos* 396a30, 397b (LCL); Ricardo Salles, "Chrysippus on Conflagration and the Indestructability of the Cosmos," in *God and Cosmos in Stoicism*, ed. Ricardo Salles (Oxford: Oxford University Press, 2009), and Thomas Aquinas, *Commentary on Aristotle's Physics*, trans. Richard J. Blackwell et al. (London: Routledge & Kegan Paul, 1963), 519.

Aquilonem carceri	as it destines the north wind
Eolo nolente	to prison against the will of Aeolus.
deputans; sic ceteri	Thus the remaining
glaciales spiritus diffugiunt repente.	icy winds disperse on the sudden.
redit calor etheri,	Warmth returns to the upper air
dum caligo nubium rarescit Sole Taurum tenente.	as the mist of clouds thins out with the sun in Taurus.
Sic beati spes, halitus flagrans oris tenelli,	So is the hope of the blessed, when the wafting breath
dum acclinat basium,	of a tender mouth inclines with a kiss,
scindit nubem omnium	splits the cloud of all
curarum; sed avelli	cares, which cannot be rent
nescit, ni congressio sit arcani medica duelli.	unless there is healing union in a private clash.
Felix hora huius duelli,	Happy is the hour of this clashing
cui contingit nectar adunare melli!	for the one who happens to unite nectar with honey.
quam felix unio,	How happy the union
cuius suavitatis poculo	by whose potion of sweetness
sopiuntur sensus et ocelli!	the senses and eyes are drugged asleep.

(CB 68.1, 3–5; copied by h¹)

Educated medieval Christians could clearly think and write about the seasons the way Augustine thought about sex prior to conversion, on the verge of awakening but for that very reason craving a deferral the way "a man delays shaking off sleep because his limbs are heavy with torpor and soon he enjoys all the more eagerly what dissatisfies him, although it is time to rise" (*Conf.* 8.5.12 [CCSL 27:120; WSA I/1:193]). In fact educated medieval Christians frequently wrote poetry *celebrating* the choice to remain asleep in the world rather than to experience an enlightenment whose moral strictures could seem repressive and inhumane by comparison. Others of course condemned this choice just as Augustine had, once he was fully awakened, enlightened by baptism, freed from the bonds of desire and thus "from enslavement to secular affairs [*saecularium negotiorum servitute*]" (*Conf.* 8.6.13 [CCSL 27:121; WSA I/1:194]). They interpreted the rotation of the heavens, seasonal change, and natural regeneration as evidence for a creator that wholly transcended the creation, not as evidence for the immanently self-constituting order of the *saeculum* or, worse, evidence "that the world is eternal and without beginning and that consequently it has not been made by God" (*De civ. Dei* 11.4.2, LCL).

There was never a time when medieval thinkers were ignorant of this ancient cosmology, for the simple reason that the doctrine of creation *ex nihilo* was explicitly designed to contradict it. William Elton is right that "a keystone of the accepted theology of Shakespeare's day was the paradox that God created the world out of nothing," but he is wrong to say that in Shakespeare's day this keystone was "at a time of increasing naturalism, materialism, and skepticism, in danger of crashing."[142] The conflict was ancient and entirely in the open for the whole of the Middle Ages. A much earlier increase in naturalism, materialism, and skepticism was caused by the Crusades and the influx of infidel learning that brought Christendom into renewed contact with the texts of ancient unbelievers—as we see unambiguously in the *Carmina Burana*'s Flight to Egypt. Immediately following the panegyrics to springtime, a rubric instructs the Egyptians to sing a tune, dating from the mid- to late eleventh century, in celebration of the seven liberal arts, which by then made up the curriculum of the medieval university.[143] The song names specifically Pythagoras, Socrates, Plato, and Aristotle—the last of whom would lead the Paris faculty into a labyrinth of secular deviance with the seemingly irrefutable argument that the world has no beginning or end. In 1215—only a few years before h^1 and h^2 copied the *Carmina Burana*—the Fourth Lateran Council attempted to offer a final and conclusive rejoinder to this ancient reverence for the primacy of the cosmos by making creation *ex nihilo* official church dogma.[144] To no avail. In 1277, the Bishop of Paris condemned on pain of excommunication 219 philosophical teachings still in circulation, among them the idea "that it is impossible to refute the arguments of the Philosopher [aka Aristotle] concerning the eternity of the world" because logic and all available evidence point to the same, ancient conclusion—"*mundus est eter-*

---

142. William R. Elton, *"King Lear" and the Gods* (San Marino, CA: Henry E. Huntington Library and Art Gallery, 1968), 181.
143. For broader context see Adolf Katzenellenbogen, "The Representation of the Seven Liberal Arts," in *Twelfth-Century Europe and the Foundations of Modern Society*, ed. Marshall Clagett et al. (Madison: University of Wisconsin Press, 1961), 39–55.
144. Heinrich Denzinger, *Enchiridion symbolorum, definitionum et declarationum de rebus fidei et morum* (Freiburg im Breisgau: Herder, 1937), 199, 491.

nus."¹⁴⁵ According to the Paris prohibitions these teachings had caused some faculty members to argue that "theological discussions are based on fables ... [and] that nothing is better known from knowing theology."¹⁴⁶ Secular reason trumped the mythical revelations of scripture.

What Elton does not fully appreciate, in short, is that the doctrine of creation *ex nihilo*, far from being threatened by ancient naturalism, presupposes and explicitly addresses it.¹⁴⁷ Even in the absence of a twelfth-century renascence and the return of Greek learning to the Latin West by way of Islam, medieval readers of the Fathers would have taken for granted the conflict between Christian and non-Christian cosmologies that, Elton supposes, produced our modern, secular age. According to Nietzsche—perhaps the greatest proponent of the *saeculum* ever to have lived—it was Abrahamic monotheism, in combination with Platonism, that created modernity's signature problem: namely, its nihilism. By this he meant creation *ex nihilo* insofar as that doctrine and the intimately related story of the Fall were designed by moralists to deprive the world's endless becoming of innocence.¹⁴⁸

The argument that God created everything from nothing will be ultimately proven, Tertullian claims, at the final dispensation, "which is to return all things to nothing."¹⁴⁹ *Ex nihilo, in nihilum*. In the dramatization of the Flight to Egypt, we find a celebration of the world that takes into account this underlying void, as though the *saeculum* were all the more blissful *because* of its doom:

Hec nova gaudia	These new delights
sunt veneranda,	must be venerated,
festa presentia	the present festivities
magnificanda.	must be magnified.

---

145. I have relied on the Latin text in H. Denifle and E. Chatelain, *Chartularium universitatis Parisiensis 1* (Paris, 1889), 543–55, here 548 (#89, #87); translated (with a different numerical ordering derived from Pierre F. Mandonnet's 1908 edition) in Ralph Lerner and Muhsin Mahdi, eds., *Medieval Political Philosophy: A Sourcebook* (New York: Free Press of Glencoe, 1963), 345. See also Edward Grant, "The Condemnation of 1277, God's Absolute Power, and Physical Thought in the Late Middle Ages," *Viator* 10 (1979): 211–44.

146. *Chartularium universitatis Parisienses*, 552 (#152 and #153); Lerner and Mahdi, *Medieval Political Philosophy*, 352.

147. Anne M. Clifford, "Creation," in *Systematic Theology: Roman Catholic Perspectives*, ed. Francis Schüssler Fiorenza and John P. Galvin, 2nd ed. (Minneapolis, MN: Fortress Press, 2011), 214-222.

148. Nietzsche, Nachlass 1887, 9[91], NKGW VIII/2:50; English in *The Will to Power*, ed. Walter Kaufmann (New York: Vintage, 1968), §553.

149. Tertullian, *Adv. Hermogenem* 34.1 (CCSL 1:425); English in J. H. Waszink, *Tertullian: The Treatise Against Hermogenes* (Westminster, MD: Newman Press, 1956), 71.

84 CHAPTER 2

Ref. Dulcia flumina sunt Babylonis, mollia semina perditionis.	*Ref.* Sweet are the rivers of Babylon, soft are the seeds of ruin.
Concupiscentia mixti saporis ingerit somnia lenis amoris.	Longing for mixed flavors occasions dreams of soft love.
Heccine frivola cupiditatis tribuunt idola captivitatis.	These frivolities of lust are granted by the idols of captivity.

(CB 228.IV.1–2)

If we take the transcription without modification, these words belong to yet another lyric sung by the Egyptian retinue, although Stephen Wright has plausibly speculated that an entrance for the Babylonians has been omitted and they should be the ones to sing it.[150] Whatever the case, the lyric reinforces the traditional pairing of Babylon with Egypt as one of two places, in the words of Chrysostom, "most in the whole earth . . . burnt up with the flame of ungodliness [*asebeias*]."[151] The song also deviously evokes a well-known psalm; where, in the original, the ancient Israelites had hung up their harps by the rivers of Babylon, sat down and wept—while consoling themselves with the thought of Babylonian infants dashed against rocks (Ps 137.1–2, 9)—the *Carmina Burana*'s unbelievers instead take pleasure in the flux of sensory experience, following Augustine's gloss that the *flumina Babylonis* represent "all the things that are here and are loved and pass away."[152] Whatever comes into being but, being imperfect, passes into oblivion is the paradise that the senses make presently available.

---

150. Stephen K. Wright, "The Play of the King of Egypt: An Early-Thirteenth-Century Music-Drama from the *Carmina Burana* Manuscript," *Allegorica: A Journal of Medieval and Renaissance Literature* 16 (1995): 47-71 at 69n.
151. Chrysostom, *Hom. in Matt.* 8.3 (PG 57:84); English in *A Select Library of the Nicene and Post-Nicene Fathers*, ed. Schaff, 10:51.
152. Augustine, *En. in Ps.* 136.3 (CCSL 40:1965; WSA III/20:224). Cf. *En. in Ps.* 109.20.

The same lyric contains the first mention in the play of the captivating idols that will later fall to the ground before Christ's presence "and thus"—in the words of Pseudo-Matthew—"clearly show themselves to be nothing."[153] Anticipation of the moment when the Christ icon would enter and demonstrate the vapid ephemerality of everything that had theretofore seemed replete with beauty and meaning must have provided a special frisson for any participants in the habit of celebrating the world as though it were of considerable significance, despite its signifying nothing. The rubric gives the performers great freedom to milk the encounter: "Let all the idols of Egypt fall down [corruant]; let the ministers set them back up repeatedly and burn incense while singing" (CB 228.V, rubric). The indefinite cycles of falling, restoration, and ongoing song underscore the idols' springlike persistence even as they recall the eternal recurrence that the doctrine of creation *ex nihilo* ought to have vanquished but seems instead to have promulgated further in negative form by intensifying the sensuous allure of an ever-beckoning, unbelieving, vapid world—one that may well be ultimately destined for annihilation but is therefore all the more worth savoring.

Christ's entrance in other words inspires a newfound and terrible attentiveness to everything beautiful that has been, or is going to be, utterly destroyed:

Audi, rex Egiptiorum,	Hear, king of Egypt
lapsa virtus idolorum,	the idols' strength has lapsed,
destituta vis deorum	the forsaken power of the gods
iacet cum miseria.	lies in misery.
iam delubra ceciderunt,	Now the temples have collapsed,
simulacra curruerunt,	the statues have fallen,
di fugati fugierunt,	the hunted gods have fled,
heu, cum ignominia.	alas, in disgrace.

(CB 228.V.17–24)

Like every staged destruction of the idols, this play, too, gives the lie to the moment it memorializes. The images and shrines whose destruction it both celebrates and mourns—"alas"—have been resurrected in the ludic festivities surrounding Christ's birth, where they are allowed to restore a certain dignity to "the frivolities of desire [*frivola cupiditatis*]" (CB 228.IV.2.1–2). After the shrines collapse and the gods have vanished, the idols are set up again so that they may be once again overcome: "and let the idols fall down

---

153. Ps-Mt 23, *Evangelia Apocrypha*, ed. Tischendorf, 91; trans. Elliott, 96.

again [*iterum corruant*]," says the second of three rubrics instructing them to topple. No sooner has the King of Egypt despaired of his gods than he begins to sing: "Behold, let Egypt worship the new god with his mother" (CB 228.V.56). The implication at the time, for some of those involved, must have been that the king has merely accepted the stronger, more exquisite idol and is thus not without solace for the death of his gods.

At least some of the idols that fell and were set back up apparently remained standing until the moment of Egypt's conversion, at which point we see the final iteration of their demise: "And let all the idols be thrown to the ground. This is the end of the King of Egypt. Then let the King of Babylon rise up" (CB 228.V.57–VI). A number of extraordinary things happen over the course of this rubric. The first is that, notwithstanding Christ's apparent triumph over idolatry, another royal idolator rises up to contest his supremacy, while Christ himself is neither seen nor heard from again. Indeed the play will end in Beckettian confusion with unnamed voices nominally addressing Herod—long since putrefied—but in fact leveling at the audience a conventional *memento mori*, if not also an echo of the carpe diem recorded in the Wisdom of Solomon: "Listen, we sing to you of how worthless you will be / When you are nibbled by worms and decay in rot" (CB 228.VII.7–8). The second extraordinary thing is that the genre changes from a play of the Nativity to a play of the End Times, as the manuscript's source text shifts to a mid-twelfth-century drama preserved by an abbey fifty miles to the west of Benediktbeuern, the Tegernsee *Ludus de Antichristo*. The latter has survived independently, more or less intact, as München MS 19411, and paints an especially detailed portrait of a widespread figure.[154] In a previous book I tried to describe the medieval Antichrist and his significance for early theater history, but I did not fully grasp that figure's bearing on the question of secularization. Antichrist stands above all for the devolution of Christianity, so long as history lasts, into the worship of images, money, and fiction by people with motives that are entirely "of the world [*de mundo*]" (1 Jn 4:5, Vulg.)—fear, greed, self-interest, love of power, and physical pleasure, or, as John Foxe would come to summarize the tradition, "pomp, extravagance, lust, savagery, doctrine, poisonings, crimes, trickeries and trumperies."[155] Antichrist is a way for Christians to prove that other

---

154. Latin text in Young 2:371–87; *The Play of Antichrist*, trans. John Wright (Toronto: Pontifical Institute of Medieval Studies, 1967).
155. John Foxe, *Two Latin Comedies by John Foxe the Martyrologist: Titus et Gesippus, Christus Triumphans*, ed. and trans. John Hazel Smith (Ithaca, NY: Cornell University Press, 1973), 351; Leo, *Tragedy as Philosophy*, 45–80; Margreta de Grazia, *Four Shakespearean Period Pieces* (Chicago: University of Chicago Press, 2021), 157–61.

Christians have no religion at all but are, instead, fully immersed in secular pursuits. Because any one Christian could look upon any other as a devotee of Antichrist all believers learned to live with the knowledge that, in someone else's eyes, what they believed in was nothing more than an empty *simulacrum* of the godhead. The premodern condition is in this case both prelude to and model for the disintegrations more commonly associated with postmodernity: "the loss of a center, the devaluation of absolute values, the dissolution of Being as stability of principles both unquestioned and unquestionable . . . because now, more than any time in the past, many cultures openly clash with one another in this world to defend their validity."[156] Vattimo is talking here about Europe in the twenty-first century, but the sentiment chimes with Europe in the twelfth. And it provides a valuable gloss on Nietzsche's decision, despite his repudiation of Christianity, to align himself with a product of the medieval Christian imagination by calling himself the Antichrist. It was by this means that he embraced the "the world," which, he insisted, accounted for the whole of existence: "a monster of energy, without beginning, without end; a firm, iron magnet of forces that does not grow bigger or smaller, that does not expend itself but only transforms itself. . . . enclosed by 'nothingness' as by a boundary; not something blurry or wasted, not something endlessly extended, but set in a definite space as a definite force, and not a space that might be 'empty' here or there, but rather as force throughout, as a play of forces and waves of forces, at the same time one and many."[157] This is not quite the eternal cosmos of the Stoics, Epicureans, or Peripatetics, but it owes a great deal to their model—and even more to Christianity for endowing the world with the demonic power to replace God as the only thing worthy of adoration.

The Flight to Egypt in the *Carmina Burana* borrows passages from the Tegernsee Antichrist foregrounding the skepticism, debate, and violence that were the constitutive condition of the Middle Ages, thanks to the spread of monotheism: "That god is rightly considered voracious [*cupidus*]," sings the Babylonian retinue, "Who, while the other gods are spurned, wants to be worshipped alone" (CB 228.VI.5–6). In the following "conflict between Paganism, the Synagogue and the Church" (CB 228.VI.9, rubric), only Paganism and its adherents are allowed to speak:

---

156. Gianni Vattimo, "Nihilism as Postmodern Christianity," in *Transcendence and Beyond: A Postmodern Inquiry*, ed. John D. Caputo and Michael J. Scanlon (Bloomington: Indiana University Press, 2007), 44-48 at 46. See also Bruce Holsinger, *The Premodern Condition: Medievalism and the Making of Theory* (Chicago: University of Chicago Press 2005).

157. Nietzsche, Nachlass 1885, 38[12], NKGW VII/3:338; *Will to Power*, §1067.

Gentilitas contra eas cantet:	*Let Paganism sing against the others:*

Deorum immortalitas est omnibus colenda,	The immortality of the gods must be revered by all;
eorum et pluralitas ubique metuenda.	and their multitude must be feared everywhere.
Comitatus suus respondeat:	*Let her followers reply:*
Stulti sunt et vere fatui, qui deum unum dicunt	They are fools and true buffoons who say there is one god,
et antiquitatis ritui proterve contradicunt	and violently speak against the rites of antiquity.
Gentilitas:	*Paganism:*
Si enim unum credimus, qui presit universis,	For if we believe in one god who rules all things,
subiectum hunc concedimus contrarie diversis . . .	Then we concede he is subject in contrary ways to opposites . . .
Finxit invidia hanc singularitatem,	Envy fabricated this lone being,
ut homo coleret unam divinitatem.	So that humanity would worship one god.

(CB 228.VI.rubric, 9–14, 17–18)

Medieval clerics would have known that *invidia* and *cupiditas* were two of the chief sins associated in scripture with idolatry.[158] They would have known that the verb used here of envy—*fingo, fingere, finxi, fictum*—was the hallmark activity of unbelievers and idol makers. By placing these terms in the mouths of pagans and directing them against Christianity, the play found a way to highlight that Christians were the ones who "best qualified as idolators" given their addiction to painting, statuary, and theater.[159] The stage pagans further lodge against Jesus the criticism that he is himself a source of negative, desacralizing energy on account of his wholly human attributes: envy, desire, not to mention the "jealousy" with which this god, according to scripture, is synonymous (Ex 34:14). We are not far here from a description of Christianity as a form of *ressentiment* that can generate positive values only by negating, designating as evil, and demonizing the values that historically precede it—values which it

---

158. Gal 5:19–21 (*invidia*); Col 3:5 and Eph. 5:5 (*cupiditas*).
159. Camille, *Gothic Idol*, 150.

nonetheless replicates in all-the-more tantalizing, all-the-more haunting forms of recompense.

"One still relishes the exit from antiquity, Christianity, as an entrance to it," writes Nietzsche, "as a goodly piece of the old world itself, as a glittering mosaic of ancient concepts and ancient value judgments."[160] Early and medieval Christians may have smashed the idols, but they also refashioned the fragments into a postmodern collage. The pieces were ancient, but their new arrangement introduced a great shock. In Christianity's tireless argument that the gods were a product of the human imagination, its insistence on the world's transience and on the primacy of our appetitive drives in the absence of true divinity, it endowed the *saeculum* with the characteristics that could enthrall anyone baptized into its system of values. Some of those born Christians, like Nietzsche, became advocates for godless secularity, not despite but because of the unholy affirmations that the world was said to occasion among its greatest adherents.

Egypt in *Antony and Cleopatra*

The image of worldly indulgence at the heart of Shakespeare's *Antony and Cleopatra* was intimately familiar to audiences schooled from the pulpit on the seductions of Egyptian secularity: "Thus do our full gorged fat franked worldlings huggle themselves in ease," preached Richard Jefferay at Paul's Cross on October 7, 1604:

> they stretch themselves upon their beds of ivory, they invent unto themselves diverse kinds of music, they drink wine in bowls, and eat the fattest of the calves from the stall. . . . It is with them as it is storied of Cleopatra, who falling in love with Marcus Antonius, was so enamored and besotted in his love, that when she could not enjoy him as she would, she took two asps and set them to her breasts . . . so our worldlings being in love with their paramour *Mundus immundus*, the filthy world, and not able to enjoy it so fully or freely as they would, set asps unto their breasts, place the vanities of the wicked world so near their hearts, that they become senseless.[161]

To Christians across more than a millennium, Egypt symbolized this secular mode of valuation. Its credo was by turns Epicurean and, after the sixteenth

---

160. Nietzsche, Nachlass 1885, 41[4], NKGW VII/3:413; *Will to Power*, §419.
161. Richard Jefferay, *The sonne of Gods entertainment by the sonnes of men set forth in a sermon at Paules Crosse the seauenth of October. 1604.* (London, 1605), 39.

century, "Machiavellian" insofar as the only meaningful addendum to sensuous indulgence was the struggle for power. You enjoyed the world without any regard for God and fought with others to dominate a small corner of it.

Shakespeare based his account primarily on Thomas North's translation of Plutarch's *Lives* (1579), as earlier rendered into French by Jacques Amyot (a French bishop). The ascetical Christian viewpoint had already crept into both translations but is heavily accented in Shakespeare's play—for example in Octavius's rational, disciplined revulsion at secular hedonism: "From Alexandria / This is the news," he says when describing Antony's sojourn in Egypt:

> he fishes, drinks, and wastes
> The lamps of night in revel; is not more manlike
> Than Cleopatra, nor the Queen of Ptolemy
> More womanly than he . . .
>
> You shall find there
> A man who is the abstract of all faults
> That all men follow.
>
> (1.4.3–9)

Antony's "libertine" commitment to "Epicurean cooks" (2.1.23–25) and to his favorite "Egyptian dish" (2.6.128), Cleopatra, clearly marks him as a devotee of the *saeculum* incarnate. Meanwhile the Roman alternative to Egypt is no less worldly: Antony can give himself over to an irrational dalliance or think strategically about ways to rule his "moiety of the world" (5.1.19). Either way he is doomed to find himself abandoned by his god (4.3), while the more calculating Octavius proves to be the superior power—partly on account of his ability to prophesy the Pax Romana that will accompany Christ's birth: "The time of universal peace is near" (4.6.5). When Charmian asks the soothsayer to predict a happy future, she too unwittingly anticipates the events of the New Testament: "Let me have a child at fifty to which Herod of Jewry may do homage" (1.2.29–30). Like *King Lear*—another play ostentatiously set in a pre-Christian era but suffused with reminders of the gods' supersession—*Antony and Cleopatra* caters more than a little to Christian jingoism. From the perspective of Shakespeare's pious contemporaries, as Margreta de Grazia has shown, ancient societies living outside scripture's sphere of influence could not help but indulge, with tragic results, in gross secularity.[162]

Both *Antony* and *Lear* draw a number of parallels between pagan and Christian society on the scriptural grounds that humanity's preference for

---

162. de Grazia, *Four Shakespearean Period Pieces*, 145–76.

EGYPT AND THE INVENTION OF THE *SAECULUM*   91

secularity persists beyond Christ's advent and indeed can only get worse, so long as the world lasts. Antony's fear that "a right gypsy hath at fast and loose / Beguiled me to the very heart of loss" (4.12.28–29) echoes Tudor legal concerns that ancient Egypt had infiltrated England in the form of gypsies or "persons calling themselves Egyptians" who "deceived the people of their money" by soothsaying and by "their old-accustomed devilish and naughty practices and devices, with such abominable living as is not in any Christian realm to be permitted, named or known."[163] "The witch" (4.12.47) Cleopatra would have been at home among the sorceresses of Renaissance demonology insofar as she too fed the appetites of her onlookers with specious forms of worldly enchantment—her "grave charm" (4.12.25), her dark sexual deviance, her histrionic excess, and so forth.[164] "Cleopatra," in the words of Thomas Nashe, suffered from an unwitting allegiance to Satan, "the warden of the witches and jugglers."[165] Just as Eden had its serpent, so too did Egypt and England. The devil encouraged all lovers of the flesh to embrace the "joy o' th' worm" (5.2.278).[166]

A Jacobean audience watching the lovers' fall was supposed to believe that they had succumbed to sin by caving to their appetites—which is to say, in Antony's case, that he had been unmanned by making "his will / Lord of his reason" (3.13.3–4). The noblest non-Christians might have had the urge to escape from Egypt, but they lacked the grace to follow reason's dictates: "These strong Egyptian fetters I must break," says Antony, "or lose myself in dotage" (1.2.122–23). For pagans indifferent to Moses and lacking the sacraments, such resolve could only be futile. Antony might "play the penitent" (2.2.98), but he has no path to a true change of heart. Regardless of how often he confesses his tragic flaw or "error" (*hamartia* in Aristotle's *Poetics*), he lacks the means to remedy his "sin" (*hamartia* in the New Testament). His only option is the one that his appetites choose

---

163. 1 and 2 Philip and Mary, c. 4, "An Act against certain Persons calling themselves Egyptians," in *Anno primo & secundo Philippi & Mariæ actes* [etc.] (London, 1555); reaffirmed with clarification by 5 Elizabeth I, c. 20 in *Anno quinto reginæ Elizabethe* [etc.] (London, 1562). In *The Gypsies Metamorphosed*, Cleopatra is called "the *gypsies' grand-matra*"—see *The Cambridge Edition of the Works of Ben Jonson*, ed. David Bevington et al. (Cambridge: Cambridge University Press, 2012), 5:492 (line 105).
164. Charles Zika, "Fears of Flying: Representations of Witchcraft and Sexuality in Early Sixteenth-Century Germany," *Australian Journal of Art* 8 (1989): 19–47; Stuart Clark, *Thinking with Demons: The Idea of Witchcraft in Early Modern Europe* (Oxford: Oxford University Press, 1997), 11–30.
165. Thomas Nashe, *'The Unfortunate Traveller' and Other Works*, ed. J. B. Steane (New York: Penguin, 1985), 118.
166. See Drew Daniel, *Joy of the Worm: Suicide and Pleasure in Early Modern English Literature* (Chicago: University of Chicago Press, 2022).

for him; he "becomes his flaw" (3.12.34), loses out to his worst self, and, like his paramour, falls prey to the delusion that suicide alone offers an exodus from worldly bondage.

For all that, Antony also "becomes his flaw" in the decorative sense of making his weakness appear beautiful, even glorious. One benefit of living beyond the reach of scripture—according to scripture—is that character flaws cannot be moralized, no matter how fatal. For "where no law is, there is no transgression" (Rom 4:15, Bishops 1568). Antony and Cleopatra are among early modern England's greatest spokespeople for this viewpoint. In them the scriptural commonplace that fornication leads to idolatry (e.g., Num 25; Ws 14:12; Rom 1:24–25; Col 3:5) receives if anything a positive rather than a negative valuation. Their erotic compulsion is the epitome of secularity because it sanctifies the beloved and transforms the human body into a phantasmatic object of worship. Lovers do this all the time in Shakespeare, but nobody does it quite like Cleopatra, if only because she loves a man of imperial, hence godlike stature:

> I dreamt there was an emperor Antony.
> O, such another sleep, that I might see
> But such another man! . . .
> His face was as the heavens, and therein stuck
> A sun and moon which kept their course and lighted
> The little O, the earth . . .
> His legs bestrid the ocean; his reared arm
> Crested the world; his voice was propertied
> As all the tuned spheres, and that to friends;
> But when he meant to quail and shake the orb,
> He was as rattling thunder. For his bounty,
> There was no winter in't; an autumn it was
> That grew the more by reaping. His delights
> Were dolphin-like: they showed his back above
> The element they lived in. In his livery
> Walked crowns and crownets; realms and islands were
> As plates dropped from his pocket.
> Dolabella: Cleopatra—
> Cleopatra: Think you there was or might be such a man
> As this I dreamt of?
> Dolabella: Gentle madam, no.
>
> (5.2.75–93)

EGYPT AND THE INVENTION OF THE *SAECULUM* 93

The earliest Christians were notorious for puncturing the illusion of the imperial cult and refusing its "gospel"—a word coopted by the New Testament from the periodic announcements in the Greek East that a deceased emperor had been deified.[167] The Christian critique is anticipated by Dolabella, as it had been in *Julius Caesar* when the assassins object that "this man / Is now become a god" (1.2.122–23). Indeed the same criticism was continually lodged against Jesus Christ by infidels, with the result that affecting shock at those who dared to divinize the wrong human became a shared position of pagans and Christians alike. Every believer occupied a position of atheism or unbelief in relation to the devotion of someone else.

Christians, as we've seen, had long insisted that the worship of anyone other than Jesus was a way of exalting here-and-now existence, consequences be damned. Antony appears in this light as a martyr to the world. He believes that Cleopatra—theatrically costumed "in th' habiliments of the goddess Isis" (3.6.17)—is for all her inadequacy sufficiently godlike to earn his adoration and self-sacrifice. His willingness to accept and even exacerbate the most painful consequences of magnifying Egypt both looks back to and anticipates a tragic, Dionysian worldview. From this perspective, mere being in the world "is counted *blessed enough* to justify monstrous amounts of suffering."[168] *Antony and Cleopatra* intimates that a god more ancient than Christ—however fickle, imaginary, and immanent to the *saeculum*—still dances through humans whenever they are so intoxicated by life that they cease to make good strategic calculations, particularly when it comes to the behaviors necessary for salvation in a heavenly afterlife:

> Boy: Come, thou monarch of the vine,
> Plumpy Bacchus with pink eyne!
> In thy vats our cares be drowned;
> With thy grapes our hairs be crowned.
> All: Cup us till the world go round!
> Cup us till the world go round!
>
> (2.7.113–18)

In this gratuitous, bacchanalian song, Dionysus manages to speak his truth against the Crucified. Wine is *his* gift to humanity. Unlike the Eucharist, it is neither symbol nor blood. It is a drug. He bids you drink enough to make the world spin.

---

167. Hans-Joseph Klauck, *The Religious Context of Early Christianity: A Guide to Graeco-Roman Religions*, trans. Brian McNeil (Edinburgh: T&T Clark, 2000), 296–98.
168. Nietzsche, Nachlass 1888, 14[89], NKGW VIII/3:58; *Will to Power*, §1052 (modified).

Chapter 3

The Secularization of the Liturgy

Peter of Blois and the Music of Egypt

The one author to whom we can most likely ascribe a number of unique erotic lyrics in the *Carmina Burana* is Peter of Blois (c. 1130–c. 1211); a songster and secular cleric, he became archdeacon of Bath, chancellor to the Archbishop of Canterbury, then chaplain and secretary to Henry II and Eleanor of Aquitaine.[1] In addition to what he calls his "love songs" (*Ep.* 76, PL 207:234B), he wrote verses of repentance for a life wasted in devotion to Venus, a collection of sermons, a variety of theological treatises, and a popular compendium of letters that was mandatory reading at Oxford by the fourteenth century. Taken together his extant writings have occasionally suggested "the shadowy outline of a Petrarch or Erasmus" in the same way that the twelfth century has been said to prefigure (or even realize) many of the developments that are credited to later renascences:[2] the recovery of

---

1. C. Wollin, ed., *Petri Blesensis Carmina*, CCCM 128 (Turnhout: Brepols, 1998), is joined by Konrad Vollmann, ed., *Carmina Burana: Texte und Übersetzungen* [etc.] (Berlin: Deutscher Klassiker, 2011) in ascribing to Peter CB 29–31, 33, 63, 67, 72, 83, 84, and 108; see also Peter Dronke, *The Medieval Poet and His World* (Rome: Edizioni di storia e letteratura, 1984), 281–339, esp. 320–36, and *Love Lyrics from the Carmina Burana*, ed. and trans. with a commentary by P. G. Walsh (Chapel Hill: University of North Carolina Press, 1993), xvii–xix.
2. R. W. Southern, *Medieval Humanism and Other Studies* (Oxford: Blackwell, 1970), 106.

antiquity by a flourishing intellectual culture, the formation of a mercantile class, increased urbanization, scientific progress, the centralization of power in courts across Europe, rampant persecution—all culminating in the kind of "crisis" or "revolution" usually associated with modernity and its long, on-going process of secularization.[3]

Two letters in Peter's compendium provide the basis for connecting him to the *Carmina Burana* (among other manuscripts), and both paint a vivid portrait of the ways that secular music had intruded into the religious life of the twelfth century. The first is to William of Aulnay, a friend for whom Peter felt "an affection of love" since adolescence (*Ep.* 57, PL 207:171C). William's side of the exchange has been lost to history but its general contents can be inferred from Peter's response. His old friend has recently entered a monastery with the express hope that he might "evade the temptations of the world [*saeculi*]" (*Ep.* 57, PL 207:171D), yet he now finds himself newly enticed by its lures and "surrounded by more miserable temptations than before" (*Ep.* 57, PL 207:172A). Neither William nor Peter seems very well cut out for the pious Middle Ages traditionally envisioned as a backdrop for modernity. They are not naïve believers blithely entranced by celestial visions, incapable of imagining a desacralized world, but Christians for whom the *vita saecularis* is so overpowering that a life devoted to God can barely hold a candle to it. Profane attractions, Peter tells William, increase in appeal the more you try to deny them: "The world fights fiercely against its deserters; and it becomes more troublesome as it lies in wait for those who, having put up a fight, escape the lures of a secular life. For even after Israel's exodus from Egypt Pharaoh burns more violently" (*Ep.* 57, PL 207:172A). Similar references to the Exodus story occur frequently in Peter's corpus and demonstrate some of the long-range consequences of the patristic interpretation that we examined in the last chapter. Anyone trying to escape from "the Egypt of this world [*saeculi*]" (*Serm.* 51, PL 207:711C) has to be forever on guard against a heightened sense of taste for the old fleshpots. Constant longing for a less transcendent experience than the cloister affords, in this paradigm, is a defining feature of Christianity.

Peter assumes without question that many of his contemporaries do not care in the least to cultivate a life of spiritual reflection. On the contrary they

---

3. Thomas N. Bisson, *The Crisis of the Twelfth Century: Power, Lordship, and the Origins of European Government* (Princeton, NJ: Princeton University Press, 2015), 350; R. I. Moore, *The First European Revolution c. 970–1215* (Oxford: Blackwell, 2000); Edward Grant, *The Foundations of Modern Science in the Middle Ages: Their Religious, Institutional, and Intellectual Contexts* (Cambridge: Cambridge University Press, 1996).

choose to pursue secular prosperity with a zeal that rivals sacred devotion. Plenty of people become "martyrs to the world [*saeculi*], professors of worldliness [*mundi*], the court's disciples" by taking unabashed pleasure in the marketplace and the new centers of power that are thronged with "actors, prostitutes, gamblers, castrati, sweet-talkers, confectioners, mimes, bearded maskers, *insatiable maws, that whole sort*."[4] Peter draws a link here between the Roman decadence once satirized by Horace and the contemporary entertainment industry to which he and his brother, William of Blois, directly contributed—one by composing salacious song lyrics, the other by writing "comedies and tragedies" (*Ep.* 76, PL 207:235A).[5] Their joint participation in courtly amusement considerably strengthens the suspicion among theater historians—most recently Carol Symes—that the thriving world of Latin song and music drama "threatens the accepted paradigm of slow secularization" according to which the beginnings of our modern, irreverent theater lie in the vernacular and are not fully realized before Shakespeare.[6] As I'll try to show over the course of this chapter, both the profane lyrics and sacred drama of the twelfth century feed off a vibrant, cosmopolitan culture that inspired would-be believers to breathtaking heights of secularity. "We who should conquer the world through faith," Peter admits in more than one of his sermons, "are conquered by it through unbelief [*infidelitatem*]" (*Serm.* 22, PL 207:627A).

Only at the end of Peter's letter to William on the terrible thrill of the *saeculum* do we learn the reason that his old friend has written. Crushed by ennui and longing to return to the world, William has asked for a few of Peter's "amorous juvenilia and adolescent trifles, to relieve the tedium" (*Ep.* 57, PL

---

4. *Ep.* 14b, in Lena Wahlgren, *The Letter Collections of Peter of Blois: Studies in the Manuscript Tradition* (Göteborg: Acta Universitatis Gothoburgensis, 1993), 155, 161–62: "histriones, candidatrices, aleatores, caupones, dulcorarii, nebulatores, mimi, barbatores, baratrones, hoc genus omne." The final allusion is frequently amended to reflect the surviving manuscripts of Horace's *Serm.* 1.2.2; I borrow the translation of *caupones* as "castrati" from Martin W. Walsh, "Babio: Toward a Performance Reconstruction of Secular Farce in Twelfth-Century England," in *England in the Twelfth Century: Proceedings of the 1988 Harlaxton Symposium*, ed. Daniel Williams (Woodbridge, UK: Boydell Press, 1990), 219–40.
5. For William of Blois's one extant play, see *Commedie latine del XII e XIII secolo*, ed. Feruccio Bertini et al. (Genoa: Instituto di filogia classica e medieval, 1998), 6:11–109; English in *Seven Latin Comedies*, trans. Alison Goddard Elliott (New York: Garland, 1984), 104–24. On Peter's prominence among the lyricists of his day, see *Moralisch-satirische Gedichte Walters von Chatillon: Aus deutschen, englischen, französischen und italienischen Handschriften*, ed. Karl Strecker (Heidelberg: C. Winter, 1929), 41.
6. Carol Symes, "The Performance and Preservation of Medieval Latin Comedy," *European Medieval Drama* 7 (2003): 29-50 at 31; see also Symes, *A Common Stage: Theater and Public Life in Medieval Arras* (Ithaca, NY: Cornell University Press, 2007), esp. 37–38; Martin W. Walsh, "Babio"; Roger Sherman Loomis, "Some Evidence for Secular Theatres in the Twelfth and Thirteenth Centuries," *Theatre Annual* 3 (1945): 33–43; Loomis and Gustave Cohen, "Were There Theatres in the Twelfth and Thirteenth Centuries?" *Speculum* 20, no. 1 (1945): 92–98; E. K. Chambers, *The Mediaeval Stage* (Oxford: Clarendon, 1903), 2:68–106.

207:172C). William evidently hoped that a handful of harmless bagatelles in celebration of the immanent fulfillment on offer in the world might provide a salve to the wounds of devotion. Peter expresses a reluctance to comply, out of fear, he says, that his compositions "may be inclined to excite and to nurture your temptations. Therefore I'm omitting the lascivious songs and sending you instead a few in a more mature style" (*Ep.* 57, PL 207:172C). And yet the lyrics that follow, rather than erasing the secular modes of valuation that characterize the songs of his youth, dwell at length on the belatedness of his relinquishing the world and the potential futility of joining a spiritual struggle that he is likely to lose:

Olim militaveram	Once I enlisted
pompis huius seculi,	in the pomp of this world
quibus flores obtuli	to which I sacrificed the flowers
mee iuventutis;	of my youth.
pedem tamen retuli	But I have turned back
circa vite versperam,	in the evening of my life
nunc daturus operam	and am about to give myself
milicie virtutis.	to warfare on behalf of virtue.
	(CCCM 128:231)

The future participle in the penultimate line would likely have solicited a smile from a reader of Augustine: Lord, give me chastity—but not yet (*Conf.* 8.7.17). The speaker has turned his back on the world but leaves his commitment to virtue ever so slightly deferred and, even then, qualified by the recognition that, whenever he does manage at last to consign himself to the fullness of piety, he will still be engaged in constant battle with the competing demands of the *saeculum*.

Those demands often have the upper hand in Peter's writing. One of the three penitential songs in the *Carmina Burana* now attributed to him on the basis of various parallels with the lyrics that he sent to William advises its aging addressee to abandon youthful passions. Here too Egypt is deployed as a stand-in for the sensuous world of aesthetic perception, with its incorrigible appetites and unseemly license, its bittersweet but instructive transience:

Salva saltem ultimam	Save at least this last
vite portiunculam	little portion of your life

offerens celestibus	by offering to the heavens,
pro iuvente floribus	in place of the flowers of youth,
senectutis stipulam!	the husk of old age!
Forsan ludo Veneris	Perhaps by the play of Venus
ultra vires ureris	you are inflamed to the point of exhaustion
ut amoris tedium	so that the tedium of love
tibi sit remedium . . .	might be your remedy . . .
Ut stes pede stabili	So that you may stand on steady feet
sine casu facili,	without risk of falling,
cave precipitium,	avoid the precipice
devitando vitium.	by avoiding vice.
sed si te vexaverit	But if she harasses you,
aut si comprehenderit	or if she embraces you—
Egyptia,	the Egyptian woman—
mox pallia	then leave your cloak behind
fugitivus desere.	and run like a fugitive.[7]

The "Egyptian woman" is presumably the wife of Potiphar, from whom Joseph fled with such suddenness that "his cloak [*pallio*]" remained in her hand after she tried but failed to seduce him.[8] One conventional gloss saw in her an allegory for how closely "the enticements of the flesh hold us" and held up Joseph as a model of Christian rectitude: "a chaste man [who] prefers to break all bonds rather than subject himself to indecency."[9] The person we see in Peter's poem, exhausting himself sexually in the hope that his exertions might culminate in the satiety of boredom, is perhaps in the end less evocative of Joseph than of Antony as described elsewhere in Peter's compendium: "a man gifted with exceptional virtue, excepting the glory of temperance" and therefore drunkenly "enthralled to his love

---

7. CB 29.1.10–3.9; CCCM 128:373–74 gives a slightly different text.
8. Gen 39:12 (Vulg.). A song that Peter sends to William, *"In nova fert animus"* (CCCM 128:251) contains another allusion to the wife of Potiphar, as noted by Dronke, *Medieval Poet*, 324.
9. Gloss on Gen 39:12, in *Biblia Latina cum Glossa Ordinaria: Facsimile Reprint of the Editio Princeps Adolph Rusch of Strassburg 1480/81*, ed. Karlfried Froehlich and Margaret T. Gibson (Turnhout: Brepols, 1992), 1:92.

for Cleopatra."¹⁰ Whether biblical or classical, the blandishments of the twelfth-century *Egyptia* were supremely hard to resist, if only because those who tried to escape found themselves further enraptured in body and spirit; for "we remember the fishes that we did eat in Egypt gratis: the cucumbers come unto our mind, and the melons and leeks and onions and garlic. Our soul is dry, our eyes behold nothing else but manna" (Num 11:5–6, DR). Properly interpreted, explains Baldwin—the Archbishop of Canterbury whom Peter served as chancellor—these mouths that water at the memory of Egypt even when offered manna from heaven are "a figure of our time" (PL 204:761A).

What seems to have made the entanglements of Egypt so difficult to break was the age-old suspicion that nothing can redeem any part of your life (least of all the last) save perhaps for one last orgy of indulgence: "Our time is the passing of a shadow," says the infidel credo found in the Book of Wisdom. "Come therefore, and let us enjoy the good things that are" (Ws 2:5–6, DR).¹¹ Hedonistic sayings of this sort—born "of infidelity touching pain or reward after death," according to the commentators of the Douai-Rheims—were widespread in antiquity and seem to have been supercharged in the Middle Ages by monotheists' relentless hammering on the fleetingness of life and the nothingness of the world. Christians happening upon any number of ancient tombstones with inscriptions that denied the possibility of an afterlife would have recognized the sentiment even if they were supposed to reject it: "Eat, drink, indulge in lust—for everything is naught";¹² "I was nothing, I am nothing: and you who live, / eat, drink, play [*lude*], come!"¹³ After all, Paul himself conceded, "if the dead are not raised, let us eat and drink, for tomorrow we die" (1 Cor 15:32). He was quoting both Isaiah 22:13 and a contemporary slogan that, according to Hans-Joseph Klauck, captured "how

---

10. *Ep.* 218 (PL 207:498C). Doubt has been cast on the attribution of this letter to Peter (Cotts, *Clerical Dilemma*, 285–86), but it is nonetheless indicative of an age that knew Antony and Cleopatra through a variety of sources: Horace's *Ode* 1.37, for example, and a Pseudo-Ambrosian history, drawn largely from Josephus, which this letter probably echoes; see Ps-Ambrose, *De excidio urbis Hierosolymitanae* 1.28 (PL 15:1988A): "Antonium, jam totum Cleopatrae amoribus deditum." Cf. Karsten Friis-Jensen, "The Reception of Horace in the Middle Ages," in *The Cambridge Companion to Horace*, ed. Stephen Harrison (Cambridge: Cambridge University Press, 2007), esp. 293 on mss. of the *Odes*, with further citations.
11. See also Fr. W. Freiherr von Bissing, *Altägyptische Lebensweisheit* (Zürich: Artemis, 1955), 142, 144; Siegfried Schott, *Altägyptische Liebeslieder: Mit Märchen und Liebesgeschichten* (Zürich: Artemis, 1950), 138.
12. Plutarch, *On the Fortune of Alexander* 336c (LCL)—the inscription on Sardanapalus's tomb.
13. Hieronymus Geist and Gerhard Pfohl, *Römische Grabinschriften* (Munich: E. Heimeran, 1969), 164 (no. 435), with many more examples of the "Pessimismus der Materialisten."

a great many people . . . perceived their life."[14] That perception could not die with the Christianization of the wider Mediterranean if only because scripture memorialized the ancient rejection of eternal life, even as Christians harped constantly on the transience of existence. "For what is your life?" asks the epistle of James. "It is a vapor appearing for a little while, and afterward it shall vanish away" (Jas 4:14, DR); "Let everyone be without worry for the future or past," says a bacchanalian lyric in the *Carmina Burana*. "Death is ahead, things perish" (CB 201.2.3). Every human "cometh forth as a flower, and is cut down"—to quote a passage from the book of Job that was read throughout the Middle Ages in the Office of the Dead—"he fleeth also as a shadow, and continueth not."[15]

It was not lost on Peter of Blois any more than it was lost on Paul that the resurrection of the dead was a very big *if* and a possibility for which the evidence was scant.[16] We find arguments for and against in scripture, in the liturgical dramatizations that first emerge around Easter, and in a song that Peter sends to William consisting of a dialogue between an admonisher of the court and a courtier. In one manuscript each viewpoint is given a speech prefix that marks the lyric's indebtedness, if not to drama then to the dialectical style of argumentation roiling the universities at that very moment—"the quality of *sic et non*," in Peter Dronke's words, that Peter of Blois exemplifies "perhaps more remarkably than any of his contemporaries."[17] I'll make the case later in this chapter that the music drama of the *Carmina Burana* excels at tarrying with the negative every bit as much as Peter's songs, but I want to dwell here on this striking lyric for the sake of comparison:

Grata est in senio	It's nice in old age,
religio,	religion,

---

14. Hans-Joseph Klauck, *The Religious Context of Early Christianity: A Guide to Graeco-Roman Religions*, trans. Brian McNeil (Edinburgh: T&T Clark, 2000), 80.
15. Job 14:2; *Officium defunctorum* (Munich, 1712), 35 (lectio 5); preserved in *The Book of Common Prayer 1559: The Elizabethan Prayer Book*, ed. John E. Booty (Charlottesville: Published for the Folger Shakespeare Library by the University of Virginia Press, 2005), 309–10.
16. Caroline Walker Bynum, *The Resurrection of the Body in Western Christianity, 200–1336* (New York: Columbia University Press, 1995), consigns the "skeptical position" to footnotes (see 139n68 and 230n3).
17. Dronke, *Medieval Poet*, 287. See 304–7 for the Latin text with accompanying translation of Oxford Bodl. MS. Add. A. 44, s. XIII in., fol. 61r–v.

iuveni non congruit.	it doesn't suit the young.
Carnis desiderio consencio;	To the body's craving I consent;
nullus enim odio carnem suam habuit.	no one has ever hated his own flesh.
Neminem ab inferis revertentem vidimus—	We've never seen anyone come back from below —
certa non relinquimus ob dubia.	we will not abandon certainties for dubious tales.
Sompniator animus respuens presencia gaudeat inanibus;	Let the spirit sunk in dreams reject the life that's here and enjoy inane things;
quibus si credideris, expectare poteris Arturum cum Britonibus!	if you can believe those, you might as well expect the return of Arthur with his British legions![18]

The courtier mashes up the Pauline dictum that "no one ever hated his own flesh" (Eph 5:29, Vulg.) with the carpe diem from Wisdom—"there is no one known to have returned from below [*ab inferis*]" (Ws 2:1, Vulg.)—in order to celebrate material embodiment at the expense of eternity. His position is effectively an inversion of the Augustinian commonplace that faith alone can awaken us from the somnambulism of corporeal existence. In this case it is the *believer*, "sunk in dreams," who devotes himself to empty tales of resurrection, just as the quixotic reader of romance accepts the fiction of Arthur's promised return. The courtier sees the Christian faith as a sign of senescence but, amidst his mockery, does not wholly begrudge the admonisher's dotage. If you can believe it, you might as well enjoy! There's a certain pathos to the admonisher's rejoinder that the riches of an earthly life "will vanish instantly, as does a dream when one awakens" (CCCM 128:271) since, for the courtier, precisely this critique of the secular world's evanescence forms the basis for treasuring it. As much as Peter strives in his other writings to occupy the sober position of outward piety, he seems to have felt keenly the allure of

---

18. *"Quod amicus suggerit"* (CCCM 128:271); trans. Dronke, *Medieval Poet*, 306.

the alternative—hesitating "between the religious life and the world," in the words of R. W. Southern, "between faith and unbelief."[19] Even when speaking from the pulpit *in propria persona* and urging his listeners to abandon "the vanity of vanities," Peter does not invariably adopt the posture of a steadfast believer shepherding the doubtful toward eternal verities; instead, he counts himself among "us secular people—we who are not only in the world but from the world . . . who are often inebriated to the point of nausea by the cup of Babylon."[20]

The *Carmina Burana* is filled with depictions of, and by, this type of Christian—the type, in short, who eats, drinks, and fucks with relish; who listens now to liturgical song, now to "the music of Egypt," and struggles to know which is more ravishing.[21] "In the polemics of twelfth- and thirteenth-century preachers," writes Sylvia Huot, "the dangers of secular lyric are its very similarities to sacred music: the responsory format of the carol, its function as communal celebration, its discourse of love and desire."[22] Huot means by this what most preachers generally meant: namely, that people's devotion to secular performance—to erotic lyrics, musical accompaniment, dancing, and playacting—could replace their devotion to a cappella church music with an eerily similar but more accessible, pleasing, and worldly spectacle. Evidently preachers like Peter of Blois also had to grapple with the further realization that church music in and of itself did not necessarily place believers heavenward on a ladder stretching from the sensible world to an eternal reality best apprehended mathematically through pure reason (a liturgical ideal espoused by several authorities we'll explore shortly). Any number of Christians seem to have sensed that a pious devotion to church music did not always differ from humanity's most ancient and untamed passion for immanent gratification. What if the liturgy itself was no less human in origin than any other bacchanalia? After all, "if Christ is human and not God," Peter concedes in a treatise meant to address Jewish unbelief,

---

19. Southern, *Medieval Humanism*, 129.
20. *Serm.* 65 (PL 207:752B): "*Verum nobis saecularibus, qui non solum in saeculo, sed ex saeculo sumus . . . qui de calice Babylonis saepius inebriamur ad nauseam.*"
21. *Serm.* 64 (207:749B); traditionally attributed to Peter of Blois but excluded from his corpus by Rolf Köhn, "Pierre de Blois," in *Dictionnaire de Spiritualité* (Paris: Beauchesne, 1985), 12.2:1514. Cf. Cotts, *Clerical Dilemma*, 234n76.
22. Sylvia Huot, *Allegorical Play in the Old French Motet: The Sacred and the Profane in Thirteenth-Century Polyphony* (Stanford: Stanford University Press, 1997), 17.

"then to believe in him is idolatry."[23] The same suspicion lies at the root of the argument between Augustine and Archisynagogus in the Nativity play of the *Carmina Burana*, where their dialectical exchange occurs in song and is explicitly concerned with the equivalence between liturgical hymns and secular show tunes.

So far as the Middle Ages knew, humans had been finding solace in theater music from time immemorial because they could not help but regress from the worship of God to the faithless veneration of temporal fulfillment: "For the apostate angel," writes Peter, "knows how to use complex artifice and exquisite frauds to bring the congregation of saints into the theater [*in theatrum*], the people of redemption into a secular play [*fabulam saeculi*], and the school of innocence into ridicule" (*Ep.* 134, PL 207:402B). The theater was widely understood as a worldly venue for music that believers were perpetually drawn to attend—and even to emulate within their own rituals. "Against the prohibition of the law you dare to plant a grove of idolatry next to the altar of the lord," says Peter in the second letter of major importance to our knowledge of his career as a songwriter:

> Alas, alas, the prince of this world has been ejected from the gates and we reduce him to sirens' songs and to the delusions of rhythmic compositions [*rhythmorum deliramentis*]. With your invitation pagans have come into the inheritance of the Lord. Pagans—or rather, the customs of pagans—have entered into the sanctuaries of God, who warned us against their penetration of his church. Even I once devoted myself to trifles, to love songs, but through the grace of him who separated me from my mother's womb, I rejected those things at the threshold of youth. The serpent of Moses devoured in me the serpents of Pharaoh, when the delight of sweet theology removed the study of vanity. (*Ep.* 76, PL 207:234AB)

Here in a nutshell is what I take to be the medieval dialectic of secularization. The worldly attitude associated with Egypt, idolatry, pleasure, delusion, youth, vanity, trifles, and love songs squares off against the properly religious attitude of maturity, reason, and the enlightened pleasures, such as they are, of "sweet theology." My sense is that we owe at least one experience of modern secularity to the patristic and medieval theologians who insisted in ever more refined ways that it is entirely possible to reject the consolations of church ritual and to devote oneself instead to human-made,

---

23. *Contra perfidiam Judaeorum* 10 (PL 207:837D); cf. #67 in Elizabeth Revell, ed., *The Later Letters of Peter of Blois* (New York: Published for The British Academy by Oxford University Press, 1993).

CHAPTER 3

aesthetic phenomena that have no transcendent meaning. In fact it was entirely possible in the Middle Ages to disavow secular music and to accept in its place the consolations of church ritual only to sense on occasion that the ritual itself offered nothing more than a histrionic delirium. Either way the theater was to die for.

Various explanations have been put forward for the curious fact that the recipient of this particular letter and its author share the same name—Peter of Blois. The ingenious speculation first advanced by Reto Bezzola and Peter Dronke that the exchange is a rhetorical, fictive device similar to Petrarch's invention of an alter ego in his *Secretum* has been pretty well laid to rest, I think, by R. W. Southern's demonstration that there really was another Peter of Blois alive at the same moment: the archdeacon of Dreux, who once likened his place at the cathedral school at Chartres to that of Prometheus, chained to his rock.[24] Even so, the existence of two Peters of Blois does little to quell the impression that, in writing to Peter the archdeacon of Dreux, Peter the archdeacon of Bath wrote as though gazing into a mirror.[25] Their exchange gives new life to the quip by John of Salisbury—who heard directly from Peter, the archdeacon of Bath, about "the other me [*me alterum*]" (*Ep.* 114, PL 207:342)—that there was some question whether an archdeacon could be saved.[26] The lower orders were notorious for producing many of the songsters loosely referred to at the time as wandering scholars or goliards, usually in documents issued by a higher authority hoping to stave off their "secular infiltrations" of the liturgy and their constant, ludic questioning of orthodox doctrine.[27] According to Peter of Blois, for example, Peter of Blois is "an earthly, carnal, animal man" who "calls the word of God hard, insipid, infantile" (*Ep.* 76, PL 207:236B–C) and who has spent all of his days, well into

---

24. Richard Southern, "The Necessity for Two Peters of Blois," in *Intellectual Life in the Middle Ages: Essays Presented to Margaret Gibson*, ed. Lesley Smith and Benedicta Ward (London: Hambledon Press, 1992), 103-18. Wollin responds to Southern's suggestion that the archdeacon of Dreux may have written the erotic lyrics now ascribed to the archdeacon of Bath with the reminder that we have no extant lyrics from the archdeacon of Dreux to provide a basis for comparison, whereas the points of contact with the verses included by the archdeacon of Bath in his letter to William of Aulnay are extensive (CCCM 127:20).
25. Cotts, *Clerical Dilemma*, 126.
26. John of Salisbury, *The Letters of John of Salisbury: The Later Letters (1163–1180)*, ed. W. J. Millor and C. N. L. Brooke (Oxford: Clarendon, 1979), 24–25; cited in Cotts, *Clerical Dilemma*, 10.
27. Edmund A. Bowles, "Were Musical Instruments Used in the Liturgical Service During the Middle Ages?" *Galpin Society Journal* 10 (1957): 40-56 at 48. Cf. Canon 9 of the Council of Trier in 1227 in *Sacrorum conciliorum nova, et amplissima collectio*, ed. Joannes Dominicus Mansi (Venice, 1779), 23:33, which specifically prohibits "vagrant scholars or goliards from singing verses on the *Sanctus* and *Agnus Dei*, as it impedes the priest and scandalizes those listening."

old age, wrapped "in the fables of pagans, in studies of the philosophers, even in civil law" (*Ep.* 76, PL 207:233A), perfectly happy "to sing illicit love songs and to boast of corrupting virgins" (*Ep.* 76, PL 207:233C).

We find in the *Carmina Burana* and elsewhere a number of songs written in celebration of rapacious deflowering: "I transcend humanity and glory to be raised among the number of those above when I touch her soft breast."[28] From one perspective, this speaker is a conventional son of unbelief who declines to mortify his members the better to pursue with savage relish "fornication, uncleanness, lust, evil concupiscence" (Col 3:5–6, DR). From another, he is someone who would transcend humanity by taking at face value the Augustinian claim that humans can "be deified" (*deificatos*) through participation in the life of the Omnipotent, here by mimicking God's ravishment of a virgin.[29] The speaker in other words repurposes the tropes of Marian devotion to suggest that Christianity's promise of transcendence, as captured in myriad depictions of the Annunciation, is at bottom the apotheosis of sexual conquest and worldly power. Perhaps the truly "heady and subversive message" of the medieval dialectical arts, to recur once more to Dronke, is not merely that, in them, "the absolutist claims of contrasting outlooks are made relative" but that the glory of the Christian religion is shown to originate in and to reflect the secularity of the world, most of all where the burning words of the liturgy approximate the lost glamour, emptiness, and cruel beauty of pagan mythology.[30] Peter's denunciation of Peter—like Augustine's denunciation of Augustine in the *Confessions*—constitutes an especially colorful, troubling moment in the long Christian history of treating music as the *saeculum*'s most seductive representative while at the same time insisting that genuine worship be accompanied by song, on the model of the scriptural lyrics celebrating God's impregnation of a virgin (the *Ave Maria* and *Gloria*). Settling accounts with secular music in the twelfth century meant coming to terms with the vacuous entertainments that Christians assumed as a matter of course had attended the primitive approximations of religion preceding

---

28. "*Sevit aure spiritus*" (CCCM 128:435); see also Arundel 8.31–35, in *The Oxford Poems of Hugh Primas and the Arundel Lyrics*, ed. C. J. McDonough (Toronto: Centre for Medieval Studies by the Pontifical Institute of Medieval Studies, 1984), 86. CB 84, an otherwise close approximation, omits this stanza. See also Jonathan Seelye Martin, "Rape, the Pastourelle, and the Female Voice in CB 185," in *Revisiting the Codex Buranus: Contents, Contexts, Compositions*, ed. Tristan E. Franklinos and Henry Hope (Woodbridge, UK: Boydell Press, 2020), 149–70.
29. *En. in Ps.* 49.2 (CCSL 38:575 WSA III/16:381); see also *En. in Ps.* 52.6; *De civ. Dei* 9.23; *Tr. Joh.* 48.9, and Henry Chadwick, *Boethius: The Consolations of Music, Logic, Theology, and Philosophy* (Oxford: Clarendon, 1990), 210–11.
30. Dronke, *Medieval Poet*, 304, 310, respectively.

the Nativity, when childish pagans played on their crude instruments in honor of gods whose passions were in essence all too human. At times of great cultural ferment and so-called renascence, what Christians repeatedly found most disconcerting was the endurance of these histrionic, overpowering performances not only despite Christ's advent but in celebration of it.

The Birth of Liturgy from the Spirit of Music

Music came into being before the creation of humanity, "when the morning stars sang together" (Job 38:7a, AV) and "the sones of God sungun joyfuli" (Job 38:7b, later Wycliffite). All but inaudible outside the sonic revelations memorialized in scripture, this choir of "ministering spirits [*leitourgika pneumata*]" (Heb 1:14, AV) was thought to have provided the model for the terrestrial liturgy of the church.[31] The *Sanctus* of the Mass, for example, quoted Isaiah and John's vision of the Seraphim crying out *Holy, Holy, Holy* (Is 6:3; Rev 4:8) and so earned the medieval moniker *hymnus angelicus*. Another angelic hymn, the *Gloria*, was similarly presumed to replicate what the shepherds heard on Christmas, when, alongside a new star, "suddenly there was with the angel a multitude of the heavenly army, praising God and saying, Glory in the highest to God: and in earth peace to men of good will" (Lk 2:13, DR).[32] Thereafter liturgical song was supposed to elevate humanity to the cosmic level.

Christianity inherited from ancient Greece a readymade explanation for the musical connection between heaven and earth. Of all the arts studied in antiquity, music best corresponded to the transcendent realms most distant from the *saeculum* on account of its inherently mathematical structure. This kinship with the immutable, abstract ratios of "measure and number and weight" (Ws 11:21, DR) could lift the mind above merely aesthetic stimulants to the realm of philosophy—a term supposedly coined by Pythagoras for the study of the immaterial constants that alone constitute true Being.[33] His invention of the monochord seemed to have produced a standard of

---

31. Reinhold Hammerstein, *Die Musik der Engel: Untersuchungen zur Musikanschauung des Mittelalters* (Bern and Munich: Francke, 1962), esp. 17–22, 33–38; Richard Rastell, "The Musical Repertory," in *The Iconography of Heaven*, ed. Clifford Davidson (Kalamazoo: Medieval Institute Publications, Western Michigan University, 1994), 162-96.
32. David Flusser, "Sanctus und Gloria," in *Abraham Unser Vater: Juden und Christen im Gespräch über die Bibel, Festschrift für Otto Michel zum 60. Geburtstag*, ed. Otto Betz et al. (Leiden: Brill, 1963), 129-52.
33. Boethius, *De instit. musica* 2.2; Latin in *Anicii Manlii Torquati Severini Boetii De institutione arithmetica libri duo, De institutione musica libri quinque*, ed. Gottfried Friedlein (Leipzig, 1867); English in Anicius Manlius Severinus Boethius, *Fundamentals of Music*, trans. Calvin M. Bower, ed. Claude V. Palisca (New Haven, CT: Yale University Press, 1989). All further citations are to these editions by section number.

measurement for ultimate reality, "a kind of rule to such fixed and enduring inquiry that no researcher would be misled by the evidence" (Boethius, *De instit. musica* 1.11). It was an astrolabe for the ear that enabled as never before a clear understanding of the numerical laws governing the motions of the planets and stars, together with the soul's relation to the body: "These [motions] each one of us should follow, rectifying the revolutions within our head, which were distorted at our birth, by learning the harmonies and revolutions of the universe," explains Plato in the *Timaeus*—the only dialogue of his to circulate in the Latin world before the twelfth century (*Timaeus* 90d, LCL). Its influence continued to be felt well into the Copernican age and contributed directly to a major discovery. In the *Harmonice mundi* (1619), Johannes Kepler celebrates the *Timaeus* for converting Genesis "to the philosophy of Pythagoras" and then produces what we now call his third law while attempting to prove mathematically that the harmony of the spheres is entirely real.[34]

The text of the *Timaeus* was able to penetrate so deeply into Latin Christendom thanks to the partial translation and extensive commentary by Calcidius, an early fourth-century intellectual about whom we know very little, save that his dedication to Plato rivaled whatever affiliation he may have felt for Christianity.[35] The reasons for the commentary's extraordinary hold on the next millennium are manifold, but one key to the successful assimilation of its Pythagorean-Platonic musicology into Christian thinking is its condemnation of any musical experience unencumbered by a studious pursuit of transcendence: "Harmony," Plato teaches, has not been given to us as "an aid to irrational pleasure [*hēdonēn alogon*]" (*Timaeus* 47d, LCL). On the contrary it should be used to restore troubled souls to order and balance. Calcidius expands this remark so as to differentiate "the music in which the mob [*vulgus*] delights, and which sometimes gives rise to vices when performed for the sake of pleasure" from "the divine music that is never disposed to separation from reason and intelligence."[36] The juxtaposition effectively served as a template over the *longue durée* of the Middle Ages to defend the liturgy from

---

34. Johannes Kepler, *The Harmony of the World*, trans. E. J. Aiton et al. (Philadelphia, PA: American Philosophical Society, 1997), 301.
35. See Peter Dronke, *The Spell of Calcidius: Platonic Concepts and Images in the Medieval West* (Florence: SISMEL edizioni del Galluzzo, 2008), and Gretchen Reydams-Schils, *Calcidius on Plato's "Timaeus": Greek Philosophy, Latin Reception, and Christian Contexts* (Cambridge: Cambridge University Press, 2020).
36. Calcidius, *On Plato's "Timaeus,"* ed. and trans. John Magee (Cambridge, MA: Harvard University Press, 2016), 542–43. For a less censorious view of music, see Macrobius, *Commentary on "The Dream of Scipio,"* trans. William Harris Stahl (New York: Columbia University Press, 1952), 185–89, 193–95.

everything that it shared with the ever-fluctuating, superficial world of sensuous experience. At the same time the contrast awakened an almost insuperable suspicion that liturgical melodies might themselves be the most captivating of all human-made phenomena insofar as they promised to deliver a world beyond sense perception but forestalled its true apprehension by acting as an all too material stand-in. Certain Christians from late antiquity onward have periodically discovered, in any event, that the attempts of their fellow believers to perform "divine music" have devolved into a hedonistic theater devoid of spiritual content—particularly at Christmas, when, according to Innocent III (c. 1160–1216), "theatrical plays [*ludi theatrales*] are put on in certain churches."[37] The liturgy has always been in danger of collapsing into its constitutive opposite—a scripted performance by paid professionals, full of songs and gestures artificially designed to move an audience toward no end other than enjoyment.

Take for example the struggle of Boethius (c. 477–524). He bequeaths to the Middle Ages a standard taxonomy for distinguishing between the harmony of the spheres (*musica mundana*), the harmony of body and soul (*musica humana*), and, at the bottom of the hierarchy, the harmonies that were associated above all with secular song (*musica instrumentalis*).[38] Like Plato and Calcidius, he militantly disentangles the transcendent promise of music from the popular tunes that were played and enjoyed despite their lack of spiritual merit. Ever "since the human race has become lascivious and impressionable," Boethius complains, "it is taken up totally by dramatic and theatrical modes [*scenicis ac theatricalibus modis*]" (*De inst. musica* 1.1). He himself once had a penchant for composing in a similar vein according to the *Consolation of Philosophy*, which opens with a lyric admitting his former

---

37. PL 215:1070–71; Emil Friedberg, ed., *Corpus iuris canonici* (Leipzig, 1881), 2:452; see also the prohibitions of "*ludos theatrales . . . in ecclesia, & alios ludos inhonestos*" from 1227 in *Concilia germaniae* [etc.], ed. P. Josephus Hartzheim (Cologne, 1760), 529. Lawrence M. Clopper, *Drama, Play, and Game: English Festive Culture in the Medieval and Early Modern Period* (Chicago: University of Chicago Press, 2001) would have us set aside the literal meaning of these passages (and many others like them) but his interpretation of the evidence is apologetic and often wrong. See the next section of this chapter and cf. Alexandra F. Johnston, "Pleyes of Myracles," *English* 64, no. 244 (2015): 5–26; John Parker, *The Aesthetics of Antichrist: From Christian Drama to Christopher Marlowe* (Ithaca, NY: Cornell University Press, 2007), 63–65, 83, 85; Gina M. di Salvo, *The Renaissance of the Saints after Reform* (Oxford: Oxford University Press, 2023), 25–26 and appendix 1, which contains many British documents testifying to the link between *ludi*, interludes, and dramatic plays, e.g., "Magnum ludum vocatum saynt christeans play."
38. *De inst. musica* 1.3; for discussion see David S. Chamberlain, "Philosophy of Music in the *Consolatio* of Boethius," *Speculum* 45, no. 1 (1970): 80–97.

addiction to secular *carmina*: "the glory, once, of my happy green youth."[39] When imprisonment brought him abruptly to old age, his "mangled Muses" began dictating "elegiacs" instead, on the model of late Ovid.[40] Only with the appearance of Lady Philosophy does he absorb at last how deep his devotion has been to the lowest kind of song. She expresses indignation that he has allowed himself to be inspired by a "chorus" of "theater-whores"—"sirens, sweet to the point of ruin."[41] Normally the Muses work their degrading enchantments most effectively on "the mob [*vulgo*]," but in this case they have managed to beguile the highly educated Boethius like any other "profane person [*profanum*]"[42]—a word meaning ignorant or uninitiated yet still carrying the force of its etymology: in front of or outside the temple (*profanum*), hence readily associated with what Tertullian calls "the profane pleasures of secular shows."[43] Boethius is supposed to know that a real student of music needs more than an ability to write rhythmical lyrics, to play well on an instrument, and to perform songs on stage. Those accomplishments are mere works of the hand, and "works of the hand are nothing unless they are led by reason" (*De inst. musica* 1.34).

Boethius derives his appeal to reason and his antitheatricalism from the Platonic tradition but clearly echoes in this instance the scriptural critique of handmade idols as nonentities. The prophets had occasionally extended their ire to worldly music and the lascivious faction of music lovers who drank to excess while singing fake devotions; woe unto you "who play the wantons in your couches . . . you that sing to the voice of the psalter," laments Amos. "They have thought themselves to have instruments of song, that drink wine in phials and are anointed with the best ointment" (Am 6:4–5, DR; cf. Ez 26:13). The prophets carved out by means of this condemnation the negative image of a more ascetic piety that they hoped might hold a place for the psaltery free from lush cavorting: "Wo to you that risen togidere eerli to [pur]sue drunkennesse, and to drinke til to eventid, that ye brenne with wyn," says Isaiah. "Harpe and giterne and tympan and pipe and wyn ben in youre feestis;

---
39. *Consolatio* 1 M. 1.7 (CCSL 94:1). A brief record of Boethius's life, evidently by Cassiodorus, says that he wrote pastoral poetry (*carmen bucolicum*) in his youth: Hermann Usener, *Anecdoton Holderi: Ein Beitrag zur Geschichte Roms in ostgothischer Zeit* (Bonn, 1877), 4; Chadwick, *Boethius*, 23.
40. *Consolatio* 1 M. 1.3–4 (CCSL 94:1); on the Ovidian heritage, see Helga Scheible, *Die Gedichte in der Consolatio philosophiae des Boethius* (Heidelberg: C. Winter, 1972), 12–16.
41. *Consolatio* 1 P. 1.8, 11, 12 (CCSL 94:2–3).
42. *Consolatio* 1. P. 1.10 (CCSL 94:2).
43. Tertullian, *De cultu feminarum* 1.8.4 (CCSL 1:350; ANF 4:17): *"profanae spectaculorum saecularium voluptates."*

and ye biholden not the werk of the Lord" (Is 5:11–12, later Wycliffite).[44] To Christian readers, scripture seemed to have drawn an explicit link between these drunken concerts and the bacchanalian festivities pursued by the Jews when, after fashioning the Golden Calf, they sat down to eat and drink and then "rose up to play [*ludere*]" (Ex 32:6, DR). Both wine and music "make a joyful heart," explains Ben Sira. "But the love of wisdom is above both" (Sir 40:20, DR). Indulging in either was to drink up emptiness, whether by ear or mouth.

By the early Middle Ages any liturgical attempt to replicate the music of angels rested on a well-established body of polemical literature accusing every *other* musical performance of being a fleshly indulgence unconnected to reason or genuine reverence: "If people spend their time with auloi, psalteria, dancing and leaping, clapping hands like Egyptians, and in other similar dissolute activities," writes Clement of Alexandria, "they become altogether immodest and unrestrained, senselessly beating on cymbals and drums, and making noise on all the instruments of deception. Obviously, it seems to me, such a banquet has become a theater of drunkenness."[45] The problem with treating the religious, festive culture of non-Christians as an image of rank unbelief and rampant playfulness—"opinion combined with irrational sense perception," in the words of Calcidius—became acute when the same festivity, and even the same melodies, made an appearance in Christian devotion, as though Christians themselves were so weak of faith that they could not hope to move beyond material gratification.[46] Of particular concern to the Fathers (and to later reformers) were the enormously popular revels held in honor of the saints: "Not only were the pagan ceremonies continued in them with their great pomp," writes Johannes Quasten, "but the people also saw in them a substitute for the all-night vigils in honor of the gods, to which converts from paganism were still deeply attached."[47] The patristic condemnation of these residual pagan activities transformed them

---

44. For analysis, see Joseph Blenkinsopp, *Isaiah 1–39: A New Translation with Introduction and Commentary* (New York: Doubleday, 2000), 205–15, 373–75.
45. Clement of Alexandria, *Paedagogus* 2.4 (PG 8:440; ANF 2:248); quoted by James McKinnon, "The Meaning of the Patristic Polemic Against Musical Instruments," *Current Musicology* 1 (1965): 69-82 at 71.
46. Calcidius, *On Plato's "Timaeus,"* 40–41 (28a).
47. Johannes Quasten, *Music and Worship in Pagan and Christian Antiquity*, trans. Boniface Ramsey (Washington, DC: National Association of Pastoral Musicians, 1983), 169. See also James W. McKinnon, "Desert Monasticism and the Later Fourth-Century Psalmodic Movement," *Music & Letters* 75, no. 4 (1994): 505–21, esp. 513; Ramsay MacMullen, *Christianizing the Roman Empire, A.D. 100–400* (New Haven, CT: Yale University Press, 1984), 75–77, 85; and E. Catherine Dunn, *The Gallican Saint's Life and the Late Roman Dramatic Tradition* (Washington, DC: Catholic University of America Press, 1989), esp. 56–59, 62, 101.

into something new in Western history. They became a *secular* undertaking (because directed toward worldly ends) with an uncanny or even demonic ability, despite their fundamental vapidity, to offer rewards that were just as compelling as a properly sanctified liturgy. Such saturnalia sometimes left participants too drunk by morning to greet "the Sun of Justice," Ambrose complains, as they reached for the psaltery instead of their psalter.[48]

Worse, Augustine worries, they reach for the psalter only to find that it commands them to play "those same instruments of the theater [*organa theatrica*]" that "vigils in the name of Christ" had been instituted to banish.[49] "Confess ye to our Lord on the harp [*cithara*]," commands David, "on a psalter[y] of ten strings sing to him" (Ps 32:2, DR). If the Psalms seemed to call literally for such puerile revelry, the Fathers concluded, then the Psalms should not be read literally. "Figuratively the body can be called a cithara and the soul a psaltery," writes Pseudo-Origen in a representative passage.[50] It was possible on the basis of this kind of reading to design a liturgy, with the psalter at its center, that entirely excluded musical instruments like the psaltery, as well as the musicians who knew how to play them.[51] Divine worship thereafter consisted of an unaccompanied body that had been subjected to special discipline—above all vocal instruction—so that a well-trained voice might achieve a certain transcendence: spirit's release, as it were, from fleshly entombment. Today we call vocal music lacking all accompaniment *a cappella* because that was the only kind of music licensed to play in the chapel, save for the occasional organ, which was itself voice-like in its bellows and tubing. "Our singers," writes Amalarius of Metz in his treatise on the liturgy, "hold neither cymbals nor lyres nor citharas in their hands, nor any other

---

48. Ambrose, *De Elia et Jejunio* 15.55 (PL 14:717B).
49. Augustine, *En. in Ps.* 32, en. 2.5 (CCSL 38:350; WSA III/15:396).
50. Ps-Origen, *Selecta in psalmos* 32.2–3 (PG 12:1304); translated in *Music in Early Christian Literature*, ed. James McKinnon (Cambridge: Cambridge University Press, 1987), 38; discussion in Bruce W. Holsinger, *Music, Body and Desire in Medieval Culture: Hildegard of Bingen to Chaucer* (Stanford: Stanford University Press, 2001), 37.
51. Christopher Page, "The English *a cappella* Heresy," in *Companion to Medieval and Renaissance Music*, ed. Tess Knighton and David Fallows (New York: Shirmer Books, 1992), 23–29, esp. 27; Carla Casagrande and Silvana Vecchio, "Clercs et jongleurs dans la société médiévale (XIIe et XIIIe siècles)," *Annales: Histoire, Sciences Sociales* 34, no. 5 (1979): 913–28, esp. 924n2 and n7; Bowles, "Were Musical Instruments Used in the Liturgical Service During the Middle Ages?"; McKinnon, "Meaning of the Patristic Polemic"; Helen Waddell, *The Wandering Scholars*, 6th ed. (Garden City, NY: Doubleday Anchor, 1955), esp. 272 for the accusation that some sing in church "after the manner of worldly poets [*saecularium poetarum modo*]" and thereby corrupt the service "with tragic stylings" [*tragico sono*]"; J. D. A. Ogilvy, "'Mimi, scurrae, histriones': Entertainers of the Early Middle Ages," *Speculum* 38, no. 4 (1963): 603–19; also Jerome, *Ep.* 107 (CSEL 55:299).

kind of musical instrument."⁵² The absence of *musica instrumentalis* provided the church with its lone best hope of imitating celestial song rather a theatrical performance.

The fragility of that hope finds its greatest expression in Augustine. For him, music can escape the taint of theatricality only when experienced as a branch of *scientia*—by which he means a form of knowledge, located in the mind rather than the body, that takes as its object the unified, immutable laws of the cosmos. Proper music appreciation is therefore a course of instruction largely unsuited to adolescence—or to adolescent peoples—since only in adulthood does a person or people become sufficiently disentangled "from carnal senses and carnal literature" to be able to adhere with the love of unchangeable truth "to the one God and Lord of all things."⁵³ Augustine acknowledges that there are other schools of thought, filled with "tumultuous tongues rejoicing in the debates of agitated voices and the sound of applause" (*De musica* 6.1.1), but he hopes to bring them around to his way of thinking by adopting the ascetic idiom of late antique Pythagorean-Platonic music theory. He has written his treatise on music, he says, specifically "for those who, devoted to secular literature [*litteris saecularibus*], are entangled in great errors and wear out their good minds with trifles, not knowing what they enjoy there" (*De musica* 6.1.1). His ultimate goal is to move "from the corporeal to the incorporeal" (*De musica* 6.2.2) until reaching the highest, unchangeable things that reside beyond the *saeculum*

> where there is no time, because there is no change, and from which the times are created and set in order and modified in imitation of eternity, while the celestial rotation returns to the same place and recalls the celestial bodies to the same place and—through the days and months and years and lustra and the other orbits of the stars—obeys the laws of equality and unity and order. So terrestrial things are subject to celestial, and their time circuits join together in rhythmical succession as if for a song [*carmina*] of the universe.⁵⁴

---

52. Amalarius of Metz, *De ecclesiastis officiis* 3.3 (PL 105:1106C–D).
53. Augustine, *De musica* 6.1.1, in CSEL 102, and Martin Jacobsson, *Aurelius Augustinus, De musica liber VI: A Critical Edition with a Translation and an Introduction* (Stockholm: Almqvist and Wiksell, 2002), 6–7; all further citations from book 6 are to this edition by chapter and section number. I have benefited from Robert Catesby Taliaferro's translation of Augustine's *De musica* in *The Immortality of the Soul, the Magnitude of the Soul, On Music, The Advantage of Believing, On Faith in Things Unseen*, trans. Ludwig Schopp et al. (Washington, DC: Catholic University of America Press, 1947), 153–379.
54. Augustine, *De musica* 6.11.29; cf. *Ep.* 138.5; *De civ. Dei* 11.18.

The way to tune into the empyrean is to participate in the Christian liturgy. Its musical numbers can be shown through metrical analysis to encapsulate the abstract ratios of the cosmos—as exemplified, for Augustine, by the Ambrosian hymn *Deus creator omnium*.[55] At the same time a person has to avoid carnal music, epitomized for Augustine by the theatrical songs that can offer no meaningful instruction in the art of harmony: "Actors [*histriones*] can in no way be students of, or learned in, music," he explains, despite their ability to "satisfy the popular ear with pleasure" (*De musica* 1.6.11). Lacking any grasp of *scientia*, actors receive at best the "theatrical rewards" that arise from "the power of chance and the judgment of the ignorant"—namely, "applause," "money and glory" (*De musica* 1.6.12). They do not love music for its abstract mathematical properties but for "outside advantages" (*De musica* 1.6.12).

Still, Augustine admits, clerical performances of liturgical song had sometimes so stimulated "the pleasures of the ear"—particularly "when sung by a sweet voice, skilled in the art [*artificiosa*]"—that his old love of being an "auditor" in the theater welled up within him to the point that he risked falling for the corporeal experience of listening in real time rather than rationally apprehending timeless reality.[56] As a young man he had found himself fluctuating wildly "between dangerous pleasure and the experience of health" when listening to liturgical melodies, at times so captivated by the "gratification of the flesh" as "to wish that every air of the pleasant songs to which David's Psalter is often set were banished both from my ears and those of the church itself" (*Conf.* 10.33.50 [CCSL 27:181; WSA I/1:270]). In the end he reconciled himself to the surface charms of the liturgy only so that, "by the delights of the ear, a weaker mind may swell with the affect of piety" (*Conf.* 10.33.50 [CCSL 27:182; WSA I/1:270]). He thought that the church, in other words, could still avail itself of the most primitive secular techniques—same as any non-Christian venue—so long as the purpose was to sway mentally infirm members of the assembly. Weak in faith, generally doubtful, all too content to rely on sense perception, these would-be Christians were allowed a sop to their bodily appetites with the expectation that they might one day rise above the liturgy's most sensuous, musical blandishments, leaving behind its theatrical structure as something fundamentally opposed to true Christianity.[57]

---

55. *De musica* 6.2.2; see Brian P. Dunkle, *Enchantment and Creed in the Hymns of Ambrose of Milan* (Oxford: Oxford University Press, 2016), 110–12.
56. *Conf.* 10.33.49, 3.2.2 (CCSL 27:181, 27; WSA I/1:269, 76), respectively.
57. Cf. Donnalee Dox, *The Idea of the Theater in Latin Christian Thought: Augustine to the Fourteenth Century* (Ann Arbor: University of Michigan Press, 2004), 43.

Seen from this perspective, even a deliberate amplification of the theatrical qualities of the liturgy could be defended as an inducement to faith, charitably extended to the spiritually unfledged. So for example when Aethelwold of Winchester compiled the *Regularis concordia* in the second half of the tenth century—"at a time when laxity, simony, and secularization of offices had eroded respect for Christian worship"[58]—he defended the monks' adoption of music drama as "a practice worthy to be imitated for the strengthening of the faith of the unlearned mob and recent converts."[59] Aethelwold seems to have envisioned the monks' performance as a way of assuaging the doubts of newly, imperfectly converted people at a moment when neophytes had every reason to question the most basic doctrines; uncountable populations still lay beyond the reach of the gospel or were actively resisting its message despite a thousand years of preaching. To the Viking invaders that periodically ravaged the British Isles, "the Virgin Birth seemed ridiculous," writes Johannes Geffcken, "the weakness of Christ, his torment on the cross were unintelligible."[60] If we add to Geffcken's list of improbable fictions the Resurrection—reports of which initially sounded to Christ's disciples like "crazy talk [*deliramenta verba*] and they did not believe it" (Lk 24:11, Vulg.)—we have the subjects for the earliest, most widespread liturgical reenactments that arose in honor of Easter and Christmas. All of them contain extensive depictions of incredulity and unbelief, presumably toward the end of demonstrating how such doubts had been overcome in the earliest days of the church and thus how they might be overcome again, if only people could be persuaded to accept the aesthetic consolations of music drama as compensation for Christ's temporary absence and for the failure of his advent to introduce into world history the peace on earth promised by the *Gloria*. *Whom do you seek?* is the question posed by every visit to the sepulcher. *He is not here* is the lesson.

---

58. Michal Kobialka, *This Is My Body: Representational Practices in the Early Middle Ages* (Ann Arbor: University of Michigan Press, 1999), 74. The "secularization" referred to here is the imposition on the monastic office of a model drawn from nonmonastic (hence "secular") churches, though this specialized usage is not without resonance for the process of secularization in a more general sense. See also Carol Symes, "The History of Medieval Theatre / Theatre of Medieval History: Dramatic Documents and Performance of the Past," *History Compass* 2 (2009): 1032–48, esp. 1039–40, and Symes "The Medieval Archive and the History of Theatre: Assessing the Written and Unwritten Evidence for Premodern Performance," *Theatre Survey* 52 (2011): 29–58, esp. 30.

59. *Regularis concordia Anglicae nationis monachorum sanctimonialiumque: The Monastic Agreement of the Monks and Nuns of the English Nation*, ed. and trans. Thomas Symons (London: Nelson, 1953), 44 (modified): "*ad fidem indocti vulgi ac neophytorum corroborandam.*"

60. Johannes Geffcken, *The Last Days of Greco-Roman Paganism*, trans. Sabine MacCormack (Amsterdam: North Holland Publishing, 1978), 308.

We may want to take these dramatizations of the events outside the empty tomb as a celebration of Christ's triumph over death and a proffer of immortality to anyone willing to believe in the gospel, but we should probably also see in them a key witness to the self-conscious need for medieval Christians to prove—or barring that, to pretend—that the Resurrection actually happened; a need, in other words, to explore fully the doubts inspired by Christ's death and the disappearance of his body in what originally appeared to be an instance of grave-robbery, staged to look like a resurrection (Mt 27:62–64; Jn 20:2, 13–15). Setting that episode to music and restaging it over and over became a peculiar testimony to the power of theatrical fabrication, its ability to reflect on and offer some temporary solace for Christ's unavailability. The *Regularis concordia* repeatedly stresses the overtly theatrical counterfactuals of the liturgy. While the third lesson is read during the Easter services, one of the brethren is to enter "as if for some different purpose" and to position himself "stealthily" beside "a part of the altar that is vacant [*vaccum*]" and that may therefore function as "a representation [*assimilatio*], as it were, of the sepulcher."[61] While the third respond is sung, three others enter "and go to the place of the sepulcher, step by step, in the likeness [*ad similitudinem*] of people searching for something. For these things are done in imitation [*ad imitationem*] of the angel seated on the tomb and of the women coming with perfumes to anoint the body of Jesus."[62] After the announcement of his absence—*non est hic*—and some further lines instructing the Maries to spread the word of his resurrection, the cleric dressed as an angel sings an antiphon revealing that the sepulcher is just as vacant as its representation: "*Come and see the place*, and then, rising and lifting up the veil, he shall show them the place void of the cross [*locum cruce nudatum*]."[63] The veil, which turns out to have concealed nothing, is now laid to rest across the altar.

After the tenth century, such dramatizations of the vacant tomb appear with increasing frequency and elaboration. Walther Lipphardt's nine-volume edition of *Lateinische Osterfeiern und Osterspiele* gathers together a massive array of extant texts while attempting to preserve a distinction between the ones explicitly designed for liturgical performance (the *Osterfeiern* or "Easter ceremonies") and those that appear to have broken free from the liturgy (the *Osterspiele* or "Easter plays") and to have thereby made a step in the direction

---

61. *Regularis concordia*, ed. Symons, 49, 44.
62. *Regularis concordia*, ed. Symons, 49–50.
63. *Regularis concordia*, ed. Symons, 50.

of what E. K. Chambers calls "secularization."[64] For all of the criticism that Chambers's account has received in the last half century (most of it pious scolding), his point in this case seems to me worth savoring. The process was not merely a matter of religious plays moving beyond the confines of the church or passing to the laity but of religious authorities grappling with the realization, firstly, that the liturgy had come to emulate secular entertainment and, secondly, that the emulation could no longer be channeled to orthodox ends during the high holidays.

Medieval thinkers labored hard to maintain a distinction between liturgical performances and mere plays—*Feiern* vs. *Spiele*—but they did so precisely because they could see the distinction between the sacred and the profane breaking down, always in the direction of profanity. Consider, for example, a passage from Herrad of Landsberg (c. 1130–1195) as she tries to describe the relation between an acceptable dramatization of the Nativity during the Christmas liturgy and the carnivalesque state of affairs that had come to attend its performance:

> On the holy Feast of Epiphany or the Octave, ever since the Fathers of old, certain imaginary reenactments [*imaginaria*] have been prescribed as a religious observance [*religio*]—the star leading the Magi in search of the new-born Christ, Herod's cruelty and his fraudulent cunning, the soldiers being dispatched to kill the children, the lying-in of the Virgin and the angel warning the Magi not to return and other additions for these days—so that the faith of believers might be strengthened, the divine grace better worshipped, and the unbeliever excited by the spiritual office itself to divine adoration. What now? What goes on in some of the churches of our time? . . . The house of God is confounded by mixing laypeople and clerics, feasting, drinking, buffoonery, unbecoming jokes, seductive plays [*ludi placesibiles*], the clang of weapons, the uproar of brothels, the undisciplined invasion of all vanities.[65]

It is no small thing for the history of theater that by the twelfth century a person could believe that "the Fathers of old" *recommended* play-

---

64. *Mediaeval Stage*, 2:68–105. The *Feiern/Spiele* distinction originates with Wilhem Meyer; for critique see Young 1:411–12.

65. Herrad of Hohenbourg, *Hortus deliciarum*, ed. Rosalie Green et al. (Leiden: Brill, 1979), 2:492; discussion and translation in Nils Holger Petersen, "The Notion of a Missionary Theatre: The *ludus magnus* of Henry of Livonia's Chronicle," in *Crusading and Chronicle Writing on the Medieval Baltic Frontier: A Companion to the Chronicle of Henry of Livonia*, ed. Marek Tamm et al. (London: Routledge, 2020), 229–44 at 240. I borrow "seductive plays" from him.

ing dramatic scenes (*imaginaria*) as part of the liturgical rites (*religio*) of Christmas. Herrad's great fear—indeed her great insight—was that the tradition of using music drama to strengthen the faithful and to convert the incredulous had opened the door to a process of secularization that the authorities could no longer turn to their advantage. So-called believers now arrived at church the way Augustine had arrived in Carthage, craving to be titillated "by contact with sensible-objects" (*Conf.* 3.1.1 [CCSL 27:27; WSA I/1:75]), addicted to immediate fulfillment and lacking any real moral compass beyond a fatally fragmented self and its interests, specifically hoping to see salacious things—the uproar of brothels!—performed "imaginatively [*imaginarie*]," "in play for show [*in ludo spectaculi*]" (*Conf.* 3.2.3 [CCSL 27:28; WSA I/1:77]). Nor was Herrad alone in discovering that Christians had found far too many ways to cater to the widespread hunger for audiovisual, fleshly stimulation: "And this ridiculous dissipation is called religious observance!" exclaims Aelred of Rievaulx apropos of a liturgical reenactment of the Nativity (c. 1141–1142) that had gone so far as to incorporate musical instruments. He uses the same term—*religio*—that Herrad thought dated from the Fathers, but he does so only to mock the idea that a musical reenactment of the Nativity might count as devotion: "Meanwhile the mob [*vulgus*] stands marveling at the sound of puffed cheeks, the clashing of cymbals, the harmony of pipes, trembling and stupefied . . . until you would think they had come not to prayer but to a theater."[66] The vulgar taste for theatrical music decried by Calcidius, Augustine, and Boethius has so deeply penetrated the liturgy, according to Aelred, that people no longer observe a difference between sacred worship and music drama.

The dramas of the *Carmina Burana* are among our most lavish testimonials to this theatricalization of the liturgy. I will have more to say about the Nativity play in coming pages but want to linger on the Easter *ludus immo exemplum dominice resurrectionis* ("play or image of the Lord's Resurrection") copied into the manuscript sometime in the thirteenth century. Contrary to the assertions of Michael Norton that the word *ludus* is found "only in works that have no clear liturgical connection" and that "the continuum between liturgy and drama recognized by contemporary scholars is a contemporary construct," here we have a *ludus* whose open-

---

66. Aelred of Rievaulx, *Speculum caritatis* 23 (PL 195:571–72); English in Aelred of Rievaulx, *The Mirror of Charity*, trans. Elizabeth Connor (Kalamazoo, MI: Cistercian Publications, 1990), 211 (modified).

ing rubric stipulates a performance "after singing Matins on Easter [*Cantatis matutinis in die pasche*]" (CB 15*) and whose ensuing action explores the intimate relationship between liturgical music and theatrical fiction.[67] The play opens with the Jewish priests' worry that the followers of Jesus will respond to the calamity of his death by stealing his corpse in order to create the appearance of a *deus ex machina*: "the disciples—seducers, rather— / are contriving the ruin of a people [*machinantur ruinam populi*] " (CB 15*.12–13). After some haggling over the price for guarding the tomb—"lest people believe that he lives" (CB 15*.39)—Roman soldiers circle the grave singing together:

Non credimus Iesum resurgere,	We do not believe that Jesus is risen,
sed, ne corpus quis possit tollere,	but to prevent someone from taking the body,
providemus per has vigilias.	we provide this vigil.
Schăwe propter insidias!	Beware of crafty stratagems!
	(CB 15*.51–4)

Various arguments against the Resurrection are added by other soldiers— "Human reason [*humana ratio*] does not conclude that he has risen . . . If he could rise from the dead, he could have remained alive!" (CB 15*.63–64, 67–68)—each of them ending in the same musical refrain: Beware of *insidias*, a word that means literally "ambushes" but applies to a large range of deceptive frauds, as when Cicero counsels orators against a sing-song delivery for fear that excessive "rhythm" would seem "like a trick [*insidiarum*] to catch the ear" (*Orator* 51.170, LCL). The layers of irony are sufficiently thick in these lines that it is hard to know when to stop peeling them back. At first the joke is clearly on the soldiers who find themselves holding a

---

67. Michael Norton, *Liturgical Drama and the Reimagining of Medieval Theater* (Kalamazoo: Medieval Institute Publications, Western Michigan University, 2017), 110n80 and 102. For a more persuasive discussion, see Richard D. McCall, *Do This: Liturgy as Performance* (Notre Dame, IN: University of Notre Dame, 2007); Petersen, "The Notion of a Missionary Theatre," in *Crusading and Chronicle Writing*, esp. 232: "few would deny some kind of continuity between certain performative medieval liturgical practices and later forms of theatre"; Sarah Beckwith, "Ritual, Church and Theatre: Medieval Dramas of the Sacramental Body," in *Culture and History, 1350–1600*, ed. David Aers (Detroit, MI: Wayne State University Press, 1992), 65–89, and John Parker, "Religion, Ritual and Myth," in *A Cultural History of Tragedy*, ed. Rebecca Bushnell, vol 2: *In the Middle Ages*, ed. Jody Enders et al. (London: Bloomsbury, 2020), 81–98.

"vigil" in anticipation of an event that they do not believe is coming. By the same token they are not wrong, from the perspective of "human reason," to have decided that the truths of the faith are impossible to differentiate from fiction. That is why Christian truths, such as they are, are particularly well suited for song and playacting. Those truths appear, at bottom, counterfactual and incredible. Here the likeness to a playful fiction has been transformed from an argument against Christian doctrine into an advertisement for the wonder that awaits those who learn to suspend their unbelief in preposterous happenings.[68]

Then come the special effects. Great thunder is heard, two people dressed as angels appear, the soldiers fall "as if dead," and the angels "announce that Christ has risen, by singing" (CB 15*.70). The artificiality of the staging at this point seems to have become part of the message. Rather than allaying all doubt once and for all, the angels' song opens the way for a series of scenes in which nearly everyone—Christian and infidel alike—expresses profound skepticism that Jesus has risen: "The disciples are disturbed," chant the Maries upon entry, "and exceeding pain holds us while he is absent [*absente eo*]" (CB 15*.106). Each of the three Maries then sings in succession an aria ("*cantet sola*" [CB 15*.107–110]) consisting of two words: *O Deus*—an oath of frustration doubling as a profession of faith and the answer to the question they later ask in chorus: Who can possibly help to roll away the stone? The action shifts abruptly back to the court of Pilate, where the soldiers describe the appearance of the angel and his announcement of the risen Christ, at which point the Jews shower the soldiers with gifts so that they will keep quiet (cf. Mt 28:13–15), and the manuscript breaks off mid-strophe. It is a silence for the ages.

Judging from the Klosterneuburger Osterspiel—a complete Easter play closely related to CB 15*—we can guess what is likely to have happened next. The apostles hear the good news, such as it is, and sing a lament:

Isti sunt similia deliramentorum,	Those [words] sound like delusions,

---

68. See Julie Orlemanski, "Who Has Fiction? Modernity, Fictionality, and the Middle Ages," *New Literary History* 50, no. 2 (2019): 145–170.

nec persuasibilia	they are not convincing
mentibus virorum	to the minds of men.[69]

Peter and John hasten to the tomb, John discovers the shroud and "wonders" in song whether Christ has risen or if "someone has taken him" (ll.144–45). Peter delivers the shroud to the rest of the disciples, and they sing an even more pessimistic version of John's grieving astonishment:

Monumentum vidimus vacuum	We have seen the vacant memorial
nec in eo vidimus mortuum;	but have not seen a corpse in it;
sed nescimus, si resurrexerit,	We do not know if he has risen
an aliquis eum abstulerit.	or if someone has taken him.

(ll. 148–51)

Unlike the earliest version of the *Visitatio* in the *Regularis concordia*, here the *quem queritis* (l. 92) does not bring the play's cycle of anguish and uncertainty to a close but, instead, sets into motion a renewed spiral of doubt with Mary Magdalene's *planctus*—a common medieval vehicle for conveying inconsolable grief or insatiable longing and one that in this case probably harkens back to the soliloquies of Seneca.[70] "Pain grows, my heart rises at the absence of my loyal master [*magistri pii absentia*]" (ll. 162–63), laments Mary, implying that Jesus, in addition to being betrayed, was himself a kind of betrayer for having defaulted on his promises. Her own sense of duty remains undiminished: "They have taken my lord," she says to the first person she sees, "and I do not know where they have put him" (ll. 171–73). It does not exactly diminish the pathos of her predicament that Jesus has slipped into the play without her knowing, "disguised as a gardener [*quasi in Specie Hortulani*]" (l. 168), as though trifling with her despair in order to cure it. When he speaks her name "*in Specie Christi*" (l. 178), she tries but cannot touch him. Is he actually there, resurrected in the flesh, or is it all a simulacrum (*species*)? Either way Christ has appeared only to announce yet another, more permanent disappearance, and Mary will not see him again in this world. She exits without saying a word, then returns for a final

---

69. Walther Lipphardt, ed., *Lateinische Osterfeiern und Osterspiele* (Berlin: de Gruyter, 1976), 5:1707–8 (ll. 135–39). All further citations of the Klosterneuburger Osterspiel are to this edition by line number.
70. See the laments in CB 13*.27–28, rubric; CB 16*.114–17, 148–65, 248–302; CB 14* and CB 100; Peter Dronke, "Laments of the Maries: From the Beginnings to the Mystery Plays," in *Intellectuals and Poets in Medieval Europe* (Rome: Edizioni di storia e letteratura, 1992), 457–490; on Seneca in the Middle Ages, see Parker, "Religion, Ritual, and Myth."

"chorus" (l. 235) in which all the women and apostles venerate the shroud—equal parts stage-prop and relic—for the absence it reveals: "The body of Jesus was *not* discovered in the tomb!" (l. 234). On that, at least, believers and unbelievers were in agreement.

The *Ave Maria* as *Ludus*

Between the tenth-century dramatization of the *Visitatio sepulchri* recorded in the *Regularis concordia* and the thirteenth-century Easter *ludus* added to the *Carmina Burana*, scholastic attitudes to the practice of playing underwent a sea change. One early witness to the shift is Hugh of St. Victor (c. 1096–1141), an Augustinian canon who laid out for his students at the abbey a comprehensive account of the fields of study then available in Paris: "The book," he explains by way of preface, "instructs a reader of both secular and divine writings."[71] On the secular side of things, he complements the seven liberal arts of the classical tradition with seven arts "that are called mechanical," following a model first proposed by John Scotus Eriugena in the ninth century.[72] As a reader of Greek, Eriugena was familiar with mechanics as the field of knowledge responsible for a range of ingenious automata, many of which were used to produce the "contrived religious wonders" of antiquity—moving cultic statues, coin-operated sacrificial vessels that flowed with water upon receipt of payment, to say nothing of the various contraptions needed on stage to produce a *deus ex machina*.[73] It was partly as a result of the link to theater and pagan worship that the word "mechanical" was

---

71. Hugo von Sankt Viktor, *Didascalicon de studio legendi: Studienbuch*, ed. and trans. Thilo Offergeld (Freiburg: Herder, 1997), 106 (praefatio). All translations are my own but I have benefited from Hugh of Saint-Victor, *Didascalicon: A Medieval Guide to the Arts*, trans. Jerome Taylor (New York: Columbia University Press, 1961), and Franklin T. Harkins and Frans van Liere, eds., *Interpretation of Scripture: Theory: A Selection of Works of Hugh, Andrew, Richard and Godfrey of St Victor, and of Robert of Melun* (Turnhout: Brepols, 2012), 61–202.
72. Hugo von Sankt Viktor, *Didascalicon* 2.20, ed. Offergeld. For Eriugena's contribution, see Stephen Parcell, *Four Historical Definitions of Architecture* (Montreal: McGill-Queen's University Press, 2012), 53–58.
73. Steven J. Scherrer, "Signs and Wonders in the Imperial Cult: A New Look at a Roman Religious Institution in the Light of Rev 13:13–15," *Journal of Biblical Literature* 103, no. 4 (1984): 599–610 at 600; Lucian, *Alexander the False Prophet* 17 (LCL); Bennet Woodcroft, ed. and trans., *The Pneumatics of Hero of Alexandria from the Original Greek* (London, 1851), 37–38; cf. Edward Grant, "Henricus Aristippus, William of Moerbeke and Two Alleged Medieval Translations of Hero's *Pneumatica*," *Speculum* 46, no. 4 (1971): 656–69; Marie Boas, "Hero's *Pneumatica*: A Study of Its Transmission and Influence," *Isis* 40, no. 1 (1949): 38–48; Kara Reilly, *Automata and Mimesis on the Stage of Theatre History* (New York: Palgrave Macmillan, 2011), esp. 23–28; Elly Rachel Truitt, *Medieval Robots: Mechanism, Magic, Nature, and Art* (Philadelphia: University of Pennsylvania Press, 2015).

etymologically derived in Latin Christendom not from its actual root (the Greek *mēchanē*) but from the biblical terms for a faithless infidel or "adulterer" (*moichos*/*moechus*)—the sort of person whose affections were easily transferred from God to works-of-the-hand, as exemplified by Israel when "she committed adultery [*moechata esset*]" (Jer 3:8, Vulg.) by whoring herself before idols.[74] What's striking about Hugh's description of the mechanical arts is his pointed refusal to describe them as idolatrous. Instead he mentions in passing that they are indeed "adulterate"—but only, he explains, because "they concern the work of an artificer [*de opere artificis*], which takes its form from nature" (*Didascalicon* 2.20, ed. Offergeld). As such they are both necessary and legitimate. In fact the survival of humanity depends on them: specifically, fabric-making, armament, commerce, agriculture, hunting, medicine, and—for the first time in Christian intellectual history—*theatrica*, or what Hugh also calls "the science of playing [*scientia ludorum*]" (*Didascalicon* 2.27, ed. Offergeld).

Hugh notably excises all the sneering references to "the immodesty of theater [*impudicitia theatri*]" and "the debauchery of play [*luxuria ludi*]" that he found in Isidore of Seville (the primary source for his description), while keeping *theatrica*, alone of the mechanical arts, firmly rooted in the unbelieving past.[75] Theater is the place where "people *used to* convene for the performance of plays" (*Didascalicon* 2.27, ed. Offergeld, my emphasis). It is the place where, long ago, "exploits were recited either in songs or with visors or masks or puppets."[76] It lent its name to all manner of sport and entertainment not, he explains, because playing occurred primarily in theaters—he lists various other arenas, including banqueting halls, amphitheaters, and temples—but

---

74. Martin of Laon, *Scholica graecarum glossarum*, under *moechus*, in M. L. W. Laistner, "Notes on Greek from the Lectures of a Ninth Century [sic] Monastery Teacher," *Bulletin of the John Rylands Library* 7, no. 3 (1923): 421–456, esp. 439; noted in Hugh of St. Victor, *Didascalicon*, trans. Jerome Taylor, 191n64.
75. Isidore, *Etym.* 18.59; Latin in *Isidori Hispalensis episcopi Etymologiarum sive originum libri XX*, ed. W. M. Lindsay (Oxford: Clarendon, 1911); English in *The "Etymologies" of Isidore of Seville*, trans. Stephen A. Barney et al. (Cambridge: Cambridge University Press, 2006), 370 (modified); Casagrande and Vecchio, "Clercs et jongleurs dans la société médiévale (XIIe et XIIIe siècles)," 919; Wladyslaw Tatarkiewicz, "Theatrica, the Science of Entertainment: From the XIIth to the XVIIth Century," *Journal of the History of Ideas* 26, no. 2 (1965): 263–72; Symes, *Common Stage*, 8–10; Parcell, *Four Historical Definitions of Architecture*, 70.
76. *Didascalion* 2.27, ed. Offergeld: "*In theatro gesta recitabantur, vel carminibus, vel larvis, vel personis, vel oscillis.*" I have translated as literally as possible but the terms are open to a certain amount of interpretation; see Tatarkiewicz, "Theatrica, the Science of Entertainment," 264; Glending Olsen, "Interpretations," in *A Cultural History of Theater*, vol. 2: *In the Middle Ages*, ed. Jody Enders (London: Bloomsbury Academic, 2017), 131; Symes, *Common Stage*, 9–13.

because theater was more frequented and popular (*celebrior*) than the others. He acknowledges that playing (*ludendum*) could extend far beyond the performance of drama to include throwing dice, wrestling, racing, even boxing, and he admires how the ancients counted such a wide variety of games among the "legitimate activities" (*legitimas actiones*) for refreshing mind and body. His claim—contrary to the ascetic thrust of patristic Neoplatonism—is that secular play need not be considered inherently sinful and can in fact confer indispensable benefits. As an innocuous form of pleasure, it is capable of preventing the harm that arises from indulging in the truly dangerous excesses on offer in the world.

Only a few decades before the *Didascalicon*—around 1100—Honorius Augustodunensis noted approvingly the likeness between ancient tragedians and the celebrants who perform "in the theater of the church [*in theatro ecclesiae*]."[77] Hugh himself does not go quite that far, but he would have known that some of the theatrical activities attributable to pagans ("they sang songs in praise of the gods") were at that very moment also the provenance of Christian clerics—*and* of the professional musicians who were called minstrels (*ioculatores*), mimes (*mimi*), and actors (*histriones*). While Hugh passes over the resemblance between clerics and players in strategic silence, other theorists soon found ways to exempt certain forms of secular performance explicitly from the traditional calumny, and thus to exonerate, in a roundabout fashion, the clerics who had been influenced by the latest repertoire. It could now be said of Augustine's loathed *histriones*, according to Peter the Chanter (d. 1197), that they "sing with instruments or sing of exploits [*de gestis rebus*] to give relaxation or perhaps to give instruction" and that such activities "border on being legitimate [*vicini sunt excusationi*]."[78] Peter's note of indulgence was followed by several other scholars in his circle, most notably Thomas of Chobham, a subdean of Salisbury; his penitential, written circa 1213–1230, would have considerable influence for the next century.[79]

---

77. *Gemma animae* 1.83 (PL 172:570B); trans. David Bevington, *Medieval Drama* (Boston: Houghton Mifflin, 1975), 9; discussed in Parker, *Aesthetics of Antichrist*, 122–25.
78. Latin and trans. in Christopher Page, *The Owl and the Nightingale: Musical Life and Ideas in France, 1100–1300* (Berkeley: University of California Press, 1990), 22.
79. *Thomae de Chobham summa confessorum*, ed. F. Broomfield (Louvain: Éditions Nauwelaerts, 1968); mistaken by Chambers, *Mediaeval Stage*, 2:262–63, for Thomas of Chobham, the Bishop of Salisbury (d. 1313)—an error repeated by Clopper, *Drama, Play and Game*, 30. See Helen F. Rubel, "Chabham's [sic] Penitential and Its Influence in the Thirteenth Century," *PMLA* 40, no. 2 (1925): 225–39, and Page, *Owl and the Nightingale*, 23–24, whom I follow closely; Clopper omits both.

He explains that *histriones* can be divided into multiple types, all of them "damnable" save for one: those called *"ioculatores* who sing the deeds of princes and the lives of saints and give people comfort either when they are ill or when they are troubled" but who scrupulously avoid "lascivious songs" and mixed-sex dancing—unlike all the other *histriones*, who "play in indecent scenes [*ludunt in imaginibus inhonestis*]."[80] We can see in this passage inklings of the decisive step that Augustine and the other antitheatrical Fathers had been at pains to prevent the church from taking—namely, toward social acceptance of professional musicians. By 1259 the shift had occurred in no uncertain terms and likely reflected a growing realization among the highest authorities that the theatricalization of the liturgy was by then irreversible: "There are other, more serious sins than spectacles and plays [*spectacula & ludi*]," writes Pierre de Tarentaise (soon to be known as Innocent V). "Those are the ones that ought to be forbidden to penitents by Augustine."[81]

The orthodox apology for the pleasure of playing achieves its most sophisticated expression in Aquinas (c. 1225–1274) and Bonaventure (1221–1274). As the body grows weary from incessant labor, Aquinas argues, so does the soul from constantly striving to ascend to an incorporeal reality. Precisely because "attractive sensible objects" (*bona sensibilia*) are so congenial to humans, it is tiresome for us to be constantly breaking our attachments and transcending the sensorium through reason; in fact, this striving after transcendence will kill us, just as the bow will soon snap that is drawn, over and over, without respite.[82] "Pleasure is rest for the soul"—a needed reprieve from seeking higher realities, comparable to the way that physical relaxation gives the body a release from and reward for labor.[83] We cannot in any meaningful way live without it: "Play [*ludus*] is necessary for the intercourse of

---

80. *Thomae de Chobham summa confessorum*, 292; trans. Page, *Owl and the Nightingale*, 23 (modified). Chobham here uses for illicit drama the same term—*imaginaria*—that Herrad of Landsberg employs for acceptable liturgical reenactments of the Nativity. Clopper's rendering of the word in Herrad as "symbolic representations" (*Drama, Play and Game*, 47) but in Chobham as "fantasies" (31)—while insisting that they refer to totally different forms of play, despite the explicit overlap in terminology—is a good example of the strain required to make the evidence support his argument. His claim that the term *ludus* has no connection to drama ignores the plays of the *Carmina Burana* and the overwhelming counterevidence provided by scholastic theologians.
81. In IV. Sent. Dist. XVI, Quaest. Unica, art. 3, [part] 3 in *Innocentii Quinti pontificis maximi, ex ordine praedicatorum assumpti, qui antea Petrus de Tarantasia dicebatur, in IV. librum sententiarum commentaria* [etc.] (Ridgewood, NJ: Gregg Press, 1964 [originally published in 1651]), 4:172; repeated by Aquinas, *Scriptum Super Sententiis*, lib. 4, d. 16, q. 4, a. 2, qc. 2, arg. 3.
82. *Summa theol*. 2a2ae, q. 168, art. 2, resp., in *Summa theologiae: Latin Text and English Translation, Introductions, Notes, Appendices, and Glossaries*, vol. 44: *Well-Tempered Passion (2a2ae. 155–70)*, trans. Thomas Gilby (New York: McGraw-Hill, 1972), 216–17.
83. *Summa theol*. 2a2ae, q. 168, art. 2, resp., trans. Gilby, 44:216–17, speaking of *delectatio*.

human life."⁸⁴ Where Thomas Chobham had reached the limit of his tolerance at giving money to actors and had agreed with the dictum (attributed to Jerome) that doing so was a sacrifice to demons, Aquinas argues by contrast that the "profession of acting [*officium histrionum*]" is both lawful and worthy of compensation: "Those who support them [i.e., *histriones*] in due season do not sin, but rather act justly by rewarding them for their services."⁸⁵ Actors were like ministers, tending to the people with a secular liturgy (*officium*). They deserved the fruits of their own offertory.

By the thirteenth century the church had gone a long way toward overturning the antitheatrical consensus summarized and affirmed by Peter Lombard in this unforgiving sentence: "Whoever wishes to obtain the perfect grace of remission should abstain from plays and secular spectacles [*a ludis, a spectaculis saeculi*]."⁸⁶ Bonaventure, for his part, argues that the "source of all enlightenment [*illuminationis*]" emanating from on high extends even to the "the light of the mechanical arts" and grants a number of advantages to "artificial figures, which are, as it were, exterior to man and intended to supply the needs of the body."⁸⁷ He quotes Hugh of St. Victor by name and repeats his list of the mechanical arts but differentiates *theatrica* from all the others by virtue of its uselessness, or what latter-day theorists have come to call aesthetic autonomy—a doctrine clearly articulated by Aquinas in his redefinition of *ludus*: "Things done in play are not ordered to anything else, but are sought for their own sake."⁸⁸ Bonaventure takes Horace's famous adage in the *Ars poetica* to mean that poets want *either* to instruct their audi-

---

84. *Summa theol.* 2a2ae, q. 168, art. 3, resp., trans. Gilby, 44:222–23: "*ludus est necessarius ad conversationem humanae vitae.*"
85. *Summa theol.* 2a2ae, q. 168, art. 3, resp., trans. Gilby, 44:222–23; Page, *Owl and the Nightingale*, 16 (on Jerome). Cf. John W. Baldwin, "The Image of the Jongleur in Northern France Around 1200," *Speculum* 72 (1997): 635–63, esp. 639–41.
86. *Sententiarum* lib. 4, dist. 16, chap. 2 (87), 5; text in *Magistri Petri Lombardi Parisiensis episcopi Sententiae in IV libris distinctae*, 3rd ed. (Grottaferrata: Editiones Collegii S. Bonaventurae ad Claras Aquas, 1981), 2:339; English in Peter Lombard, *The Sentences: Book 4—On the Doctrine of Signs*, trans. Giulo Silano (Toronto: Pontifical Institute of Medieval Studies, 2010), 91; citing Ps-Augustine, *De vera et falsa poenitentia* 15.31 (PL 40:1126).
87. Bonaventure, *Opera omnia*, edita studio et cura PP. Collegii a S. Bonaventura (Quaracchi, 1891), 5:319; English in *Saint Bonaventure's "De Reductione Artium Ad Theologiam*," trans. Emma Thérèse Healy, 2nd ed. (Saint Bonaventure, NY: The Franciscan Institute, Saint Bonaventure University, 1955), 21 (modified).
88. Thomas Aquinas, *An Exposition of the On the Hebdomads of Boethius*, trans. Janice L. Schultz and Edward A. Synan (Washington, DC: Catholic University of America Press, 2001), 5; cf. Theodor Adorno, *Aesthetic Theory*, trans. Robert Hullot-Kentor (Minneapolis: University of Minnesota Press, 1997), 1, 104, 204–205, 228; Max Weber, MWG I/22.2:410; English in *Economy and Society: An Outline of Interpretive Sociology*, ed. Guenther Roth and Claus Wittich (Berkeley: University of California Press, 1978), 1:608.

ence (by providing some sort of moral edification) *or* to please it (by offering a momentary release from the labor of spiritual betterment). Only one art, however, exists *exclusively* "for consolation and pleasure [*delectationem*]," without any eternal benefit whatsoever. "It is *theatrica*, or the art of plays [*ars ludorum*], which includes every mode of playing [*ludendi*], whether with song, instrumental music [*organis*], fictions [*figmentis*] or pantomime [*gesticulationibus corporis*]"—and, some manuscripts add, "choruses [*choreis*]" (*Opera omnia*, 5:319). Because theater grants a certain freedom from both the work-a-day world of mere subsistence and from moral improvement, "it is one of a kind," all the more necessary as it is totally gratuitous (*Opera omnia*, 5:320). With its unique proffer of sanctuary, theater legitimizes the phantom delights of the *saeculum* while also functioning as a proxy for spiritual experience.

It did not take long for someone to follow this line of thinking to its logical conclusion and to argue that the transcendence celebrated by Pythagorean-Platonic musicology was in actuality an immanent effect of earth-bound voices and instruments, projected into the heavens, and that there was nothing particularly wrong or blameworthy in placing such high value on secular music. In a stunning treatise, Johannes de Grocheio (c. 1255–1320) infers from the vibrant mechanical arts of Paris that the harmony of the spheres is a myth, the stars are completely silent, and the soul's relation to the body is without musical significance.[89] He casts aside the old Boethian taxonomy in favor of various new subdivisions, following "the usage of the moderns [*usum modernorum*]," while giving pride of place to the popular *musica vulgaris* against which the traditional musicology had been explicitly formulated.[90] This modern, secular category subsumes all other types of music by disclosing their true purpose: "They mitigate the suffering to which all humans are born."[91] *Musica vulgaris*, in other words, is a primary *source* of the liturgy's power.[92] Indeed the treatise is "so deeply imbued with the idea of constructive pleasure in secular music," according to Christopher Page, that it does not bother once to condemn *ioculatores*, *histriones*, or *mimi* but instead, when it names them, does so

---

89. Ernst Rohloff, ed., *Die Quellenhandschriften zum Musiktraktat des Johannes de Grocheio* (Leipzig: Deutscher Verlag für Musik, 1972), 122. English in Johannes de Grocheio, *Concerning Music (De musica)*, trans. Albert Seay (Colorado Springs: Colorado College Press, 1972), 10–11. I have relied whenever possible on Christopher Page, "Johannes de Grocheio on Secular Music: A Corrected Text and a New Translation," *Plainsong and Medieval Music* 2, no. 1 (1993): 17–43.

90. Rohloff, *Quellenhandschriften*, 138; Page, "Johannes de Grocheio on Secular Music," 35.

91. Rohloff, *Quellenhandschriften*, 130; Page, "Johannes de Grocheio on Secular Music," 22.

92. Rohloff, *Quellenhandschriften*, 124; Page, "Johannes de Grocheio on Secular Music," 21. Cf. Constant J. Mews, "Questioning the Music of the Spheres in Thirteenth-Century Paris: Johannes de Grocheio and Jerome de Moravia OP," in *Knowledge, Discipline and Power in the Middle Ages: Essays in Honour of David Luscombe*, ed. Joseph Canning et al. (Leiden: Brill, 2011), 95–117, esp. 101.

only to praise their accomplishments.[93] If *musica vulgaris* provided a foundation for ecclesiastical music, and if secular musicians could be celebrated for putting on "plays [*ludi*]" before powerful magnates, why should anyone take offense that the clergy, too, indulged in the popular taste for music drama?[94]

The songs and plays of the *Carmina Burana* are among the deepest of surviving inquiries into the relationship between clerical performance and the *officium histrionum*. "Play, let one play, all play! [*Lude, ludat, ludite*]" (CB 172.1)—that is a commandment reverberating throughout the whole manuscript, and the religious plays are in no way exempt. As in Hugh of St. Victor's definition of *theatrica*, the term *ludus* can cover a great many activities. Two of the plays added in the thirteenth century are titled *ludi* (the longer Passion [CB 13*] and the Easter play [CB 15*]), but the same term also appears in portions of the manuscript copied earlier, where it can mean playing dice, as in the *Officium lusorum* or "Liturgy of Gamesters" (CB 215), which parodies the ubiquity of clerical drinking and gambling.[95] *Ludus* can mean playing on a psaltery while singing the "songs of Ovid" (CB 216.1.3, 2.3, 8); flirtation ("I play with Celia," [CB 88.1]); sex ("Come play with me!" [CB 90.1.2]); or indeed rape: "Let's play a game [*ludum faciamus*]" (CB 185.7.3), as one speaker says to his victim, echoing a notorious assault in Terence (*Eunuchus* 585–86, LCL). "Do not be ashamed that you have played," counsels a poem by Peter of Blois, "but that you have not stopped playing [*sed ludum non incidere*]" (CB 33.1.1–2).[96] As part of an overall program for improving the priesthood, Peter encourages his reader neither to give nor to take anything from "an actor [*histrio*]" (CB 33.4.7), so that, having sublimated all ludic impulses, "you may minister unsullied at the altar / of the unsullied Virgin" (CB 33.2.9–10).

Even then, you might still be playing. The most iconic liturgical performance of Marian devotion—the *Ave Maria*—is itself described as a play (*ludus*) in the *Carmina Burana* by the rubric setting the stage for the entrance of the angel and Virgin:

> When this is over let the acting area be given up by the prophets— either let them withdraw or be seated in their places out of deference to the play [*propter honorem ludi*]. Then let an angel appear to Mary as

---

93. Page, *Owl and the Nightingale*, 40.
94. Rohloff, *Die Quellenhandschriften*, 136; Page, "Johannes de Grocheio on Secular Music," 31 (modified).
95. See Martha Bayless, *Parody in the Middle Ages: The Latin Tradition* (Ann Arbor: University of Michigan Press, 1996), esp. 99–105.
96. Quoting Horace, *Ep*. 1.14.36; cf. CCCM 128:94–95; for the music, see Miriam K. Whaples, ed. and trans., *Carmina Burana: Twenty Songs from the Benediktbeuern and Florence MSS in One, Two and Three Parts for Voices and Instruments* (Macomb, IL: Roger Dean, 1975), 42.

she is laboring in the manner of a woman [i.e., sewing] and say, *Ave Maria, gratia plena!* (CB 227.110–11, rubric)

The neumes accompanying the *Ave Maria* suggest that it was sung to a known liturgical melody, performed here explicitly as "play" (*ludus*). The actor-clerics involved might well have imagined they were reenacting the historical origins of a prized hymn in praise of the Virgin (just as they will later illustrate the origins of the *Magnificat* and *Gloria*), but they were at the same time forging an unmistakable link between liturgical music and the *officium histrionium*. Was not every sacred performance of the *Ave Maria* a play or *ludus* in which Christians sang the supposed words of an angel to the wonder and delight of an audience?

One way of understanding the repertoire of songs, liturgical skits, and drama that has come down to us under the aegis of the goliards is to see in it a form of music that denies the difference between sacred and profane performances—not simply because "the unexampled hold of minstrelsy on the popular ear might be turned to the service of religion," as Chambers tends to understand the conflation, but because the service of religion was easy to expose as a form of minstrelsy.[97] In the *Carmina Burana* the goliardic impulse leads even further, to an exploration of the sex appeal at the heart of the liturgy. A manuscript so invested in the preservation of erotic poems and pagan rape fantasies, which also labels the exchange between Mary and the angel "a play" (*ludus*), cannot help but invite highly charged comparisons, and some of them would have been considerably strengthened by recent developments in scriptural exegesis: "O blessed Mary," exclaims Rupert of Deutz (c. 1125) in his commentary on the Songs of Songs. "The inundation of joy, the power of love, the torrent of pleasure overwhelmed you totally, possessed you totally, intoxicated you inwardly, and you sensed 'what eye has not seen, nor ear heard, nor has entered into the heart of man,' [1 Cor 2:9] and you said, 'Kiss me . . . ' [Sg 1:1]."[98] This line of thinking is not far

---

97. Chambers, *Mediaeval Stage*, 1:46. On goliardic "liturgical skits" see David Wulstan, *The Emperor's Old Clothes: The Rhythm of Mediaeval Song* (Ottawa, ON: Institute of Mediaeval Music, 2001), 211.

98. *Commentaria in Cantica Canticorum* 1.1 (CCCM 26:10); E. Ann Matter, *The Voice of My Beloved: The Song of Songs in Western Medieval Christianity* (Philadelphia: University of Pennsylvania Press, 1990), 35, 159–163; see also John Brückmann and Jane Couchman, "Du 'Cantique des cantique' aux 'Carmina Burana': Amour sacré et amour érotique," in *L'Érotisme au Moyen Âge: études présentées au troisième colloque de l'Institut d'études médiévales*, ed. Bruno Roy (Montreal, QC: Aurore, 1977), 35–50; Emma Maggie Solberg, *Virgin Whore* (Ithaca, NY: Cornell University Press, 2018), esp. 36–40 where she cites Rupert and gives a variety of parallel passages in Latin and the vernacular, e.g. the angel's winking joke in N-Town that Mary's "body shal be so fulfylt with blys / That she shal sone thynke this sownde credible" (36). The orgasmic pleasure of hearing the *Ave Maria* in this case provides the grounds for Mary's faith in the angel's proclamation.

removed from the contemporaneous lyric tradition recorded in the *Carmina Burana* that would hail a virgin in Marian terms—"Ave, most beautiful one, precious jewel . . . glory of virgins, virgin of fair fame . . . light of lights . . . rose of the world"—only to decline the ascent to incorporeal realities in favor of a profane "Helen, a noble Venus" (CB 77, stanza 8).[99] Indeed when, at the end of the Nativity play, Mary flees to Egypt, there to encounter a group of pagans singing a *conductus* in praise of Venus (possibly while playing musical instruments before idols that had been erected in the church for this very purpose *by the clergy*), the effect is not to draw a contrast but rather to stress a complex likeness.[100] We see here "the union of the farcical, even the obscene, with the religious feeling" that existed historically, according to Nietzsche, "in the festivals of Demeter and Dionysus, in the Christian Easter and mystery plays."[101] The Nativity play as a whole suggests that in overcoming pagan idols the church had not so much converted unbelievers as opened itself to their bawdy love of playacting. The anti- and pro-theatricalists of the Middle Ages appear to have differed mainly in the degree to which they were willing to tolerate a centuries-long process of secularization, which some tried to slow, some to control, and some to enjoy—but that none could undo.

The Doubts of Archisynagogus and the Devil

Few authorities in the history of Christianity have had a more profound "love of playing [*amore ludendi*]" than Augustine (*Conf.* 1.19.30 [CCSL 27:16; WSA 1/1:59]). Before he was old enough to attend the theater, he was delighted, he says, to study dramatic set pieces in school, such as the scene from Terence where a young man is inspired to rape a virgin by observing a painting of the moment when Jove "played a game [*luserat . . . ludum*]" with Danaë.[102] As pagan gods did to mortals, so plays did to Augustine: "Theatrical spectacles ravished me [*rapiebant*

---

99. Barbara Newman, *Medieval Crossover: Reading the Secular Against the Sacred* (Notre Dame, IN: Notre Dame University Press, 2013), 9–10; Waddell, *Wandering*, 223.
100. On the so-called *Ludus de rege Aegypti*, which depicts the fall of the idols (CB 228), see chapter 2. For the possibility that *conducti* were performed with musical instruments, see Christopher Page, *Voices and Instruments of the Middle Ages: Instrumental Practice and Songs in France 1100–1300* (Berkeley: University of California Press, 1986), 86. The *Conductus Danielis* in the Beauvais *Ludus Danielis* (performed at Christmas) unquestionably involved instrumental accompaniment (Young 2:290–306, esp. 302–303). Two songs by Peter of Blois included in the *Carmina Burana* are *conducti*—CB 30 and 108.
101. NKGW IV/2:116; English in *Human, All Too Human*, trans. R. J. Hollingdale (Cambridge: Cambridge University Press, 1996) §112.
102. Terence, *Eunuchus* 585–86 (LCL); the lines immediately adjacent to these are quoted from memory by Augustine in *Conf.* 1.16.26 (CCSL 27:14; WSA I/1:56).

me spectacula theatrica]," he writes, remembering in particular how overwhelmed he felt by the "lovers on stage while they enjoyed themselves in disgraceful deeds."[103] Eventually he cast off with revulsion these overpowering, secular pleasures so as to devote himself instead to liturgical music, and yet there he was, roughly eight centuries later, sitting down "in the front part of the church" (CB 227.1, rubric) to watch along with the prophets and Archisynagogus a dramatic reenactment of Mary's divine ravishment.[104] This disgraceful deed, minus the disgrace, had become a central preoccupation of the liturgy, and the pleasure it aroused was by then all the more palatable for being inspired by an apparent fiction. Indeed there is probably no better example than the Nativity play in the *Carmina Burana* of the degree to which the Fathers' antitheatricalism had been overcome by medieval clerics eager to draw connections between their most exalted celebrations and the ancient pleasure of enacting mythological fantasies to the accompaniment of music. In fact the pleasure could be heightened by airing fully the most radical doubts about the Nativity's basis in reality.

According to the opening rubric, after Augustine is seated, the stage should be split between believers and what another, roughly contemporaneous drama calls *Iudea incredula* (Young 2:142): "Let Augustine have on his right side Isaiah and Daniel and the other prophets, but on the left Archisynagogus and his Jews" (CB 227.1, rubric). The momentary tableaux vivant would have recalled the widespread iconography of *Ecclesia* in debate with *Synagoga*, while also catering to a renewed interest in written dialogues between Christians and Jews.[105] Despite the Christian triumphalism of these traditions,

---

103. *Conf.* 3.2.2, 3.2.3 (CCSL 27:27-28; WSA 1/1:76-77), respectively.
104. For other plays in which Augustine appears, see Edélestand du Méril, *Origines latines du théatre moderne* (Paris, 1849), 55.
105. Paul Weber, *Geistliches Schauspiel und kirchliche Kunst in ihrem Verhältnis erläutert an einer Ikonographie der Kirche und Synagoge* (Stuttgart, 1894); Margaret Schlauch, "The Allegory of Church and Synagogue," *Speculum* 14, no. 4 (1939): 448–64; Lewis Edwards, "Some English Examples of the Mediaeval Representation of Church and Synagogue," *Transactions (Jewish Historical Society of England)* 18 (1953–55): 63–75; Avery Dulles, *A History of Apologetics* (New York: Corpus, 1971), 32, 97–98, 105–8; Heinz Schreckenberg, *Die christlichen Adversus-Judaeos-Texte und ihr literarisches und historisches Umfeld (1.-11.Jh)* (Frankfurt am Main: Peter Lang, 1982); Schreckenberg, *Die christlichen Adversus-Judaeos-Texte (11.-13. Jh.): mit einer Ikonographie des Judenthemas bis zum 4. Laterankonzil*, 2nd ed. (Frankfurt am Main: Peter Lang, 1991); Anna Sapir Abulafia, *Christians and Jews in the Twelfth-Century Renaissance* (London: Routledge, 1995), esp. 77ff. and Abulafia, *Christians and Jews in Dispute: Disputational Literature and the Rise of Anti-Judaism in the West (c. 1000–1150)* (London: Routledge, 2016); Christopher A. Lee, "Augustine vs. Archisynagogus: Competing Modes of Christian Instruction in the Benediktbeuern *Ludus de nativitate*," *Florilegium* 23, no. 2 (2006): 81–97; Nina Rowe, *The Jew, The Cathedral and the Medieval City: Synagoga and Ecclesia in the Thirteenth Century* (Cambridge: Cambridge University Press, 2011), esp. 239–241; Constant Mews, "St. Anselm and Roscelin: Some Texts and Their Implications. I. the *De Incarnatione Verbi* and the *Disputatio inter Christianum et Gentilem*," *Archives d'histoire doctrinale et littéraire du moyen âge* 58 (1991): 86–98.

there was at the time palpable anxiety that, after more than a thousand years, the synagogue had not been sufficiently vanquished: "Wherever they went, Jews brought with them levels of literacy and a depth of learning that far surpassed anything that their Christian neighbors could show," writes R. I. Moore of the high Middle Ages:

> The denigration of Judaism, its characterization as a source of heresy, idolatry and immorality, was one aspect of the general assault on the older literate cultures with which the new clerical intelligentsia of Latin Christendom consolidated its own culture hegemony. In this context, the attack on the Jews had a further advantage for those who conducted it, since it eliminated the most immediate and authoritative challenge to the authority of Christian masters in the exposition of the scriptures. In doing so, it also removed from the arena of competition for place and influence at the courts a potential elite much better qualified for that role by its mastery of the essential skills of literacy, numeracy and legal acumen than the Christian clerks who were so desperate to fill it.[106]

Not far beneath the surface of the high-brow, dialectical debates in which a Christian author impersonates a fictional Jew so as to promulgate a pro-Christian agenda is a bleak history of pogroms and massacres.[107] Where argumentation failed, violence was at the ready to prove Christian supremacy, just as it had been from Constantine forward whenever the church came into contact with obdurate atheists and unbelievers.

And yet the staged impersonation of such infidels, Jewish or otherwise, also allowed Christians to explore in the open an otherwise unspeakable skepticism of church dogma: "No one is allowed to inquire into what should be believed among his own people," says Abelard's Philosopher in a debate with a Jew and Christian, "or to doubt what everyone affirms, without fear of punishment."[108] The fear was naturally stronger in some than in others—Abelard himself was notorious for boldness and had no small influence on

---

106. R. I. Moore, *The First European Revolution c. 970–1215* (Oxford: Blackwell, 2000), 150, 156; see also Jeremy Cohen, *The Friars and the Jews: The Evolution of Medieval Anti-Judaism* (Ithaca, NY: Cornell University Press, 1982); Gilbert Dahan, *The Christian Polemic Against the Jews in the Middle Ages*, trans. Jody Gladding (Notre Dame, IN: University of Notre Dame Press, 1988); Miri Rubin, *Gentile Tales: The Narrative Assault on Late Medieval Jews* (New Haven, CT: Yale University Press, 1999).
107. Schlauch, "Allegory of Church and Synagogue," 461.
108. Peter Abelard, *A Dialogue of a Philosopher with a Jew, and a Christian*, trans. Pierre J. Payer (Toronto: Pontifical Institute of Mediaeval Studies, 1979), 26.

the goliards—but the easiest way for the timid to evade condemnation was to attribute to non-Christians a searing indictment of the church's most cherished articles of faith, particularly since there was no shortage of instances when infidels had in fact lodged the criticisms attributed to them.[109] Odo of Tournai (1060–1113) admits that he composed his dialogue not in response to incredulous Jews but to "Catholics who take the position of the Jew."[110] It is unlikely that this describes Christians on the verge of converting, adopting the law, and being circumcised; on the contrary, he was probably targeting a more disconcerting population—those people who in no way believed that Judaism was a true religion but nonetheless felt that the Jews, in rejecting the divinity of Jesus, had had good reasons. Like the pagans of old who were persuaded by Christians to deny the existence of the gods but stopped short of converting (as we saw in Eusebius), Odo's "Jewish" Catholics appear to have adopted the position of the stereotypical infidel—the position, that is, of someone with no faith whatsoever. Any Christian who played Archisynagogus was actively promulgating the atheist's viewpoint. In contrast to the Jews of contemporary dialogues, who tend as a rule to affirm the law of Moses against the gospel, Archisynagogus does not offer a single positive defense of *any* religion. Instead he takes an Aristotelian view of natural law and reason in order to argue that the Virgin Birth is pure "illusion [*phantasma*]" (CB 227.85, 98). He is *incredulitas* personified.

We have many instances of the kind of Christmas play that Archisynagogus and Augustine watch together, and its history is not without significant bearing on the way that both of them are figured in the *Carmina Burana*. The earliest script appears as a *lectio* at various points in the Christmas liturgy, drawn more or less verbatim from a fifth-century sermon attributed to Augustine.[111] Its purpose had been to underscore and sometimes augment the degree to which the Hebrew prophets had predicted and could thus authenticate the Virgin Birth; at the same time it conscripted testimonials

---

109. Bernhard Blumenkranz, *Juifs et chrétiens dans le monde occidental, 430–1096* (Paris: Peters, 2006), 52–53, 256–65, 279, points out that the "Jewish" position in Christian apologetic literature can overlap so closely with that of Christian heretics that it's hard to know where the objections actually originated.

110. Odo of Tournai, *"On Original Sin" and "A Disputation with the Jew, Leo, Concerning the Advent of Christ, the Son of God,"* trans. Irven M. Resnick (Philadelphia: University of Pennsylvania Press, 1994), 97; cited by Lee, "Augustine vs. Archisynagogus," 83n11.

111. Ps-Augustine, *Contra Judaeos, paganos et Arianos sermo de symbolo* (PL 42:1115–30); now attributed to Quodvultdeus (CCSL 60:227–258); for a partial English rendering see Edward Noble Stone, *A Translation of Chapters XI–XVI of the Pseudo-Augustinian Sermon Against Jews, Pagans and Arians, Concerning the Creed* (Seattle: University of Washington Press, 1928).

from pagan sources—most notably Nebuchadnezzar, Virgil, and the Sybil—in order to condemn the "unbelievers" (CCSL 60:249) responsible for the death of Jesus and to attack the Arian blasphemers who argued that Jesus was less than God (CCSL 60:234–47, 254–55). At some point Balaam was added to the parade of biblical prophets, and the prophecies were set to music. By the time a costumed cleric came to sing Balaam's prediction that "a star will arise out of Jacob" (variously interpreted as a reference to Mary or the star of Bethlehem, but either way prefiguring the birth of Jesus), musical harmony had been collaborating for a long while with the rational testimony of the heavens to buttress the case for the Incarnation.[112]

Unlike every other surviving procession of prophets, the cumulative effect of their songs in the *Carmina Burana* is not to place the legitimacy of Jesus beyond question but to make unbelievers go wild with histrionic indignation.[113] "Let Archisynagogus with his Jews, having heard the prophecies, clamor; and let him speak while ribbing his companions, moving his head and his whole body and tapping the ground with his foot, imitating the gestures of a Jew in all ways [*imitando gestus Iudei in omnibus*]" (CB 227.44–45, rubric). One thing we can infer from the decision of the Fourth Lateran Council (1215) to require all Jews to wear an identifying badge on their clothing is that few people at the time had any confidence they could reliably discern from a person's behavior (*gestus*) whether or not he was Jewish. In fact, without the badge, Jews could be mistaken for priests.[114] What then could it possibly mean to "behave like a Jew in all ways"? If the model for these antics was not readily discernable in actual Jews, another despised group, notorious for obscene gesticulation, must have provided the clerics with mannerisms to imitate—namely, the *histriones* who "distort their bodies with shameless jumps or shameless gestures [*per turpes gestus*]" and who were "damnable unless they relinquish their trade."[115] Precisely this kind of performance was condemned by Aelred of Rievaulx when he saw in another twelfth-century Nativity play a *Christian* performer's "whole body violently agitated by histri-

---

112. For the "star from Jacob" as a foretelling of Mary (in her role as *stella maris*), see Bede, *Explanatio in quartum librum Moisis* 23–24 (PL 91:371C); as a foretelling of the star of Bethlehem, see Ambrose, *Exp. ev. Luc.* 2.48 (PL 15:1570A) and Young 2:150.
113. For a comprehensive collection see Karl Young, "Ordo Prophetarum," *Transactions of the Wisconsin Academy of Sciences, Arts and Letters* 20 (1921): 1–82.
114. Solomon Grayzel, *The Church and the Jews in the XIIIth Century: A Study of Their Relations During the Years 1198–1254, Based on the Papal Letters and the Conciliar Decrees of the Period*, rev. ed. (New York: Hermon Press, 1966), 321, 335.
115. *Thomae de Chobham summa confessorum*, ed. Broomfield, 291.

onic gestures—contorted lips, rolling eyes, hunching shoulders—and drumming fingers to keep time with every single note."[116] More or less the same description appears in commentaries on Lombard's condemnation of "plays and secular spectacles" as an explanation of what exactly the Jews had been doing when "they rose up to play" before the Golden Calf (Ex 32:6; 1 Cor 10:7): "play is passionate gesticulation in dances [*ludus est gesticulatio libidinosa in choreis*]," offer Albert the Great and Bonaventure.[117] Archisynagogus's tapping his foot and bobbing his head would have recalled this foundational moment of faithless histrionics toward a highly ironic end. Even the scholastics who were most tolerant of *histriones* were nonetheless unanimous in wanting to exclude from permissible, Christian performances the madcap gesticulations and the "excessive laughter" (CB 227.69) associated by Aquinas with "superfluous play."[118] By making such behavior *Jewish*, the performers of the Nativity in the *Carmina Burana* gave it free reign. Archisynagogus's outbursts are figured as a tumultuous misrule far exceeding anything Christians would ever dare to perform—except that Christians are the ones performing it, in church, in a manner that is clearly modeled on their own yuletide riots. After Archisynagogus's first disruption, a boy bishop wanders briefly into the play from the Feast of Fools for the express purpose of calling the kettle black: "Their speech is empty," he says of the Jews, "whom frenzy and the freedom of wine rile up" (CB 227.53–54).

Archisynagogus's ability to integrate into a nominally sacred drama the extreme style of acting normally reserved for the most contemptible, secular forms of performance makes him one of the great antiheroes of the twelfth-century stage—on par with his near contemporary, the Tegernsee Antichrist.[119] And yet he is perhaps most thrilling and dangerous when using the restrained tone that he shares with the "sober voice" (CB 227.90) of Augustine. The last we hear from him, he has joined the play-within-the-play as an actor working opposite Herod—already famous in the Middle Ages,

---

116. *Speculum caritatis* 23 (PL 195:571C): "Interim histrionicis quibusdam gestibus totum corpus agitatur, torquentur labia, rotant, ludunt humeri; et ad singulas quasque notas digitorum flexus respondet." Aelred of Rievaulx, *Mirror of Charity*, 210.
117. D. Alberti Magni, *Commentarii in IV Sententiarum (Dist. I–XXII)* (Paris, 1894), 632 (dist. 16, A, art. 43, 1); Bonaventure, *Opera omnia*, ed. PP. Collegii a S. Bonaventura, (Florence, 1889), 4:401 (dist. 16, pt. 1, dub. 13). Cf. Rubel, "Chabham's Penitential," 234–35.
118. *Summa theol.* 2a2ae, q. 168, art. 3, in *Summa theologiae: Latin Text and English Translation*, trans. Gilby, 44:220–21.
119. For the borrowings from the Tegernsee Antichrist in CB 228 and the range of possible dates for the Nativity play (1160–1230), see chapter 2.

as in *Hamlet*, for overacting. Faced with *that* example of histrionic excess, Archisynagogus drops the minstrelsy schtick and speaks instead "with great wisdom and eloquence" (CB 227.229)—a trick he likely uses against Augustine, too, when not melodramatically mocking him. The most disconcerting thing about this particular stage villain may not have been the flamboyant, indecorous histrionics, in other words, but the suggestion that even a pious performance is still a performance and therefore, at bottom, also mere theater.

"Tell me," Archisynagogus sings in response to Balaam's prediction of the Virgin Birth, "what announcement does this whited wall make? / Tell me, what is asserted by this decomposition of truth?" (CB 227.45–46). The phrase "whited wall" (*dealbatus paries*) was originally aimed by Paul against his persecutors (Acts 23:3, Vulg.); coming here in such close proximity to the word "decomposition" (*caries*), it also recalls the condemnation by Jesus of "whited sepulchers" (Mt 23:27)—which is to say, it recalls a scriptural condemnation of the double-speak employed professionally by actors (*hypocrites*). Who is the greater hypocrite here, Archisynagogus implicitly asks, the indecorous Jewish *histrio* or the decorous Balaam, a gentile prophet that "loved the wages of doing wrong but was rebuked for his own transgression" (2 Pt 2:15–16; cf. Rev 2:14)? The stage-prophets trying to prove with a song that Mary's pregnancy had begun "without the seed of man" (CB 227.1) had succeeded only in demonstrating that the Christian faith requires a mindless embrace of fantastical music and theatrical fiction—about which, as a consummate actor, Archisynagogus clearly knows plenty: "O what simple-mindedness compels them to be devoid of wisdom!" (CB 227.51). Christians who claimed to have been enlightened by baptism had in fact remained as children, enchanted with song and ritual movements no different at bottom from the dances of any idolator. Thus do "unbelievers [*infideles*]," Anselm once noted, "deride our simplicity"—they call the Virgin Birth a "fiction [*figmentum*]."[120]

The same cleric or choirboy who performs as the angel in the *ludus* of the *Ave Maria* likely doubles as the angel who appears before the shepherds to wow them with the *Gloria*. Before that traditional showstopper, the angel shares a *sic-et-non* exchange with the devil that has no parallel in extant medieval drama. Entering with the usual tidings of great joy, instead of singing

---

120. *Cur Deus Homo* I, 3-4, in *S. Anselmi Cantuariensis Archiepiscopi opera omnia*, ed. Franciscus Salesius Schmitt (Edinburgh: Thomas Nelson, 1946), 2:50, 52; English in *St. Anselm: Basic Writings*, trans. S. N. Deane, 2nd ed. (La Salle, IL: Open Court Publishing, 1962), 196, 198.

the *Gloria* in accordance with scripture, he goes markedly off-script to contradict Archisynagogus's earlier denials of Jesus's divinity:

Magnum vobis gaudium, pastores, annuntio:	I proclaim to you shepherds great joy:
Deus se circumdedit carnis vestre pallio,	God has wrapped himself in the cloak of your flesh;
quem mater non peperit carnali commercio,	His mother did not beget him by means of fleshly congress,
immo virgo permanens mater est ex filio.	On the contrary, the mother is an eternal virgin by virtue of the son.

(CB 227.218–21)

This description of the body as a costume or "cloak" for the godhead is awkwardly reminiscent of Archisynagogus's advice to Herod to approach the Magi under "the cloak of love [*sub amoris pallio*] (CB 227.205), as though the angel were inviting the shepherds to credit the Incarnation as a form of divine, hypocritical showmanship. Before the angel can break into the *Gloria* to make good on his claims through music, he is interrupted by the appearance of the devil, who warns the shepherds against believing any further claptrap about the Incarnation:

Tu ne credas talibus, pastorum simplicitas!	You simpleminded shepherds, do not believe such things!
scias esse frivola, que non probat veritas.	You should know that those things, which the truth disproves, are silly.
quod sic in presepio sit sepulta Deitas,	For the Godhead to be buried in a manger
nimis est ad oculum reserata falsitas.	is too much, an open falsehood before your very eyes!

(CB 227.222–25)

The word "buried" (*sepulta*) echoes the long-standing, frequently dramatized connection between the Maries' visit to the sepulcher and the shepherds' visit to the manger, where two midwives, drawn from Pseudo-Matthew, also ask, "Whom do you seek?"[121] Rather than accepting that Christ's birth foreshadows

---

121. Young 2:4–24; Hammerstein, *Musik der Engel*, 74.

his subsequent rebirth through resurrection, the devil argues that Mary, like every mother, gives birth astride a grave. The doctrine of incarnation is not only an obvious fiction but a blasphemous desecration of the very idea of *Deitas*.

The angel intervenes to encourage the shepherds to seek out the baby buried in the manger nonetheless. He continues to withhold the *Gloria*, however, which gives the devil time to offer a critique of the way that angelic song deploys aesthetic embellishments in lieu of rational proof:

Simplex cetus, aspice, qualis astutia eius, qui sic fabricat vero contraria;	You simple people! Look how crafty he is who fabricates things contrary to the truth
utque sua phaleret nugis mendacia,	and, so that he may decorate his lies with trifles,
in rhythmis conciliat, que profert, omnia.	reconciles in rhythmic compositions everything he asserts.

(CB 227.230–34)

The word *rhythmis* can mean "songs," "lyrics," or, more literally, "rhythmic compositions" and had a connection in Neoplatonic music theory to the rational structure of the cosmos; at the same time it could also be used as a synonym for the "tropes" inserted into the conventional hymns of the Mass (specifically, the *Kyrie* and *Gloria*) or for secular songs "in the newer, accentual verse, often with highly complex rhyme and rhythmic schemes."[122] The latter were what Peter of Blois had in mind when he castigated Peter of Blois for reducing the Lord "to sirens' songs and the delusions of rhythmic compositions [*rhythmorum deliramentis*]" (*Ep.* 76, PL 207:234AB). The same term that described the transcendent properties of a liturgical hymn, in other words, could be applied with equal justice to empty show tunes.

The devil's point is that the *Gloria* cannot be readily differentiated from the secular performances that theologians had traditionally denounced as a fraud designed by unscrupulous *histriones* to "soften, weaken and dupe the minds of their hearers."[123] The familiar polemic against popular music—which stretches from the prophets and Plato through Augustine, Calcidius, and Boethius to

---

122. Whaples, *Carmina Burana: Twenty Songs*, v; Domino du Cange et al., *Glossarium mediæ et infimæ latinitatis*, vol. 7 (Niort, 1886), under *rythmus*; Joannes Rothomagenesis, *Le "De officiis ecclesiasticis" de Jean d'Avranches, archevêque de Rouen (1067–1079)*, ed. René Delamare (Paris: A. Picard, 1923), xix, lxix, xci, cxxxix. For patristic usage, see e.g. Martianus Capella 9, §967–69, in *The Marriage of Philology and Mercury*, trans. William Harris Stahl et al. (New York: Columbia University Press, 1977), 373, and Augustine, *De musica*, trans. Robert Catesby Taliaferro, 234n11.
123. Robert Courson, *Summa*, in Page, *Owl and the Nightingale*, 195, contextualized on 25.

twelfth-century antitheatricalists like Aelred of Riveaux and Robert Courson—is here in the *Carmina Burana* directed against a centerpiece of the liturgy, as though it, too, were merely another theatrical mode. The *Gloria* itself, according to the devil, circumvents reason, gratifies the flesh, and thus reroutes a person's focus from divine to earthly matters. The clerics whose musical performances decorate (*phaleret*) the apparent falsehood of the gospel effectively dupe (*falleret*) their audience (the manuscript uses the latter spelling but grammatically requires the former). We should note in particular how the angel's alleged deception is addressed above all to "simple people"—an echo of the Neoplatonic condescension toward the irrational *vulgus*—though here the term "people" (*c[o]etus*) could apply equally to a "congregation," as if the whole assembly watching the drama, long accustomed to hearing angelic hymns sung in the liturgy, suffered from the same immature addiction to rhythm, melody, and spectacle that Christianity was supposed to overcome, not apotheosize. Instead, it appeared to have exalted theatrical diversions—the *ludus* of the *Ave Maria*, the *rhythmus* of the *Gloria*—to the status of divinity.

After hearing the devil's sermon, the unlettered shepherds start to wise up. Is it possible, they wonder, that someone might cynically deploy the sensuous allure of music in order to manipulate the credulous?

quedam vox insinuat de nato filio;	Some voice insinuates something about a newborn son,
verum in contrarium ab hoc suscipio,	twisting the truth into its opposite; from which I suspect
quod audita resident iuncta mendacio.	that the things we've heard are akin to a lie.

(CB 227.234–37)

For the Fathers and the early Middle Ages, performing the liturgy exclusively by voice (*vox*) rather than on instruments was supposed to forestall the accusation that church music abetted worldly pleasure, while still allowing for just enough sensuous gratification to help neophytes accept hard doctrines. Here, thanks to the disenchanting critique of the devil, the whole machinery of Christian performance is exposed as no less mythical, no less illusory, no less fictive and fleshly than the bacchanalia of pagans: "You rave too much [*debaccharis nimium*]," he tells the shepherds, "if you believe that these things are certain" (CB 227.245).[124] Merely

---

124. See Richard of St. Victor (d. 1173), *In circumcisione Domini* (PL 177:1036), for a condemnation of the rapturous, Dionysian ravings ("*hodie debacchationis suae furiis rapti*") that are here equated with the *Gloria*.

the appearance of an irresolvable conflict between the messages of the angel and the devil puts the shepherds into a state of confused delirium: "My mind, hardly sober, / does not know which of these views is stronger!" (CB 227.275–76).

At last the hosts of heaven gather to sing the *Gloria*, and their performance intoxicates the shepherds beyond all measure with the luxurious sounds of the liturgy. If the argument between the devil and the angel—or, for that matter, between Archisynagogus and Augustine—can in fact be settled, it is settled here in the church's favor by the clergy's professional training as singers:

Ad hanc vocem animi produco suspirium,	At this voice of spirit I catch my breath!
ex hac intus habeo citharizans gaudium.	From this I have within the joy of citharas playing!
. . . adoremus filium!	Let us adore the son!

(CB 227.251–52, 254)

It had long been the goal of the church to capitalize on the seemingly spiritual immateriality of the human breath to act as a guarantor that a cappella music was closer to the songs of angels than to the *officium histrionum*. Here the two have been fused, as though the power of the *Gloria* stemmed from the shepherd's internalization, or bodily recollection, of the *musica instrumentalis* that the liturgy excluded: "I have within the joy of citharas playing!" Whenever these instruments appear elsewhere in the *Carmina Burana*, they invariably accompany and promote all the pagan indulgences that had led to their ban from sacred performance. In spring when people sing the praises of Venus, a man in love with a virgin who is "brighter than a star" begs that she will answer his "prayer [*votum*]" and make him "blessed [*beatum*]" through sexual congress, lest he be forced to ravish her as Apollo tried to overpower Daphne: "I am equal to the cithara of Apollo in vernal sweetness."[125] That a purely vocal, liturgical song in honor of the Virgin might produce in a shepherd's heart—after every possible warning—the same venereal "joy of citharas playing" that we see in the secular bucolic tradition completes the manuscript's reclamation of the libidinal power of instrumental music.

It is probably no accident that the string player or *citharedus*, of all secular musicians, was the one that even fairly censorious theorists of the twelfth century had come to exempt from damnation. Christopher Page offers many germane reasons—the tendency of the *citharedus* to perform saints lives as

---

125. CB 61.14.1, 10.4–5, 1a, respectively; see Peter Dronke, *Medieval Latin and the Rise of the European Love Lyric*, 2nd ed. (Oxford: Clarendon, 1968), 1:305 and cf. CB 121.

well as secular *gesta*; the perception that without recreation to relieve the burden of everyday living, a commonwealth could not profit; the sense that the life of a city or state involved "a vast common enterprise that hallowed any work which contributed to its needs."[126] Indeed the sanctification of everyday life—together with the growing sense that the *saeculum* offers benefits and forms of meaning on par with traditionally sacred enterprises—is precisely what Charles Taylor means by "a secular age." We can see this type of secularization in the twelfth century because professional minstrels—and their highly talented goliardic counterparts in the liturgy of the high holidays—had forced a concession from theologians: Christian authorities came to a grudging respect for the worldly musician only when it was no longer possible to ignore how much of his showmanship had infiltrated their own rites of worship. When the shepherd in the *Carmina Burana* hears the *Gloria* and suddenly experiences a cithara "within" (*intus*), he is discovering what it means to feel in his viscera the immanent value of earthbound singing, regardless of whether the singing happens in or outside the church and irrespective of its eternal benefits. By the twelfth century, when the participants in the liturgy ended a hymn by singing *in saecula saeculorum*, any number of them were acknowledging that they had found in the sensuality of liturgical song the only sweet-ever-after they were likely to know.

Post-twelfth-century iconographical depictions of the shepherds often show them playing wind instruments and thus priming themselves through earthly, ludic pastimes for the auditory revelation from heaven that is soon to befall them.[127] Even when not playing instruments they were still closely associated with music by virtue of their penchant for secular singing. In the Towneley Second Shepherds' Play, for example, their receptivity to the *Gloria* is foreshadowed by their brief attempt at a song that is painfully truncated by Mak's ill behavior. When the divine interlude hits them they are at once wonderstruck and notably analytic, as they consider how to replicate the angels' musicianship:

> *2 Pastor*: Say, what was his song?
> Hard ye not how he crakyd it,
> Thre brefes to a long?
> *3 Pastor*: Yee, Mary, he hakt it:
> Was no crochett wrong,

---

126. Page, *Owl and the Nightingale*, 36.
127. Helen Cooper, *Pastoral: Medieval into Renaissance* (Ipswich, UK: Brewer, Rowman & Littlefield, 1977), 54–55.

Nor nothyng that lakt it.
1 Pastor: For to syng us emong
Right as he knakt it,
I can.
2 Pastor: Let se how ye croyne!
Can ye bark at the mone?
3 Pastor: Hold youre tonges! Have done!
1 Pastor: Hark after, than.[128]

It has often been observed that the shepherds employ here a fairly precise language for the mechanics of polyphonic music. They are discussing, writes Nan Cooke, "celestial music in terms of earthly practices," specifically using the terminology of the *ars nova*.[129] "Hakt it," "crakt it," "knakt it," "three briefs to a long" with "no crochett wrong"—these are the most up-to-date terms shared by the musicologist, the choirmaster, and the professional secular musician for describing a three-part harmony sung in 6/4 time with short notes and plenty of trilling.[130] ("Shakespeare's shepherd revelers in *The Winter's Tale*," notes Helen Cooper, "are 'three-part song-men all.'")[131] One response to the permeable boundary in the Second Shepherds' Play between sacred and secular playing, liturgy and theater, would be to say that the *Gloria* fulfills the ideal foreshadowed by the shepherds' earlier, disappointed attempt to sing a worldly three-part harmony.[132] What strikes me, by contrast, is how the shepherds have translated the production of a miracle into a teachable technique that they already know. From this perspective it's remarkable how little the *Gloria* changes anything. Prior to revelation, the shepherds had sung a secular song to while away the longest night of winter, and they appear to do the same thing afterwards, when they exit singing yet again: "To sing we are bun [bound]" (l. 1087). Nothing in the play tells us *what* they sing on their way out but I think we can surmise it is not the *Gloria*. The stronger likelihood is that the play's grand finale is a contemporary carol of the sort that featured jolly shepherds drawn from

---

128. Martin Stevens and A. C. Cawley, eds., *The Towneley Plays* (Oxford: Published for the Early English Text Society by the Oxford University Press, 1994), 1:153–54.
129. Nan Cooke, "Music in the *Secunda Pastorum*," *Speculum* 26, no. 4 (1951): 696–700 at 697.
130. Garrett P. J. Epp, ed., *The Towneley Plays* (Kalamazoo: Medieval Institute Publications, Western Michigan University Press, 2017), 445–46.
131. Cooper, *Pastoral*, 55.
132. See e.g. Martin Stevens, "Language as Theme in the Wakefield Plays," *Speculum* 52, no. 1 (1977): 100–117, esp. 116.

the pastoral tradition and that scandalized reformers for transforming the *Gloria* into *terly terlow*:

> Of angeles ther came a great commpanie,
> With mirthe and joy and great solemnitye,
> The[y] sange "terly terlow"
> So mereli the sheppards ther pipes can blow.[133]

Those lines are from the closest text we have to a version of the *Officium pastorum* that Shakespeare might have seen.[134] If so, he could have taken from it (among other sources) a lesson that Shakespeareans have not always recognized as part of his medieval inheritance. By relegating all adherents of prior religions to the status of unbelievers—while also accusing many Christians themselves of being "sons of unbelief" in hot pursuit of fulfillment through sex, food, drink, the arts, and "secular ambition" (1 Jn 2:16, Vetus Latina)—the church created a vision of the godless world that modernity stepped into. It created above all the sense that any effort to transcend the *saeculum* by locating a particular set of lyrics beyond mortal experience could itself be challenged, disenchanted, and evacuated as nothing more—and nothing less—than humanity's visceral love of music. "Had she oones [once] wett hyr whystyll," Mak says of his wife's ability to find inspiration for song in strong drink, "She couth syng full clere / Hyr *Paternoster*" (ll. 150–52). What audiences saw in the Second Shepherds' Play prior to Christ's arrival—the merciless landlords, the conspiring couple, the thievery, the consolation of music—was also a vision of the world *after* his disappearance. The overarching question was whether Christ's coming had made any difference other than to expose every promise of deliverance from the world as a fiction, a song and dance, a fool's errand.

---

133. Pamela King and Clifford Davidson, eds., *The Coventry Corpus Christi Plays* (Kalamazoo: Medieval Institute Publications, Western Michigan University, 2000), 111.
134. Beatrice Groves, *Texts and Traditions: Religion in Shakespeare 1592–1604* (Oxford: Clarendon, 2007), 36–39; Stephen Greenblatt, *Will in the World: How Shakespeare Became Shakespeare* (New York: Norton, 2004), 36–38.

CHAPTER 4

The Disenchantment of Astrology

Yahweh Versus the Sky Gods

The Hebrew Bible repeatedly forbids the worship of celestial bodies, "whether the sun or the moon or any of the host of heaven" (Dt 17:3), because the sun and moon and whole host of heaven were things that people commonly treated as higher beings.[1] Emptying the sky of its divinities was an essential step in the process of disenchantment that Jan Assmann has termed "the Mosaic distinction"[2]—that violent line of desacralization, in constant need of redrawing, meant to separate the worship of Yahweh from idolatry, magic, and what the early rabbinate called *avodat kokhavim u-mazalot* ("worship of the stars and signs of the zodiac").[3] The diatribes of the prophets

---

1. Cf. Dt 4:19; 2 Kgs 23:5, 11; Job 31:26; J. Edward Wright, *The Early History of Heaven* (New York: Oxford University Press, 2000), esp. 63; J. W. McKay, *Religion in Judah Under the Assyrians* (London: SMC Press, 1973), 45–59; Othmar Keel and Christoph Uehlinger, *Gods, Goddesses, and Images of God in Ancient Israel*, trans. Thomas H. Trapp (Edinburgh: T&T Clark, 1998), esp. 261.
2. Jan Assmann, *Moses the Egyptian: The Memory of Egypt in Western Monotheism* (Cambridge, MA: Harvard University Press, 1997), proposes an early version of the Mosaic distinction; he refines the idea in *The Price of Monotheism* (Stanford: Stanford University Press, 2010) and *The Invention of Religion: Faith and Covenant in the Book of Exodus* (Princeton, NJ: Princeton University Press, 2018).
3. Philip S. Alexander, "'The Parting of the Ways' from the Perspective of Rabbinic Judaism," in *Jews and Christians: The Parting of the Ways A.D. 70 to 135*, ed. James D. G. Dunn (Grand Rapids, MI:

against "those who gaze at the stars" (Is 47:13) articulate the "exclusionary negation" by means of which Yahwistic puritans first defined themselves—and have had to redefine themselves, over and over, as they inevitably discover their brethren returning to more traditional, perceptible objects of veneration overhead.[4] Not long after the death of Jesus, for example, Stephen attacked his fellow Jews for having turned "in their hearts . . . back to Egypt" (Acts 7:39) such that God had given them up "to worship the host of heaven" (Acts 7:42)—in particular "the star of your God Rephan, [and] the images that you made to worship" (Acts 7:43).[5] The hostility of the prophets and rabbis to astrology had not prevented would-be believers in Yahweh from casting horoscopes, or from incorporating images of the zodiac into temple mosaics, or even from embroidering the high priest's garments with a "replica of the whole heaven"—in the words of Stephen's contemporary, Philo—so that "the universe may join with man in the holy rites and man with the universe."[6] From the perspective of the New Testament, astrolatry had so infiltrated the synagogue there was little choice but to condemn it.[7]

The Fathers were well aware that the church could also be credibly accused of offering sanctuary to the *'ovedei kokhavim* or "star worshippers" generally known in the Greco-Roman world as *genethliaci, mathematici, astrologi,* and *magi.* The potential for embarrassment was made increasingly acute over

---

Eerdmans, 1999), 1–25, esp. 6; Emmanuel Friedheim, "Sol Invictus in the Severus Synagogue at Hammath Tiberias, the Rabbis, and Jewish Society: A Different Approach," *Review of Rabbinic Judaism* 12, no. 1 (2009): 89–128 at 107–8; M. Hadas-Lebel, "Le paganisme à travers les sources rabbiniques des IIe et IIIe siècles—Contribution à l'étude du syncrétisme dans l'empire romain," in *Aufstieg und Niedergang der römischen Welt* II, vol. 19, part 2, ed. Wolfgang Haase (Berlin: de Gruyter, 1979), 397–485, esp. 415–17.
4. Assmann, *Price of Monotheism*, 21.
5. "Rephan" (whatever the spelling) has no parallel in ancient literature but likely refers to Saturn or "Sakkuth" (Am 5:26), in whose honor Jews were sometimes said to rest on Saturday. See *Amos: A New Translation with Notes and Commentary*, trans. Francis I. Andersen and David Noel Freedman (New York: Doubleday, 1989), 533–34; Augustine, *De consensu* 1.22.30; F. J. Foakes-Jackson and Kirsopp Lake, eds., *The Beginnings of Christianity: Part I: The Acts of the Apostles* (London: Macmillan, 1933), 4:79–80; Kocku von Stuckrad, "Jewish and Christian Astrology in Late Antiquity: A New Approach," *Numen* 47, no. 1 (2000): 1–40, esp. 29–30.
6. Philo, *On Dreams* §215-16 (LCL); see also Josephus, *Jewish Antiquities* 1.2.3 (LCL) and *Jewish War* 5.217–18 (LCL); Iris Fishof, "The Many Faces of the Zodiac," in *Written in the Stars: Art and Symbolism of the Zodiac*, ed. Iris Fishof (Jerusalem: The Israel Museum, 2001), 28–92, esp. 34, 37; Steven Fine, *Art and Judaism in the Greco-Roman World: Toward a New Jewish Archaeology* (Cambridge: Cambridge University Press, 2005), 196–205.
7. Cf. Gal. 4.3, 8–10; Jon D. Levenson, "Is There a Counterpart in the Hebrew Bible to New Testament Antisemitism?" in *Divine Doppelgängers: YHWH's Ancient Look-Alikes*, ed. Collin Cornell (University Park, PA: Eisenbrauns, 2020), 159-178; Todd Penner, *In Praise of Christian Origins: Stephen and the Hellenists in Lukan Apologetic Historiography* (New York: T&T Clark, 2004), esp. 312n105.

the fourth and fifth centuries by the gradual cooptation of winter solstice (December 25 on the Julian calendar) as the day to observe Christmas, notwithstanding the lack of scriptural warrant and the date's former role as the festival of *Sol Invictus*.[8] "You celebrate the solemn feast days of the nations, such as the kalends and solstices," Faustus accuses orthodox Christians. "From their life you have in fact changed nothing."[9] The Fathers demurred but could see in their congregations evidence that the church was not wholly innocent. Leo the Great (c. 400–461) excoriates the "damnable perversion" of church-goers arriving for Christmas services only to turn "themselves around towards the rising sun, and bow down to honor its shining disk."[10] Maximus of Turin (c. 380–c.465) similarly complains of his congregants' Christmas revels. They give themselves over "to pagan feasts" out of ignorance of the fact that those who follow the Lord "cannot rejoice with the world [*cum saeculo*]."[11] Eating, drinking, and, worst of all, dancing in honor of the solstice can only encourage a person "to ignore the existence of God [*ignorare quod deus est*]," as though the solar cycle itself were reason enough to celebrate the passage of time.[12]

Before the spread of Christianity, these Saturnalian activities had not been widely considered secular riots. It took a profoundly untraditional, disenchanting insight to claim that the seasonal festivity connected to the solstice was in no way a sacred enterprise and that those who continued to walk "aftir the cours of this world [*secundum saeculum mundi*]"—merrily regarding the cosmos as the sum total of all being—were in fact "sones of unbileve" and "with outen God" (Col 3:6; Eph 2:2, later Wycliffite). One of the chief effects of the gospel, according to the Fathers, was to break and

---

8. The first mention of December 25 as Christ's birthday is found in the *Chronograph of 354*; text in *Chronica minora saec. IV, V, VI, VII*, ed. Theodor Mommsen (Berlin, 1892), 1:56; discussed in Michele Renee Salzman, *On Roman Time: The Codex-Calendar of 354 and the Rhythms of Urban Life in Late Antiquity* (Berkeley: University of California Press, 1990), 149–53.
9. Augustine, *Contra Faust.* 20.4 (CSEL 25:538; WSA I/20:263).
10. Leo the Great, *Serm.* 27.4–5; Latin in Léon le Grand, *Sermons*, ed. and trans. Dom René Dolle (Paris: Éditions du Cerf, 1964), 1:156–58; English in St. Leo the Great, *Sermons*, trans. Jane Patricia Freeland and Agnes Josephine Conway (Washington, DC: Catholic University of America Press, 1996), 113. See also *Serm.* 22.6.
11. Maximus of Turin, *Serm.* 63 (CCSL 23:266); English in *The Sermons of St. Maximus of Turin*, trans. Boniface Ramsey (New York: Newman Press, 1989), 155; see also *Serm.* 98 and *Serm.* 62 (a more positive evaluation of solstice); Ps-Ambrose, *Serm.* 6 (PL 17:614–17); Jerome, *Tractus sive homiliae in psalmos* 148.3 (CCSL 78:344); further references in Hugo Rahner, *Greek Myths and Christian Mystery*, trans. Brian Battershaw (New York: Harper & Row, 1963), 145–54; E. K. Chambers, *The Mediaeval Stage* (Oxford: Clarendon, 1903), 1:234–48, esp. 243.
12. Maximus of Turin, *Serm.* 63 (CCSL 23:266); trans. Ramsey, 155.

secularize people's formerly religious attachments, such that the cosmos could be at last, in Weber's terminology, conclusively *entzaubert*—which is to say, shorn of magic.[13] If the church continued to subordinate its liturgical calendar to astral calculations, that was merely to show that it had the power to turn to genuinely spiritual uses the pagan fascination with natural motion: "Let us keep this day as a festival," Augustine preaches apropos of Christmas, "not like the unbelievers [*infideles*], because of the sun up there in the sky, but because of the one who made the sun."[14] A limited respect for celestial bodies and seasonal change could help to raise human affections "from things seen, corporeal and temporal, to things unseen, spiritual and eternal," but only so long as believers were able to grasp, when contemplating the cosmos, its radical impermanence and lack of inherent meaning (*Ep.* 55.8.13 [CCSL 31:245; WSA II/1:223]). On the final day, the sun's radiance will expire, the starlight fade, the moon's splendor set, all things cease, and the earth perish (*De civ. Dei* 18.23, LCL). Christians who want to ascend the ladder of spiritual similitude toward transcendence have to accept that solar radiation merely *appears* to be the source of all life on earth. In fact the sun is but a fleeting shadow, whose only value lies in the tenor of which it is a bare, empty vehicle.

When the Fathers read that a star, of all things, announced this gospel directly to a group of *magi*—virtually synonymous at the time with astrologers or "astromyenes" (Mt 2:1, later Wycliffite)—they assumed that the news had come at the cost of a terrible disillusionment. Astral worship had been discredited by the star of Bethlehem in the same way that Christ's birth sounded the death knell for every god, oracle, and idol.[15] "Its strangeness caused amaze-

---

13. MWG I/22.2:273; English in *Economy and Society: An Outline of Interpretative Sociology*, ed. Guenther Roth and Claus Wittich (Berkeley: University of California Press, 1978), 1:506.
14. *Serm.* 190.1 (PL 38:1007; WSA III/6:38). Cf. Augustine, *Serm.* 186.1, 190.1 (PL 38:999, 1007; WSA III/6:24, 38).
15. See Plutarch, *The Obsolescence of Oracles* 419B–D (LCL); interpreted by Theodoret of Cyrrhus, *Graecarum affectionum curatio* 10.6, 8, 10, in Théodoret de Cyr, *Thérapeutique des maladies helléniques*, trans. Pierre Canivet (Paris: Éditions du Cerf, 1958), 2:362–64 and Eusebius, *Praeparatio evangelica* 5.16–17, in *Eusebius Werke*, ed. Édouard des Places, 2nd ed. (Berlin: Akademie, 1982), 8.1:252–56; trans. Edwin Hamilton Gifford, *Preparation for the Gospel* (Oxford: Clarendon, 1903), 1:204–7; Sharon Lynn Coggan, *Pandaemonia: A Study of Eusebius' Recasting of Plutarch's Story of the "Death of Great Pan"* (PhD. diss., Syracuse University, 1992). See also Athanasius, "Life of St. Anthony," in *Early Christian Biographies*, ed. Roy J. Deferrari, trans. Mary Emily Keenan (Washington, DC: Catholic University of America Press, 1952), 203: "Tell me, therefore, where now are your oracles? Where are the incantations of the Egyptians? Where are the delusions of the magicians? When did all these lose their power and cease but at the coming of the cross of Christ?"

ment," writes Ignatius, and "all magic and every kind of spell were destroyed."[16] At the star's first appearance, according to Origen, the demons who helped astrologers to make on occasion accurate predictions "lost their strength and became weak; their sorcery was confuted and their power overthrown."[17] Magi across the world consequently experienced an impotence without precedent. Casting about for a way to explain the cessation of earthly enchantment, a group from the East followed the new star to the source of their enervation. In Jerome's telling, it guided them to the one "who would destroy all the power of their art."[18] Augustine likewise thought that a primary virtue of the nova was its ability to expose magic as species of con-artistry, poetry, or play. The demons behind astral divination worked through natural, worldly means in the same way that "theatrical performers" (*theatrici artifices*) used stage magic to produce the appearance of divinity.[19] The star of Bethlehem tore the veil that had enchanted the enchanters, shredding their mistaken reverence for the cosmos: "This star confounded the futile calculations and divinations of the astrologers," according to Augustine, "when it pointed out to star-worshippers the creator of heaven and earth as the proper object of worship" (*Serm.* 201.1 [PL 38:1031; WSA III / 6:87]). It convinced astrolators, where nothing else could, that whenever people venerate the stars as though the cosmos were divine, in fact "no god whatsoever is worshipped or prayed to."[20] The star of Bethlehem thus brought about "the enlightenment of the Magi [*Magorum illuminatio*]" because they—unlike the Jews—discovered in the heavens a reason to abandon their superstitious devotion.[21] The Magi took the first step on the road to Epiphany— "through deserts, all the way waste and desolate," as Lancelot Andrewes would come to put it before King James in a Christmas sermon—by accepting the loss of everything that they had once held sacred.[22]

---

16. Ignatius, *Letter to the Ephesians* 19.3, in *The Apostolic Fathers: Greek Texts and English Translations*, ed. Michael W. Holmes (Grand Rapids, MI: Baker Books, 1999), 148–49.
17. *C. Celsum* 1.60 (PG 11:769C); English in Origen, *Contra Celsum*, trans. Henry Chadwick, rev. ed. (Cambridge: Cambridge University Press, 1980), 54. Max Weber, MWG I / 22.2:303; *Economy and Society*, 1:527: "That Christ broke the power of the demons by the force of his spirit . . . was, in the early period of Christianity, one of the most important and influential of its messages."
18. Jerome, *Comm. in Esaiam* VII.xix.2 / 4 (CCSL 73:278); English in *St. Jerome: Commentary on Isaiah*, trans. Thomas P. Scheck (New York: Newman, 2015), 347.
19. *De divinatione daemonum* 4.8 (CSEL 41:606); English in *Saint Augustine: Treatises on Marriage and Other Subjects*, ed. Roy J. Deferrari, trans. Ruth Wentworth Brown (Washington, DC: Catholic University of America Press, 1955), 429.
20. *De civ. Dei* 5.1 (LCL); see also 5.9, responding to Cicero, *De divinatione* 2.42–47 (LCL); Sextus Empiricus, *Against the Professors* 5 (LCL); Tamsyn Barton, *Ancient Astrology* (London: Routledge, 1994), 52–56.
21. *Serm.* 200.3 (PL 38:1029; WSA III / 6:84); repeated by Aquinas, *Summa theol.* 3a, Q. 36, art. 8, reply 3.
22. Lancelot Andrewes, *Sermons*, ed. G. M. Story (Oxford: Clarendon, 1967), 109.

In the course of discrediting astromancers, Augustine describes in some detail the advantages of a fully secularized astronomy. As a kind of physics gone astray, astrology can be turned back toward the end of producing real knowledge so long as people avoid looking to the stars "to extract something of relevance to our own actions and experiences, like the maniacs who cast horoscopes"; one should concentrate instead only on "as much as relates to the stars themselves [*quantum ad ipsa pertinet sidera*]."[23] Heavenly bodies "themselves," observed without credulity, contain a great deal of practical information. For example they provide a way to increase agricultural yields by allowing farmers to know the timing of the seasons, thus when to sow and when to reap. Observing the stars "as farmers and sailors do, or to locate parts of the world and to direct a course there and back, as pilots of ships do or those who cross through sandy deserts in interior regions to the south without any certain path" is indispensable to the food supply and to global trade routes (*Ep.* 55.8.15 [CCSL 31:245–46; WSA II/1:223]). Without the sun, moon, and stars, secular civilization as Augustine knew it could not have come into existence, and he appreciates how astronomy might continue to grant humanity, for the time being, mastery over the environment.

Augustine's most prescient insight into the possibilities afforded by a disenchanted astrology is the realization that a person with sufficient skill could chart by its means the history of the *saeculum* as such, from beginning to end, in strictly mathematical terms: "As well as the demonstration of things in the present, it [i.e., astronomy] has something in common with narration of the past, because one may systematically argue from the present position and movement of the stars to their outermost courses in the past. It also makes possible systematic predictions about the future, which are not speculative and conjectural but firm and certain."[24] When directed "systematically" (*regulariter*) toward the past, astronomy had become central to the science of chronology; when directed to the future, its ability to make firm, certain and (we would say) *objective* calculations formed the basis of computus—"the only applied science of Western Europe" for much of the Middle Ages, insofar as it gave the church the most authoritative means of knowing when, based on the astronomical data contained in the New Testament, to celebrate Holy Week.[25] "The orbit of the moon, which is

---

23. *De doct. Christ.* 2.46.113; Latin and English in Augustine, *De doctrina Christiana*, ed. and trans. R. P. H. Green (Oxford: Clarendon, 1995), 109; see Franz Cumont, *The Oriental Religions in Roman Paganism* (New York: Dover, 1956), 184, for "physics gone astray."
24. *De doct. Christ.* 2.46.113, ed. and trans. Green, 109.
25. Immo Warntjes, "Isidore of Seville and the Formation of Medieval Computus," in *A Companion to Isidore of Seville*, ed. Andrew Fear and Jamie Wood (Leiden: Brill, 2020), 457-523 at 459.

regularly used to fix the annual celebration of our Lord's passion, is familiar to very many people," notes Augustine. "But very few have any knowledge, free from error, about the rise or setting or any other movements of the other heavenly bodies."[26] Because the gospels had bound the Crucifixion to the first full moon following the vernal equinox (aka Passover) and placed the Resurrection on a Sunday, the church needed a highly specialized, technical ability to coordinate the lunar and solar calendars with the days of the week such that the whole of Christendom could celebrate Easter uniformly on the basis of calculations that were mathematically valid, empirically verifiable, universally binding, and thus, so to speak, catholic.[27]

A secularized astrology, in other words, was the only standard of measurement that the church trusted to calculate the dates of moveable feasts. As the sun and moon moved, so did Christian festivities—not in accordance with ancient superstition but in harmony, rather, with the measurable order of the cosmos. The equations and instruments necessary for accuracy were indeed familiar "to very few," as Augustine says, but already in his lifetime the church had handed over its liturgical calendar to the professional *mathematici* whose learning would eventually produce Copernicus—a university-trained astronomer and Polish canon preoccupied with the "accurate prediction of the occurrences of holy days."[28] This interest in computus, when combined with a theory of motion first pioneered by theorists of the sacraments, is what gives Copernicus his "specific medievalness."[29] By the early Middle Ages monasteries had become especially fruitful astronomical laboratories since the varying day length over the course of the year rendered it impossible, without careful observation of the stars, to know when "one ought to awake and pray to the Lord."[30] Merely keeping the canonical hours

---

26. *De doct. Christ.* 2.46.112; ed. and trans. Green, 109 (modified).
27. The synoptic gospels place the Crucifixion on the day after Passover (Mt 27:1; Mk 1:15; Lk 22:66), John on Passover itself (Jn 18:28, 19:14); all agree that the Resurrection was on Sunday (Mt 28:1; Mk 16:2; Lk 24:1; Jn 20:1).
28. Robert S. Westman, "The Copernicans and the Churches," in *God and Nature: Historical Essays on the Encounter between Christianity and Science*, ed. David C. Lindberg and Ronald J. Numbers (Berkeley: University of California Press, 1986), 76-113 at 77.
29. Hans Blumenberg, *The Genesis of the Copernican World*, trans. Robert M. Wallace (Cambridge, MA: MIT Press, 1987), 475.
30. Gregory of Tours, *De cursu stellarum ratio* 16, in *Gregorii Turonensis Opera*, ed. W. Arndt and Br. Krusch (Hannover, 1885), 2:863; discussion in Stephen C. McCluskey, "Gregory of Tours, Monastic Timekeeping, and Early Christian Attitudes to Astronomy," *Isis* 81, no. 1 (1990): 8-22; James A. Weisheipl, "Curriculum of the Faculty of Arts at Oxford in the Early Fourteenth Century," *Mediaeval Studies* 26 (1964): 143-85, esp. 172-73.

(to say nothing of all-night vigils before feast days) made Christian monks particularly adept at predicting the date of Easter. And because the same calculations could be run in reverse—"to argue from the present position and movement of the stars to their outermost courses in the past"—monks became highly motivated to determine how many years had transpired since Christ's advent. There were several possibilities in circulation throughout late antiquity, but we owe the placement of his arrival at what we now call year 1 of the Common Era to Dionysius Exiguous, an early sixth-century Scythian astronomer-monk stationed in Rome. This particular year seems to have called to him because in it, his calculations showed, the full moon had coincided with the vernal equinox of the Julian calendar (March 25). For many Christians this date served as the new year, plus the date of creation, the Annunciation, and the Crucifixion—a striking conjunction, in Dionysius's eyes, that produced what would eventually become "the most successful dating system the world has ever known."[31]

The global success of the BC/AD divide resulted from more than a thousand years of conquest and evangelism. "We wish to reduce all the calendars to solar years and to the years of the Latins," proclaims Roger Bacon in the thirteenth century, "which are the years of Christ."[32] Writing after centuries of crusade, Bacon felt keenly the advantage that an accurate, astronomically based computus and chronology would give to the church universal. The course of history from creation to the present might be set in order with respect to Christ, Bacon explains, "so that all sects of pagans, idolaters, Tartars, heretics and other unbelievers [*infidelium*] may be destroyed through a certification of the time of the savior."[33] There was, Bacon knew, considerable ongoing debate about the starting point of the Christian era, as much among Christians themselves as between them and everyone else.[34] There were equally charged debates about when to celebrate, in any given year, the events of Christ's life: "Unbelieving philosophers [*philosophi infideles*]," Bacon writes, "Arabs, Hebrews, and Greeks who live among Christians, as in Spain and Egypt and parts of the East and many other regions of the world

---

31. Georges Declercq, "Dionysius Exiguus and the Introduction of the Christian Era," *Sacris Erudiri* 41 (2002): 164–246 at 165; see also 245–46.
32. *The Opus Majus of Roger Bacon*, ed. John Henry Bridges (London: Williams and Norgate, 1900), 1:188; English in *The Opus Majus of Roger Bacon*, trans. Robert Belle Burke (Philadelphia: University of Pennsylvania Press, 1928), 1:209.
33. *Opus Majus*, ed. Bridges, 1:188; trans. Burke, 1:208.
34. See Peter Verbist, *Duelling with the Past: Medieval Authors and the Problem of the Christian Era, c990–1135* (Turnhout: Brepols, 2010).

abhor the stupidity that they see in the ways that Christians calculate the times for their solemnities."³⁵ For Bacon, these conflicts made it imperative for Christian counting to be regularized and for the calendar to be reformed, so that the church could direct the full "potency of mathematics [*potestas mathematicae*]" toward "the conversion of unbelievers [*infidelium*] and the repression of those who cannot be converted."³⁶ At the end of the day there was no science more essential than astronomy to the Catholic ambition to remove from the world all diversity of opinion about the true course of history: "No one can certify in regard to times except the astronomer, nor can any other science [*scientia*] than astronomy certify in regard to them."³⁷ Bacon knew all too well that in debates about the true faith, to be persuasive against the forces of unbelief, one had to rely on *more* than faith; one needed to be able to observe empirical phenomena and to make mathematical predictions on the basis of those observations. Indeed one needed to be able to say that "the philosophers who have been led by the exercise of their reason alone"—absent any faith whatsoever—"agree with us."³⁸

The increased enthusiasm for astronomical observation, mathematics, logic, and reason following the twelfth-century recovery of ancient learning had the effect of further indebting the church to the very forms of unbelief that it had hoped to vanquish: "Medieval theologians imported logic and natural philosophy into theology to such an extent," writes Edward Grant, "that they effectively secularized it."³⁹ Natural philosophy in the Middle Ages gains "a right," in the words of Hans Blumenberg, "that contains a high degree of imaginative freedom precisely as a result of its employment of elements that have not been theologically dogmatized. Reason's self-assertion against theological absolutism is not carried out primarily by throwing off obligations but by a subversive twisting of the functional orientation of the theological contents themselves."⁴⁰ Christmas dramas featuring the Magi are a particularly vivid witness to this type of secularization insofar as they were designed to show that the church had made its first inroads with the most learned astrologers of the day by teaching them that the stars were just stars, nothing more—save for the one above Bethlehem: "The Magi were the first fruits of the gentiles," Augustine preaches, "and we are a nation of gen-

---

35. *Opus Majus*, 1:285; trans. Burke, 1:306; see also Amanda Power, *Roger Bacon and the Defence of Christendom* (Cambridge: Cambridge University Press, 2010), 107–8.
36. *Opus Majus*, ed. Bridges, 1:253; trans. Burke, 1:276.
37. *Opus Majus*, ed. Bridges, 1:188; trans. Burke, 1:208–9.
38. *Opus Majus*, ed. Bridges, 1:254; trans. Burke, 1:276.
39. Edward Grant, *God and Reason in the Middle Ages* (Cambridge: Cambridge University Press, 2001), 289.
40. Blumenberg, *Genesis of the Copernican World*, 157.

tiles."[41] By the eleventh century their conversion was frequently dramatized by means of a star "hanging from a cord [*pendentem in filo*]" as part of the liturgical rite on Epiphany (January 6).[42] The episode was explicitly imperialist; in being overcome by the King of Kings, the Magi offered a glimpse into the pan-Christian future when Christ would at last "crush the rulers of foreign peoples and the whole earth will be his possession."[43] Originally "from the East" (Mt 2:1), they were often described on stage as "kings" coming specifically *ex Arabitis*—which is to say, from the regions whose scientific acumen and military might could inspire at that moment no small feelings of inferiority among Christians.[44] When these wise men laid down their crowns before Christ alongside their gifts, they were thought to have lent to the church the full authority of astronomy in its struggle against the infidel at a time when the infidel had allowed Christian intellectuals to recover Ptolemy, Euclid, the astrolabe—and to discover, with those, a new science.[45]

Shakespeareans have traditionally been keen to defend the unique prerogatives of the London commercial stage by associating its aesthetic power with the scientific discoveries of the sixteenth and seventeenth centuries: "Shifts within communities of knowledge in early modern England could be seismic," writes Carla Mazzio, and "would have found a rather hospitable home, a local habitation and a name, as it were, in the theatre—where clashing systems, thesis and antithesis, conjecture and refutation are the stock and trade of dramatic vitality."[46] Since Shakespeare wrote during "a period in history when distinctly visual demonstrations of scientific effects were often inseparable from the work of theatre" (ibid.), scientists, players, and playwrights shared with one another a kindred mindset; thus, in the words of Sophie Chiari and Mickaël Popelard, the "analogous 'procedures of thought' . . . which bind together scientific and literary discourses, practices and mentalities within a single episteme (in the Foucauldian sense of the

---

41. *Serm.* 200.1 (PL 38:1028; WSA III/6:83). Repeated by Aquinas, *Summa theol.* 3a, Q. 36, art. 6.2.
42. Young 2:35, from the use of Limoges, of uncertain date but probably after 1100.
43. Paris, Bibl. Nat. MS lat. 904, Grad. Rothomagense saec. xiii, fol. 28v–30r; ed. Young 2:436 (see also 2:44).
44. Young 2:69; see also 2:51, 78, 86, and Bacon, *Opus Majus*, ed. Bridges, 1:332; trans. Burke, 1:350–51, specifying that the Magi were Arabs.
45. Edward Grant, *The Foundations of Modern Science in the Middle Ages: Their Religious, Institutional, and Intellectual Contexts* (Cambridge: Cambridge University Press, 1996); James Hannam, *God's Philosophers: How the Medieval World Laid the Foundations of Modern Science* (London: Icon Books, 2009).
46. Carla Mazzio, "Coda: Scepticism and the Spectacular—On Shakespeare in an Age of Science," in *Spectacular Science, Technology and Superstition in the Age of Shakespeare*, ed. Sophie Chiari and Mickaël Popelard (Edinburgh: Edinburgh University Press, 2014), 239.

word)."[47] I largely share this aspiration to coordinate the histories of science and theater but cannot help wondering when Shakespeare's allegedly distinct "episteme" began. Did it really emerge sui generis, without meaningful antecedents, as though *ex nihilo*? The question has frequently been met among early modernists with a shrug of indifference: "What would be the point," asks Mary Thomas Crane, "of showing that early modern literature was backward looking?"[48] Indeed would it not imperil the hard-won privileges of modernity as formulated over and against the Middle Ages? And yet more than one historian of science has come to suspect that the modern "faith in the possibility of science," to borrow from Alfred North Whitehead, "is an unconscious derivative from medieval theology."[49] Medieval theologians were key players, that is, in the seismic transfer of authority from theology to natural philosophy.[50] One result of acknowledging this history is to shatter the truism of Shakespeare studies that the stars play a different role in medieval drama than they do in the London theater: "Roman superstition and medieval belief in the powers of celestial prophecy remained attached to ominous as well as numinous moments of divine revelation," writes François Laroque, for example. "Not so astrology in the early modern period, since it was linked to astronomy, mathematics and medicine."[51] Through a similar juxtaposition Jonathan Bate has counted Shakespeare's contemporaries among "the first to separate astronomy (the empirical observation of the stars) from astrology (the art of divining the influence of the stars on people and events)."[52] How can that claim possibly be sustained when the separation of astronomy from astrology—as well as astronomy's links to mathematical calculation, empirical observation, agriculture, navigation, and medicine—is a demonstrable inheritance from the Middle Ages? We can see in the Nativity play of the *Carmina Burana* the same debunking of so-called judicial astrology that has been celebrated for its modernity in *King Lear*, and we can see it there because plays about the Magi were the beneficiaries of the patristic commonplace that "magic was discredited at the

---

47. Chiari and Popelard, "Introduction," in *Spectacular Science*, 7.
48. Mary Thomas Crane, *Losing Touch with Nature: Literature and the New Science in Sixteenth-Century England* (Baltimore, MD: Johns Hopkins University Press, 2014), 2.
49. Alfred North Whitehead, *Science and the Modern World* (New York: Macmillan, 1925), 19.
50. Brad Gregory, *The Unintended Reformation: How a Religious Revolution Secularized Society* (Cambridge, MA: Belknap Press, 2012).
51. François Laroque, "The 'Science' of Astrology in Shakespeare's Sonnets, *Romeo and Juliet* and *King Lear*," in Chiari and Popelard, *Spectacular Science*, 29–30.
52. Jonathan Bate, *Soul of the Age: A Biography of the Mind of William Shakespeare* (New York: Random House, 2009), 59.

advent of Christ" (Young 2:30). Like the Easter plays that were painstakingly timed to coincide with astronomical observation, a Nativity play performed on winter solstice implicitly asked its audience to consider the stars as a universal, homogenous standard for measuring time, which the church alone had the wisdom to value dispassionately.

Because medieval Christians regularly found in "the whole machine of the world [*totam mundi machinam*]" a witness to the mathematical genius of the creator, they often treated the natural philosophy pioneered by unbelievers as an all-too-adequate stand-in for biblical theology.[53] In the process they managed to extend to the *saeculum* some of the reverence officially due to the transcendent godhead: "For no one would search for god or aspire to a state of piety," writes Calcidius in the early fourth century, "if he had not first viewed the heavens and stars and nourished a love of knowing both the causes of things and the origins of those that have their coming-to-be in time; and these matters pertain ultimately to the inquiry into nature."[54] By means of such reasoning Calcidius managed to produce a massively influential work on the cosmos that seemed to its medieval readers "essentially of secular orientation," in Peter Dronke's words, and that inspired a host of subsequent texts—from Boethius to Eriugena and Bernardus Silvestris—whose "force and fascination . . . is bound up with their freedom of spirit, their refusal to rely on explicit Christian doctrines as vehicles for their conceptions."[55] Readers could learn from Calcidius all manner of information absent from the Bible: that the earth is spherical (§63, ed. Magee [222–23]), for example; that "in comparison with the vastness of the universe" the world we inhabit has "the proportions of a point" (§64 [224–25]); that the moon is closest to the earth; that Venus and Mercury intervene between the earth and sun; and that Mars, Jupiter, and Saturn (in that order) are increasingly distant (§72 [236–37]). In fact the only explicit reference to scripture in the whole of his commentary suggests that the Magi had been saved as much by their secular learning—which enabled them to detect the appearance of a nova among the regular celestial rotations—as by the "recent birth of a god" that the nova signified.[56]

---

53. Bacon, *Opus Majus*, ed. Bridges, 1:127; trans. Burke, 1:148.
54. Calcidius, *On Plato's "Timaeus,"* ed. and trans. John Magee (Cambridge, MA: Harvard University Press, 2016), 539 (§264), commenting on *Timaeus* 47a.
55. Peter Dronke, *The Spell of Calcidius: Platonic Concepts and Images in the Medieval West* (Florence: SISMEL edizioni del Galluzzo, 2008), 6, xv, respectively.
56. Calcidius, *On Plato's "Timaeus,"* §126, ed. Magee, 331 (modified). For a less aggressively Christianizing translation, see Gretchen Reydams-Schils, *Calcidius on Plato's "Timaeus": Greek Philosophy, Latin Reception, and Christian Contexts* (Cambridge: Cambridge University Press, 2020), 194.

It was, at any rate, possible by the thirteenth century to believe that the full depths of the world were best plumbed *per experimentum*—in the terminology of Roger Bacon—ideally through the use of *instrumenta*, such as the lens, which could correct for the limitations of human vision. In fact theater and science were already joined by the twelfth century; plays performed in glazed churches foregrounded the spectacular effects of light passing through a medium that was increasingly central to the theory of optics and that became in time the single most important astronomical instrument after the astrolabe. The widespread use of glass windows in sacred spaces and of convex crystals for purposes of magnification (as reading aids and in reliquaries)—to say nothing of the liquid-filled glass vessels in the tavern culture lovingly extolled in the songs of the *Carmina Burana*—all helped to make Bacon's optical discoveries possible. By his own account, he routinely watched rays of light "penetrating" glass and being refracted by it, in the same way that God had impregnated Mary, according to a medieval commonplace that we'll examine shortly. Indeed it was the medieval culture of glazing and grinding optical aids that made the Benediktbeuern Abbey—from which the *Carmina Burana* was taken in 1803—a particularly suitable target for secularization. It contained a ready-made set-up that was easily transformed into a foundry for the production of precision lenses. The intellectual and material histories to which the *Carmina Burana* bears witness do not only call into question when exactly the modern "scientific" episteme might be said to begin. They beg us to question whether or not we ourselves have ever left the Middle Ages, given that so many of our disenchantments, debunkings, and secularizations—indeed our perpetual sense of having to break, at last, from the superstitions of the past in order to see without distortion our fragile, temporary place in the vastness of space—are themselves a bequest from medieval Christianity.

The Magi in the *Carmina Burana*

The star of Bethlehem makes two appearances in the Nativity play of the *Carmina Burana*. The first is to the Sybil, who sings her prophecy "with excited gestures while gazing at the star [*inspiciendo stellam*]" (CB 227.15–16, rubric).[57] The original Sybilline oracles had been gradually replaced in late

---

57. Original text in Johannes Geffcken, *Die Oracula Sibyllina* (New York: Arno Press, 1979), 28 (2.34–38) and 111–12 (5.155–61); English in James H. Charlesworth, ed., *The Old Testament Pseudepigrapha*, trans. J. J. Collins (Garden City, NY: Doubleday, 1983–85), 1:345–46, 397. For other instances of the star appearing twice, see Young 2:48–49.

antiquity by another corpus of writings jointly composed from the second century onward by Jews and Christians in order to denounce the Roman Empire and thus "promote the cause of monotheism."[58] By the time of the *Carmina Burana*, the Sibyl had long since joined Virgil, Nebuchadnezzar, and Balaam in liturgical processions during the Christmas season as one of the gentile voices lending support to Christ's divinity, largely on the strength of Augustine's appreciation for her prophecies. He notes with interest that, despite her paganism, she refrains from saying anything positive about "the worship of false or feigned gods, but rather speaks against them and their worshippers in such a way that we might even think she ought to be reckoned among those who belong to the city of God."[59] Here is an instance of pagan critical thinking, Augustine imagines, that anticipates Christ's coming disenchantments with a clear-sighted vision of the world's radical impermanence: "The sun's radiance is torn away, the chorus of the stars is ruined / The sky dissolves, the moon's splendor will set . . . all things will cease, the earth broken into pieces will perish."[60] These apocalyptic lines likely conclude the prophecy that the Sibyl sings in the Nativity play, though the scribe has indicated only the beginning of the famous acrostic from which they're taken (spelling out *Jesus Christ Son of God Savior*)—with the result that modern editions of the play often do not bother to print anything beyond the first five lines or trail off with the words *et cetera*. Whether the stage-Sibyl got to the end times or not, the animosity of her prophecy to any conception of the world's permanence was a central, disillusioning interpretation of winter solstice among medieval Christians. Not even the sun can remain unconquered. One day it too will be "turned to darkness" (Jl 2:31), when both "heaven and earth will pass away" (Mt 24:35).

The Sibyl repeatedly stresses that the message conveyed by the star of Bethlehem is without precedent—a new testament, as it were, that does not require any prophecies older than her own: "This newness of the star," she proclaims, "bears new tidings" (CB 227.16). When she gives those tidings a specific content—that "a new king," for example "will create a new age [*nova secula*]" (CB 227.27)—the emphasis falls on Christ's radical viola-

---

58. Hans-Joseph Klauck, *The Religious Context of Early Christianity: A Guide to Graeco-Roman Religions*, trans. Brian McNeil (Minneapolis, MN: Fortress Press, 2003), 204.
59. *De civ. Dei* 18.23 (LCL). Cf. Lactantius, *Div. Inst.* 6.1.
60. Augustine, *De civ. Dei* 18.23 (LCL); repeated in Ps-Augustine, *Contra Judaeos, Paganos et Arianos sermo de symolo* (PL 42:1126); sung by the Sibyl at CB 227.32. For the Greek text, see *Sibylline Oracles* 8.223–33, in Geffcken, *Oracula Sibyllina*, 155–56; Charlesworth, *Old Testament Pseudepigrapha*, 1:423; the last word of the acrostic in the Greek text is "cross" rather than "savior."

tion of archaic pieties in a world superstitiously opposed to innovation. In Jesus, "everything old has passed away" (2 Cor 5:17), and only the people capable of adapting to the change—only those able to *let go* of their past beliefs—will have a place in the *nova secula*. The star of Bethlehem does not simply announce this historic break; its imperviousness to every past interpretive framework radically decenters humanity. The star's appearance thus becomes one of those "modern things [*moderna*]" (CB 227.80)—to borrow a term from Archisynagogus—that tears the fabric of every inherited paradigm and disrupts all prior cosmologies. Through the new star, we're repeatedly told, emerges our first glimpse of a virgin epoch, one liberated at last "from the threshold of error [*ab erroris limine*]" (CB 227.4).

When the star appears again to the Magi, it is once again the very latest thing: "Its newness," exclaims one of them, "carries a new message" (CB 227.124). What exactly the message communicates proves difficult for them to determine at first because the star "did not appear to anyone of old" (CB 227.128) and therefore cannot be adequately explained by "the language of the old school [*lingua secte veteris*]" (CB 227.132). The star's fundamental *weirdness* (another way of translating *novitas*) leaves all three of them "speechless [*elinguem*]" (CB 227.133), able only to say how little anything they might say could capture the shock of its perverse revelation. Their inability to ascribe a clear meaning to it, even though they are "not unlearned in the stars" (CB 227.200), reveals the heretofore invisible limit of all astrological learning. By exposing that limit, the star casts an enigmatic light onto the truth that surpasses it. Everything that astrologers used to revere—"the power . . . / of Mars, Venus, the Sun, Mercury, / the mercy of Jupiter, the decline of Saturn" (CB 227.142–44)—has been eclipsed, as the old pantheon now pales in comparison with the new star's radiance.

Its effects consequently throw them into a sublime fit of "worry" and "doubt" (*cura, dubium*) (CB 227.139–40) that splits the difference between atheism and a new form of worship: "I am repeatedly torn at a crossroad of anxieties [*Per curarum distrahor frequenter quadruvium*]," one moans, "suffering a shipwreck of mind and reason / When I see this star bearing a sign" (CB 227.121–23). Once upon a time the stars had been signposts eternally fixed in the firmament, and a wise man could steer by the "constancy, order, symmetry and calm which are associated with divine things," in the words of Ptolemy.[61] The bizarreness of a *new* star—not to mention one in motion,

---

61. *Ptolemy's Almagest*, trans. G. J. Toomer (New York: Springer, 1984), 37.

leading to fantastic happenings in a faraway land—opens the possibility that supposedly eternal truths are either different than supposed or, more frightening still, perpetually subject to change in light of new information. The Magi of the *Carmina Burana*, in a manner of speaking, are the first Copernicans. Their discovery marks the moment when old standards begin to lose their coherence, the old gods their power; when a new point of reference in the sky redefines what counts as a sign of divinity.

The "crossroad" (*quadruvium*) tearing the mind of the magus apart would have been written *quadrivium* in classical Latin but has been assimilated to the variant spelling that the earliest manuscripts of Boethius's *De arithmetica* had used for the four branches of learning pioneered by pagan mathematicians: arithmetic, geometry, and those twinned studies for ear and eye, music and astronomy.[62] Knowing the "course and nature of the stars," to say nothing of their imperceptible sounds, required looking into "their number" (CB 227.153)—less in the sense of counting the innumerable than of calculating their most prominent movements with sufficient mathematical precision to predict their future positions and theorize relations between them.[63] "Teachers of secular literature [*saecularium litterarum*]," Cassiodorus explains, thus "made it possible through theoretical texts to ascertain what was earlier regarded as hidden from view in the nature of the world," though prior to the star of Bethlehem infidel philosophers had routinely mistaken the order immanent to the *saeculum* as an autonomous source of value.[64] They imagined that the cosmos produced its own physics, which they could visualize in equations and astral maps. In the words of Paul, "they became vain in their cogitations . . . and they changed the glory of the incorruptible God into a similitude of the image of corruptible man, and of fowls and four-

---

62. Plato, *Republic* 530d (LCL). On *quadrivium* vs. *quadruvium*, see Michael Masi, *Boethian Number Theory: A Translation of the "De Institutione Arithmetica"* (Amsterdam: Rodopi, 1983), 71n3; on the medieval curriculum, Pearl Kibre, "The *Quadrivium* in the Thirteenth-Century Universities (with Special Reference to Paris)," in *Arts libéraux et philosophie au Moyen Âge: Actes du Quatrième Congrès International de Philosophie Médiévale, Université de Montréal* (Montreal: Institut d'études médiévales, 1969), 175-91; Kibre, "The Boethian *De Institutione Arithmetica* and the Quadrivium in the Thirteenth-Century University Milieu at Paris," in *Boethius and the Liberal Arts: A Collection of Essays*, ed. M. Masi (Berne: Peter Lang, 1981), 67-80.
63. See Stephen C. McCluskey, *Astronomies and Cultures in Early Medieval Europe* (Cambridge: Cambridge University Press, 1999), 35; Edward Grant, "Cosmology," in *Science in the Middle Ages*, ed. David C. Lindberg (Chicago: University of Chicago Press, 1978), 265-302; Olaf Pedersen, "Astronomy," in Lindberg, *Science in the Middle Ages*, 303-37.
64. *Exp. Ps.* 80.4 (CCSL 98:750); English in *Cassiodorus: Explanation of the Psalms*, trans. P. G. Walsh (New York: Paulist Press, 1990), 2:295; see also Cassiodorus, *Institutes* 2.5.2.

footed beasts and of them that creep" (Rom 1:21b, 23, DR). When stargazers mistook the dots of the dome for mimetic patterns—a bull, a lion, a virgin, and so forth—and then went about trying to predict and manipulate their influence (sometimes with the help of magical amulets engraved with the zodiac), they divinized the "science of images" that the Decalogue had proscribed. "The mindlessness of pagans is to be marveled at," writes Isidore of Seville (c. 560–636). "They set not only fish, but even rams and goats and bulls, bears and dogs and crabs and scorpions into the sky."[65] Having become proficient at determining mathematically the future positions of the sun, moon, and stars, they came to believe they could predict the fate of individual humans "by means of malicious computations, which is called 'astrology' [*mathesim*]" (*Etym*. 3.71.39).

The star of Bethlehem at once dispels and repurposes this ancient superstition; it "takes up" astrology in order to purify its functions. As a result future stargazers could be especially esteemed for their ability to "draw minds entangled in secular wisdom [*saeculari sapientia*] from earthly matters and set them in contemplation of what is above" (*Etym*. 3.71.41) yet also especially plagued, on account of their attentiveness to the cosmos, by association with unbelief, enchantment, and other idolatrous modes of picture-thinking. Their dual reputation predates Christianity but serves there as a complex sort of wish fulfillment. Through the Magi, Christianity's originality could be constructed at the expense of cosmological views it was supposed to discredit, even where it depended on those views and had to maintain them—usually in a reinvented, phantasmatic form—as a witness to its own supremacy. One result of this strategy was that pagan astrology counted as *scientia* when Christians used its contributions toward ends they valued (as in computus, chronology, agriculture, navigation, and medicine) but as superstition or witchcraft when its more expedient function was to demonstrate how far Christianity had advanced beyond a mistaken reverence for the cosmos.

The image of the Magi in the Nativity play of the *Carmina Burana* is for this reason fundamentally two-sided or even dialectical. *Mathesis, astrologia, astronomia*—all of these terms for a mathematical knowledge of the heavenly motions could count either as demonic charlatanry or as true knowledge;

---

65. *Etym*. 3.71.32; Latin in *Isidori Hispalensis Episcopi Etymologiarum sive Originum Libri XX*, ed. W. M. Lindsay, 2 vols. (Oxford: Clarendon, 1911), n.p.; English in *The "Etymologies" of Isidore of Seville*, trans. Stephen A. Barney et al. (Cambridge: Cambridge University Press, 2006), 106. All further references are to these editions by chapter and section numbers.

hence also the ambivalence of *magos*—a Greek word normally reserved for frauds like Simon Magus but almost always taken in the Nativity episode to mean "sages" or "wise men," as for example in every early English Bible, save only the later Wycliffite, which preserves their most likely original calling by referring to them as "astromyenes."[66] Often the word goes untranslated, as though the term for magician were an exotic title for majestic persons; the Nativity play of the *Carmina Burana* uses *magi* interchangeably with *reges*, following the idea that kings had been prophesied to bring gifts to Christ (Ps 71:10–11, Vulg.). The promotion of the Magi to royalty was particularly useful in making the *translatio imperii et studii* of Christ's coming reign plainer to see. In the Nativity play, for example, it eventually dawns on the astronomer-magician-kings, with something like defeated resignation, that the failure of their astral semiotics to interpret the new star must in itself portend "the birth of a king, than whom no greater may ever come, / whose will the whole world, conceding, will serve" (CB 227.151–52). In this way they finally manage to fold the new (*novus*) into what they think they already know (*novimus*): "When the beam of a comet appears" (CB 227.154–55)—which, actually, it hasn't, since the nova over Bethlehem is no comet—"the ends of certain princes are shown" (CB 227.156). In failing to grasp the meaning of the heavens and then mistaking the star of Bethlehem for a comet, they nonetheless manage to foresee correctly the end of their own imperium.

A major question at the crossroad of this play is whether or not the Magi's prediction of Christ's universal dominion, and with it, the end of astrology, could ever come to pass. The awkward result of having learned from Dionysius Exiguus "to discover, without any error, the years of the Lord" (PL 69:1249A–B) was that Christians in the twelfth century were able to form a fairly good approximation of the number of centuries that had transpired since Christ had proclaimed the coming of his Kingdom and, with it, an end to magic. The years were in the thousands, and it was necessary, for the time being, still to keep counting: "Where is the promise of his coming? For since the fathers fell asleep, all things continue as they were fro[m] the beginning

---

66. Mt 2:1; Acts 8:9–24 (Simon Magus), 13:6–11 (Bar-Jesus), 19:13–19 (magicians of Ephesus); see also Jerome, *Comm. in Dan.* 2.2; C. S. Mann, "Epiphany—Wise Men or Charlatans?" *Theology* 61 (1958): 495–500; Gerhard Friedrich, ed., *Theological Dictionary of the New Testament*, trans. and ed. Geoffrey W. Bromiley (Grand Rapids, MI: Eerdmans, 1968), 4:356–59; Huge Kehrer, *Die Heiligen Drei Könige in Literatur und Kunst*, 2 vols. (Leipzig: E. A. Seemann, 1908–1909); for a more recent discussion with bibliography, see Ulrich Luz, *Matthew 1–7: A Commentary*, trans. Wilhelm C. Linss (Edinburgh: T&T Clark, 1990), 127–41; Richard Kieckhefer, *Magic in the Middle Ages*, 3rd ed. (Cambridge: Cambridge University Press, 2022), 44–48.

of the creation" (2 Pt 3:4, AV). Everybody knew that Christendom was riven by faction and perpetually at war with unbelief; that the power attributed to idols had not been wiped out; that astrological predictions based on the stars had not ceased but lived on and had become if anything increasingly vibrant.

The secularization of pagan religion in other words allowed medieval Christians to apprehend as never before the widespread, nefarious, but also highly seductive persistence of nondivine enchantment—and to question whether their own forms of worship were perhaps equally indebted to worldly enticement. From the casting of horoscopes, for instance, it was a short step to the "malicious art" of casting spells. These were chanted—sometimes explicitly in imitation of the stars' influential music—and therefore went by the name *carmina*.[67] One particular incantation in the *Carmina Burana* specifically invokes the legendary names of the Magi (Caspar, Melchior, and Balthasar), along with Pharaoh's sorcerers, to work against the serpent "whose hubris dragged down a third of all the stars," lest those fallen astral powers "corrupt the vessel of Christianity" (CB 54.2.5–6, 5.18–19). Depending on the Christian you asked, these spells either epitomized the most demonic aspect of paganism or were a useful technology well worth borrowing toward approved ends—exorcism, in this case.[68] The Magi are called upon in this particular *carmen*, as in the Nativity play, to bear witness to the purity of Christianity even as the need for such witnesses risks corrupting the faith with a supplementary, non-Christian magic—or what John of Salisbury calls "the violence of a charm [*violentia carminis*]."[69] The Magi symbolize the supersession of pagan enchantment by a more enlightened faith, while their very presence in a spell of this sort openly perpetuates a form of wizardry that was as widely condemned as it was enthusiastically

---

67. Isidore of Seville, *Etym.* 8.9.9. For the classical usage of *carmen* as charm, spell, or incantation, see e.g. Pliny, *Natural Hist.* 28.3.12, 28.4.18 and 21, 28.5.29. See also John Haines, "Why Music and Magic in the Middle Ages?" *Magic, Ritual, and Witchcraft* 5, no. 2 (2010): 149–72; Madeline Pelner Cosman, "Machaut's Medical World," in *Machaut's World: Science and Art in the Fourteenth Century*, ed. Madeline Pelner Cosman and Bruce Chandler (New York: New York Academy of Sciences, 1978), 1–36; Béatrice Delaurenti, *La Puissance des Mots*, *"Virtus Verborum": Débats doctrinaux sur le pouvoir des incantations au Moyen Âge* (Paris: Éditions du Cerf, 2007), esp. 61–67, 159–60, 217–29, 368–79, 383-5, 455–65 on astrology and music in medieval incantations.

68. Charles Burnett, "Talismans: Magic as Science? Necromancy Among the Seven Liberal Arts," in *Magic and Divination in the Middle Ages: Texts and Techniques in the Islamic and Christian Worlds*, ed. Charles Burnett (Aldershot, UK: Ashgate, 1996), 1–15; Bert Hensen, "Science and Magic," in *Science in the Middle Ages*, ed. David C. Lindberg (Chicago: University of Chicago Press, 1978), 483–506.

69. *Policraticus* 1.10 (CCCM 118:56); English in *Frivolities of Courtiers and Footprints of Philosophers* [etc.], trans. Joseph B. Pike (Minneapolis: University of Minnesota Press, 1938), 40 (modified).

practiced.⁷⁰ The Nativity play itself, we saw in the last chapter, depends on the power of the *Gloria* to provoke belief in dubious or confusing assertions about the ultimate reality; it depends, that is, on the highly ambiguous power of a liturgical song to *enchant*. Whether the incantations of the prophets, the heavenly choir and, by extension, the charming numbers of the liturgy were anything more than idolatrous magic persisting under the guise of an allegedly enlightened faith is an abiding preoccupation of the play and a question that it poses openly in the figures of Archisynagogus and the Devil. From their perspective—which is voiced in the play *by Christians*—Christ's advent represents the triumph of a new irrationalism.

"If astrology was reborn suddenly and with such profusion in the twelfth century," writes Guy Beaujouan, "it was not because the attitude of the ecclesiastical authorities had changed."⁷¹ They continued to police the boundary between computus and astrology all the more as both practices shared the same technologies. "What had changed was that, thanks to the Arabs, Latins had learned to use astronomical tables and to calculate the longitude of the planets for any time whatever, past present, or future—the precondition of an astrology which truly believed in itself" (ibid.). Thanks to Islam, Latin-speaking Christians had also rediscovered the astrolabe, which was used to advance the cause of both astrologers and computists.⁷² Two hundred miles to the west of Benedikbeuern in another Benedictine monastery, for example, the noted *musicus* Hermann of Reichenau used an astrolabe and the astronomical theory of unspecified *moderni* to correct errors in the old liturgical calendars that now seemed "glaringly obvious" and that risked making the church's celebrations look "ridiculous to Jews and Muslims"⁷³—especially when the latter were a

---

70. For medieval critiques of astrology and witchcraft more generally, see e.g. Rabanus Maurus, *De magicis artibus* (PL 110:1095–1110A) and *Poenitentium liber* 23–24 (PL 112:1417A–1418A); John of Salisbury, *Policraticus* 1.9–12; 2.18–19, 24–26, 28 (CCCM 118:56–61, 106–17, 137–47,164–69); *Caesarii Heisterbacensis monachi ordinis cisterciensis dialogus miraculorum* [etc.], ed. Josephus Strange (Cologne, 1851), 1:274–340; English in Caesarius of Heisterbach, *The Dialogue on Miracles*, trans. H. von E. Scott and C. C. Swinton Bland, vol. 1 (London: Routledge, 1929), book 5; William of Auvergne, *De universo* IIIa–IIae, chaps. 22–26, in *Guilielmi Alverni Episcopi Parisiensis, Mathematici Perfectissimi, Eximii Philosophi, Ac Theologi Præstantissimi, Opera Omnia* (London, 1674), 1059–74; analysis in Lynn Thorndike, *A History of Magic and Experimental Science* (New York: Columbia University Press, 1923), 2:338–71; see also Henry Charles Lea, *A History of the Inquisition of the Middle Ages* (London: Macmillan, 1922), 3:437–46, and Kieckhefer, *Magic in the Middle Ages*, 232–51.
71. Guy Beaujouan, "The Transformation of the Quadrivium," in *Renaissance and Renewal in the Twelfth-Century*, ed. Robert L. Benson and Giles Constable (Toronto: University of Toronto Press, 1991), 463–87 at 480.
72. See Arno Borst, *Astrolab und Klosterreform an der Jahrtausendwende* (Heidelberg: Carl Winter, 1989), esp. 77–98.
73. McClusky, *Astronomies and Cultures*, 180, 201. See also T. J. H. McCarthy, *Music, Scholasticism and Reform: Salian Germany, 1024–1125* (Manchester: Manchester University Press, 2009), 23–30, 55–108.

primary source for the new astronomy and periodically bested their Christian adversaries on the battlefield, if not also in the arguments over doctrine that the Nativity play stages. To conservative authorities such innovations were patently un-Christian and patently offensive, most of all when "some of our moderns . . . have been said to inscribe their novelties into the Easter charts and to disregard the path of the Fathers"—notwithstanding that the path of the Fathers had been shown by the new learning to wander into demonstrable error.[74]

Archisynagogus and the Devil speak directly to Christians' embarrassment by the incoherence of their rituals and doctrines when seen from the perspective of unbelievers, and they speak at a time when many nominal believers entertained that perspective with unnerving enthusiasm. Some, such as Frederick II—Holy Roman Emperor from 1194 to 1250 and the "first European" to suit Nietzsche's taste—actively reached out to infidels to gain a better knowledge of the heavens.[75] Following the precedent of his grandfather, Friedrich Barbarossa, he defended Jews against accusations of ritual murder, even welcoming them into his court as translators of Greek and Arabic texts.[76] He solicited information directly from his contacts in the Muslim world—forged in part by the Crusades, which his client-poet Walter von der Vogelweide helped celebrate (CB 211, stanza 6)—and surrounded himself with natural philosophers. These included most prominently a translator of Ptolemy, Michael Scot, who spoke of "'the new astrology' as proudly as writers today now speak of the new chemistry or the new history."[77]

The Magi of Benediktbeuern represent, in this light, more than the adherents of a long dead religion driven to nonplus by the discovery that discredited their faith in the heavens—though they are also that. They reflect as well the long persistence of a pagan curriculum whose compatibility with Christian theology had always been subject to debate and which, at this very moment, was having one of its periodic, contentious revivals.[78] We see evidence of the most recent rebirth throughout the *Carmina Burana*: the frontispiece invoking the supremacy of Fortuna, poems by Ovid, Juvenal, an ode in the voice of

---

74. From an anonymous treatise around 1175; Latin in Charles Homer Haskins, *Studies in the History of Mediaeval Science* (Cambridge, MA: Harvard University Press, 1924), 87.
75. NKGW II/6:123; English in Nietzsche, *Beyond Good and Evil: Prelude to a Philosophy of the Future*, trans. Walter Kaufmann (New York: Vintage, 1989), §200.
76. For the Hohenstaufens' defense of their Jewish subjects, see *Church, State, and Jew in the Middle Ages*, ed. Robert Chazan (New York: Behrman House, 1980), 118–22 (Frederick I), 124–26 (Frederick II).
77. Charles H. Haskins, "Science at the Court of the Emperor Frederick II," *American Historical Review* 27, no. 4 (1922): 669–94 at 684. The broad outlines of Haskins's portrait seem to me more or less in tact despite the critiques: see, e.g., David Abulafia, *Frederick II: A Medieval Emperor* (Hammondsworth, UK: Allen Lane/The Penguin Press, 1988), 256–58, 261–65.
78. See R. I. Moore, *The First European Revolution c. 970–1215* (Oxford: Blackwell, 2000); *Renaissance and Renewal in the Twelfth Century*, ed. Robert Louis Benson et al. (Cambridge, MA: Harvard Uni-

Epicurus, phrases suggestive of Lucretius (allegedly still lost).[79] Not long after the Magi exit, the Holy Family flees to Egypt, where the king and his court praise the "seven rivers" (CB 228.III.1.2) of the liberal arts flowing from the headwaters of philosophy, calling out by name Aristotle, Plato, Socrates, and Pythagoras. Missing from that list but arguably the unnamed star of the show is the Greco-Egyptian astronomer Ptolemy, whom the Middle Ages frequently mistook for one of his Macedonian namesakes and therefore depicted as the "king of Egypt." He was the progenitor of the astronomical model whose accuracy allowed monks to calculate nocturnal hours and feast days.[80]

The star of Bethlehem in the Nativity play of the *Carmina Burana* converts the Magi to a supposedly more enlightened religion at the very moment when Christians were rediscovering how much more pagan astronomers had known about the heavens before the empire was Christianized and this knowledge was lost. Any progress represented by Christ, however novel, therefore has to figure as the extension or fulfillment of secular science—the little-known secret toward which learned pagans had always been striving, the truth that their texts and traditions, if correctly interpreted, had all along foretold. "How right the book of Wisdom is to find fault with the investigators of this world [*inquisitores huius saeculi*]," exclaims Augustine. "For if they were capable, it says, of so much that they could appraise and weigh up the world [*aestimare saeculum*], how is it that they did not all the more easily find its Lord? [Ws 13:9]."[81] The Magi were the very first of those devoted to the *saeculum* to have the scales drop from their eyes. They were consequently available in Nativity plays to confirm Christianity's superiority to a non-Christian legacy whose blessing Christians craved and whose learning they cultivated whenever possible.

---

versity Press, 1991); *Rebirth, Reform, and Resilience: Universities in Transition, 1300–1700*, ed. James M. Kittelson and Pamela J. Transue (Columbus: Ohio State University Press, 1984); R. W. Southern, *Medieval Humanism and Other Studies* (Oxford: Blackwell, 1970); Brian Stock, *Myth and Science in the Twelfth Century: A Study of Bernard Silvester* (Princeton, NJ: Princeton University Press, 1972); dated but still useful is Charles Homer Haskins, *The Renaissance of the Twelfth Century* (Cambridge, MA: Harvard University Press, 1927), esp. on astronomy.

79. See *Love Lyrics from the Carmina Burana*, ed. and trans. P. G. Walsh (Chapel Hill: University of North Carolina Press, 1993), xxviii, 18, 27.

80. Isidore, *Etym.* 3.26.1: "Ptolemy, king of Alexandria"; Hugo von Sankt Viktor, *Didascalicon* 3.2, in *Didascalicon de studio legendi: Studienbuch*, trans. Thilo Offergeld (Freiburg: Herder, 1997), 220: "Ptolemy, king of Egypt, revived astronomy"; these and others are discussed by Charles Burnett, "Images of Ancient Egypt in the Latin Middle Ages," in *The Wisdom of Egypt: Changing Visions Through the Ages*, ed. Peter Ucko and Timothy Champion (London: UCL Press, 2003), 65–99, esp. 86–87; Jutta Tezmen-Siegel, *Die Darstellungen der septem artes liberales in der Bildenden Kunst als Rezeption der Lehrplangeschichte* (Munich: Tuduv-Verlagsgesellschaft, 1985), 113, 274n69, plates 13, 38, 55.

81. *De Genesi ad litteram* 5.16.34 (CSEL 28.1:160; WSA I/13:293). Augustine quotes the same passage from Wisdom in *Conf.* 5.3; *Ep.* 55.4.7; *De doct. Christ.* 2.21; *Serm.* 68.1; *De diversis quest.* 45 (*adversus mathematicos*); *De anima* 4.5.

Medieval Optics and the Annunciation In Vitro

Twelfth-century clerics frequently defended the Annunciation against the implication that God had deflowered or even raped Mary by claiming to see in the moment of insemination something as gentle as sunlight passing through a window. They took inspiration from a late fifth- or sixth-century sermon, attributed at the time to Augustine, that tried to counter the objections of "an unbelieving Jew [*Judaeus incredulus*]" and of a Manichean who were appalled at the prospect of sexual congress between God and a mortal female, thus convinced that the Virgin Birth was a degrading "fantasy [*phantasma*]."[82] The counterargument met these unbelievers on their own turf in the secular world of sense perception, making a case for belief by comparison: "Sunlight penetrates a window pane [*Solis radius specular penetrat*]," preaches Pseudo-Augustine. "The beam does not therefore break the glass: is it possible that the entrance—or exit—of the godhead defiled the integrity of the Virgin?"[83] Twelfth-century readers found several reasons to linger over this analogy. Most importantly, it suggested that proclamations of the gospel could in some cases be confirmed by physics; if "God is light" (1 Jn 1:15), then his interactions with humans should involve not only spiritual enlightenment but the characteristics of solar radiation (*solis radius*). Those characteristics could then be shown to interact with an optical instrument that was central to Christian worship, so as to allay doubts about the legitimacy of Jesus. Already by the fifth century, a believer wanting to defend the truth and decency of the Annunciation against infidel critics could point to any number of churches where the windows had been not only glazed but pigmented.[84] Penetration, acceptance, love—none of this has to be ugly, carnal, or difficult. "Glass is not violated [*violatur*] by the sun," explains an anonymous author writing around 1200: "nor is the Virgin deflowered while she is blessed with progeny."[85] When you gaze at a depiction of the Virgin in a windowpane, the medium is the message.

We have no evidence before the ninth century that pigmented glass was shaped into iconic figurations of any kind, much less of the Annunciation,

---

82. Ps-Augustine, *Serm.* 245.2 (PL 39:2197); sometimes subtitled *De mysterio Trinitatis et Incarnationis*, the sermon survives in manuscripts as early as the eighth century but is probably a couple of centuries older according to H. Barré, "Le Sermon 'Exhortatur' est-il de Saint Ildefonse?" *Revue Bénédictine* 67 (1957): 10–33, esp. 18–19; further bibliography in J. Machielsen, *Clavis patristica pseudepigraphorum medii aevi* (Turnhout: Brepols, 1990), 1:210 (item 1030).
83. Ps-Augustine, *Serm.* 245.4 (PL 39:2197).
84. Francesca Dell'Acqua, "Early History of Stained Glass," in *Investigations in Medieval Stained Glass: Materials, Methods, and Expressions*, ed. Elizabeth Carson Pastan and Brigitte Kurmann-Schwarz (Leiden: Brill, 2019), 23–35.
85. *Pictor in Carmine: Ein Handbuch der Typologie aus der Zeit um 1200: Nach MS 300 des Corpus Christi College in Cambridge*, ed. Karl-August Wirth (Berlin: Gebr. Mann, 2006), 136.

but the growing importance of glazing in connection to Marian devotion is attested as early as Venantius Fortunatus (c. 530–600), a successful poet and courtier largely based in Gaul, where his writing found an enthusiastic audience among local elites.[86] The church, he writes, "has imitated Mary—she enclosed the light in her womb, it enclosed the day."[87] He may have been thinking of burning candles in this instance, but other poems suggest the type of building that "captures light beams through eye-shaped glass windows and, by the artisan's hand [*artificisque manu*], has enclosed the day in its fortress."[88] As glazing became more and more widespread, comparisons between it and the Virgin Birth multiplied.[89] Five windows from the third quarter of the twelfth century that were central to a Marian devotional program at the Arnsteiner Abbey—and that include an exceptional homage to the *artificis manum* in depicting the glazier, Gerlach, as he inscribes his name on the glass—show multiple parallels with a German prayer to Mary from the same period that was preserved in the abbey's library.[90] This so-called *Arsteiner Mariengebet* explicitly celebrates the glazier's achievement as a way of combating unbelief in the Virgin Birth:

Sint du daz kint gebære,	When you bore the child,
bit alle du wære	you were in all ways
luter unde reine	clear and pure
van mannes gemeine.	from the company of men.
Swenen so daz dunket unmugelich,	Whoever thinks this is impossible,
der merke daz glas, daz dir is gelig:	should consider the glass which is similar to you:

---

86. Michael Roberts, *The Humblest Sparrow: The Poetry of Venantius Fortunatus* (Ann Arbor: University of Michigan Press, 2009), 6.
87. Venance Fortunat, *Poèmes*, ed. and trans. Marc Reydellet (Paris: Les Belles Lettres, 1994), 1:35–36 (1.15.57–58).
88. Venance Fortunat 2.10.13–14, ed. Reydellet, 1:67; cf. 3.7.47 (p. 97).
89. Herbert L. Kessler, "'Consider the Glass, It Can Teach You': The Medium's Lesson," in *Investigations in Medieval Stained Glass*, ed. Pastan and Kurmann-Schwarz, 143–57, esp. 146; Brigitte Kurmann-Schwarz, "'Fenestre vitree [. . .] significant Sacram Scripturam': Zur Medialität mittelalterlicher Glasmalerei des 12. und 13. Jahrhunderts," in *Glasmalerei im Kontext: Bildprogramme und Raumfunktionen: Akten des XXII. Internationalen Colloquiums des Corpus Vitrearum, Nürnberg, 29. August-1. September 2004* (Nürnberg: Germanisches Nationalmuseum, 2005), 61–73.
90. Bruno Krings, *Das Prämonstratenserstift Arnstein a.d. Lahn im Mittelalter (1139–1527)* (Wiesbaden: Selbstverlag der Historischen Kommission für Nassau, 1990), 228–29 and 474–84 (on Gerlach's windows and the *Mariengebet*), 202–203 (on the fate of the library at the time of the monastery's secularization in 1803). See also Jeffrey Hamburger, "The Hand of God and the Hand of the Scribe: Craft and Collaboration at Arnstein," in *Die Bibliothek des Mittelalters als dynamischer Prozess*, ed. Michael Embach et al. (Wiesbaden: Reichert, 2012), 53–80, esp. 61.

| daz sunnen liet schinet durg mittlen daz glas, | the sunlight shines directly through the glass, |
| iz is alinc unde luter sint, als iz e des was. | it is intact and clear as it was before.[91] |

The panes in which Gerlach depicted the Annunciation have been lost but would have shown how glass could be "similar to" Mary in a double sense: both by depicting her and by remaining unbroken while shot through with light. Evidently such depictions were needed as evidence in favor of belief because Christians had to live with the widespread impression that the Virgin Birth was clearly "impossible." The prayer could have claimed that this impossibility demonstrates the absolute power of God to suspend the laws of nature; instead, it secularizes the divinity, together with the founding miracle of Christianity. Mary's insemination is here explained with reference to reason, empirical evidence, and physical causation.

There was some concern that relying on sunlight and glass as a bulwark against unbelief conceded too much to skeptics. Just as liturgical hymns promised to raise humanity to the celestial harmonic sphere but perpetually risked devolving into theater music (as we saw in the previous chapter), so too, some twelfth-century clerics suspected, the veneration of celestial light as captured in glass risked idolizing handmade, visual artifacts—not to mention transforming Marian devotion into a kind of sun worship. The same Cistercians who excluded statuary from the cloister at Cluny, for example, also forbade the use of stained glass, for reasons expounded by Bernard of Clairvaux: "There is here (in contemplation), as I think, no need or use for material, sense-transmitted images of Christ's flesh or cross or any other representations which belong to the weakness of His mortality."[92] However useful for instructing the unlearned and doubtful, glass remained for the Cistercians intractably rooted in carnal finitude, as demonstrated to them by scripture. When Jesus rebuked the Pharisees for ritually cleaning their plates and chalices (but not their spirits), the Gloss explains that "chalice" here refers to a "glass vase" and signifies "the fragility of the human body."[93]

---

91. *Kleinere deutsche Gedichte des 11. und 12. Jahrhunderts*, ed. Albert Waag and Werner Schröder (Tübingen: M. Niemeyer, 1972), 173; translation in Kessler, "Consider the Glass," 146 (modified).
92. Serm. 45 on the Song of Songs, Sect. IV, para. 6; *S. Bernardi opera*, ed. Jean Leclercq (Rome: Editions Cistercienses, 1958), 2:53; trans. in *St. Bernard's Sermons on the Canticle of Canticles* (Dublin: Browne & Nolan, 1920), 2:17; quoted by Meredith Lillich, *Studies in Medieval Stained Glass and Monasticism* (London: Pindar Press, 2001), 312.
93. Gloss on Lk 11:39 in *Biblia Latina cum Glossa Ordinaria: Facsimile Reprint of the Editio Princeps Adolph Rusch of Strassburg 1480/81*, ed. Karlfried Froehlich and Margaret T. Gibson (Turnhout:

Hence the deeper meaning behind Christ's prayer that his Father might "take away this cup from me" (Mk 14:36, AV)—the cup, made of glass, signified the breaking of his body in death.[94] Indeed the brittleness of glass largely explains why its use as a material for the chalice and paten in the Mass was repeatedly forbidden—perhaps not incidentally in a canon that directly precedes a ban on women approaching the altar or touching the chalice on account of the same "fragility."[95] (This prohibition effectively ruled out the ordination of women.) When virgins are compared directly to glass, it's usually to point out how easily they are entered and broken: "glass is shattered by a stone; a virgin joined to a man will not remain innocent."[96] The medieval ban on glass for use in the Mass was despite its ubiquity in the earliest ceremonies and notwithstanding that the Holy Grail had itself probably been a glass drinking vessel. Alongside the tendency to fracture, it was the cheap commonness of glass that made it unsuitable as a receptacle for Christ's blood in the Middle Ages. Excavations of medieval sites abound in fragments of the glass containers used by apothecaries and alchemists as urinals.[97] Wine-filled glass vessels held pride of place in every barroom bacchanalia and were therefore excluded from the Eucharist: "How happy is the life of a lush," sings an unknown songster of the *Carmina Burana*, "while the wine shimmers in a glass of ruddy hue [*in vitro subrubei coloris*]" (CB 197.3.1, 4). Glass was an ambiguous symbol of chastity, in short, because it was also a sign of material impermanence, carnal indulgence, and earthly vicissitude more generally. The goddess who presides over the frontispiece of the *Carmina Burana* (figure 1) is asked in one poem, "Why do you fail, glassy Fortuna? [*Fortuna vitrea*]" (CB 6*.3.5), following the ancient adage that "Fortuna is made of glass; just when she glitters, she breaks."[98] She is fickle, even slutty in her tastes. Or as Ovid puts it in a poem that also appears in the manuscript, "Fortuna gives good but not durable gifts" (CB 18.3.1).

Christians who invoked the metaphor of sunlight passing through glass to defend the miracle of the Virgin Birth were employing a method outlined by

---

Brepols, 1992), 4:183. Cf. Augustine, *Serm.* 17.7 (PL 38:128/WSA III/1:370): "Aren't we all more fragile than if we were made of glass?"

94. Gloss on Tob 6:3 (quoting Mk 14:36), in *Biblia Latina cum Glossa Ordinaria*, 2:336.

95. *Concilia Galliae*, c. 18 (CCSL 148a:101); *Eutychiani Papae Exhortatio ad presbyteros* (PL 5:165B); see also *Sacrorum conciliorum nova, et amplissima collectio*, ed. Joannes Dominicus Mansi (Venice, 1769), 14:891.

96. Evagrius, *Sententiae* 2 (PL 20:1187D); quoted and attributed to Augustine by Symphosius Amalarius, *Forma institutionis canonicorum et sanctimonialium*, bk. 2 (PL 105:937D).

97. Ruth Hurst Vose, "From the Dark Ages to the Fall of Constantinople," in *The History of Glass*, ed. Dan Klein and Ward Lloyd (London: Orbis, 1984), 39–66, esp. 47; cf. the Canon's Yeoman's Tale 791–94, in *The Riverside Chaucer*, ed. Larry Benson, 3rd ed. (Boston: Houghton Mifflin, 1987), 273.

98. Publilius Syrus, *Sententiae* 219 (LCL *Minor Latin Poets*): "*Fortuna vitrea est: tum cum splendet frangitur.*"

Figure 1. München, Bayerische Staatsbibliothek, Clm 4660

Augustine. Secular phenomena, though lacking in divinity of any kind, are nonetheless useful in thinking through theological doctrine by way of *"spiritualium similitudines"* (*Ep.* 55.8.15 [CCSL 31:246; WSA II/1:223]). Metaphor allows a person to move from what can be known by sense perception to the imperceptible realities apprehensible only by the mind through mere likeness. One sees the fullness of the godhead through a glass, darkly. The usefulness of such comparisons is their ability to suggest that God's miracles—despite surpassing human understanding—are nonetheless worthy of belief by a reasonable person because they are compatible to a degree with everyday observation: "Do you not see that a ray of the sun shines through the medium of glass," a Christian asks an incredulous Jew in a dialogue from the second quarter of the twelfth century, "and yet the glass remains wholly intact?"[99] Such questions probably reflect contemporary debates between learned clerics and a variety of unbelievers (Jews, Muslims, heretics), but they also provide a

---

99. Ps-William of Champeaux, *Dialogus inter Christianum et Iudeum de fide catholica* (PL 163:1055A).

venue for doubts that otherwise orthodox Christians were exploring amongst themselves with no little vigor as part of their training in dialectics. If, as Margaret Schlauch writes, "the danger in the composition of such dialogues was that the very zeal to convert an enemy might be transformed into an opposite attitude—one perilously hospitable to his ideas," then it must have offered an even more thrilling, dangerous freedom to impersonate the infidel in church, surrounded by stained glass, and so lend him a platform to test the miracle of the Virgin Birth by means of a theatrical experiment.[100]

One of the great challenges of trying to picture Augustine's debate with Archisynagogus in the Nativity play of the *Carmina Burana* is having to fathom what Madeline Caviness calls "the performative aspects of glass in situ in Christian buildings."[101] Was Augustine's final plea for the Virgin Birth sung in front of a stained-glass depiction of the Annunciation? Or perhaps a rendering of *Ecclesia* in opposition to *Synagogus*?[102] Either way, we're facing a *mise en abyme* of contrived representations asking an audience to believe—on the basis of light's interaction with a manufactured artifact—that the Virgin Birth is neither an idolatrous fabrication nor subject to the ordinary course of nature. Here is Augustine's rejoinder to Archisynagogus's doubts:

> Just as a sun ray enters solid glass,
> And an accessible passageway serves it purely,
> Even so into the womb of the virgin the son of the father on high
> will slide and yet without harm.
>
> Ut specular solidum solis intrat radius
> et sincere transitus servit ei pervius,
> sic in aulam virginis summi patris filius
> lapsum quidem faciet, et tamen innoxius.
>
> (CB 227.102–5)

The harm to be avoided goes two ways: none to Mary's hymen, none to the godhead, despite God's "lapse" into the evanescent world of birth and death through the womb of a virgin. Yet the fact that Augustine appeals to the world of *aisthēsis* for validation reduces the godhead to a process of verification and rationalization that could as easily reopen as close debate on any

---

100. Margaret Schlauch, "The Allegory of Church and Synagogue," *Speculum* 14, no. 4 (1939): 448–64 at 464.
101. Madeline H. Caviness, "Performative Interaction of Liturgy and Light through the Medium of Painted Glass," in Pastan and Brigitte Kurmann-Schwarz, *Investigations in Medieval Stained Glass*, 175–88 at 176.
102. Emile Mâle, *L'art religieux du XIIe siècle en France*, 7th ed. (Paris: A. Colin, 1966), 166; Schlauch, "Allegory of Church and Synagogue," 455.

given miracle.[103] His exchange with Archisynagogus reflects a culture accustomed to subjecting preternatural phenomena to the explanatory power of reason in combination with empirical "observation" (*experimentum*)—as when Roger Bacon describes the unusual optical effects of "a solar ray falling through a window . . . [and] penetrating [*penetrantes*] strongly-colored glass."[104] This type of inquiry risks idolizing the *saeculum* since it grants to sunlight the reverent attention traditionally reserved for unseen realities, even as it places divine intervention within the limits of natural law. The tendency is clearly toward a secular mode of evaluation at the expense of divine mysteries. If the sun gives birth to life in the world of plants, how hard can it have been for God to do the same thing to Mary, since he is the true light?

It is perhaps easy from our current perspective to feel that the Christians who made comparisons between sunlight and the Virgin Birth "were aided," as Anna Sapir Abulafia writes, "by the severe limitations of their scientific knowledge."[105] But we should not let those limitations blind us to everything that modern optics and astronomy owe to the ancient—especially Neoplatonic—physics of light when combined with the medieval culture of glazing and grinding crystals for the express purpose of magnification. Light in the physical world is supposed to let us perceive the unchanging laws that structure our finite, mutable, epiphenomenal experience.[106] In the Middle Ages, those laws were expressed through geometry, mathematical equations, theory, and "ideas"—a term whose root in visuality (cognate with v*ideo*) rests on the ancient conviction that true intellectual understanding might begin with the eyes but requires a movement beyond bodily perception, through the corrective lens of reason, to achieve genuine insight into the ultimate and, we like to say, objective reality.[107] The eye requires both the help of reason (*logos*) and that of technological instruments (*techne*) to bring what it sees into focus. Arguably medieval Catholics put their faith, no less than we do, in what Latour calls "factish gods"—that

---

103. See Steven Justice, "Did the Middle Ages Believe in Their Miracles?" *Representations* 103, no. 1 (2008): 1–29.
104. *Roger Bacon's Philosophy of Nature: A Critical Edition, with English Translation, Introduction, and Notes, of "De multiplicatione specierum" and "De speculis comburentibus,"* ed. and trans. David C. Lindberg (Oxford: Clarendon, 1983), 8–11.
105. Anna Sapir Abulafia, *Christians and Jews in the Twelfth-Century Renaissance* (London: Routledge, 1995), 82–83.
106. David C. Lindberg, "The Genesis of Kepler's Theory of Light: Light Metaphysics from Plotinus to Kepler," *Osiris* 2 (1986): 4–42. Cf. Bacon, *Roger Bacon's Philosophy of Nature*, ed. and trans. Lindberg, xxxv–liii.
107. Rudolf Bultmann, "Zur Geschichte der Lichtsymbolik im Altertum," *Philologus* 97 (1948): 1–36, esp. n3.

is, they replaced deluded peoples' handmade fetishes and idols with facts that were generated by handmade, scientific instruments: monochords, astrolabes, or, in this case, the glazed church windows that were a precursor to the telescopic lens.[108]

The development of medieval lenses was by and large achieved through practical, artisanal means rather than a theoretical understanding of the physics of light, but the theoretical understanding began to take off in the middle of the ninth century through the recovery of Ptolemy's *Optics* and the reception of Hasan Ibn al-Haytham (c. 945–c. 1040)—known to Latin readers as Alhacen.[109] His treatise on "burning mirrors," though lost to us, was familiar to Robert Grosseteste and Roger Bacon, both of whom had already witnessed firsthand the effects of light passing through rock crystal and curved glass. As a consequence they were able to break new ground in the Latin description of reflection, refraction, and magnification: "We can so shape transparent substances," writes Bacon, "and so arrange them relative to the eye and objects that the rays will be refracted and deflected in whatever direction we wish, and thus we will see them near or far, under whatever angle we choose. Thus from an incredible distance we would be able to read the smallest letters and count particles of dust and sand."[110] Passages like this one—together with Bacon's investment in testing his hypotheses against observed experience and his interest in sharpening those observations *per instrumenta*—have made him a pivotal and often forward-looking figure in the history of science, though they are nonetheless fully a product of their time, if for no other reason than that his insights were frequently born of pondering sunlight's passage through stained glass and seeing there a frenzied, involuntary fecundity.[111] "This species," writes Bacon—using his preferred, technical term for solar rays—"produces every action in the world, for it acts on sense, on the intellect, and on all matter of the world for the

---

108. Bruno Latour, *On the Modern Cult of the Factish Gods*, trans. Catherine Porter and Heather MacLean (Durham, NC: Duke University Press, 2010), esp. 1–66.
109. A. Mark Smith, "Alhacen's Theory of Visual Perception: A Critical Edition, with English Translation and Commentary, of the First Three Books of Alhacen's 'De aspectibus,' the Medieval Latin Version of Ibn al-Haytham's 'Kitāb al-Manāẓir': Volume One," *Transactions of the American Philosophical Society*, 91, no. 4 (2001): 1–337.
110. *Roger Bacon and the Origins of "Perspectiva" in the Middle Ages: A Critical Edition and English Translation of Bacon's "Perspectiva" with Introduction and Notes*, ed. and trans. David C. Lindberg (Oxford: Clarendon, 1996), 333–35; cf. xlv and xciii–xciv.
111. *Opus majus*, ed. Bridges, 1:lxxiii, 109.

generation of things."[112] In the short term Bacon's writings seem to have spurred more innovations in iconography than in technology: Fra Lippo Lippi, in his London Annunciation (c. 1455), for example, appears to take Bacon's theory as "an ideal model for demonstrating explicitly yet without breach of decorum how the Holy Spirit 'came upon' Mary."[113] Just as sunlight causes the earth to blossom in springtime, so too did the Holy Spirit work on the womb of Mary.

The telescope turns out to be like many of the conventional markers of the unbridgeable gulf between modernity and the Middle Ages. Once you pry into its first invention, you find antecedents. No sooner had the novel instrument been announced to great fanfare in 1608 than contradictory accounts began to emerge that it had already been in existence; thus what Eileen Reeves calls the "senescence" of the telescope—upon arrival, it was already old news.[114] We know from Aristotle, Pliny, Strabo, and Ptolemy that the ancients used wells, chimneys, and sighting tubes to make the stars more readily visible, even in daylight: "The man who shades his eye with his hand or looks through a tube [δι' αὐλοῦ]," writes Aristotle, "will not distinguish any more or any less the differences of colors, but he will see farther."[115] "For when it proceeds from narrow places," explains Ptolemy—in a passage quoted by Roger Bacon—"sight is extended and elongated."[116] Pope Sylvester II (c. 946–1003) describes an armillary sphere into which he placed a tube (*fistulam*) so that, by sighting the pole star, he could orient the globe (PL 139:155). In fact we have more than one depiction of these so-called polar tubes. The earliest appears around the year 1000 and shows Pacificus of Verona, archdeacon from 803 to 844, gazing at the sky through a tube held in place against a stone window by a column (figure 2); a thirteenth-century manuscript, housed in the Scheyern Abbey until its secularization in 1803,

---

112. *Opus majus*, ed. Bridges, 1:111; trans. Burke, 1:130 (modified).
113. Samuel Y. Edgerton, Jr., *The Heritage of Giotto's Geometry: Art and Science on the Eve of the Scientific Revolution* (Ithaca, NY: Cornell University Press, 1991), 94.
114. Eileen Adair Reeves, *Galileo's Glassworks: The Telescope and the Mirror* (Cambridge, MA: Harvard University Press, 2008), 6. See also Robert Temple, *The Crystal Sun: Rediscovering a Lost Technology of the Ancient World* (London: Century, 2000): "It has always been obvious from the surviving fragments of Democritus . . . that rudimentary telescopes must have been available in antiquity" (185); Rolf Willach, "The Long Route to the Invention of the Telescope," *Transactions of the American Philosophical Society*, 98, no. 5 (2008): i–116.
115. Aristotle, *Generation of Animals* 5.1 (780b) (LCL). Cf. Pliny, *Natural History* 2.11 (LCL); Strabo, *Geogr.* 3.1.5 in *Strabonis Geographica: graece cum versione refecta*, ed. Karl F. Müller (Paris: Didot, 1853), 1:114 (for text) and 2:951 (for the proposed emendation, adopted by the Loeb, changing the manuscript's "tubes" (αὐλῶν) to "lenses" (ὑάλων).
116. Lindberg, *Roger Bacon and the Origins of "Perspectiva,"* 163.

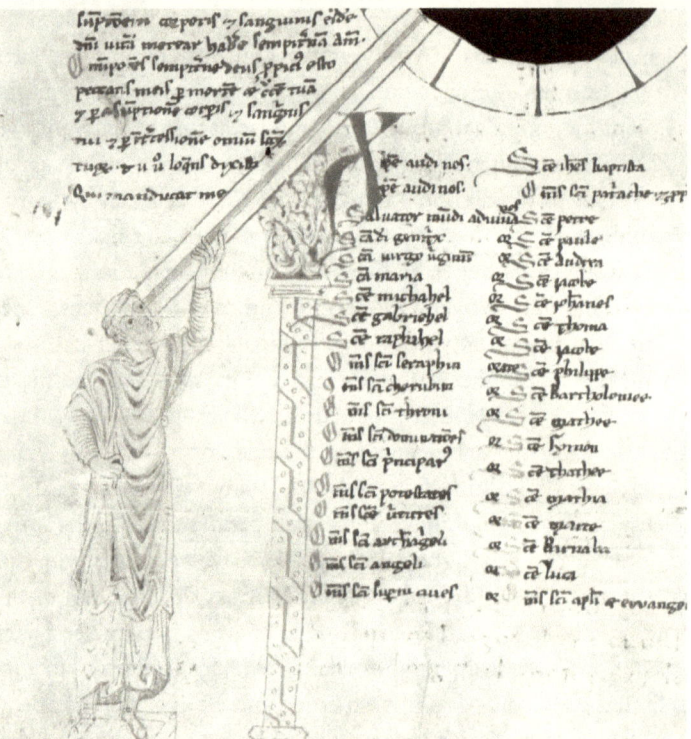

FIGURE 2. St. Gallen, Stiftsbibliothek, Cod. Sang. 18: Composite manuscript, astronomical clock of Pacificus of Verona.

has Astronomy, among the Seven Liberal Arts, seated next to a figure gazing at the stars through a telescopic tube that Robert Eisler thinks may have been constructed from parchment and glue (figure 3).[117]

Readily downplayed in histories of the telescope due to the assumed absence of lenses, these early sighting tubes would seem to challenge one of the more highly prized ways of periodizing modernity.[118] "Such pictures must give rise to the suspicion," writes Derek J. Price, "that the instrument in question is actually some sort of telescope with lenses. Although the evidence is weak it cannot be summarily discarded merely because of the great

---

[117]. Robert Eisler, "The Polar Sighting Tube," *Archives internationales d'histoire des sciences* 2, no. 6 (1949): 312–32, esp. 319.
[118]. See e.g. Blumenberg, *Genesis of the Copernican World*, 644–51.

FIGURE 3. München, Bayerische Staatsbibliothek, Clm 17405

improbability of the invention having been made so early."[119] Since he wrote those words even more evidence has come to light: for example, the discovery of a convex crystal lens ground into "an almost perfect elliptical shape" in the eleventh century for unknown purposes.[120] "Would it be totally foolhardy, then," asks Vincent Ilardi, "to speculate that one or two convex lenses might have been inserted into the sighting tubes to provide greater magnification, the latter combination anticipating the telescope later described by Kepler?"[121] Such a discovery would not have required any advanced understanding of optical theory—only great manufacturing skill, tremendous patience with the time-worn, artisanal practice of trial and error, and an almost worshipful devotion to sun- and starlight.

---

119. Derek J. Price, "Precision Instruments to 1500," in *A History of Technology*, ed. C. Singer et al., vol. 3: *From the Renaissance to the Industrial Revolution c. 1500–c. 1750* (Oxford: Clarendon, 1957), 593.
120. O. Schmidt, K.-H. Wilms, and B. Lingelbach, "The Visby Lenses," *Optometry and Vision Science* 76, no. 9 (1999): 624–30 at 629.
121. Vincent Ilardi, *Renaissance Vision from Spectacles to Telescopes* (Philadelphia, PA: American Philosophical Society, 2007), 211.

We know that some of the consumers of such products were quite learned in optical theory. The earliest translator of Copernicus in England, Thomas Digges, claimed that his father Leonard had come across "one old written book of the same Bacon's experiments" and managed to devise an optical device made from "perspective glasses."[122] These allowed him to see distant objects up close, such that he could explore "every particularity in the country round about, wheresoever the sun beams might pierce" (ibid.). Wherever sunlight penetrates, so too may the lens. Digges's claims on behalf of his father, however overblown, may well describe a successful attempt at a makeshift telescope after reading Roger Bacon. And there is at any rate no question that the younger Digges understood the value of optical instruments (astrolabe, cross-staff, lenses) when combined with arithmetic and geometry—the so-called wings, or *alae*, of mathematics referred to in the title of his treatise on the nova of 1572, which follows the hoary tradition of using astronomy to "ascend to the most distant theaters of the heavens."[123] What he saw there was the same thing people had been seeing for centuries, Christmas after Christmas, in the theater of the church: a new star, which shattered any possibility of the heavens' immutability—or any possibility, according to Tycho Brahe, of the world's eternity. Here was an augury that confirmed the earlier prophecy of the Sybil: "The heavens shall be leveled with the seas, and after these things come to pass, there shall be continual night, destruction, ruin, condemnation and eternal darkness."[124] The nova of 1572 was, in short, a reiteration of the gospel announced by the nova 1,572 years earlier: "Amongst so many troubles and commencements of greater sorrows, a new star appeared in heaven as great as the day star," Jean Hainault wrote of 1572 nova. "It was thought to be like the star which appeared to the wise men which came from the East, to worship Jesus Christ in Bethlehem, straight

---

122. Facsimile reprint in Leonard Digges, *Stratioticos: London 1579* (Amsterdam: Theatrum Orbis Terrarum Ltd. & Da Capo Press, 1968), 189–90; discussed with further citations in A. G. Molland, "Roger Bacon as Magician," *Traditio* 30 (1974): 445–60, esp. 457.
123. Thomas Digges, *Alæ seu scalæ mathematicæ quibus visibilium remotissima cœlorum theatra conscendi, & planetarum omnium itinera nouis & inauditis methodis explorari* [etc.] (London, 1573). See Stephen Pumfrey, "'Your Astronomers and Ours Differ Exceedingly': The Controversy over the 'New Star' of 1572 in the Light of a Newly Discovered Text by Thomas Digges," *British Journal for the History of Science* 44, no. 1 (2011): 29–60, esp. 45–46 and those he cites. Further discussion of Leonard and Thomas Digges in Crane, *Losing Touch with Nature*, 68–81.
124. Tycho Brahe, *Learned: Tico Brahæ his astronomicall coniectur of the new and much admired [star] which appeared in the year 1572* (London, 1632), 23.

after his birth."[125] When Kepler considered the nova of 1604, as we'll see in the next chapter, he too linked it to the star of Bethlehem; yet he all but ruled out the possibility that God had miraculously suspended the laws of physics at the moment of Christ's birth. Instead, he chose to interpret new stars throughout history as purely natural phenomena occurring at regular intervals. The tendency of medieval scholasticism to secularize miracles was at that point fully realized.

The Secularization of Benediktbeuern Abbey

The manuscript we now call the *Carmina Burana* came to the Munich *Hof- und Zentralbibliotek* from the Benediktbeuern Abbey in 1803, along with half a million other texts from monasteries secularized at the same time as part of a political settlement between France and Bavaria. Virtually overnight the influx created the preeminent research library of the German-speaking world and an inspiration for the burgeoning field of medieval studies: "Without the present catastrophe," writes Johann Christoph von Aretin—leader of the commission tasked with stripping the monastic libraries—"their treasures would never have become common property."[126] To keep the public apprised of his discoveries in real time, Aretin sent to the printer immediately upon completion open letters detailing his experience of the monasteries' final days, and he appended to each letter an annotated bibliographical entry for the most promising specimens. The resulting documentation paints the portrait of an exacting bibliophile and unabashed son of the radical Enlightenment who cannot quite square his contempt for "the frightful ignorance" of monastic librarians with his love for the texts that they kept from ruin (*Briefe* 171). He means to impose a secular mode of valuation on the last remaining vestiges of the Middle Ages but repeatedly discovers, to his great consternation, that secular modes of valuation had been operative there already for centuries. At various moments an ironic, half-joking self-awareness seems to seize him, as he dimly intuits that his mission to the monasteries merely

---

125. [Jean de Hainault], *The estate of the church, with the discourse of times, from the Apostles vntill this present* [etc.], trans. Simon Patrike (London, 1602), 609.
126. Johann Christoph von Aretin, *Briefe über meine literarische Geschäftsreise in die baierischen Abteyen*, ed. Wolf Bachmann (Munich: Langen Müller, 1971), 65. All further citations of Aretin's letters are to this edition. See also Dieter Kudorfer, "Die Säkularisation und das Bibliothekswesen—Traditionsbruch und Neuanfang für die Wissenschaft," in *Lebendiges Büchererbe: Säkularisation, Mediatisierung und die Bayerische Staatsbibliothek—Eine Ausstellung der Bayerischen Staatsbibliothek, München, 7. November 2003–30. Januar 2004* (Munich: Bayerische Staatsbibliothek, 2003), 9–20.

forces the latest orthodoxy onto monks who had had more than a millennium to practice evading unwanted oversight.

On April 12th at the Tegernsee Abbey, for example, Aretin learns from the local commissioner that the monks there are "extremely unruly and deceitful" (*Briefe* 59). It does not take him long to determine that the most valuable books catalogued by earlier visiting scholars have gone missing. When the Pater Bibliothecarius appears for questioning, he tries to blame the omissions on a prior rummaging by French soldiers. "But when one pressed him and let drop a few words about a spiritual correctional facility for recalcitrant clerics," Aretin comments, "he remarked that perhaps there could still be a few books in the Anthony chapel" (*Briefe* 60). Aretin had to overcome even steeper resistance at Benediktbeuern, the next stop on his tour three days later, largely on account of its abbot, Karl Klocker. Suspected at the time of preemptively selling the monastery's silver and gold, then hiding the money along with artworks, precious maps, and all the best books, Klocker appears also to have forged records to make the monastery's holdings appear less extensive than they were.[127] The subterfuge backfired. Aretin was inspired by it to root out valuable texts with a zeal that seemed, even to himself, almost fanatical. After finishing a successful interrogation, he jokingly admits, "we resumed our Inquisition" (*Briefe* 62).

It came as a shock to discover books that he thought the Inquisition had banned. He wanted to enlighten the Dark Ages, but found the Enlightenment, to his great surprise, already there—Helvetius, Montesquieu, Rousseau, all "in the original languages" (*Briefe* 54). At Benediktbeuern, Aretin was astounded by the monks' active exploration of contradictory, destabilizing viewpoints: "We were struck to come across here an actual repository of forbidden books that was mainly filled with Protestant theologians. We found other books banned by Rome unobstructed, and in the familiar *Monarchia Solipsorum* there was even inscribed the remark: this book is not prohibited" (*Briefe* 67). The *Monarchia* was in fact never placed on the *Index Librorum Prohibitorum*, despite its poisonous diatribes against the Jesuits and the ensuing trial of Melchior Inhofer for allegedly authoring it.[128] But other texts really were banned or had caused such scandal as to be confiscated

---

127. Wolfgang Jahn, "Die Aufhebung des Klosters Benediktbeuern," in *Glanz und Ende der alten Klöster: Säkularisation im bayerischen Oberland 1803*, ed. Josef Kirmeier and Manfred Treml (Munich: Süddeutscher, 1991), 70–77.
128. See Richard J. Blackwell, *Behind the Scenes at Galileo's Trial: Including the First English Translation of Melchior Inchofer's "Tractatus Syllepticus"* (Notre Dame, IN: University of Notre Dame Press, 2006), 44; J. Martinez de Bujanda, *Index Librorum Prohibitorum: 1600–1966* (Geneva: Librairie Droz, 2002).

upon printing—thus becoming rarities of equal interest to monks and secular appraisers (*Briefe* 171–72). Given the long history of *Büchercensur*—as yet unwritten, Aretin notes, before including among his reports some materials in support of its future composition—these texts should never have survived, and yet there they were, in a monastery of all places, ripe for the picking.[129] Like any number of his enlightened contemporaries, Aretin thought of his appropriations on behalf of the state as a public service. What the church publicly forbade but privately indulged, his secular age would publish without guilt. He is so taken by a volume from Benediktbeuern—described in his bibliography as "a collection of poetic and prose satires, mostly against the papal throne" (*Briefe* 171)—that he carries it with him en route to the next monastery. When he finds very few books there, he uses the opportunity to flesh out his report with a transcription from this "old manuscript of satires." Now known as CB 44, "The Gospel according to Mark of Silver Coins" is the first printed transcription from the *Carmina Burana*.

Aretin's derision for the monastic culture whose texts he values beyond measure serves a strategic if somewhat unconscious purpose. He needs to make a case for the monks' insufferable backwardness, hypocrisy, deceit, and ignorance to justify dispossessing them. Their medieval rule, he thinks, has instilled a censorious discipline while at the same time permitting too much. His secular mission, by comparison, would offer a corrective to the pitiless if ineffectual prohibitions of the Catholic Church by imposing more humane, enlightened, and less escapable limits. He and his fellow commissioners counted heavily on the institutional power of the Central Library to neutralize any wrongheaded, superstitious content that they shipped to Munich. By selecting for preservation only texts of value to higher learning, they relied on the library walls to curate a qualified readership. Scholars were to take the place of clerics, with the hope that scholars might put the books to better use. Aretin's success at ferreting out a vast number of texts, including many duplicates, eventually presented his superiors with a conundrum. Because the state library could archive just a fraction of what had been appropriated, they considered selling the rest, only to realize the market would disperse the seeds of medieval thinking more widely than ever before. Their fear of the past's persistence was so strong, in fact, as to be almost superstitious.

---

129. Johann Christoph Freiherr von Aretin, ed., *Beyträge zur Geschichte und Literatur, vorzüglich aus den Schätzen der pfalzbaierschen Centralbibliothek zu München*, vol. 1, part 3 (Munich, 1803), 49ff. This section of the *Beyträge* is not explicitly attributed but a contemporary reviewer assumed it was written by Aretin; see *Oberdeutsche Allgemeine Litteraturzeitung* 21 (February 18, 1806): 326.

Worrying that "the monkish spirit" would find a way to continue disseminating Christian false consciousness long after the monasteries were gone, they created an index of "pernicious literature" and had it pulped.[130] Their enlightenment, like every rational insight, cut through the darkness with a bonfire of vanities.

Once everything moveable at Benediktbeuern had been auctioned or destroyed, a disagreement erupted between the government officials who wanted to turn the buildings into a factory and the local *Aufhebungskommissar* who feared that anything less than their wholesale obliteration would leave an open invitation for the return of credulity. "So long as this hiding place of monkery stands," he warned his superiors, "its current fate resembles only a slumber, not complete death."[131] His anxiety turned out to be prescient, if not quite in the way he expected. When an industrialist purchased Benediktbeuern as the site for a glass foundry to be run by Joseph von Fraunhofer (the leading crafter of precision lenses, whose theodolites had helped Montgelas and Napoleon map Bavaria in advance of its secularization), monkery did indeed return, but it returned as the one thing the Enlightenment refused to see in religion—namely, science. Aretin was befuddled by the inexplicable "oddity" that the Dießen Abbey had an optical telegraph to communicate across Lake Ammer to neighboring villages (*Briefe* 94). At Aldersbach Abbey, he was astounded to find a colossal electrical generator (*Briefe* 142). Fraunhofer's new factory joined a time-honored Benedictine tradition of glasswork that had supplied the monks with windowpanes and reading lenses for centuries. The laborers given to maintaining Benediktbeuern's forests and fueling its kilns stayed on the premises when Fraunhofer took over, as did Pater Udalricus Riesch, the mapmaker with knowledge of the latest surveying technology, and Pater Josef Maria Wagner, who now taught optics, as he always had, to incoming apprentices.[132] Because Napoleon had blockaded imports from England—theretofore Europe's chief supplier of

---

130. Eberhard Weis, "Montgelas und die Säkularisation der bayerischen Klöster 1802/3," in *Die Säkularisation in Bayern 1803: Kulturbruch oder Modernisierung?*, ed. Alois Schmid (Munich: C. H. Beck, 2003), 152–255 at 187. See also Hermann Hauke, "Die Bedeutung der Säkularisation für die bayerischen Bibliotheken," in *Glanz und Ende*, 87–97; Rainer Braun and Joachim Wild et al., eds., *Bayern ohne Klöster? Die Säkularisation 1802/03 und die Folgen: Eine Ausstellung des Bayerischen Hauptstaatsarchivs: München, 22. Februar bis 18. Mai 2003* (Munich: Generaldirektion der Staatlichen Archive Bayerns, 2003), 122 on wholesale destruction; 128 for the sale of books as scrap.
131. Quoted in Jahn, "Die Aufhebung des Klosters Benediktbeuern," in *Glanz und Ende*, 77.
132. Myles W. Jackson, *Spectrum of Belief: Joseph von Fraunhofer and the Craft of Precision Optics* (Cambridge, MA: MIT Press, 2000), 78; Josef Hemmerle, ed., *Das Bistum Augsburg* (Berlin: de Gruyter, 1991), 1:572.

high-quality optical instruments—Fraunhofer's inventions became highly coveted. They would lead in time to some of the more significant discoveries in the sciences of geodesy and astronomy, including by mid-century the first glimpse of a new planet. There were conflicting ideas about what to call it, but after some initial bickering, the custom prevailed of naming heavenly bodies after the gods that science and Christ had together secularized, and it became Neptune.[133]

---

133. Jackson, *Spectrum of Belief*, 3.

CHAPTER 5

King Lear and the Copernican Revolution

The Disenchantment of the World

Scholarship on *King Lear* has often located in Edmund's critique of astrology a form of skepticism unknown to the Middle Ages. This "new rationality" is supposed to have collaborated with "the new philosophy," the recovery of ancient atomism, Machiavellianism, the Reformation, and the Copernican revolution, among other developments, to produce a play starkly at odds with "the relative medieval sense of security."[1] According to James Shapiro, by 1606 Shakespeare still on occasion "invokes the supernatural," but he can no longer depend on "the moral certitude" that had suffused "medieval England's now barely remembered mystery plays" and in fact withholds "the supernatural element" altogether from *Lear*, giving pride of place instead

---

1. John Danby, *Shakespeare's Doctrine of Nature: A Study of "King Lear"* (London: Faber and Faber, 1949), 42; Jonathan Bate, *Soul of the Age: A Biography of the Mind of William Shakespeare* (New York: Random House, 2009), 65; William R. Elton, *"King Lear" and the Gods* (San Marino, CA: Henry E. Huntington Library and Art Gallery, 1968), 9, respectively. See also Susan Thomas Crane, *Losing Touch with Nature: Literature and the New Science in Sixteenth-Century England* (Baltimore, MD: Johns Hopkins University Press, 2014), 123–47; François Laroque, "The 'Science' of Astrology in Shakespeare's Sonnets, *Romeo and Juliet* and *King Lear*," in *Spectacular Science, Technology and Superstition in the Age of Shakespeare*, ed. Sophie Chiari and Michaël Popelard (Edinburgh: Edinburgh University Press, 2017), 29–42; Gerard Passannante, *Catastrophizing: Materialism and the Making of Disaster* (Chicago: University of Chicago Press, 2019), esp. 114–133.

to Edmund's "debunking spirit."[2] When we read *Lear* today, writes Richard Strier, we should see the same thing William Elton saw—"a world that is truly and utterly 'disenchanted,'" one that lacks the "transcendental guarantee" of Christian theology and is therefore "thoroughly secular."[3]

Few positions could be more in line with conventional Christian thinking than to see life in polytheist Britain as a time "'without God in this world,' where no prophet, no preacher of God's word, [and] as it were, no human had dwelt."[4] Pagans living in the absence of scripture by definition had to "endure history," in the words of Joseph Wittreich, "without the promises of Revelation."[5] Nearly everything in *Lear* that has been taken for a premonition of modern secularity, according to Margreta de Grazia, is in fact an attempt to figure the world as it existed in the *milia inane* or "empty millennia" before Moses and the prophets.[6] Not least among the pleasures of watching the tragedy unfold must have been the opportunity it afforded audiences to savor everything they had gained in comparison with the grim state of striving that once reigned among infidels. "For the audience, auspiciously oriented in AD time, the possibility of redemption, in the future at least, is a given," writes de Grazia. "The tragedy assumes familiarity with the faith that it has put in abeyance." Indeed one's prospects for salvation "might be enhanced by the witnessing of what there is without them" (ibid., 174). The perverse Pietà of Cordelia in her father's arms, for example, is there to remind us, "and certainly Shakespeare's original audience," says R. V. Young, "of what the world of *King Lear* did not have."[7]

Any number of people in that audience—particularly among the learned at court—would have had reason to think that Abrahamic monotheism was responsible for the world's disenchantment. According to Raphael Holinshed, Leir's father, Baldud, was a wizard who "took such pleasure in artificial practices and magic that he taught this art throughout all his Realm," specifically the "sciences of Astronomy, and Nigromancy."[8] The king's enthusiasm

---

2. James Shapiro, *The Year of Lear: Shakespeare in 1606* (New York: Simon & Schuster, 2015), 183 (on *Macbeth*); 73, 82 (on *Lear*).
3. Richard Strier, "Shakespeare and the Skeptics," *Religion and Literature* 32, no. 2 (2000): 171–96 at 181, 189.
4. Augustine, *En. in Ps.* 28.8 (CCSL 38:170–1; WSA III/15:295), quoting Eph 2:12.
5. Joseph Wittreich, *"Image of that Horror": History, Prophecy, and Apocalypse in "King Lear"* (San Marino, CA: Henry E. Huntington Library, 1984), 120.
6. Margreta de Grazia, *Four Shakespearean Period Pieces* (Chicago: University of Chicago Press, 2021), 149.
7. R. V. Young, "Hope and Despair in *King Lear*: The Gospel and the Crisis of Natural Law," in *King Lear: New Critical Essays*, ed. Jeffrey Kahan (New York: Routledge, 2008), 253–77 at 273.
8. *Holinshed's Chronicles: England, Scotland and Ireland*, with a new introduction by Vernon F. Snow (New York: AMS, 1976; reprint of the 1807 edition), 1:446.

for stargazing and conjuring came to an end, however, when he tried "to fly in the air" and fell "upon the temple of Apollo," thus making way for the reign of Leir "at what time Joas reigned in Juda" (ibid.). At that time, we learn from scripture, Joas was laying waste not just to magic and superstition but to pagan worship as such. He "destroyed the soothsayers" and "them also that burnt incense to Baal, and to the sun, and to the moon, and to the twelve signs, and to all the host of heaven" (4 Kgs 23:5, DR). Following his encouragement, "all the people of the land entered into the temple of Baal, and destroyed his altars, and his images they brake in pieces stoutly: Mathan also the priest of Baal they slew before the altar" (4 Kgs 11:18, DR). Geoffrey of Monmouth ties the demise of Leir's father even more directly to the rise of Judeo-Christianity by linking his fall to the moment when Elijah's attacks on false worship were having their first global impact:

> At that time Elijah prayed that there should be no rain upon the earth and it did not rain for three years and six months [3 Kgs 17:1]. Bladud [sic] was a very clever man, who taught magic [*nigromantiam*] throughout the kingdom of Britain. He did not cease to work wonders [*praestigia*] until he tried to fly high through the air on wings he had made; he fell over the temple of Apollo in Trinovantum and was completely dashed to pieces. After Bladud met his fate, his son Leir became king.[9]

Leir came to the throne, that is, amidst the first tremors of the monotheist earthquake, when magicians lost their footing and the world began to lose its aura of sanctity. All of Shakespeare's audiences were more than familiar with subsequent aftershocks: the shattering of images, the eradication of saints, the secularization of church property, the loss of the traditional sacraments, the persecution of witches, and the emergence of a new orthodox conviction that "miracles are past" (*All's Well* 2.3.1). The great frisson of *Lear* in its earliest performances must have been in part the impression it gave that the disenchantments of ancient and contemporary Britain were historically conjoined.

Many in Shakespeare's day no doubt inferred from *Lear* that the tragedy of ancient unbelief had found its remedy when Britain was Christianized.

---

9. Geoffrey of Monmouth, *The History of the Kings of Britain: An Edition and Translation of "De gestis Britonum,"* ed. Michael D. Reeve, trans. Neil Wright (Woodbridge, UK: Boydell Press, 2007), 36–37. Monmouth's history circulated widely in manuscript during Shakespeare's lifetime—John Stowe's twelfth-century copy is still extant (Cotton MS Nero D VIII)—and had been translated into French. A Latin text, otherwise largely abridged, adds to Bladud's magical talents the ability to shift his shape, change one thing into another, compel the dead to speak, halt rivers from flowing, and cause earthquakes: see *Pontici Virunnii viri doctissimi Britannicæ historiæ libri sex* [etc.] (London, 1585), 6–7.

Others might just as easily have gotten the sense that Christian society was in a worse predicament than the society it replaced. The coming of Christ had demonstrated the fraudulence of the gods and the vacuity of magic but had proven impotent to counter "the cares of the world [*saeculi*]," which in addition to their ancient intrigue had now taken on the power to "choke the Word and make it fruitless" (Mk 4:19, Vulg.). According to the Pauline corpus, whose authority was at its peak following the Reformation, even devout believers could be "weak in faith" (Rom 14:1), stumble, and "fall" (1 Cor. 10:14) merely on account of "loving this world [*diligens hoc saeculum*]" (2 Tim 4:10, Vulg.). Such lapses into secularity could occur either through an unwitting substitution of worldly pursuits for genuine divinity or through a deliberate rejection of God, as when Doctor Faustus resolved to lead an "Epicurish life" out of disbelief "that there was a God, hell, or devil."[10] By figuring the *saeculum* as a godless but temporarily self-sustaining sphere and constantly warning against its fascinations, scripture assured that this sphere was always available as an alternative source of value, however fragile, doomed, fictitious, or demonic it might turn out to be. Christians were, in short, a chief vector for the secularity and unbelief that they constantly saw in others—and in themselves.

Over the course of this book I have tried to illustrate the benefits that earlier centuries reaped—and the costs that they incurred—by stripping the *saeculum* of divinity and populating it with infidels. From this perspective Edmund does not differ substantially from the *filios incredulitatis* (Col 3:6, Vulg.) whom Christians throughout the Middle Ages treated with special attentiveness. Figures of rank incredulity appear so reliably in medieval and early modern literature because they serve multiple, even antithetical purposes. For one thing, the infidel shores up the faithful in their need to believe that non-Christians by definition pursue a tragic, if luridly glamorous overvaluation of the material world. This is the role Edmund plays when he celebrates nature as his "goddess" (KL 1.2.1) while asserting his own self-interest. He is an extreme example of the unbeliever committed to the immanent allure of the *saeculum* (wealth, prestige, sex, power)—a hopeless yet attractive spokesperson for "the immediate desires of bestial creation."[11] Alternately, the infidel could provide a mouthpiece for Christians to articulate publicly an otherwise unspeakable dissent from orthodox doctrine or

---

10. *The historie of the damnable life, and deserued death of Doctor Iohn Faustus newly imprinted* [etc.], trans. P[aul] F[airfax] (London, 1592), 10.
11. G. Wilson Knight, *The Wheel of Fire: Interpretations of Shakespearean Tragedy with Three New Essays* (London: Routledge, 1989; originally published in 1930), 186–87.

popular opinion. This is the role into which Edmund has been cast by scholars who imagine that his critique of astrology was a new development, tied to recent developments in astronomy.

In fact Edmund's critique of astrology had been preached from the pulpit for centuries and parrots an especially rigid Christian dogma. Far from speaking the disruptive truth of a newly disenchanted age, Edmund refashions the patristic animus against magic that we examined in the last chapter. At the moment of Christ's advent, astrological divination was discredited as a sham religion. Christians had long been instructed *not* to believe that higher, providential powers existed in the sky overhead, and the instruction grew all the more heated the more astrology encroached on the prerogatives of the true godhead. The ancient impulse to divest the firmament of its divinities was not only ongoing in Shakespeare's lifetime but reached a fresh crescendo, as the most zealous believers intensified their commitment to the idea that *other* Christians had once again descended into an illicit relationship with astral motions. "All astrologers," writes Henry Charles Lea, "practiced their profession under liability of being at any moment called into account by the Inquisition."[12] The astrologer Roger Bolingbroke was among the first witches to be executed in England, and he returned to grace the stage in *2 Henry VI* at a time when astrologers from John Dee to Thomas Harriot and Johannes Kepler were rumored to have embraced the dark arts.

From the perspective of orthodox doctrine, any preternaturally accurate ability to assess a person's character or determine the future by casting horoscopes was the result of chance or demonic intervention. A Christian schooled in the conventions of contemporary demonology knew that demonic agency was confined to the secular world of natural causation and that it therefore amounted to nothing in comparison with the miracles of the Almighty. To help astrologers make accurate divinations, demons used the same natural indicators as computists, physicians, sailors, and farmers but with a keener sensory apparatus and a better understanding of hidden or occult causes. Demons still made mistakes, however, just like any human who was committed to predicting future outcomes through careful but nonetheless imperfect observation of the physical world; and when their

---

12. Henry Charles Lea, *A History of the Inquisition of the Middle Ages* (New York: Macmillan, 1922), 3:339–440. See also Ugo Baldini, "The Roman Inquisition's Condemnation of Astrology: Antecedents, Reasons and Consequences," in *Church, Censorship, and Culture in Early Modern Italy*, ed. Gigliola Fragnito, trans. Adrian Belton (Cambridge: Cambridge University Press, 2001), 79–110, esp. 84–85 where he lists medieval prohibitions of judicial astrology in the papal bulls of Honorius II (1225), John XII (1326), and Innocent VIII (1485)—to which should be added Sixtus V's bull *Coeli et terrae creator Deus* (1586).

expertise in natural philosophy failed, they relied on a marvelous ability to deceive. Demons were masters of spectacular, staged effects. For an idea of their talents, you only needed to consider "how many things rope-dancers and other theatrical performers have done," according to Augustine, and "how many things artisans have accomplished—especially engineers—that are to be wondered at."[13] Demonic marvels were no different. The threat posed by devils derived, in short, from their extraordinary but hardly supernatural talent for scientific prediction and for stagecraft.[14]

What this meant for astrologers and players in Shakespeare's lifetime was that both of their enterprises risked incurring the ire of Christians who had committed themselves to a very specific project of disenchantment—that of suppressing demonic magic.[15] Astrologers and players tended to flourish as a result in connection with royal courts that offered them sanctuary from persecution by inquisitors and puritans. John Dee would never have prospered, he says, had Elizabeth not "promised unto me great security against any of her kingdom, that would, by reason of any my rare studies and philosophical exercises, unduly seek my overthrow."[16] Her court extended the same protection to theater companies. Actors, like astrologers, thrived best when working in proximity to a temporal power whose regulative apparatus was least likely to confuse natural magic and various forms of play with the dark arts. Rudolf II was notorious for his occult experimentation and extended the protective cover of his imperial influence to Tycho Brahe and Kepler so that they could serve as his personal astrologers. This protection enabled some of the most significant, post-Copernican advances in astronomy even while Galileo was having "his first real brush with the Inquisition" on charges of casting horoscopes and therefore practicing "deterministic astrology."[17] Before Brahe moved to Prague, he enjoyed the patronage of Frederick II of

---

13. Augustine, *De divinatione daemonum* 4.8 (CSEL 41:606); translated by Ruth Wentworth Brown in *Treatises on Marriage and Other Subjects*, ed. Roy J. Deferrari (Washington, DC: Catholic University of America Press, 1969), 415–40 at 429.

14. Stuart Clark, *Thinking with Demons: The Idea of Witchcraft in Early Modern Europe* (Oxford: Oxford University Press, 1997).

15. On theater and the persecution of witches, see the penetrating analysis by James Simpson, *Permanent Revolution: The Reformation and the Illiberal Roots of Liberalism* (Cambridge, MA: Belknap Press, 2019), 201–56, from which I have greatly benefited even where I have taken a different tack.

16. John Dee, *The Compendious Rehearsal*, in *Autobiographical Tracts of Dr. John Dee, Warden of the College of Manchester*, ed. James Crossley, *Remains Historical & Literary Connected with the Palatine Counties of Lancaster and Chester*, Published by The Chetham Society (Manchester, 1851), 24:21; Peter J. French, *John Dee: The World of an Elizabethan Magus* (London: Routledge & Kegan Paul, 1972), 4–19.

17. Dom Paschal Scotti, *Galileo Revisited: The Galileo Affair in Context* (San Francisco: Ignatius Press, 2017), 113; Robert S. Westman, *The Copernican Question: Prognostication, Skepticism, and Celestial Order* (Berkeley: University of California Press, 2011), 376.

Denmark and Norway—the father-in-law of James VI. That is how Britain's future king came to meet Brahe and to write sonnets extolling the astrologer's acumen; these attracted the attention of Kepler, who reached out to James as a prospective patron at the same moment that Shakespeare was writing *King Lear* for a likely debut at court. Both Kepler and the King's Men mined James's *Daemonologie* for ways that they might capitalize on his interest in magic, his taste for uncovering frauds, and his refusal to condemn outright the exploration or even production of preternatural phenomena in controlled environments custom-built for observation, such as the experimental workshop, astronomer's lab, royal palace, or theatrical playhouse.[18]

Theater, Astronomy, and Magic

After an overcast week in Prague, clear skies on October 17, 1604, allowed Johannes Kepler to confirm reports that a new star had appeared in Serpentarius (the constellation now called Ophiucus). It blazed brighter than Jupiter for about two years before fading from sight, during which time he suspended work on his *Astronomia nova* (1609)—and, with that, the first two of his three laws—to issue a short vernacular report, followed by the more lengthy and learned *De stella nova* (1606).[19] The interruption gave him a welcome opportunity to ratify and update one of the most significant observations of Brahe (his erstwhile employer, chief rival, and immediate predeces-

---

18. On the overlap of the courtly *Wunderkammer*, scientific laboratory, and theater, see *Collection—Laboratory—Theater: Scenes of Knowledge in the 17th Century*, ed. Helmar Schramm et al. (New York: de Gruyter, 2005).

19. KGW 1:150–390 (*De stella nova*); 1:393–399 (*Gründtlicher Bericht von einem ungewohnlichen Newen Stern*). For a partial translation of *De stella nova* see Patrick J. Boner, "Astrology on Trial: Kepler, Pico and the Preservation of the Aspects," *Culture and Cosmos: A Journal of the History of Astrology and Cultural Astronomy* 14 (2010): 209–34; the *Gründtlicher Bericht* has been translated by Judith V. Field and Anton Postl, "A Thorough Description of an Extraordinary New Star Which First Appeared in October of this Year, 1604," *Vistas in Astronomy* 20 (1977): 333–39. Essential analysis in *Kepler's New Star (1604): Context and Controversy*, ed. Patrick J. Boner (Leiden: Brill, 2021); Owen Gingerich, "Kepler's *De Vero Anno* (1614)," in *The Star of Bethlehem and the Magi* [etc.], ed. Peter Barthel and George van Kooten (Leiden: Brill, 2015), 3–16; Westman, *Copernican Question*, 230–35, 240–43, 403–15, and passim; Patrick J. Boner, *Kepler's Cosmological Synthesis: Astrology, Mechanism and the Soul* (Leiden: Brill 2013), 69–104; Miguel A. Granada, "Johannes Kepler and David Fabricius: Their Discussion on the Nova of 1604," in *Change and Continuity in Early Modern Cosmology*, ed. Patrick J. Boner (New York: Springer, 2011), 67–92; Miguel A. Granada, "Kepler v. Roeslin on the Interpretation of Kepler's Nova: (1) 1604–1606," *JHA* 36 (2005): 299–319; Anthony Grafton, *Worlds Made by Words: Scholarship and Community in the Modern West* (Cambridge, MA: Harvard University Press, 2009), 114–36. Older but still valuable: Arthur Koestler, *The Sleepwalkers: A History of Man's Changing Vision of the Universe* (London, Hutchinson, 1959), esp. 227–427; Lynn Thorndike, *A History of Magic and Experimental Science* (New York: Macmillan, 1923–41), 5:67–98.

sor as *Mathematicus Imperialis* in the Rudolphine court), whose first book decades earlier had offered mathematical proof that the appearance of a nova in 1572 discredited the Aristotelian faith in supralunar immutability.[20] If it was new, the old cosmology held, it could not be a star; if it was a star, then it wasn't new.[21] But there it was, said Brahe, said Kepler, and it was both. Both times.

The time before then, too. The star of Bethlehem had already served as a point of comparison for Brahe's nova in 1572, but Kepler thought that "our modern star [*nostra moderna stella*]" (KGW 1:280) had the strongest connection yet by virtue of appearing in Sagittarius—one of three constellations of the zodiac, along with Aries and Leo, traditionally associated with fire—while Saturn, Jupiter, and Mars were conjoined in the same region. Kepler had already proven in his first book that Saturn and Jupiter met periodically within this so-called Fiery Trigon as part of an overall eight-hundred-year cycle.[22] In *De stella nova* he went further, linking the onset of each Trigon to personages of world historical import. He acknowledged that to make the schema work you had to allow for "fairly imprecise numbers" (KGW 1:182), but the pattern seemed to him beyond coincidence. Counting backwards from his patron—the current Holy Roman Emperor, Rudolf II—he arrived at the empire's founding by Charlemagne in 800; eight hundred years before that came Christ, then a series of Christ's precursors in eight-hundred-year increments: Isaiah, Moses, Noah, Enoch, and Adam. It was not unreasonable to imagine that yet another "catastrophe [*katastrophēn*]" (KGW 1:352.11), heralded once more by a new star, might well be in the offing at the moment of cyclical transition "about which astrologers have written so much" (KGW 1:395.9). For Kepler the ultimate question was whether the catastrophe could be associated with outward changes in the course of world history, as so many other astrologers supposed—the conversion of the New World, James's unification of Scotland and England, Rudolf's triumph over infidel Turks, and so forth—or if the change, assuming it came at all, would be a decidedly inward, global crisis of conscience on the model of Christ's first advent.

---

20. *Tychonis Brahe De nova et nullius aevi memoria prius visa stella* (Copenhagen, 1573), in *Tychonis Brahe Dani Opera omnia*, ed. J. L. E. Dreyer (Copenhagen: In Libraria Gyldendaliana, typis Nielsen & Lydiche [Axel Simmelkaer], 1913), 1:1–142; included in Brahe's *Astronomiae instauratae progymnasmata* (Prague, 1602) and translated into English as *Learned: Tico Brahœ his astronomicall coniectur of the new and much admired [star] which appeared in the year 1572* (London, 1632).
21. Edward Grant, "Celestial Incorruptibility in Medieval Cosmology 1200–1687," in *Physics, Cosmology and Astronomy, 1300–1700: Tension and Accommodation*, ed. Sabetai Unguru (Dordrecht: Kluwer Academic Publishers, 1991), 101–28.
22. KGW 1:12; English in *The Secret of the Universe = Mysterium cosmographicum*, trans. A.M. Duncan (New York: Abaris Books, 1981), 66–67.

Several publications around the turn of the century illustrate how the star of Bethlehem framed the reception of the 1604 nova.[23] Since the Incarnation had clearly occurred "at the end of the watery Trigon, and the beginning of the fiery," in the words of Richard Harvey, it was difficult *not* to anticipate something equally portentous at the start of a new Trigon: "We are most like to have a new world," he writes, "by some sudden, violent, & wonderful strange alteration, which even heretofore hath always happened, at the ending of one Trigon, & beginning of another, but now most especially is like to happen."[24] Sudden, violent, wonderfully strange—but still predictable. The same type of alteration that routinely happened, according to early modern stargazers, was destined to happen to them, only this time the alteration would be the most profound yet; their era would instantiate as never before the seismic rupture presaged over Bethlehem, accomplishing at last the final break in world history: "That blessed star, which conducted the Magi to Christ's poor but sacred nursery," writes John Bainbridge (the first Savilian Professor of Astronomy at Oxford), "doth enforce me often to think that those many new stars and comets, which have been more this last century of the world than in many ages before, did amongst other things signify that glorious light of the gospel, which hath lately illumined the whole world."[25] The present age lacked precedent only insofar as reminders of Bethlehem were happening in it with maximum frequency: at least five comets in ten years while Luther was preaching, "after which followed the happy departure of Germany, England and many other northern parts from the spiritual Babylon" (ibid.). More recent sightings gave Bainbridge hope that "the rest of Christendom before long will follow; and so at length shall be verified the prophecy of Sybilla upon occasion of these new stars: *Rome shall again become a forlorn and desert village*" (ibid.). Once Christendom as a whole caught up with the

---

23. See Margaret Aston, "The Fiery Trigon Conjunction: An Elizabethan Astrological Prediction," *Isis* 61, no. 2 (1970): 158–87; Germana Ernst, "From the Watery Trigon to the Fiery Trigon," in *"Astrologi Hallucinati": Stars and the End of the World in Luther's Time*, ed. Paola Zambelli (Berlin: de Gruyter, 1986), 265–80, esp. 266–67.
24. Richard Harvey, *An astrological discourse vpon the great and notable coniunction of the two superiour planets, Saturne & Iupiter* [etc.] (London, 1583), 40–41, 38, respectively. Similar views had already appeared in Cyprian Leowitz, *De coniunctionibus magnis insignioribus superiorum planetarum* (London, 1573; originally published in 1564) and Helisaeus Roeslin, *Theoria nova coelestium meteoron* (Strasbourg, 1578). Further discussion in Granada, "Johannes Kepler and David Fabricius," esp. 86–87n49; Thorndike, *History of Magic and Experimental Science*, 5:116–18.
25. John Bainbridge, *An astronomical description of the late comet from 18 November 1618 to 16 December following* (London, 1618), 30–31; see 5 for his cautious embrace of the heliocentric model. Further commentary by John L. Russell, "The Copernican System in Great Britain," in *The Reception of Copernicus' Heliocentric Theory* [etc.], ed. Jerzy Dobrzycki (Dordrecht: D. Reidel, 1972), 189–240, esp. 218.

critical disruption of Christ's advent, the gospel could spread further to the enlightenment of more recently discovered parts the globe, "which did long sit in most fearful darkness" (ibid.) but which had been finally uncovered, Kepler also notes, "by Christians in this, the last age" (KGW 1:347). Fulfillment could not be infinitely deferred of "the most certain prophecy of Christ our savior"—namely, that the "gospel shall be preached throughout the whole earth" (KGW 1:347; quoting Mt 24:14). The stage would then be set for "the second coming of our blessed Savior; *Forerunners whereof* (he saith) *shall be signs in the sun, moon, and stars.*"[26]

The chief obstacle to any such attempt to unite Copernican astronomy with Christian theology was its vulnerability to the standard Christian critique of astrology. Astrologers were "avid for new things" by temperament and thus found themselves perpetually looking to the sky, rather than to God, for the leading edge of a different future.[27] They consequently inspired highly moralized revenge fantasies, as in the legends of Leir's father and of Faustus. John Donne went so far as to place Kepler in hell alongside Copernicus after reading the remark in *De stella nova* that it had fallen into Kepler's care after Brahe's death "that no new thing be done in heaven without his knowledge."[28] The anti-astrological fervor reverberating throughout scripture had taken on fresh animus among humanists and was especially fierce in some Protestant circles, to the point that no strain of skepticism about the nature and meaning of the heavens was more virulent than what *sola scriptura* inspired in its most ardent English advocates.

Hardline Protestants, returning *ad fontes*, channeled with minimal dilution the monotheistic imperative to demonize, desecrate, and secularize any quasi-divine power to which others showed deference—most of all when the other was a fellow Christian still committed to the power of planets named after nonexistent deities. Paul's condemnation of the Galatians for their stargazing (Gal 4:10) inspired William Perkins to castigate "the superstition of the Popish Church" for the "heathenish conceits" that speciously invested the cosmos with the ability to determine earthly events:

---

26. Bainbridge, *An astronomical description*, 32; quoting Lk 21:25.
27. Giovanni Pico della Mirandola, *Disputationes adversus astrologiam divinatricem*, ed. Eugenio Garin (Firenze: Vallecchi Editore, 1946), 1:78: *"rerum avidi novarum."* Cf. Sheila J. Rabin, "Pico and the Historiography of Renaissance Astrology," *Explorations in Renaissance Culture* 36, no. 2 (2010): 170–80; Rabin, "Kepler's Attitude Toward Pico and the Anti-Astrology Polemic," *Renaissance Quarterly* 50, no. 3 (1997): 750–70; Nick Kollerstrom, "Kepler's Belief in Astrology," in *History and Astrology: Clio and Urania Confer*, ed. Annabella Kitson (London: Unwin, 1989), 152–70.
28. John Donne, *Ignatius his Conclave: An Edition of the Latin and English Texts with Introduction and Commentary by T. S. Healy* (Oxford: Clarendon, 1969; originally published in 1611), 7; quoting *De stella nova* (KGW 1:297); for Kepler's response, see below.

Here therefore, we must be put in mind, not to observe the planetary hours: for men suppose that the hours of the day are ruled by the planets, and hereupon, that some hours are good and lucky (as they say) and some unlucky: that men are taken with planets, and born under unlucky planets. . . . Neither must we respect our horoscope or the time of our birth, and the constellation of the heavens then, as though we could hereby know what should befall us to the end of our days. And we must not put difference of days, as though some were lucky unto us, and some unlucky, according to the course of the stars. . . . it is foolishness to ascribe the regiment of our affairs to the stars, they being matters contingent, which depend on the will and pleasure of man.[29]

People like Kepler who cast horoscopes for a living were seeking guidance not from a real but from "a supposed heaven" (ibid.). Excepting only the forms of astronomy needed for agricultural planning, seasonal markets, fairs, and ecclesiastical observance (ibid., 314), Perkins denounced every supposed influence of the heavenly motions as the epitome of human foolishness, "for no man can by learning know the operation of the stars" (ibid., 314), modern astronomers be damned. They were no better than actors, who also took monetary advantage of the human attachment to illusion. Among the many transgressors of the Mosaic commandment against theft, Perkins counted as one the person "that gets his living by casting of figures and by plays."[30] Perkins may have had in mind gambling or some other type of "play" in this case (rather than theatrical entertainments), but we know from another text that he was as glad to see astrological magic condemned as he was to see stage magic suppressed.[31]

Such regulations went hand-in-hand with the reformers' hope to impose on England an even more austere version of the disenchantment first envisioned by the Yahwistic puritans of earlier millennia. According to Philip Stubbes, Christendom had suffered too long from both "foolish star tooters" and playactors. While the latter had reduced the gospel to a laughing matter by staging fake miracles, the former had brought "the world into a wonderful perplexity" by incessantly forecasting "either a wonderful alteration of

---

29. William Perkins, *A commentarie or exposition upon the five first chapters of the Epistle to the Galatians* (Cambridge, 1604), 316–17.
30. William Perkins, *Two treatises: I. Of the nature and practise of repentance. II. Of the combat of the flesh and spirit* (Cambridge, 1593), 32–33.
31. William Perkins, *The whole treatise of the cases of conscience, distinguished into three bookes* (Cambridge, 1606), 585: "the more holy the matter is which they represent, the more unholy are the plays themselves."

states and kingdoms . . . or else a final consummation and overthrow of all things. . . . Whereas, God be thanked, at the very hour and moment when . . . these wonders and portents should have happened, there was no alteration nor change of anything."[32] The one indication that history might be nearing its last phase would not appear in the skies above but down here below in the ravings of star-addled Christians; when consulting the firmament for guidance, they "not only rob the majesty of God of his honour but also strengthen the hands of the heathen, pagans, infidels, and idolatrous people" (ibid., 61). Astrologers added their voices to the ancient chorus encouraging undue reverence for the created world, with the result that true religion had virtually disappeared from England. Every liberty since the beginning of civilization—fine apparel, infidelity, riotous living, greed, theater, minstrelsy, gambling, you name it—had become progressively worse: "There is no sin that was ever broached in any age, which flourisheth not now."[33] Nothing new had ever come into the world, save for the New Testament, and its arrival added to the old, timeworn sins of the *saeculum* one sin worse. People could now also flout the gospel, such that the Christian age was occasion to a greater impiety—and greater secularity—than ever before: "I am persuaded, neither the Libertines, the Epicures nor yet the vile Atheists ever exceeded this people in pride" (ibid., 70). Pagans had rendered their devotion to false gods—or to no gods at all—through incessant riot, but at least they had done so prior to Christ's advent. English Christians, by comparison, under the tutelage of the Catholic Church, had become even *more* committed to fleshly indulgence, according to Stubbes, as if Christ's coming offered nothing in comparison to the chimerical pleasures of their star-encased globe.

Reginald Scot's *Discoverie of Witchcraft* appeared one year after Stubbes's *Anatomie of Abuses* and shares many of its complaints against astrology as part of a broad assault on belief in witchcraft. Fundamental to Scot's outlook is the familiar patristic and scholastic idea that Christ's advent reduced magic to a class of phenomena that could be readily explained without reference to the supernatural.[34] From this Scot makes the unusual inference that demons have no power to intervene meaningfully in the chain of material

---

32. Philip Stubbes, *The second part of the Anatomie of Abuses, conteining the display of corruptions* (London, 1583), in *Philip Stubbes's Anatomy of the Abuses in England in Shakspere's Youth, A.D. 1583*, ed. Frederick J. Furnivall, part 2 (London, 1879), 57.
33. Philip Stubbes, *The Anatomie of Abuses*, ed. Margaret Jane Kidnie (Tempe: Arizona Center for Medieval and Renaissance Studies, in conjunction with Renaissance English Text Society, 2002), 61.
34. See Robert H. West, *Reginald Scot and Renaissance Writings on Witchcraft* (Boston: Twayne, 1984); Sydney Anglo, "Reginald Scot's *Discoverie of Witchcraft*: Scepticism and Sadduceeism," in Anglo, ed., *The Damned Art: Essays in the Literature of Witchcraft* (London: Routledge & K. Paul, 1977), 106–139.

causation; if the devil is at best a secular agent, forced to collaborate with the world and human frailty, then the world and human frailty alone can explain the appearance of every preternatural occurrence. The only other means of accounting for superhuman events would be to allow for the possibility of a divine miracle, but Scot endorses the Protestant commonplace that Christ had brought miracles to an end so that he "might make the new preaching of the gospel marvelous forever."[35] Were he to have allowed such phenomena to endure, the wonders recorded in the New Testament would have staled and "grown into contempt" (248). Instead, the record of those miracles bequeathed to future ages the ability to discern in any preternatural appearance a mere simulacrum of divinity. The most interesting and dangerous of such counterfeits were generated artificially by magicians and unscrupulous con artists; hence the long history of Catholic histrionics: the exorcisms, the incantations, the "blessings, cursings" (185), among all the other "cozening tricks of oracling priests and monks," who "with their counterfeit miracles" did what the clergy had done since the time of Apollo—"bewitched the people" (138). For Scot the mysteries of salvation have been truly revealed in the New Testament alone, and that is the end of true novelty. Thereafter "we are not to seek new signs and miracles but to attend to the doctrine of the apostles" (140). We should be as guarded against the imposture of Catholic divines as we are against the astrological diviners "who have received their light, and their very art from poets, without whose fables the twelve signs . . . had never ascended into heaven" (169–70). Priests, astrologers, and writers of poetry are all committed to fabricating the *effect* of the sacred and other illusions—as are the "jugglers" to whom Scot dedicates many chapters of critical scrutiny. He explains in some detail, for instance, the technical processes of legerdemain that had recently allowed a magician named Kingsfield to perform in London, before Scot's very eyes, the decollation of John the Baptist (286–87).

For all of Scot's enthusiasm for disenchantment, he stops short of the extreme anti-astrological and anti-theatrical diatribes of his Calvinist peers. In fact he goes to some lengths to protect certain forms of magic from the disdain into which he otherwise taps. On the question of "juggling," "spectacle," and "play," Scot echoes the teachings of high scholasticism on the *ars theatrica* that we examined in chapter 3: "If these things be done for mirth and recreation, and not to the hurt of our neighbour, nor to the abusing or profaning of Gods name, in mine opinion they are neither impious nor alto-

---

35. Reginald Scot, *The Discoverie of Witchcraft*, ed. Brinsley Nicholson (London: Elliot Stock, 1886; originally published in 1584), 125. All further citations are to this edition.

gether unlawful: though herein or hereby a natural thing be made to seem supernatural. Such are the miracles wrought by jugglers, consisting in fine and nimble conveyance, called legerdemain" (250). Although Scot attacks the widespread belief in witches, demonic pacts, and so forth, he is deeply appreciative of magic tricks—precisely on account of his disbelief in their ability to produce anything beyond natural, nondemonic phenomena. His descriptions of the special effects that were used to create stage magic—decapitation, stabbing, bestial transformation (as when an actor dons an ass head), and so on—can read as much like demystifications of witchcraft as a how-to manual for an acting company. His experiments in conjuring, which he undertook to prove empirically that the devil did not respond to human summons, would have given crucial reassurance to contemporary theater troupes that their incantations and curses could not accidently produce a real visitation of evil: "I for my part have read a number of their [i.e., magicians'] conjurations, but ne'er could see any devils of theirs, except it were in a play" (374). Given various echoes between his work and the magical effects required to stage surviving playscripts, it is not unthinkable that London acting companies consulted Scot to learn the tricks of the trade.[36] (Middleton borrows unambiguously from him in *The Witch*.) Scot's book, in other words, may have helped legitimize the forms of stage magic that took over English drama once representations of the godhead and figures like John the Baptist had been banished.

Scot used the same logic to defend the branches of astronomy that his Calvinist peers would have preferred to suppress: "The superstitious observations of senseless augurers and soothsayers (contrary to philosophy and without authority of scripture) are very ungodly and ridiculous. Howbeit, I reject not the prognostications of astronomers, not the conjectures or forewarnings of physicians, nor yet the interpretations of philosophers."[37] Despite the condemnations of Lactantius and Calvin, Scot avers, "surely it is most necessary for us to know and observe diverse rules astrological, otherwise we could not with opportunities dispatch our ordinary affairs" (136). Given the centrality of astrology to agriculture, navigation, and medicine, he was not prepared to rule out completely "the curious observation used by our elders, who conjectured upon nativities" (137). Even the kinds of stargazing that had been reviled as judicial astrology and persecuted by the

---

36. Pierre Kapitaniak, "Staging Devils and Witches: Had Shakespeare Read Reginald Scot's *The Discoverie of Witchcraft?*" in Chiari and Popelard, *Spectacular Science*, 43-63. See also Philip Butterworth, *Magic on the Early English Stage* (Cambridge: Cambridge University Press, 2005).
37. Scot, *Discoverie of Witchcraft*, ed. Nicholson, 138.

church could be re-classed as a legitimate form of inquiry: "in this art of natural magic," he writes (invoking a centuries-old category), "God almighty hath hidden many secret mysteries; as wherein a man may learn the properties, qualities, and knowledge of all nature. For it teacheth to accomplish matters in such sort and opportunity, as the common people thinketh the same to be miraculous; and to be compassed none other way, but only by witchcraft" (236–37). Once miracles had been removed from the world, it became possible to discern in nature some of the wonder that other Christians wanted either to restrict to God alone or condemn as the work of the devil. "Experiments of natural magic" (251)—which for Scot encompass both the inquiries of astrologers and the performances of players—are a way of exploring the *saeculum* without recourse to supernatural or demonic aid. Such experiments, according to Scot, deserve protection from persecution.

Francis Bacon and Kepler both made related arguments, and both appealed to the scriptural Magi in order to license the exploration of natural mysteries through a form of experimentation that could seem to some contemporaries all too dangerous, pantheistic, atheistic, or magical: "But I must here stipulate that magic, which has long been used in a bad sense," writes Bacon, "be again restored to its ancient and honourable meaning. For among the Persians magic was taken for a sublime wisdom, and the knowledge of the universal consents of things; and so the three kings who came from the east to worship Christ were called by the name of Magi."[38] Bacon wants to show that some modes of learned inquiry are fully compatible with Christianity despite having been targeted by overzealous Christians as forms of witchcraft: "for it is not yet known in what cases, and how far, effects attributed to superstition participate in natural causes, and therefore howsoever the use and practice of such arts is to be condemned, yet from the speculation and consideration of them (if they be diligently unraveled) a useful light may be gained, not only for the true judgement of the offences of persons charged with such practices, but likewise for the further disclosing of the secrets of nature."[39] Some people accused of being in league with the devil are actually committed to discovering chains of causation hidden in nature and have learned in this way to produce preternatural effects without mistaking them for miracles or requiring the aid of demons These people depend on magistrates to know the difference between their activities and witchcraft: "For these, and such like marvelous acts and feats, naturally, mathematically, and mechanically wrought and

---

38. *De augmentis scientiarum*, in *The Works of Francis Bacon*, ed. James Spedding et al. (London, 1858), 4:366.
39. Ibid., 296; for analysis, see Clark, *Thinking with Demons*, 254ff.

contrived," asks John Dee, "ought any honest student and modest Christian philosopher be counted and called a conjurer?"[40] If the Magi were celebrated for having the courage to follow a star to Bethlehem, how could the authorities afford to condemn contemporary magicians without due process?

One consequence of inquiring into occult causation through natural magic was to call into question the status of phenomena that others might deem supernatural. Kepler chastises the *theologi* who considered the appearance of the new star a miracle on the order of creation: "For it is the work of God alone to create *ex nihilo.*"[41] Within the confines of the created world, nothing can come of nothing—not even a new star, which had to have arisen from material processes subject to human understanding. What the nova of 1604 reveals is that one of the key miracles recorded in the New Testament was not a miracle in the technical sense of the word but rather an instance of God subordinating himself to natural law at the very moment when he took on flesh and became subject—even unto death—to the secular world. The star of Bethlehem did not come out of nowhere in defiance of regular astronomical order but rather appeared at the precise moment when astronomers would have expected to see something significant: "God had accommodated [*accommodasse*] himself, for the time being, to the rules of the Magi by igniting the star at the very moment when the Magi most expected a star" (KGW 1:280). Just as God is described throughout scripture in similitudes and metaphors with which he cannot be literally equated, so too he "prefers to act with the aid of nature, to accommodate his plans to existing, contingent circumstances," rather than to suspend the laws of physics through the exercise of his absolute power or through unmediated revelation.[42] Not even the Real Presence as defined by Luther could be real in any literal sense because God is neither ubiquitous nor "illocal"; nor does he offer ongoing miraculous interference with the ordinary course of nature.[43] Any apparent

---

40. "John Dee his Mathematical Preface," in *The elements of geometrie of the most auncient philosopher Euclide of Megara* [etc.] (London, 1570), Aij'.
41. KGW 1:267; Westman, *Copernican Question*, 385; Peter Dear, "Miracles, Experiments, and the Ordinary Course of Nature," *Isis* 81, no. 4 (1990): 663–83.
42. Amos Funkenstein, *Theology and the Scientific Imagination from the Middle Ages to the Seventeenth Century*, 2nd ed. (Princeton, NJ: Princeton University Press, 2018), 232. See also Carlo Ginzburg, "History and/or Memory: On the Principle of Accommodation," in *Thinking Impossibilities: The Intellectual Legacy of Amos Funkenstein*, ed. Robert S. Westman and David Biale (Toronto: University of Toronto Press in association with the UCLA Center for Seventeenth- and Eighteenth-Century Studies and the William Andrews Clark Memorial Library, 2008), 193–206; Robert S. Westman, "Was Kepler a Secular Theologian?" in *Thinking Impossibilities*, 34–62.
43. Aviva Rothman, "From Cosmos to Confession: Kepler and the Connection between Astronomical and Religious Truth," in Boner, *Change and Continuity*, 115–34 at 119; see 124 on accommodation. Cf. KGW 17:88–89: "Let me be an example that God rarely alters the course of nature."

miracle, such as the new star, was not an instance of divine intervention but at best an example of God accommodating himself symbolically to natural law, as though donning a costume in the *mundano theatro* (theater of the world).[44] Establishing the ultimate truth or reality of anything—whether in astronomy, theology, or theater—was intimately bound up with the interpretation of images, semiotic debate, and the regulative pressure of conflicting administrative powers.

"Let us imitate the example of the Magi [*imitemur exemplum Magorum*]," Kepler advises his readers at the end of *De stella nova*, "who because they had the prophecies of Daniel about the coming of Christ, when a marvelous star appeared around the time of the great conjunction at the start of the sixth period of triplicities, were roused to study books and, the sum of the years not disagreeing, to seek him who in their judgment was born with a star for a sign, the king of the Jews, savior of the world" (KGW 1:347). Kepler supplements the wisdom of the Magi by giving them knowledge of Hebrew prophecies so that they can serve as a proxy for modern Christian astronomers. Like the Magi, contemporary astronomers had to rectify the limitations of their models in light of new cosmological observations; they too had to subject themselves to scrupulous observation and doubt, opening themselves to the unsettling type of discovery that, as we saw in the last chapter, had been dramatized centuries earlier in the Nativity play of the *Carmina Burana*. In fact Kepler's plea to his fellow astronomers to *imitate* the Magi was not without a theatrical dimension. Remnants of the goliardic theater that had given rise to the *Carmina Burana* endured at Tübingen in an updated, humanist guise when Kepler was a student there. According to the diary of Martin Crusius (Kepler's professor of Greek), from the late 1580s to the mid-1590s students put on a play about Aeneas and Dido, a *Faustcomödie*, along with various biblical dramas: Joseph and his brothers, Tobias, Rebecca, Susanna, John the Baptist.[45] Kepler took part in at least one play of this type according to a letter he wrote years later to David Fabricius, a Lutheran pastor, astrologer, and discoverer of the first variable star (that is, a star whose brightness dims and strengthens in periodic fluctuations). Kepler sent his horoscope to Fabricius in hopes of pinpointing the cause of a sudden fever

---

44. KGW 2:16; English in Johannes Kepler, *Optics: Paralipomena to Witelo & Optical Part of Astronomy*, trans. William H. Donahue (Santa Fe, NM: Green Lion Press, 2000), 15; discussion in Raz Chen-Morris, *Measuring Shadows: Kepler's Optics of Invisibility* (University Park: Penn State University Press, 2016), esp. 33–37 for a connection to Shakespeare; see also Ann Blair, *The Theater of Nature: Jean Bodin and Renaissance Science* (Princeton, NJ: Princeton University Press, 1997), 154.

45. Edmund Reitlinger, *Johannes Kepler*, part 1 (Stuttgart, 1863), 93–94, citing Crusius's unpublished diary.

that felled him in 1591 during carnival season, when he was recovering from "a great disturbance of mind and body, on account of the excitement from a play in which I was Marian" (KGW 14:275).

There's no mention of a Marian or Mariam or Mariamne (all potentially interchangeable variants) in scripture, but one particular Mariamne in the Herodian dynasty was just then coming into fashion on the Renaissance stage throughout Europe, and she features importantly in *De stella nova*.[46] Kepler's interpretation of this figure was based on one of the many print editions of Josephus circulating in Latin and German, as was his argument that the star of Bethlehem appeared "around the time of the great conjunction at the start of the sixth period of triplicities."[47] According to Kepler's calculations, that particular conjunction had to have taken place in 7 BC—far too early to have directed the Magi to Bethlehem if Christ was born on the traditional date. According to Josephus, however, Herod died in 4 BC after having killed the two sons he shared with Mariamne the year before in a fit of paranoid rage that must have coincided, Kepler thought, with the Slaughter of the Innocents.[48] Allowing the Magi at least a year to complete their journey by Twelfth Night brought the stars into alignment and gave Mariamne a peculiar, proto-Marian quality—something that was not lost on contemporary playwrights attempting to retain and revitalize medieval dramatic traditions in places where those traditions were frowned upon. The Lutheran antipathy to staging the Passion, Corpus Christi plays, *Fastnachtspiele*, and saint plays would have made representations of Mariamne at the Herodian court a welcome substitute in Tübingen for representations of Mary and Joseph.[49] If Kepler wanted his fellow astronomers in Protestant lands to imitate the Magi, they would increasingly have to do it in real life rather than on stage—and in real life they would have to respond to the Christian invective against astrology, just as players had to manage a renewal of the old Christian invective against theater.

Both Kepler and Shakespeare survived this time of violent sectarianism and confessional conflict by offering to a powerful patron with occult interests highly sophisticated apologies for their respective forms of natural and

---

46. Maurice Valency, *The Tragedies of Herod and Mariamne* (New York: Columbia University Press, 1940).
47. KGW 1:347; Kepler came to realize the importance of Josephus's account by reading the Polish Jesuit Laurence Suslyga (KGW 1:360–90). See M. W. Burke-Gaffney, *Kepler and the Jesuits* (Milwaukee, WI: Bruce Publishing Company, 1944), 26–41.
48. KGW 1:372, 386 for Mariamne; also 379, 384–85 for her sons.
49. See Eckehard Simon, "German Medieval Theatre: Tenth Century to 1600," in *A History of German Theatre*, ed. Simon Williams and Maik Hamburger (Cambridge: Cambridge University Press, 2008), 8–37, esp. 36; Thomas I. Bacon, *Martin Luther and the Drama* (Amsterdam: Rodopi, 1976).

art magic. Kepler tried to position his science as "an enlightened offensive, a campaign against superstition, in which a purified astrology was the natural ally of a purified gospel."[50] At the same time he frequently gave voice to the view that the pseudo-religions of antiquity had prepared the way for a more accurate account of the cosmos. He argued, for example, that the pagan overvaluation of creation had provided future astronomers with an indispensable heuristic: "If previously nobody had been so silly as to conceive the hope of learning future developments from the heavens, then you too, astronomer, would never have become so clever as to have thought of investigating the heavenly motions to honor God. . . . In fact, you learned to distinguish the five planets from other heavenly bodies not from holy writ but from the superstitious books of the Babylonians."[51] Believers in scripture were empowered by the Bible to appropriate whatever wisdom they discerned in the miasma of pagan delusion and put it to better, more enlightened uses. As Kepler writes in the *Harmonice mundi* (1619)—an attempt, culminating in his third law, to prove with unprecedented mathematical rigor the ancient astrological faith in celestial harmony and a book that he dedicates to King James—"I mockingly defy all mortals with this open confession: I have robbed the golden vessels of the Egyptians to make out of them a tabernacle for my God, far from the frontiers of Egypt" (KGW 6:290).

The plundering of the Egyptians (Ex 12:35–36) was the standard point of reference whenever Christians had to defend the learning that they borrowed from infidel observations of the *saeculum* (for which "Egypt," as we saw in chapter 2, served as the paradigm). The biblical episode complemented Augustine's gloss on the Magi such that the astrological discernment of pagans could be said to have led the wisest among them to abandon their idols and embrace instead the modern, Christian universe. The pagans who first mastered cosmology by observing with utmost attentiveness the created world, as though it possessed a sanctity all its own, were brought by this obsession to apprehend the vapidity of their religious ideas and with that, a better astronomy: "In every wonderment and every desire," Kepler says in *De stella nova*, "so long as it remains uncultivated, there is an abundance of vanity [*vanitatis plurimum*]; but at the crossroad [*trivio*] that leads to philoso-

---

50. Robin B. Barnes, *Astrology and Reformation* (New York: Oxford University Press, 2016), 132; cf. Boner, *Kepler's Cosmological Synthesis*, esp. 76.

51. *Tertius interveniens* (Frankfurt am Main, 1610), in KGW 4:161; this passage is translated in Edward Rosen, "Kepler's Attitude Toward Astrology and Mysticism," in *Occult and Scientific Mentalities in the Renaissance*, ed. Brian Vickers (Cambridge: Cambridge University Press, 1984), 253–72 at 266–67.

phy, this vanity directs those it meets to a beautiful place."⁵² People accuse astronomy—"the mother who is very wise but poor"—of being superstitious because she "is supported and nourished by the ditties of her foolish daughter," that is, astrology, when in fact the relationship between the two produces great insights (KGW 1:211). Later in *Tertius interveniens*, Kepler returns to the same image of mother and child visiting a crossroads: "All curiosity and all wondering," he writes, "is in its first stage nothing but simple foolishness. Yet this foolishness plucks us by the ears and leads us through the crossroads [*Creuzweg*] that goes directly to philosophy" (KGW 4:161). He follows Brahe in arguing that the new astronomy should be *Against the Astrologers, for Astrology*—a form of natural magic that Christians ought to be able to pursue without being accused of witchcraft.⁵³

And yet accused they were. Shakespeare and Kepler would have both known about John Dee, the Elizabethan court astrologer and one-time guest of Rudolf II.⁵⁴ Ruined by accusations of conjuring at the end of Elizabeth's reign, he begged the new king to be "tried and cleared of that horrible and damnable . . . most grievous and damageable slander," and, if found guilty, "either to be stoned to death, or to be buried quick, or to be burned unmercifully."⁵⁵ James neither tried him nor readmitted him to the court, creating a vacuum for a first-rate natural magician that Kepler hoped to fill. In 1605, as a result of the Gunpowder plot, Thomas Harriot was imprisoned for allegedly casting horoscopes of the royal family. A natural philosopher of exceptional talent, a frequenter of the playhouse, and one of Kepler's most learned correspondants on the subject of refraction and optics, Harriot was interrogated personally by King James and then set free.⁵⁶ His liberation may have inspired Kepler to think that James would appreciate the argument in *De stella nova* that astrological prognostications could be made "without magic" (KGW 1:336), despite their resemblance to witchcraft.

---

52. KGW 1:211; trans. Rosen, "Kepler's Attitude Toward Astrology and Mysticism," 266 (modified); see also *De Fundamentis astrologiae certioribus* [etc.] (Prague, 1602) in KGW 4:7–35; Sheila J. Rabin, "Kepler's Attitude Toward Pico and the Anti-Astrology Polemic"; Kollerstrom, "Kepler's Belief in Astrology," in *History and Astrology*, 152–70.
53. *Tychonis Brahe Dani Opera omnia*, 1:36; see Westman, *Copernican Question*, 234–35 and 245–50 (on Pico et al.); cf. John Louis Emil Dreyer, *Tycho Brahe: A Picture of Scientific Life and Work in the Sixteenth Century* (Edinburgh, 1890), 52.
54. Peter Marshall, *The Magic Circle of Rudolf II: Alchemy and Astrology in Renaissance Prague* (New York: Walker, 2006), 110–28.
55. John Dee, *To the King's most excellent Majestie* (London, 1604), n.p.
56. Robyn Arianrhod, *Thomas Harriot: A Life in Science* (Oxford: Oxford University Press, 2019), 4; Westman, *Copernican Question*, 411–12.

Kepler was in no way immune to the risk of that resemblance. On December 29, 1615, he received a letter from his sister informing him that their mother, Katharina, had been accused of bewitching her neighbors. Others had been caught up in the proceedings, names were being named, and Kepler worried that his own might be among them, "as if I myself had been accused of forbidden arts."[57] He had good reason to worry, having written a quasi-autobiographical dream vision that defended conjuration in unusually explicit terms. The manuscript was long withheld from publication—but not, evidently, from circulation; somehow, Kepler believed, it had fallen into the hands of John Donne, leading him to predict that Kepler would be damned.[58] At last brought to press by Kepler's son under the title *Somnium, sive Astronomia Lunaris, Joannis Kepleri* (1634), portions of it seem to preserve the germ of a project begun at Tübingen, although the main body of the text was composed in 1608. According to the preface, Rudolf's embattled position at court, born partly of the emperor's fascination with the occult, had inspired Kepler to read up on the legendary founder of Prague—one Libussa, "famous for her magic art."[59] One night "after watching the stars and the moon," Kepler fell asleep and dreamt he was reading a book purchased at the Frankfurt market. Narrated by an Icelandic astronomer named Duracotas, it tells the story of how he came to learn about the moon from studying with two masters: his mother—a witch named Fiolxhilde—and Tycho Brahe.

Sworn to secrecy by her for fear of persecution, Duracotas dares to tell the tale only because of his mother's "recent death" (KGW 11.2:321; ed. Lear, 89)—a remark to which Kepler later appended a note describing how much better off his family would have been, "had I obeyed the instructions I dreamed Fiolxhilde had given" (KGW 11.2:334n8; ed. Lear, 91n8). Throughout the text Duracotas is at pains to stress the overlap between the Hven observatory and astrological witchcraft: "Brahe and his students passed the whole night with wonderful instruments [*mirabilibus machinis*] fixed on the

---

57. From Kepler's 1616 letter to the Senate of Leonberg (KGW 17:155): "*alss ob auch Ich selber verbottener Künsten bezüchtiget worden sey*"; loosely translated (without a source) in James A. Connor, *Kepler's Witch: An Astronomer's Discovery of Cosmic Order Amid Religious War, Political Intrigue, and the Heresy Trial of his Mother* (San Francisco: Harper, 2004), 7–10.

58. See Marjorie Nicolson, "Kepler, The *Somnium*, and John Donne," *Journal of the History of Ideas* 1, no. 3 (1940): 259–80.

59. KGW 11.2:321; English in John Lear, ed., *Kepler's Dream: With the Full Text and Notes of "Somnium, sive Astronomia Lunaris, Joannis Kepleri,"* trans. Patricia Frueth Kirkwood (Berkeley: University of California Press, 1965), 87. Further discussion in Elmar Schenkel, "Lunar Dreams: Religion and Politics in Literary Journeys to the Moon," in *Entangled Knowledge: Scientific Discourses and Cultural Difference*, ed. Klaus Hock and Gesa Mackenthun (Münster: Waxmann, 2012), 291–304.

moon and stars. This reminded me of my mother because she, too, used to commune constantly with the moon" (KGW 11.2:322; ed. Lear, 95). When the astronomer returned home from the observatory, his mother "delighted in the knowledge I had acquired about the sky. She compared my reports of it with discoveries she herself had made about it" (KGW 11.2:322; ed. Lear, 96). Just as the son studied with Brahe, the mother, it turns out, had received instruction from a demon, whom she eventually conjures on her son's behalf that he might learn more than he could at Hven: "My mother withdrew from me to a nearby crossroads, and after crying aloud a few words in which she set forth her desire, and then, performing some ceremonies she returned, right hand outstretched, palm upward, and sat down beside me" (KGW 11.2:322–23; ed. Lear, 100–1). A demon from "Levania" (Hebrew for "moon") answers the summons and describes how to travel to the moon, the effects of eclipses, the unevenness of its terrain, the duration of the days and seasons in both hemispheres, the nature of its inhabitants—all while receiving copious mathematical corroboration from Kepler in the footnotes.

These notes were appended to the text after Katharina's trial and seem designed to exonerate astrological witchcraft by showing its consonance with natural magic. Stressing repeatedly that his tale is an allegory (like many other dream visions), Kepler reminds his readers that *daimon* in Greek means "to know" (KGW 11.2:336; ed. Lear, 97n34)—thus any talk of demons or spirits refers to the liberal arts (KGW 11.2:336; ed. Lear, 97n35). Kepler appends a long note comparing Fiolxhilde's rites to his own teaching techniques, in particular his use of words, gestures, and a camera obscura:

> This too is a magic ceremony to which there is a correspondence in the method of teaching astronomy . . . every useful reply requires repose, attentiveness, and carefully selected words. Whenever men or women came to watch me in a particular observation which I performed frequently in Prague in those years, I would first remove myself from them to a nearby corner of the house which I had chosen for this activity. There, after shutting out the daylight, I would fashion a small window out of a tiny aperture, and put a white covering on the wall opposite . . . These were my ceremonies, my rituals. Do you want characters, too? On a black tablet I would write with a piece of chalk, in big letters, whatever seemed suited to the spectators. I would write the letters backwards (more magic!) as Hebrew is written. When the slate was hung upside down in the sun outside the house, the letters I had written would be reflected right side up against the white cloth on the wall within. (KGW 11.2:338; ed. Lear, 100nn44, 46, 47)

The only difference between witchcraft and science here is that the scientist is self-consciously theatrical: "I also used to throw in these very games [*ludos ipsissimos*], which were especially pleasing to my spectators because they knew that they were games [*quod intelligerent, ludos esse*]" (KGW 11.2:338; Lear, 101n48). If inquiry into natural processes could amount on some level to a form of play, then any accusation of practicing witchcraft had to be wildly overblown. Just as witches used occult systems of signification, so too did mathematicians, but neither deserved condemnation for the simple reason that their characters and symbols were at bottom a playful way of producing knowledge: "I play with symbols," Kepler wrote to Joachim Tanckius in 1608. "But I play in such a way that I do not forget that I am playing."[60] Scientific inquiry could thus be insulated from moral and legal attack thanks to the positive reevaluation of play (*ludus*) that we've seen among the high scholastics and in Reginald Scot's admiration for stage magic.

Scholars who have interpreted Edmund's critique of astrology as a reflection of contemporaneous advances in astronomy have effectively reversed the historical reality. His critical attitude was a familiar Christian bias, and the most significant post-Copernican innovations were made by a professional astrologer willing to sail perilously close to witchcraft. The point throughout Kepler's *Dream* is not simply to show the practical effectiveness of magical techniques even in the absence of demonic intervention; it is also to stress that any astronomer worthy of the name shares with witches a love of darkness and shadows, a passionate devotion to the moon, an unshakeable conviction that its cycles are of utmost consequence. To understand them truly one would need a knowledge so advanced, a mathematics so technical, an obsession or even a kind of possession so intense that the astronomer's art of necessity resembles demonic magic. And in some cases, Kepler allows, demons might in fact be involved—particularly when "eclipses of the sun and moon bring about so many ills" (KGW 11.2:339; ed. Lear, 102n55). To

---

60. KGW 16:158: "*Ludo quippe et ego Symbolis . . . sed ita ludo, ut me ludere non obliviscar.*" Further discussion in D. P. Walker, *Studies in Musical Science in the Late Renaissance* (London: Warburg Institute, University of London, 1978), 53–57; Robert S. Westman, "Nature, Art and Psyche: Jung, Pauli, and the Kepler-Fludd Polemic," in *Occult and Scientific Mentalities*, ed. Brian Vickers, 177–229, esp. 205; Johannes Kepler, *Discussion avec le messager céleste: rapport sur l'observation des satellites de Jupiter = Dissertatio cvm nvncio sidereo: narratio de observatis jovis satellitibvs*, trans. Isabelle Pantin (Paris: Les Belles Lettres, 1993), xcii–xciv; Paula Findlen, "Jokes of Nature and Jokes of Knowledge: The Playfulness of Scientific Discourse in Early Modern Europe," *Renaissance Quarterly* 43 (1990): 292–331, esp. 319 on theater; Nick Jardine, "God's 'Ideal Reader': Kepler and His Serious Jokes," in *Johannes Kepler: From Tübingen to Żagań*, ed. R. L. Kremer and J. Wlodarczyk (Warsaw: Studia Copernicana, 2009), 41–51; Aviva Rothman, "Kepler's Astrological Play," in Boner, *Kepler's New Star*, 129–44.

think strictly in terms of *ratio physica* ("the reasoning of physics") does not allow one to exclude conclusively the presence of witchcraft:

> Evil spirits are certainly called powers of darkness and air [e.g., Eph 6:12]. It might be believed, therefore, that they have been condemned and, so to speak, relegated to the regions in the cone of the earth's shadow. When this cone of shadow touches the moon, the demons use the cone of shadow as a ladder to invade the moon in great swarms. And when the cone of the moon's shadow touches the earth in a total eclipse of the sun, the demons return to earth through the cone. . . . These occasions are rare. Insofar as a demon is here understood to be the science of astronomy [*Daemon sumitur pro scientia Astronomica*], the assertion that there is no other way for the mind to go to the moon than by means of the shadow of the earth and *by whatever other means depend on this shadow* is a serious one. (KGW 11.2:339; ed. Lear, 102–3n55; my emphasis)

If demons and witches really exist—and if the moon plays a special role in their collaboration—then any astronomer who endeavors "to extend the boundaries of astronomy" (KGW 11.2:341; ed. Lear, 106n64) will have to agree that eclipses facilitate the casting of spells. And any astronomer worth his salt would make certain that no unusual occurrence in the lunar cycle went unobserved. Like the witches who gather "slips of yew / Silvered in the moon's eclipse" (*Macbeth* 4.1.27–28), true astronomers must also "lie in wait for lunar eclipses," Kepler writes, "and, using them as a ladder, dare the ascent to the moon" (KGW 11.2:341; ed. Lear, 106n64). He had been particularly inspired, he says, by an eclipse that occurred in October 1605, "a little before I got the idea for this book" (KGW 11.2:338; trans. Lear, 101n49).

Shakespeare took note of eclipses, too, along with the new star of 1604, in part because he had a professional stake in the interest that such portents generated among the stargazers at court. "These late eclipses in the sun and moon portend no good to us," says Gloucester. "Though the wisdom of nature can reason thus and thus, yet nature finds itself scourged by the subsequent effects" (KL 1.2.103–6, Q). Elton's first instinct was to take these topical allusions as a portrait of "pagan superstition," even while he understood that the conflict between pro- and anti-astrological discourses was "part of a continuing Renaissance debate. . . . which engaged not only [Shakespeare's] royal patron but also his probably divided audience."[61] It has been little appreciated that those who considered eclipses to be potential harbingers of ruin counted among their company the foremost astronomical authority of

---

61. Elton, *"King Lear" and the Gods*, 156.

the Copernican revolution. A thoughtful deference to astrology would have appeared utterly contemptible and totally without merit—the mere foppery of the world—less to Kepler than to the dogmatic Christians whose censure he, like Shakespeare, spent his career evading. Although Edmund has been taken as the spokesperson for a newly skeptical, more scientifically minded age, his anti-astrological diatribe does not place him on the side of the latest science but rather on the side of the zealous disenchanters who condemned the least hint of magic. Unlike Kepler's Duracotas—the son who reconciles with a parent committed to lunar influence—Edmund turns against his father and sides violently with a very old Christian orthodoxy: radical unbelief in the occult power of the heavens.

Kepler and the King's Men

In October of 1607, Kepler inscribed a copy of *De stella nova* to James I and enclosed a letter of introduction highlighting chapters of special interest.[62] By then James's views on stargazing had been widely disseminated through multiple editions of his *Daemonologie* (in English, Dutch, and Latin), though what first caught Kepler's attention must have been the king's admiration for Tycho Brahe.[63] James's father-in-law, Frederick II of Denmark and Norway, had deeded to Brahe the land for his observatory on Hven, where James and Anna paid him a visit on their honeymoon after a series of ominous storms kept her from Scotland and forced James onto the continent for the wedding. (The subsequent investigation into the cause of those tempests would result in the North Berwick witch trials, and these in turn provided the occasion for James's lengthy rejoinder to Reginald Scot in the *Daemonologie*.)[64] James was so impressed by the setup at Hven that he granted Brahe copyright over his writings in Scotland for the next thirty years and composed a series of sonnets extolling his unprecedented grasp of the cosmos. The Lord "who made all of nought" had "at the creating of this earthly ball ... pitch'd each planet in his place ... as heavenly imps to govern bodies base."[65] The planets, in other words, were designed as angelic intercessors or "heavenly imps"

---

62. KGW 16:103–4; German translation in *Johannes Kepler in seinen Briefen*, ed. and trans. Max Caspar and Walther von Dyck (Munich: R. Oldenbourg, 1930), 296–98.
63. Astrid Stilma, *A King Translated: The Writings of King James VI & I and Their Interpretation in the Low Countries, 1593–1603* (Burlington, VT: Ashgate, 2012), esp. 251.
64. Alan Stewart, *The Cradle King: The Life of James VI & I, the First Monarch of a United Great Britain* (New York: St. Martin's Press, 2003), 115–16.
65. "A Sonnet on Ticho Brahe," in *The Poems of James VI of Scotland*, ed. James Craigie (Edinburgh: Printed for The [Scottish Text] Society by William Blackwood & Sons, 1947), 2:100–101.

to help regulate life on earth. If you wanted to understand their "order, course and influence," you needed "Tycho's tools" (ibid.)—by which James meant the same state-of-the-art gear on Hven that Kepler described as *mirabiles machinae*. The use of these instruments allowed Brahe to assume such "commandment . . . over these commanders" (ibid.)—the influential astral powers—that he had managed to surpass not only Phaeton, with his doomed attempt to master the sun, but the sun-god himself: "Greater art thou," concludes James, "than Apollo clear" (ibid.). The science of astrology, practiced within the bounds of licit or natural magic, afforded Brahe the power once attributed to a mythological divinity.

A Latin translation of several lines from James's sonnet sequence, along with the grant of copyright, were placed by Kepler at the start of Brahe's posthumously published *Astronomiae instauratae progymnasmata* (1602). Kepler subsequently hoped that the king might appreciate how his own observations in *De stella nova* sifted astrological magic for its hard gem of truth. As a "Lutheran astrologer" (KGW 13:184) working in a Catholic court, Kepler seems to have imagined that his knack for walking the line between competing religious factions—as well as the line between *scientia* and superstition—might suit James's need to find the middle path among similar extremes.[66] James was, in Max Caspar's words, "Kepler's great hope in matters of creed."[67] We can tell from the letter accompanying *De stella nova* that Kepler maximized his odds of winning the king's support by doing the same thing Shakespeare was doing. He consulted the *Daemonologie* and tried to coordinate its analysis of magic, bewitchment, and astrology with his own particular enterprise.

James endorses in his treatise the Augustinian consensus among demonologists that one species of astrology has a firm basis in mathematics and plays an indispensable, predictive role in agriculture and medicine. Any person of reason rightly consults the stars (usually via an almanac) in order to determine when to plant and when to harvest, when to cup and when to bleed. Every successful harvest, like every cure for the flu, depends on anticipating the stars' impact, "knowing thereby the powers of simples, and sicknesses, the course of the seasons and the weather, being ruled by their influence."[68] What James condemns are the popular charms practiced by "daft wives" and sundry "unlearned men," which have no real efficacy but sometimes

---

66. D. Harris Wilson, *King James VI and I* (London: Jonathan Cape, 1956), 198–99; Stewart, *Cradle King*, 194.
67. Max Caspar, *Kepler*, trans. C. Doris Hellman, with a new introduction and references by Owen Gingerich (New York: Dover Publications, 1993), 252.
68. *Daemonologie* 1.4, in *Witchcraft in Early Modern Scotland: James VI's Demonology and the North Berwick Witches*, ed. Lawrence Normand and Gareth Roberts (Exeter, UK: University of Exeter Press, 2000), 367.

work anyway "by the power of the Devil for deceiving men" (ibid.). Even more threatening are the people formally schooled in the science of "natural causes" and "natural reason" who begin to seek ultimate mastery of their environment "and so mounting from degree to degree, upon the slippery and uncertain scale of curiosity, they are at last enticed . . . to satisfy their restless minds, even to seek to that black and unlawful science of *Magie*."[69] The worry is that someone legitimately "grounded in astrology"—Doctor Faustus, for example—already possesses "all the principles magic doth require" and might voluntarily enter into a pact with the devil out of a mistaken or delusional view that demonic aid gives one the godlike power to transcend nature.[70] In fact the devil can at best stage pseudo-miracles, either through his highly advanced technical prowess or the great powers of showmanship that he shares with professional actors; hence the fireworks, fake appendages, and bestial transformation that Marlowe's play foregrounds and that likely appeared at the same time in the *Faustcomödie* of Kepler's Tübingen years.[71]

It may seem counterintuitive that an astrologer vulnerable to accusations of witchcraft would make contact with an authority known to have overseen the execution of witches, but the repressive function of absolutist power was evidently less of a concern than its ability to grant sanctuary and, with that, to incite a flamboyant culture of experimentation. James's promotion of the doctrine of divine right traded heavily on the idea that "the power of all witches is restrained by the authorities of the magistrate," as Thomas Cooper (a London preacher) explains. "If once the magistrate hath arrested them, Satan's power ceaseth."[72] By enforcing a violent partition between natural magic and witchcraft, James had the unique, God-given ability to confer legitimacy on an ambiguously positioned stargazer. That James insisted so frequently on his ability to tell divine intervention from natural wonders, victims of genuine demonic possession from frauds, and legitimate actors from con men gave early modern natural philosophers and players reason

---

69. *Daemonologie* 1.3, ed. Normand and Roberts, 365
70. *Doctor Faustus: A- and B-Texts (1604, 1616): Christopher Marlowe and his Collaborator and Revisers*, ed. David Bevington and Eric Rasmussen (Manchester: Manchester University Press, 1993), 120 (1.1.140, 142).
71. On the similarities between Faustus's magic and the commercial theater, see Richard Halpern, "Marlowe's Theater of Night: *Doctor Faustus* and Capital," *ELH* 71 (2004): 455–95; William N. West, *Common Understandings, Poetic Confusion: Playhouses and Playgoers in Elizabethan England* (Chicago: University of Chicago Press, 2021), 43–45.
72. Thomas Cooper, *The mystery of witch-craft* (London, 1617), 246. Cf. James, *Daemonologie* 2.6, ed. Normand and Roberts, 399: "For where God begins justly to strike by his lawful lieutenants it is not the devil's power to defraud or bereave him of the office or effect of his powerful and revenging sceptre." On divine right and witchcraft, see Clark, *Thinking with Demons*, 549–682.

to hope that they could rely on his powers of discrimination in those cases where they were investigating (or actively producing) preternatural wonders that mimicked the works of God or Satan.[73]

In fact the King's Men actively collaborated with engineers, mechanics, architects, and natural philosophers to produce quasi-miraculous, magical effects in their court entertainments. All of these court professionals were technicians of the preternatural. Both Shakespeare and Kepler were familiar with some of the technological achievements of Cornelis Drebbel, whose expertise "in wonderful things [*wunderlichen sachen*]" (KGW 16:7) gave him access to James's inner circle. Credited with inventing the first compound microscope, as well as the submarine, Drebbel was especially interested in lens crafting and designed a machine for precision grinding. Upon arriving at James's court in 1604 he astounded the court with his magic lantern, camera obscura, improved telescopes, a perpetual motion machine, organs, clocks, thermostats, and pyrotechnics—so much so that "James entrusted him with preparing spectacular effects for court masques."[74] (If the dagger in *Macbeth* ever appeared to the audience, it could probably have done so only at court through Drebbel's magic lantern or a projector of the sort used by earlier magi, such Faustus.)[75] Jonson paints a satirical portrait of Drebbel in the figure of Vangoose, that "rare artist" who promises to bring in "some dainty new ting dat never vas nor never sall be in de *rebus natura*; dat has neder van de *materia*, nor de *forma* . . . but is a *mera devisa* of de brain."[76] He was a specialist, that is, in generating effects that seemed to

---

73. See the letter to Prince Henry from 1603 in *Letters of the Kings of England*, ed. James Orchard Halliwell (London, 1846), 2:102: "Ye have oft heard me say that most miracles now a days prove but illusions, and ye may see by this how wary judges should be in trusting accusation without an exact trial, and likewise how easily people are induced to trust wonders"; Gareth Roberts, "'An Art Lawful as Eating'? Magic in *The Tempest* and *The Winter's Tale*," in *Shakespeare's Late Plays: New Readings*, ed. Jennifer Richards and James Knowles (Edinburgh: Edinburgh University Press, 1999), 126–42, esp. 139; Michel Macdonald, ed., *Witchcraft and Hysteria in Elizabethan England: Edward Jorden and the Mary Glover Case* (New York: Routledge, 1991), xlix; George Lyman Kittredge, *Witchcraft in Old and New England* (New York: Russell & Russell, 1958), 319.
74. R. J. W. Evans, *Rudolf II and His World: A Study in Intellectual History 1576–1612* (London: Thames & Hudson, 1997), 189. See also Rosalie L. Colie, "*Some Thankfulnesse to Constantine*": *A Study of English Influence upon the Early Works of Constantijn Huygens* (The Hague: Martinus Nijhoff, 1956), 92–110.
75. See Thomas L. Hankins and Robert J. Silverman, *Instruments and the Imagination* (Princeton, NJ: Princeton University Press, 2014), 47; Anthony Grafton, *Magus: The Art of Magic from Faustus to Agrippa* (Cambridge, MA: Harvard University Press, 2023), 10–11.
76. *The Masque of Augurs* (1622) ll. 79–81, in *The Cambridge Edition of the Works of Ben Jonson*, ed. David Bevington et al. (Cambridge: Cambridge University Press, 2012), 5:593; see also Jennifer Speake, "The Wrong Kind of Wonder: Ben Jonson and Cornelis Drebbel," *Review of English Studies*, n.s. 66.273 (2014): 60–70; Robert Grudin, "Rudolf II of Prague and Cornelis Drebbel: Shakespearean Archetypes?" *Huntington Library Quarterly* 54, no. 3 (1991): 181–205; Francis A. Yates, *Theatre of the World* (Chicago: University of Chicago Press, 1969), esp. 92–111 and 169–85.

transcend the material, natural order. In fact these effects were artificially produced illusions dreamt up by a highly innovative engineer who knew how to capitalize on an observer's imagination to create the effect of supernatural intervention.

Such magic was sheer theater—which, for James, was fine within the confines of the court, the Globe, or a laboratory (all to some extent overlapping venues), but virtually nowhere else because only at court, in the theater, or in the laboratory could people be counted on to recognize that the marvels were produced through natural means by instruments and machinery acting in collaboration with a human observer. (If the aid of spirits was said to be involved—as in Dee's conjurations of Uriel or Drebbel's perpetual motion machine—the spirit was supposed to be benign, incapable of miracles, and its presence was in any case subject to debunking.) Outside these licensed amphitheaters of controlled observation a demon might more easily mislead people into thinking they were in the presence of the supernatural, and this ruse had to be discredited through "careful, and essentially negative, scrutiny."[77] According to James's demonology, Satan's faux miracles—performed in collaboration with witches—were a form of "counterfeiting" in the same way "that simple jugglers will make an hundred things seem both to our eyes and ears otherwise than they are" (*Daemonologie* 1.6, ed. Normand and Roberts, 376). The difference between a simple juggler and a witch in league with Satan was that witches lost their magic in the presence of a godly magistrate, whereas jugglers were greatly empowered by entertaining the court. No one could risk saying that actors' palpably artificial tricks, however "magical," were demonically aided marvels without running afoul of the king's theocratic pretensions. Outside the disenchanted circle of courtly influence, witchcraft was a perpetual threat. Inside, the magic of the King's Men was an art lawful as eating. To the extent that the scenes and machines of their court performances were meant to illustrate the authority of God's anointed king, they tended to do so by showcasing the royal power to dissipate the effects of unlawful magic. In Jonson's first antimasque, the King's Men dressed as witches and danced in the royal presence before finding themselves overcome and dismissed.[78]

---

77. Clark, *Thinking with Demons*, 153.
78. *The Masque of Queens* (1609), in *The Cambridge Edition of the Works of Ben Jonson*, 3:283–349. Cf. Thomas M. Greene, "Magic and Festivity at the Renaissance Court: The 1987 Josephine Waters Bennett Lecture," *Renaissance Quarterly* 40, no. 4 (1987): 636–59; I am returning here to a position with which Greene quarrels: Laura Hibbard Loomis, "Secular Dramatics in the Royal Palace, Paris, 1378, 1389, and Chaucer's 'Tregetoures,'" *Speculum* 33 (1956): 242–55. See also Clark, *Thinking with Demons*, 634–54, on courtly "spectacles of disenchantment."

Because James wanted to be the national arbiter between natural and demonic magic, his government also had to discriminate between the benign forms of play that generated mirth and the more malignant ways of manipulating spectators that involved outright deception toward nefarious ends. The year 1604 saw the adoption of the *Constitutions and Canons Ecclesiastical*, which forbade those without a license from the bishop to attempt "upon any pretense whatsoever . . . to cast out any devil or devils, under pain of the imputation of imposture or cozenage."[79] In the same year, Parliament modified the existing witchcraft statute to make hanging mandatory, without benefit of clergy, for anyone convicted of practicing magic (or rather, trying to practice it, while being deluded by the devil). Immediately upon ascension to the English throne, James empowered the Stationers to enforce a crucial division on every astrological book published in England: "we forbid all printers and booksellers, under the same penalties, to print or expose for sale, any almanacs or prophecies which shall not first have been seen and revised by the archbishop, the bishop (or those who shall be expressly appointed for that purpose), and approved of by their certificates."[80] Astrology was science so long as it was endorsed by the Anglican hierarchy; otherwise it was a fake religion. By the same logic public theater was entertainment so long as it was licensed by the Master of Revels and excluded all positive representations of divinity; otherwise it was Catholicism.

Both Kepler and the London players knew that they stood to benefit from the king's enthusiasm for legislating the difference between lawful and unlawful practices. For Kepler it was also a matter of moving from a Catholic to a Protestant court—or at any rate to a court that might support his work more reliably, as Rudolf was perpetually in arrears with Kepler's salary. The players for their part found that the crackdown on illegal forms of the occult—whether genuine traffic with the devil or the sham pretense of being bewitched—created a market for theatrical *depictions* of genuine traffic with the devil and the sham pretense of being bewitched. Likely in response to the new laws against conjuring, Marlowe's decade-old script about an astrologer's pact with the devil was finally brought into print (1604), just in time to profit from the appearance of the new star, the ban on uncertified prophecy, and the overall animus against conjuring. Within the first ten years of the seventeenth century, Shakespeare's company staged the seduction of Hamlet

---

79. Canon 72 in *Constitutions and Canons Ecclesiastical, 1604: Latin and English*, ed. J. V. Bullard (London: The Faith Press, 1934), 76; discussion in Shapiro, *Year of Lear*, 79; Elton, *"King Lear" and the Gods*, 90.
80. Quoted in Patrick Curry, *Prophecy and Power: Astrology in Early Modern England* (Princeton, NJ: Princeton University Press, 1989), 20.

by a potentially demonic ghost, the artificial bewitchment of Malvolio, the fake possession of Volpone, the witches in *Macbeth* and the *Masque of Queens*, the "demi-devil" Iago and Othello's enchanted handkerchief, the pros and cons of astrology in *King Lear*, and the con-artistry of *The Alchemist* (likely modeled on Dee's sidekick and scryer, Edward Kelley). They often performed at court, where explorations of occult causation and the generation of preternatural phenomena were welcome as nowhere else—particularly over the Christmas holidays, given the heightened appetite for disruptions and reversals of all sorts during this historically festive, playful time.[81]

Kepler claims in his letter to James to have been encouraged to write by Johann Georg Gödelmann—a prominent theorist of magic and godfather to Kepler's son, Ludwig—who thought James might particularly appreciate Kepler's "painstaking differentiation between astrological vanity and natural causes" (KGW 16:103). That differentiation, Kepler says, had allowed him to extract "a precious kernel from the foul dross" of astrological speculation, "which your majesty has generally censured" (KGW 16:103). Kepler hoped that the king, upon reading the book, "might form a somewhat more liberal opinion concerning the sympathy between the sublunary world and the celestial harmonies" (KGW 16:103). What gave Kepler hope is worth dwelling on. He claims that the king had provided a persuasive explanation for the efficacy of the floating test, which "was otherwise generally doubted" (KGW 16:103). The practice was doubted because it required binding a suspected witch and throwing her into water. If she sank, she was innocent; if she floated or "swam," as though by magic, she was a witch for a reason that Kepler found refreshingly unexpected. As James argued in his *Daemonologie*, "water shall refuse to receive them in her bosom that have shaken off them the sacred water of baptism" (*Daemonologie* 3.6, ed. Normand and Roberts, 424). Puritanical doubters like Perkins found this line of thinking just as superstitious and magical as the witchcraft it was supposed to combat since it attributed to all water a lingering sacramental quality, when in fact "the element out of the use of the sacrament, is no sacrament, but returns again to his common use."[82] Kepler by contrast felt that James's analysis "confirmed the experiment's validity [*experimentii firmetur authoritas*]" (KGW 16:103). While no doubt designed to flatter, Kepler's appreciation for this argument cannot be easily disentangled from his interest in testing hypotheses against

---

81. Leah Marcus, *Puzzling Shakespeare: Local Reading and its Discontents* (Berkeley: University of California Press, 1988), 154–55.
82. William Perkins, *A discourse of the damned art of witchcraft* [etc.] (Cambridge, 1610), 208; see also Robert Bartlett, *Trial by Fire and Water: The Medieval Judicial Ordeal* (Oxford: Clarendon, 1986), 144–52.

observable data—an interest that he hoped James might share. Kepler seems to have imagined that James could be equally swayed by the empirical data contained in *De stella nova*: "All the more may one wish for the same [validation] concerning some astrological experiments" (KGW 16:103). In fact this wish and the flattery go hand in hand: Kepler means to impress on James his understanding of the hierarchy that will structure any future relationship between them. He is in effect following the same strategy that John Dee had tried when he volunteered for trial, live burial, or burning and thus showed his willingness to submit fully to the sovereign's discrimination in all matters related to magic. If Kepler, like Dee or Harriot, should ever be suspected of witchcraft, his letter implies, he is willing to drown for it. Such daring deference could purchase tremendous latitude for speculation and experiment.

Kepler's overture bore fruit, eventually. After he publicly dedicated the *Harmonice mundi* (1619) to James, he entrusted delivery to a *"Doctore Theologo Namens Donne"* who was visiting Linz at the time on a diplomatic mission to the Holy Roman Emperor.[83] Later that same year Kepler was invited to the London court by Sir Henry Wotton (whose infatuation with the new star Jonson mocks in *Volpone*), but by then war had broken out between James's son-in-law (the Elector Palatinate) and the emperor upon whose favor Kepler still depended.[84] Meanwhile Kepler was urgently needed at home to defend his mother in court from the accusations of witchcraft that, he feared, his demonological treatise on lunar astronomy had helped to inspire. He did not in this case advocate for the floating test. Instead he moved to Württemberg and composed a painstaking rebuttal of each of the charges. It was true that she had tried to have the skull of Kepler's father exhumed so that it could be cast in silver and gifted to Kepler's brother as a drinking vessel. Although skull flagons were characteristic of sorcery, they could also serve as sacred relics, and at any rate, drinking from one would serve as a *memento mori*, the importance of which Katharina had learned from sermons.[85] It was not true that she had lamed the local butcher by teaching him an invocation to the sun-god. "Some particular words," Kepler explains, "whether the names of God or his creatures, poetical phrase like 'salve Sol' or 'light of the sun' etc.—just like 'salve festa dies'—are not diabolical words, or pagan . . . but rather expressions

---

83. KGW 16:215; quoted in Wilbur Applebaum, "Donne's Meeting with Kepler: A Previously Unknown Episode," *Philological Quarterly* 50, no. 1 (1970): 132–34.
84. Sir Henry Wotton, *Reliquiae Wottonianae, or A Collection of the lives, letters and poems* (London: Roycroft, 1672), 291. Ben Jonson, *Volpone, or The Fox*, ed. Brian Parker, rev. ed. (Manchester: Manchester University Press, 1999), 132–33 (2.1.37–38). Westman, *Copernican Question*, 409.
85. Ulinka Rublack, *The Astronomer and the Witch: Johannes Kepler's Fight for his Mother* (Oxford: Oxford University Press, 2015), 170–74.

of the Holy Trinity, which to the honorable judge suffices almost to guarantee that they were well-intended and to rule out any suspicion of an attempt at the devil's work."[86] Kepler, it seems, was defending his mother with the argument that superstition and the bogus enchantments of the pagan *saeculum* had persisted into the present *by way of* Christianity. If Christianity had successfully neutralized or at any rate redirected the power of incantation to a proper devotional object, what was to be feared from his mother's use of such formulae? This is the type of argument that only someone steeped in demonology could make, and it was an argument that inquisitors had been trained to respect.

Kepler did not mention it in the court papers, but an invocation to the sun-god (*salva Sol*), though admittedly ineffectual, mirrored his own commitment to a sun-centered universe. He thought it was almost a matter of indifference whether one ascribed "the motion of the earth around the sun to physical, or if you prefer, metaphysical reasons."[87] Heliocentrism recommended itself as the most likely physical model for the same theological and astrological reasons that had motivated Christians to celebrate Christmas on solstice: "the sun in the middle of the moving stars, himself at rest and yet the source of motion," writes Kepler, "carries the image of God the Father and Creator. . . . He distributes his motive force through a medium that contains the moving bodies even as the Father creates through the Holy Ghost."[88] From Kepler's perspective, the great achievement of Copernicus— a canon who wanted to expand the observation of Martianus Cappella that Mercury and Venus "do not travel around the Earth at all, but circle the Sun in wider revolutions"—was to bring the cosmos into alignment with the irrepressible astrological symbolism of Christian theology.[89]

---

86. Johannes Kepler, *Opera Omnia*, ed. Ch. Frisch (Frankfurt, 1870), 8.1:538; see also Rublack, *Astronomer and the Witch*, 202.

87. *Mysterium cosmographicum*, Praefatio (KGW 1:9); English in *The Secret of the Universe*, trans. Duncan, 63 (modified). Further discussion in Robert S. Westman, "The Copernicans and the Churches," in *God and Nature: Historical Essays on the Encounter between Christianity and Science*, ed. David C. Lindberg and Ronald L. Numbers (Berkeley: University of California Press, 1986), 76–113; Peter Barker and Bernard R. Goldstein, "Theological Foundations of Kepler's Astronomy," *Osiris* 16 (2001): 88–113.

88. Letter to Maestlin, 3 October 1595 (KGW 13:35). See also Edwin Burtt, *The Metaphysical Foundations of Modern Physical Science: A Historical and Critical Essay*, rev. ed. (London: Routledge & Kegan Paul, 1951), 47–51; Job Kozhamthadam, *The Discovery of Kepler's Laws: The Interaction of Science, Philosophy, and Religion* (Notre Dame, IN: University of Notre Dame Press, 1994), 192–93.

89. Martianus Capella, *De nuptiis Philologiae et Mercurii* 8.857, in *Martianus Capella*, ed. James Willis (Leipzig: B. G. Teubner, 1983), 324; English in *The Marriage of Philology and Mercury*, trans. William Harris Stahl et al. (New York: Columbia University Press, 1977), 333; cited by Copernicus, *De Revolutionibus* 1.10, in *De revolutionibus libri sex*, ed. Heribert M. Nobis (Hildesheim: Gerstenberg, 1984), 19; see also Edward Grant, *Planets, Orbs and Spheres: The Medieval Cosmos, 1280–1687* (Cambridge: Cambridge University Press, 1994), 312–13.

Whether Shakespeare ever came across any form of the heliocentric model (in either its ancient, medieval, or modern variants) is not easily settled. Mary Thomas Crane's argument that "Shakespeare does not seem to have been particularly interested in astronomy" is belied by the wide range of astrological references across his corpus, some of which are notably up to date.[90] Poins jokes about "the fiery Trigon" (*2 Henry IV* 2.4.263), Gloucester worries about recent eclipses, and Edmund alludes to the new star of 1604. All of these were of great concern to people at court whose interests Shakespeare needed to pique. The contention that he presupposed a geocentric view of the universe draws its best support from Ulysses's brief description of the cosmos: "The heavens themselves, the planets and *this centre*," he says, "observe degree, priority and place" (*Troilus* 1.3.85–86, my emphasis). And yet the Ptolemaic model had always had to coexist with Christianity's cooptation of earlier forms of sun worship; the celebration of Christmas on winter solstice and Easter on the first Sunday after the first full moon following the vernal equinox gave the sun far greater prominence and centrality than the earth in the Christian cosmos. Copernicans could and did borrow from this symbolic heliocentrism to give their astronomical model protection from doubters—as does Ulysses, when he follows the reference to the earth as "this centre" with the observation that the sun holds pride of place in the middle of the universe:

> And therefore is the glorious planet Sol
> In noble eminence enthroned and sphered
> Amidst the other[s].[91]

So while there may not be "any *unambiguous* and *direct* references to the heliocentric model of the universe in Shakespeare's plays," the ambiguity and indirection of the reference we have is of a piece with the Copernican age.[92] Shakespeare shared with the Copernicans of his day a deep fascination with astrology and, in the case of Kepler specifically, with demonology. Both Shakespeare and Kepler furthermore looked to James to stave off prosecution despite their commitment to practices that zealous Christians at the time wanted to abolish. It was through the power of an absolutist, theocratic magistrate alone that the King's Men found shelter to explore the

---

90. Crane, *Losing Touch with Nature*, 124.
91. *Troilus* 1.3.93–95; see David H. Levy with Judy A. Hayden, "An English Renaissance Astronomy Club? Shakespeare, Observation and the Cosmos," in *Literature in the Age of Celestial Discovery: From Copernicus to Flamsteed*, ed. Judy A. Hayden (New York: Palgrave Macmillan, 2016), 75–90, esp. 80.
92. Crane, *Losing Touch with Nature*, 206n4, my emphasis.

occult causation of apparent miracles in an age when genuine miracles were supposed to have ceased.

The Maidenliest Star in the Firmament

The Hebrew prophets feature prominently in Geoffrey of Monmouth's chronicle: Madden—the third ruler of Britain—is paired with Samuel "the prophet"; Ebraucus with David, Nathan and Asaph; Rud Hudibras with Haggai, Amos, Jehu, Joel, and Azariah; Leir's father, Bladud, with Elijah; and Cordeilla with Isaiah and Hosea.[93] These pairings coordinate the chronology of the pagan world with the unfolding of Abrahamic monotheism in order to anticipate the triumph of the latter over the former, as when Bladud's magical powers fail him and he crashes midflight into the temple of Apollo. Holinshed omits direct reference to the prophets but retains the fall of Leir's father—now an expert in "astronomy" as well as "nigromancy"—and dates Leir's reign with reference to the iconoclastic regime of Joas.[94] Christians familiar with these references would have known enough to infer that they were witnessing in *Lear* the effects on the world of an exceedingly painful revelation: "I the Lord do all things my self alone," announces Isaiah. "I only spread out the heaven . . . by my own self" (Is 44:24, Bishops 1568). With no other god before him, he alone pitched Mercury, Venus, Mars, Jupiter, and Saturn in their places. He alone determined their significance, and their significance humbled the truths of the wicked: "I destroy the tokens of witches" (Is 44:25, Bishops 1568). This destruction, William Perkins notes, had been especially bad for "the astrologers of Chaldea," who were once considered wise but then had their wisdom exposed as foolish trickery.[95] Their divinations were sheer hocus pocus. "In like sort, God forbiddeth his people of England to give credit, or fear the constellations & conjunctions of stars and planets which have no power of themselves" (ibid.). The disenchantment already at work in the world when Leir assumed the throne—though long stymied by the relapse of the Catholic Church into magic—was being violently reasserted in Perkins's day.

It had to be reasserted because people born after Christ, like people born after the prophets, all too often chose the empty fictions and vain calculations of the *saeculum* over the arrival of a Kingdom whose coming had so far

---

93. *Pontici Virunnii viri doctissimi Britannicæ historiæ* [etc.] (London, 1585), 6; Monmouth, *History of the Kings of Britain*, ed. Reeve, 34–37, 44–45.
94. *Holinshed's Chronicles: England, Scotland and Ireland*, with a new introduction by Vernon F. Snow (New York: AMS, 1976; reprint of the 1807 edition), 1:446.
95. William Perkins, *Foure great lyers, striuing who shall win the siluer whetstone. Also, a resolution to the countri-man, prouing is vtterly vnlawfull to buye or vse our yeerly prognostications* (London, 1585), n.p.

KING LEAR AND THE COPERNICAN REVOLUTION

defied all prophecy and whose reality was therefore rejected by all manner of infidels: "We know that in all nations sorcery or witchcraft hath borne sway," Calvin preaches, "yea, and the more sway for the rejecting of God's truth."[96] Scripture warns its readers against the ongoing threat of magic, according to Calvin, "lest we should fall into such a maze as the wretched infidels are in, yea and proceed so far as to wander quite away, when we have once forsaken his word" (ibid.). Protestants were especially keen to turn the scriptural critique of magic against the Catholic sacraments, but they were hardly alone in believing that the process of Christianization was on the brink of failure. Both the Protestant and Catholic Reformations were equally committed to "the abolition of magic and the eradication of a wide range of popular cultural forms as 'superstition.'"[97] Indeed the rampant intramural conflicts among Christians, together with Christendom's extramural conflicts with unbelievers, strengthened the dread that humanity as a whole had come to prefer the superficial marvels of the natural world to the genuine miracles performed by God: "Witness the Muslims in Africa and Asia, the heretics of Germany, France, and Britain, and the apathetic Catholics," writes Martín Del Río (a Jesuit scholar whose study of magic is cited by Kepler and Jonson). "In these areas, magic is immensely strong."[98] True Christians—whether Protestant or Catholic—had to double down on the scriptural condemnation of magic, to look inward and repent, so as to forgo "heresies, atheisms, enchantments, scandals and vices."[99]

King Lear trades on the widespread suspicion that the disillusioning aspects of Christ's coming were being forgotten, such that a massive cultural campaign against superstition, astrology, and magic was urgently needed if a truly global enlightenment was ever going to come into being. Lear's invocation of the stars in his curse on Cordelia, for example, presents an image of pre-Christian witchcraft recognizable to many as precisely the type of enchantment whose supernatural status demanded mockery and total debunking—all the more so, as it was still ubiquitous:

> For by the sacred radiance of the sun,
> The mysteries [F2] of Hecate and the night,
> By all the operation of the orbs

---

96. *The sermons of M. Iohn Caluin vpon the fifth booke of Moses called Deuteronomie* [etc.], trans. Arthur Golding (London, 1583), 670.
97. Clark, *Thinking with Demons*, 530.
98. Martín Del Río, *Investigations into Magic*, ed. and trans. P. G. Maxwell Stuart (Manchester: Manchester University Press, 2000), 26–27. For Kepler's borrowings, see *Somnium* (KGW 11.2:336; Lear, *Kepler's Dream*, 98n38); for Jonson's, see *The Masque of Queens*, in *The Cambridge Edition of the Works of Ben Jonson*, 3:332–36, 347.
99. Crepet, *Deux Livres*, fo. 408v; quoted in Clark, *Thinking with Demons*, 532.

> From whom we do exist and cease to be,
> Here I disclaim all my paternal care,
> Propinquity and property of blood.
>
> (KL 1.1.110–15)

Because he cannot swear by God, Lear appeals instead to what he considers the totality of all being—the cosmos from which we are born, to which we return, and with which we can collaborate to a limited extent through magic. Lear's wording is likely modeled on similar curses that appear in classical literature: Dido calls on the Sun and Hecate, as do Medea and Phaedre.[100] Plutarch explains that Hecate, like the moon, operates at the boundary between the earth and the heavens and is therefore well-positioned to intercede between human affairs and higher powers (*Obsolescence of Oracles* 416e–f, LCL). According to Ovid's Medea, she comes when called by incantation "to the aid of the spells and arts of magicians," who hope to bend the moon's influence to their purposes.[101] Kepler's *Somnium* is indebted to this tradition, which similarly furnishes Edmund with a readymade accusation against Edgar when he claims to have seen his brother

> in the dark, his sharp sword out,
> Warbling of wicked charms, conjuring the moon
> To stand's auspicious mistress.
>
> (KL 2.1.37–39, Q)

One way to ward off the baleful effects of such charms was to offer Hecate gifts at a crossroads—hence her epithets as three-personed, the goddess of the three-way meeting, or "triple Hecate" (*Midsummer Night's Dream* 5.1.391). Christians had continued to render devotion "to the gods of the trivium" out of an enduring conviction that humanity's well-being, if not its very existence, depended on the cosmos, despite the manifold efforts over more than a millennium to dispel such magical thinking.[102] Likely as a result of Middleton's revisions, Hecate makes an appearance in *Macbeth*, too, although this

---

100. Virgil, *Aeneid* 4.609 (LCL); Seneca, *Medea* 7, 577, 832, 840 (LCL) and *Phaedre* 412 (LCL).
101. Ovid, *Metamorphoses* 7.195 (LCL): "*cantusque artisque magorum.*" Prospero quotes from this speech when he abjures his magic (*Tempest* 5.1.33ff.). Cf. *The XV. Bookes of P. Ouidius Naso, Entitled Metamorphosis* [etc.], trans. Arthur Golding (London, 1587), 90.
102. Valerie I. J. Flint, *The Rise of Magic in Early Medieval Europe* (Princeton. NJ: Princeton University Press, 1991), 89; Bernadette Filotas, *Pagan Survivals, Superstitions and Popular Cultures in Early Medieval Pastoral Literature* (Toronto: Pontifical Institute of Mediaeval Studies, 2005), 208–10; Peter Mortenson, "Friar Bacon and Friar Bungay: Festive Comedy and Three Form'd Luna," *English Literary Renaissance* 2 (1972): 194–207, esp. 202–4; Frank Ardolino, "The Protestant Context of Peele's Old Wives Tale," *Medieval and Renaissance Drama in England* 18 (2005): 146–165, esp. 150.

play is not set in a pagan world and does not need to be, since those who conjured by her name were considered legion throughout Christendom.

James understood that reports of such conjurations could not be taken at face value. They might, like Edmund's report of Edgar's magic, be lies meant to smear a rival or, like Lear's invocation of the sun and moon, the attempt of a "lunatic" (KL 3.7.46) to enlist higher powers in his own delusional enterprise. If these astrological curses seemed to work, they worked at bottom only by seeming—which is to say, "by the power of the devil for deceiving men, and not by any inherent virtue in these vain words and freits [i.e., superstitious formulae]" (*Daemonologie* 1.4, ed. Normand and Roberts, 367). James draws here on a skeptical attitude toward the efficacy of language, derived from Aristotle and Augustine, that runs throughout Renaissance demonology and that Protestants found especially inspiring: "That which is in nature nothing but a bare signification," writes William Perkins, "cannot serve to work a wonder, and this is the nature of all words."[103] Since language had been "invented only to show or signify some thing" (ibid., 137) it was impossible for spells, charms, or curses to have any kinetic effect on the material world; and in fact Lear's invocation of the sun, moon, and Hecate to preserve him in his loathing of Cordelia proves to be ineffectual when he begs her forgiveness. Astrology, among all the dark arts, was especially bankrupt, not only when conjurors swore by astral powers but when they claimed to know how the "signs" in the heavens influenced the body: "And how can it stand with reason, that in a firmament feigned by poets and philosophers, a forged sign, which indeed is nothing, should have any power or operation on the bodies of men?" asks Perkins (ibid., 89). Legitimate sciences proceed by way of axioms and precepts that can be confirmed "by observation and experience" (ibid., 84), but the stars are too vast, too complex, and too mixed to afford meaningful inferences.

If the astrological conjuring in *Lear*, along with all the other god references, can seem on account of their futility "entirely 'disenchanted'"—to recur to Richard Strier—we should remember that righteous Christians were the ones most committed to the eradication of magic. They were the ones who thought that believers in astrology—including believers who outwardly professed to be Christians—had put their faith in the starry firmament to the point of terrifying themselves with mistaken ideas about its power. Those who did not believe preached the gospel of Edmund. In the early seventeenth century, visceral disgust at the astrological foppery of the world had been fully integrated into the secularizing viewpoint of Christianity; this

---

103. Perkins, *A discourse of the damned art of witchcraft*, 136–37.

viewpoint fervently condemned how "we make guilty of our disasters the sun, the moon and the stars, as if we were villains on necessity, fools by heavenly compulsion, knaves, thieves, and treacherers by spiritual predominance; drunkards, liars and adulterers by an enforced obedience of planetary influence; and all that we are evil in by a divine thrusting on" (KL 1.2.120–26, Q).[104] No element of the astrologers' "curious science," in the words of Stubbes, exercised skeptical Christians more than its denial of human accountability—notwithstanding the doctrine of predestination, whose similarity to astrological fate made Christians all the more hostile to the stars' alleged dominion: "Belief in providence," writes Max Weber, "is the consistent rationalization of magical divination, to which it is related, and which for that very reason it seeks to devalue as completely as possible, as a matter of principle."[105] In the Christian view, humans are base by nature, lecherous, given to every form of license but, for all that, no less personally responsible for their depravity. If the fault is in our stars, Stubbes asks, "why should the homicide, the murtherer, adulterer, or wicked person be punished, whereas he might say, it was not I, it was *Planetarium injuria*, the force of the planets that compelled me to sin?"[106] For Stubbes, as for Edmund—as indeed for Edmund Spenser—"it is the manner of men, that when they are fallen into any absurdity . . . they are always ready to impute the blame thereof unto the heavens, so to excuse their own follies and imperfections."[107] In the words of Shakespeare's curiously puritanical villain, it is "an admirable evasion of whoremaster man, to lay his goatish disposition on the charge of stars" (KL 1.2.126–28, Q).

Of all the Christian references in this ostensibly pagan play—and of all the topical allusions to contemporary England—Edmund's concluding remarks on astrology are among the most pointed: "Fut, I should have been that I am had the maidenl[i]est star in the firmament twinkled on my bastardy" (KL 1.2.131–33, Q). The freshly coined superlative here for the newest star in heaven probably refers to the same astral development that inspired Kepler to write *De stella nova*: "When these words were first spoken," notes F. G. Butler, "a virginal star—a nova—was twinkling in the sky above an audience

---

104. Warren Smith, "The Elizabethan Rejection of Judicial Astrology and Shakespeare's Practice," *Shakespeare Quarterly* 9, no. 2 (1958): 159–76.
105. MWG 1/22.2:297; English in Max Weber, *Economy and Society: An Outline of Interpretative Sociology*, ed. Guenther Roth and Claus Wittich (Berkeley: University of California Press, 1978), 1:523.
106. Stubbes, *Second Part of the Anatomie of Abuses*, in *Philip Stubbes's Anatomy of the Abuses*, ed. Furnivall, 61.
107. Edmund Spenser, *A View of the State of Ireland: From the First Printed Edition (1633)*, ed. Andrew Hadfield and Willy Maley (Oxford: Blackwell, 1997), 1.

fearfully sensitive to such phenomena."[108] As in Kepler's treatise, the new star is both the youngest in the firmament (hence "maidenliest") and yet unnervingly reminiscent of an earlier star that announced a virgin birth (hence "maidenliest" in another sense) and that notoriously cast its light upon a bastard. "Fut"—a colloquial shortening of "Christ's foot"—follows a pattern long established by the Nativity plays in which shepherds who knew nothing of the revelation about to be writ large across the heavens swore in advance by their coming savior. Even that fleeting mention of Christ is suppressed in the folio, probably in accordance with the 1606 Act to Restrain Abuses of Players. The disappearance would be minor were it not part of a much broader push over the course of the sixteenth and seventeenth centuries to eliminate from the stage certain kinds of religious content—the latest in a long line of secularizations prompted by the oldest of theological motives: namely, to demonize popular piety as a form of worldliness and unbelief. Any biblical drama featuring the "maidenliest star in the firmament" over Bethlehem had become as taboo as judicial astrology.

Freed from astral influence, Edmund cannot escape the lingering demands of an old Christian script: "Pat he comes, like the catastrophe of the old comedy. My cue is villainous melancholy with a sith [sigh, F] like them o'Bedlam.—O, these eclipses do portend these divisions" (KL 1.2.134–35, Q). I will have more to say in the next chapter about the transformation of St. Mary of Bethlehem into the asylum known as Bedlam but want to register briefly how mention of it here ties Edmund, despite his nominal antiquity, to various processes of secularization that occurred in the sixteenth century. Not only had the monasteries been dissolved but the dramatic representations of Christ—"a begger of Bedlem, borne as a bastard" (York 32.106)—had been forcibly suppressed. For all of Edmund's celebrated modernity, he draws inspiration from forms of drama that were no longer in fashion; in fact the type of soliloquy in which he speaks—a villain leveling with the audience about his deception of everyone else—comes from the cycle plays.[109]

"Catastrophe" means literally "overturning" and had been used dramaturgically since antiquity to signify a crucial plot twist—often a tragedy's final resolution, though by the Renaissance it was applicable to "the end or

---

108. F. G. Butler, "Novas, Eclipses and the English Stage, 1598–1608," *Shakespeare in Southern Africa* 10 (1997): 33–43 at 39. F3 first emends "maidenlest" to "maidenliest."
109. John Parker, *The Aesthetics of Antichrist: From Christian Drama to Christopher Marlowe* (Ithaca, NY: Cornell University Press, 2007), 113–16; Neil Corcoran, *Reading Shakespeare's Soliloquies: Text, Theatre, Film* (London: Bloomsbury, 2018), 69.

shutting up of a comedy," as well, "or any thing else."¹¹⁰ The term had been taken up by contemporary astrologers to describe an astral development, such as the new star, that might augur "a renewal of maximum contention" (KGW 1:352). Helisaeus Roeslin—one of Kepler's correspondents—argued for example that James's accession and the subsequent unification of England with Scotland had coincided with the Fiery Trigon and the appearance of a new star because the world was at last reaching its promised end: "A catastrophe will arise on account of all the things that have occurred in Christendom over many years," he writes. Long had the astronomers kept watch, but now at last the great event "is coming to be in England."¹¹¹ Despite Kepler's defense of the Trigon's "particular power for stirring (I do not say compelling) the nature of sublunar things" (KGW 1:181) and despite his support for "the utility of the doctrine of Trigons in the history of the age of the world" (given the Trigons' correspondence with so many historic figures—above all Christ), he tries to accommodate Pico della Mirandola's critique of the attempt to tie celestial events to specific happenings on earth. Kepler suggests that the new star conveys something "a bit more modest [*paulo plus ruboris*]" and that people should react to its appearance "most righteously in accordance with that star of the Magi" (KGW 1:321–22). They should take to heart the admonitions of the gospel, "descend into themselves and examine their sins, acknowledge their errors and crimes and be converted to true repentance" (KGW 1:354–55). Kepler in this case follows a strategy devised by late scholastic theorists of magic when faced with preternatural phenomena or dire omens whose interpretation might seem to require recourse to superstition. Whatever occult mechanisms lay behind an omen or apparent miracle, its meaning in the end could be referred to the conscience on the grounds that the book of nature is filled with semiotic prompts for an inward feeling of remorse; from this source commonly spring the abrupt shifts in world history that are a regular element in the ordinary course of things.¹¹² Using nothing but material causation and forgoing all miracles, God could inspire people to confront their own nature—and to change.

"Woe that too late repents!" (KL 1.4.249, F) is probably the most openly Christian leitmotif in *King Lear*. Lear and Gloucester both come to regret how they've treated their children, and even Edmund resolves at the end of

---

110. John Florio, *A World of Words* (London, 1598), 63; thanks to Margreta de Grazia for this reference; see de Grazia, *Four Shakespearean Period Pieces*, 161.
111. Helisaeus Roeslin, *Iudicium, oder Bedencken* (Strasbourg, 1605), sig. Aiij^r; for discussion see Granada, "Kepler v. Roeslin," 302.
112. Clark, *Thinking with Demons*, 445–56, esp. 452; Westman, *Copernican Question*, 393.

the play to do "some good... despite mine own nature" (KL 5.3.241–2, F). In this preoccupation with repentance, Shakespeare follows the anonymous *Leir* and the medieval dramatic tradition at a time when the sacrament of penance—among all but two others—had been eliminated on the grounds that it was nothing more than a "means to enchant and bewitch... innocent simple souls, and so to offer them up for a prey to their great idol at Rome."[113] Accusations that penance and, more specifically, the words of absolution were a form of magic exploded during the Reformation, as Protestants labored to see the old Catholic spell broken.[114] Like so many traditional observances, the rituals of remorse had been consumed over the course of the sixteenth century by their age-old proximity to the emptiness of performance, or—if the rituals were not completely empty—by the strategic self-assertion they made possible under a show of humility. Witness Richard III, "sealed in [his] nativity, / The slave of nature and the son of hell" affecting regret out of pure self-interest by wetting "with repentant tears" the graves of those he had buried (*Richard III* 1.3.229–30). Fear of the hypocrisy on display here is why Kepler urges his fellow Christians to be converted by the nova "to *true* repentance." Suspicion of what Luther had called "gallows repentance" or "Judas repentance"—faking remorse in the hope of escaping punishment—was by the early seventeenth century a standard gripe against the sacrament of penance.[115]

Edmund seems at first to be cut from the same Machiavellian cloth as Richard III. When betraying Gloucester toward the end of getting the family estate, he feigns a grudging remorse at having been forced to expose his father's treason: "How malicious is my fortune, that I must repent to be just!" (KL 3.5.9–10). A similar type of fake regret was practiced by Plexirtus, the character in Sidney's *Old Arcadia* on whom Edmund is based.[116] Achieving absolution and making satisfaction for your wrongs, in the Protestant tradition, does not transcend the taint of a means–end transaction; it cannot cleanse your behavior of all negative imputation. On the contrary, it opens

---

113. John Gee, *The foot out of the snare with a detection of sundry late practices and impostures of the priests and Iesuits in England* [etc.] (London, 1624), 51.
114. Thomas Tentler, *Sin and Confession in the Age of Reformation* (Princeton, NJ: Princeton University Press, 1977), 294; Lea, *History of the Inquisition*, 2:13. For the loss of the sacrament of penance, see Sarah Beckwith, *Shakespeare and the Grammar of Forgiveness* (Ithaca, NY: Cornell University Press, 2011), esp. 85–93.
115. See John Parker, "Antinomian Shakespeare: Confession and English Drama across the Reformation Divide," in *Shakespeare and Judgment*, ed. Kevin Curran (Edinburgh: Edinburgh University Press, 2016), 175–94; Parker, "Faustus, Confession, and the Sins of Omission," *ELH* 80, no. 1 (2013): 29–59.
116. Sir Philip Sidney, *The Countesse of Pembrokes Arcadia*, ed. Albert Feuillerat (Cambridge: Cambridge University Press, 1963), 213.

the penitent to the charge of committing a deeper, more conniving evil—that of pretending to be sorry in order to gain tactical advantages. Shakespeare's other representations of penance in *Measure for Measure* and *Romeo and Juliet* draw from the same well, such that shrift explicitly serves the ends of deceit. The duke of dark corners manages to secure a bride for himself by posing as a mendicant friar and hearing confessions; the willingness of "star-crossed lovers" to meet secretly for romantic trysts under pretense of being confessed leads to their illicit marriage and deaths. The sacrament of penance, besides abetting false magic, is in the words of *Romeo and Juliet*'s source text, "the key to whoredom."[117]

Had *Lear* followed its source in the case of Edmund's repentance, we would expect to see more of the same—a fake demonstration of remorse that would seem simultaneously pre-Christian and typical of Catholics. Instead the play shows something that is, in its way, more optimistic. At the moment of his death, for the first time, Edmund does not appear to be running a con, and audiences have reason to trust the appearance if only because his repentance has no consequence. The timing fulfills Lear's early dictum—woe to him that repents too late—but the belatedness and ineffectuality also safeguard the sincerity of Edmund's remorse from contamination by success. He has nothing more to gain, and in fact gains nothing. That alone, after all his machinations, can make something he says sound genuinely selfless. He begins to long for something above or beyond or against his natural inclinations to take possession of his life—to long, that is, for a will within himself to act *against* the self.

Is this not a foreshadowing of the grace that would be available to humanity after the maidenliest star of the firmament twinkled on Christ's bastardy? The fundamental problem with astrology, according to the traditional Augustinian critique, is that it dooms proponents to a life of impenitence by encouraging them to deny personal responsibility. Even serious Calvinists officially committed to double predestination could hold to a version of this view: "It is foolishness to ascribe the regiment of our affairs to the stars, they being matters contingent, which depend on the will and pleasure of man."[118] Of course the will to pleasure, from the same perspective, is a form of enslavement that leaves a person beholden to an inborn temperament and goatish disposition—the inherent depravity of humanity. But God has the power to override innate, physiological instincts using mysterious backdoors

---

117. *The tragicall historye of Romeus and Iuliet* [etc.], trans. Arthur Brooke (London, 1562), n.p. ("To the Reader").
118. Perkins, *A commentarie or exposition, vpon the fiue first chapteres of the Epistle to the Galations*, 317.

he placed in the human animal at its making so as to allow even the worst sinners to feel remorse. Thus the inordinate appreciation among early modern Protestants, as well as Catholics, for any spasm of regret that went beyond a person's habitual leanings. You could devote yourself to the *saeculum* by virtue of your ingrained appetites, inflict untold damage, and yet still form an intention to deny nature and strengthen your moral fiber. The extraordinary lesson of Edmund is that you could do this without ever hearing the gospel, so long as you did not believe in astrology.

CHAPTER 6

Medicine and the Secularization of Miracles

The War Against Miracles

A standard sixteenth-century justification for secularizing England's religious houses held that they had already been relinquished to the world by an impious clergy. Assets supposedly dedicated to God had come to feed human appetites—for money, sex, food, and art especially. Parliament noted in 1536 that for the space of "two hundred years and more" efforts had been made "for an honest and charitable reformation of such unthrifty, carnal, and abominable living, yet nevertheless little or none amendment is hitherto had."[1] Instead of adhering to the faith, "a great multitude of religious persons do rather choose to rove abroad in apostasy" (ibid.), as though there were no difference between taking orders and abandoning Christianity. The temporal power was not so much despoiling the church as putting to better use what little remained after an irreversible wave of secularization had already dissolved its properties, "now being spent, spoiled, and wasted for increase and maintenance of sin" (ibid., 259). Ample incomes from rent and tithes were to be reallocated for the benefit of the commonwealth rather than the cloistered, "as in erecting of grammar schools . . . the further aug-

---

1. "Act for the Dissolution of the Lesser Monasteries, A.D. 1536," in *Documents Illustrative of English Church History*, ed. Henry Gee and William John Hardy (London: Macmillan, 1921), 258.

menting of the Universities, and better provision for the poor and needy."[2] The King's New School in Stratford-upon-Avon, founded by Edward VI and the most likely site for Shakespeare's education, was the direct result of this movement. The public theaters in which his company played were built in the Liberties formerly attached to monastic estates, and his private venue, the Blackfriars, was a secularized Dominican priory.[3] Desacralization prepared the literal grounds for Shakespearean drama.

Early modern secularizers were especially keen to eliminate the representation, performance, and authentication of miracles. We find repeatedly in the injunctions of Protestant Tudors the demand to "take away, utterly extinct, and destroy all shrines . . . pictures, paintings, and all other monuments of feigned miracles, pilgrimages, idolatry, and superstition."[4] To Protestant eyes, the material artifacts associated with the cult of the saints (icons, relics, and so forth) had replaced the transcendence of the deity with "works devised by men's fantasies" (ibid., 419–20; cf. 431). Especially contemptible to reformers was the expectation that pilgrims might experience a miracle cure for dire illness after making a donation in the presence of an icon or sanctified corpse. The considerable sums spent on these quack remedies, Protestants argued, ought to be redirected to charity, if not also to hospitals staffed by trained physicians. Seekers of miraculous healings were told that "it shall profit more their soul's health, if they do bestow on the poor and needy, [that] which they would have bestowed upon the said images and relics."[5] It was better to die of affliction than to imperil one's eternal salvation by seeking a cure "at the tombs & statues of saints."[6] Medical care was of course a vital necessity, but the London hospitals ostensibly committed to relieving the sick and lame were devoted instead to the "maintenance of canons, priests and monks, to live in pleasure," according to Richard Gresham, the Lord Mayor of London at the time of the dissolution.[7] These institutions

---

2. "Act Dissolving the Chantries, A.D. 1547," in Gee and Hardy, *Documents*, 329.
3. Irwin Smith, *Shakespeare's Blackfriars Playhouse: Its History and Its Design* (New York: New York University Press, 1964); Herbert Berry, *Shakespeare's Playhouses* (New York: AMS, 1987), esp. 2–8, 27–29; Steven Mullaney, *The Place of the Stage: License, Play, and Power in Renaissance England* (Chicago: University of Chicago Press, 1988), 55.
4. "The Injunctions of Elizabeth, A.D. 1559," in Gee and Hardy, *Documents*, 428; for other instances of the concern inspired by "feigned miracles," see *Documentary Annals of the Reformed Church of England*, ed. Edward Cardwell (Oxford, 1839), 1:81, 194, 234.
5. "The First Royal Injunctions of Henry VIII, A.D. 1536," in Gee and Hardy, *Documents*, 271.
6. William Perkins, *A discourse of the damned art of witchcraft* [etc.] (Cambridge, 1608), Epistle Dedicatory.
7. Letter to Henry VIII in BL, Cotton MS, Cleopatra E, 4; John Strype, ed., *Ecclesiastical Memorials* [etc.], vol. 1, part 1 (Oxford, 1822), 410. Discussion in Susan Brigden, *London and the Reformation* (Oxford: Clarendon Press, 1991), 293–94.

ought to be handed over to the secular authorities, he argued, along with "all the lands, tenements, and revenues appertaining and belonging to the said hospitals" (ibid.). Rather than receiving the faux ministrations of sham clerics, the sick could then be tended "by physicians, surgeons, and potecaries, which shall have stipend and salary only for that purpose" (ibid., 411). Doctors were to replace divines so that medicine, rather than miracles, might offer meaningful care for infirm bodies.

Doctors were further entrusted with care for the mind, whose location in the brain made it uniquely vulnerable to humoral disturbances emanating from the vital organs and blood. The mad could no more be cured by saints, said the Anglican church, than demoniacs could be healed by the miracle of exorcism. Would-be faith healers—whether saints, cunning men and women, or dissident priests—were all impotent to remedy the mentally afflicted in defiance of the laws of human physiology, and there was nothing inspired or supernatural about the affliction. The speaking in tongues, the extraordinary strength, the insensitivity to pain—these had secular explanations, so long as the evaluating authority had an adequate grasp of natural philosophy. To the extent that devils might be involved in mental illness (to say nothing of the cure), they played upon weaknesses inherent to human psychology so as to interfere with appearances. They produced preternatural effects not so much in the world, writes Michel Foucault, as in the space between the world and cognition, "along the length of this surface, which is that of 'fantasy' and the senses, where nature is transformed into an image."[8] The whole of their power, such as it was, lay in illusion and the inherent frailty of brain chemistry—"the dampest of all the parts of the body," according to the *Malleus Maleficarum*, therefore the most susceptible to imbalances arising from vapors, fumes, and other spirits, particularly when subject to lunar influence (hence *lunacy*).[9] Devils intent on driving people to distraction could do so only by preying on those already prone to deranged thinking because devils were subject to the bedrock principle of Hippocratic medicine that madness comes from the brain's moisture.[10] The miraculous restoration of sanity regularly attributed to saints and exorcists obeyed the same principle and could therefore be dismissed as the result of a natural development whose mechanisms in no way required divine intervention.

---

8. Michel Foucault, "Les déviations religieuses et le savoir médical," in *Hérésies et sociétés dans l'Europe pré-industrielle 11e–18e siècles*, ed. Jacques Le Goff (Paris: Mouton, 1968), 19–29 at 21.

9. Henricus Institoris and Jacobus Sprenger, *Malleus Maleficarum*, ed. and trans. Christopher S. Mackay (Cambridge: Cambridge University Press, 2006), 1:278 (Latin), 2:108 (English); Cf. *Macbeth* 4.1.28.

10. Hippocrates, *The Sacred Disease* 17 (LCL).

Physicians trained at university in the theories of Galen, the Canon of Avicenna, and Constantine the African, among others, had been tasked for centuries before Shakespeare with drawing the line between natural and supernatural phenomena in the trials of saints, heretics, witches, and demoniacs—not despite but because of the medical preference for strictly natural, physiological explanations of preternatural phenomena. Already by the twelfth century the customary bias of physicians, according to John of Salisbury, was to grant "excessive authority to nature" at the expense of "nature's Author"—often "by opposing faith"—if only because their expertise in natural causation had accustomed them to the regular occurrence of wondrous cures, up to and including what looked like resurrection, through routine medical therapies.[11] They knew that people who seemed to have been possessed and then miraculously cured could in fact have been suffering from more banal ailments, such as the "falling sickness, which always supposeth the loss of sense and judgment" or "the passion, which we call Hysterica or Suffocation of the Matrix," and in that case healing could be achieved through nonsupernatural means.[12] By appointing physicians to test demoniacs and to authenticate the miracles that attended the restoration of their wits, inquisitors had lent an exceptional privilege to secular medicine, one that led English doctors and bishops at the close of the sixteenth century to turn against faith healing as a whole: "The learned physician who hath first been trained up in the study of philosophy, and afterwards confirmed by the practice and experience of all manner of natural diseases," writes Edward Jorden in a treatise with no small bearing on *Lear*, "is best able to discern what is natural, what not natural, what preternatural, and what supernatural."[13] He meant by this that learned physicians had a unique authority to rule out the supernatural and to dissolve the preternatural into the natural while eliminating the possibility of demonic interference. In fact their long-standing reputation for incredulity had grown to the point of inviting the accusation that they had abandoned Christ for Galen and become "Atheists, mere Naturians."[14]

---

11. John of Salisbury, *Policraticus* 2.29 (CCCM 118:170); English in *Frivolities of Courtiers and Footprints of Philosophers* [etc.], trans. Joseph B. Pike (Minneapolis: University of Minnesota Press, 1938), 149 (modified).
12. [Michel Marescot], *Discours veritable sur la faict de Marthe Brossier de Romorantin, pretendue demoniaque* (Paris, 1599), 19; English in *A true discourse, upon the matter of Martha Brossier of Romorantin, pretended to be possessed by a devill*, trans. Abraham Hartwell (London, 1599), 14.
13. Edward Jorden, *A briefe discourse of a disease called the suffocation of the Mother, written upon occasion which hath beene late taken thereby, to suspect possession of an evill spirit, or some such like supernaturall power* [etc.] (London, 1603), 5v-r.
14. Henoch Clapham, *An epistle discoursing upon the present pestilence* (London, 1603), A3v; quoted in F. David Hoeniger, *Medicine and Shakespeare in the English Renaissance* (Newark: University of Delaware Press, 1991), 303.

As for religion, it was "the general scandal" of the medical profession, writes Thomas Browne, that doctors had "none at all."[15] So long as their reliance on nothing but natural philosophy could effect the same types of cures that were sometimes considered miraculous—for conditions that were often considered demonic—they were bound to leave the impression that their training had rendered both God and demons superfluous. "They say that miracles are past," remarks an old Lord in *All's Well that Ends Well*. "And we have our philosophical persons, to make modern and familiar, things supernatural and causeless" (2.3.1–3). People trained specifically in the philosophy of medicine were in other words capable of replicating miraculous healings without any need for a miracle. Helen, daughter of the "famous" physician Gerard de Narbon (1.1.26), has so deep an understanding of the occult properties inhering in nature—drawn from the tenets "both of Galen and Paracelsus" (2.3.11)—that she alone can cure a king whose recovery seems otherwise beyond the realm of natural possibility.

Black bile—*mēlaina cholē* in Greek, *succus melancholicus* in Latin—was a major cause, in addition to *passio hysterica*, of a variety of psychological disturbances. Its sufficiency as an explanation for alleged cases of possession led some of Shakespeare's more learned contemporaries to recommend strictly medical treatment (or, treatment failing, confinement at Bedlam) and to argue against both demonic causation and the miracle of exorcism.[16] "*Melancholicum est sedes daemonum*, a melancholic brain is the chair of estate for the devil," writes Samuel Harsnett, then chaplain to Richard Bancroft, the Bishop of London.[17] A leading figure in the Anglican attack on the feigned miracles of exorcists, a licenser of books for the press, and future Archbishop of York, Harsnett was an essential liaison between the world of learned demonology and Shakespeare, who borrowed extensively from his book against possession and the pseudo-miracles performed by Jesuits. Similar apothegms about "the

---

15. Thomas Browne, *Religio medici* (London, 1642), 1.
16. Levinus Lemnius, *Occulta naturae miracula* (Antwerp, 1559), 102r; Girolamo Maggi, *Variarum lectionum seu miscellaneorum libri IIII* (Venice, 1564), 202v–203r; Girolamo Cardano, *De rerum varietate libri XVII* (Avignon, 1558), 384–85, 728–41; *Witches, Devils and Doctors in the Renaissance: Johann Weyer, "De praestigiis daemonum,"* ed. George Mora et al., trans. John Shea (Binghamton, NY: Medieval & Renaissance Texts and Studies, 1991), 180–81; Reginald Scot, *The Discoverie of Witchcraft*, ed. Brinsley Nicholson (London: Elliot Stock, 1886 [originally published in 1584]), 12; Robert Burton, *The Anatomy of Melancholy* [etc.] (London, 1621), 260; see also Jean Céard, "Folie et démonologie au XVIe siècle," in *Folie et Déraison à la Renaissance* [etc.] (Brussels: Éditions de l'Université de Bruxelles, 1976), 129–48; Sydney Anglo, "Melancholia and Witchcraft: The Debate between Wier, Bodin, and Scot," in *Folie et Déraison à la Renaissance*, 209–228; Noel L. Brann, *The Debate Over the Origin of Genius During the Italian Renaissance* (Leiden: Brill, 2002), 333–34.
17. Samuel Harsnett, *A declaration of egregious popish impostures* (London, 1603), 132.

melancholic brain" appear throughout early modern medical and demonological literature, often toward the end of showing that melancholic people are the most susceptible to demonic influence, but Harsnett follows Reginald Scot in arguing that blackened brain matter by itself is enough to account for every apparent miracle, every alleged possession, every witch's confession, and the unshakeable credulity of every witch hunter. Jean Bodin—widely considered the most ingenious defender of witch burning—may have once been a man of towering intellect, Harsnett concedes. But the great man's cerebral tissues had been weakened by age and transformed by black vapors into the *"veram sedem daemonum*, the theater and sporting house for devils to dance in: for he hath in his brain, such strange speculations, fantasms, and theorems for devils, as a man may see a great deal of madness mixed with his great wit" (ibid.). According to Harsnett, the diseased mind and the theater were both venues in which demonic or even supernatural phenomena might seem to happen, but such happenings, whatever they were, were never demonic, much less supernatural. The human imagination by itself had the power to transform nature into an otherworldly experience.

For both Foucault and Charles Taylor, every medical debate about the origins of madness before the modern age (whether we date its onset from the Enlightenment or the Reformation) had to be resolved in favor of demonic or divine causation. There could be no escape from the closed loop of Christian belief because medieval medicine accepted fundamentally the interventions of demons, along with the interventions of God, as part of the fabric of everyday experience. The only question was how to differentiate these types of interventions, and the question could be invariably settled by knowing the difference between natural causes and what Jorden calls "the immediate finger of the Almighty."[18] Knowing precisely how medieval medicine had formulated this difference, however, led Jorden and the Anglican authorities in London at the start of the seventeenth century to take the position that virtually every instance of demonic possession, along with the miracle cure afforded by exorcists, was decidedly human in origin and usually the result of fraud or a physical pathology. "The indirect result of the controversy over the legitimacy of spiritual healing," writes Michael MacDonald, "was that the secular alternative, medical psychology, was established as the only acceptable alternative in the eyes of the orthodox elite."[19] Long before the enlightened age of madness, that is, demonological reasoning was already well on its way toward what Taylor calls "the

---

18. Jorden, *A briefe discourse*, 2r; cf. Ex 8:19 and Lk 11:20.
19. Michael MacDonald, *Mystical Bedlam: Madness, Anxiety, and Healing in Seventeenth-Century England* (Cambridge: Cambridge University Press, 1981), 177.

therapeutic turn, the move from a hermeneutic of sin, evil or spiritual misdirection, to one of sickness," such that body and mind could be reduced to objects best handled by medical experts.[20] Neo-Hippocratic physicians and the latest Paracelsian "Empiriks" could both explain away an apparent case of "supernatural soliciting" (*Macbeth* 1.3.143) as a fantasy of otherworldly powers—the result of a heat-oppressed brain, wishful thinking, willful blindness, or (as we will see vividly in Harsnett) a disillusioned form of role-play. When it came to diagnosing "Bedlam beggars" (KL 2.2.185) or a "lunatic King" (KL 3.7.46), doctors before and after the Reformation were predisposed to take the position of ancient pagans like Edmund and Lear. "Nature" was their "goddess" (KL 1.2.1, 1.4.267). They did not search beyond her for ultimate causes.

We owe to Abrahamic monotheism—and to Christianity in particular—the idea that an exclusive commitment to nature can replace God; the idea, in other words, that a desanctified, secular sphere exists and is an easy substitute for religion because it supplies a sufficient explanation for observable experience. Before the coming of the law, the prophets, and Christ, veneration of nature was supposed to have been the closest thing to God that infidels had. The whole purpose of Christ's miracles, from the perspective of Archbishop Whitgift, Bancroft, and Harsnett (among others), was to make natural wonders look godless by comparison, so as to preserve for the true divinity alone an absolute transcendence. Indeed by the time of *Lear*, the orthodox Anglican position was that the apostolic age had left behind a world bereft of its sacred aura and largely impervious to divine intervention: no gods, no miracles, and very little magic beyond the weak prestige of legerdemain. It was the duty of the true believer *not* to believe in such devices. Real faith attended to the eternal divine and awaited a second advent while moving through a world whose processes were devoid of sanctity.

Both Catholic and Puritan opponents of this mindset were quick to point out that its fervor for desacralization, which up to a point everybody shared, when taken too far led to the most profound, unsettling, and impious unbelief: "Atheists abound in these days and witchcraft is called into question," writes John Popham (a godly opponent of the Anglican hierarchy). "Which error is confirmed by denying dispossession, & both these errors confirm atheists mightily . . . If neither possession nor witchcraft (contrary to what hath been so long generally and confidently affirmed), why should we think that there are devils? If no devils, no God."[21] Scholars writing in the shadow

---

20. Charles Taylor, *A Secular Age* (Cambridge, MA: Belknap Press, 2007), 620.
21. Quoted in D. P. Walker, *Unclean Spirits: Possession and Exorcism in France and England in the Late Sixteenth and Early Seventeenth Centuries* (London: Scolar Press, 1981), 71–72.

of Lucien Febvre, Foucault, and Taylor have been inclined to suppose that people like Popham and his Catholic counterparts could in no way imagine how "faithless atheists" might really think.[22] But Puritans, Catholics, and Anglicans all knew that it was possible to give yourself entirely to natural causation as a guiding regulative principle. They knew the credo in favor of the "Epicures life" from reading scripture, along with its denial of an afterlife (Ws 2:6, DR, marginal gloss). They knew that thinkers ranging from Plato to al-Qāsim b. Ibrāhīm, Anselm, Maimonides, and Aquinas had needed proofs of God's existence to counter the unbelievers who denied it.[23] And they knew that such unbelievers walked among them: Christopher Marlowe was reportedly "able to show more sound reasons for atheism than any divine in England" in the same decade that an "atheist" was hauled before the High Commission of York and announced to the judge, "My Lord, if any here can prove there is a God, I will believe it."[24]

Late twentieth- and early twenty-first-century scholars have had great difficulty believing in the existence of these atheists, and yet Shakespeare's contemporaries had no difficulty at all finding throughout history "infidels and carnal men" who were "following only nature and reason" (Mk 5:3, DR annotation). The millennia-old insistence that God utterly transcended natural law had carved out a deep respect for secular evaluations, since these alone gave the divine power a verifiable standard to surpass. Believers tasked with appraising the reality of an alleged miracle, if they hoped to be persuasive, had no choice but to make their arguments with reference to the limits imposed by worldly causation. In trials of saints and witches, a fundamental purpose of the proceedings was to falsify the appearance of supernatural intervention so as to prevent charlatans, magicians, and the mentally compromised from becoming subject to veneration—an issue, as we'll see, that is central to the trial of Jesus in the York cycle. There, as in *Lear*, a "begger of Bedlem" appears to be mad but is also capable of performing various preternatural feats. The speculation about occult causation and mental competence that consumes Jesus's interrogators is a direct reflection of the late medieval and early modern *inquisitio*. For most audiences of the York cycle and all audiences of *Lear*, Bedlam was furthermore the name for the former

---

22. Harsnett, *A declaration*, 248 (quoting a now lost Catholic treatise).
23. See Sarah Stroumsa, "The Religion of Freethinkers of Medieval Islam," in *Atheismus im Mittelalter und in der Renaissance*, ed. Friedrich Niewöhner and Olaf Pluta (Wiesbaden: Harrassowitz, 1999), 45–59.
24. Constance Kuriyama, *Christopher Marlowe: A Renaissance Life* (Ithaca, NY: Cornell University Press, 2002), 215 (the first Cholmeley report), and *The triall of Maist. Dorrell, or A collection of defences against allegations not yet suffered to receiue convenient answere* [etc.] (Middelburg, 1599), 88, respectively.

priory outside London whose secularization in the late fourteenth century produced Europe's first insane asylum. The early appearance of this "playhouse of Folly" offered sixteenth- and seventeenth-century actors a model for the examination of human psychology.[25] Both Bedlam and the London stage provided venues to inspect the limits of reason, to watch the imagination shape perception, to investigate the problem of demonic possession, to contemplate the mind's susceptibility to corruption as well as its need for an array of therapies—miraculous, medicinal, or fictional, as the case might be. Both Bedlam and the London stage resulted from processes of secularization that long predated the Reformation but that Protestants willfully accelerated—first and foremost by extending the fate of the Bethlehem Priory to a vastly wider range of church property, such that any number of dissolved monastic estates now welcomed visitations from customers willing to pay for a preternatural spectacle, whether at Bedlam, the Globe, or Blackfriars.

The Birth of an Asylum

The Priory of St. Mary of Bethlehem was founded just outside the walls of London in 1247 by Simon fitzMary, an on-again, off-again sheriff and onetime alderman plagued by allegations of embezzlement alongside "many other evil and detestable actions which he had secretly been guilty of against the city."[26] His surname means literally "son of Mary" and may explain on more than one level what the land grant calls his "special and peculiar devotion to the church of the glorious Virgin."[27] A matronymic, if that's what it is, would indicate that his mother, like her virginal namesake, had given birth to a bastard.[28] The grant is explicit about his intention to honor Bethlehem in particular—"the place ... where the hosts of the army of heaven sang a new hymn, *Gloria in excelsis Deo* ... whither a new star drew the kings by whom the king of kings wanted to be adored."[29] All members of the Bethlehemite

---

25. Mullaney, *Place of the Stage*, 71.
26. *Chronicles of the Mayors and Sheriffs of London A.D. 1188 to A.D. 1274 ... The French Chronicle of London A.D. 1259 to A.D. 1343*, trans. Henry Thomas Riley (London, 1863), 16–17; Latin in *De Antiquis Legibus Liber: Cronica Maiorum et Vicecomitum Londoniarum*, ed. Thomas Stapleton (London, 1846), 15–16. For background see Nicholas Vincent, "Goffredo de Prefetti and the Church of Bethlehem in England," *Journal of Ecclesiastical History* 2 (1998): 213–35; Jonathan Andrews et al., *The History of Bethlem* (London: Routledge, 1997), 27–33.
27. Latin in Louis Chevalier Lagenissière, *Histoire de l'Évêché de Bethléem* (Paris, 1872), 85; English in James Howell, *Londinopolis an historicall discourse or perlustration of the city of London, the imperial chamber, and chief emporium of Great Britain* [etc.] (London, 1657), 65–66.
28. Edward Geoffrey O'Donoghue, *The Story of Bethlehem Hospital from Its Foundation in 1247* (New York: E. P. Dutton, 1914), 5; Andrews et al., *History of Bethlem*, 28.
29. Lagenissière, *Histoire*, 85.

order had to wear "the sign of the star publicly on their cloaks and capes," unlike any other habit, and we know from other sources that their liturgy broke from tradition by incorporating the *Gloria* into every mass, no matter the occasion, "even for the dead, since it was in that town . . . that this hymn was first sung."[30] The new song and the nova had together proclaimed a god so almighty, and a dominion so lacking in precedent, that the proclamation thereafter needed constant renewal if the news was going to spread.

The further it spread, the more incredulity it met. By the time of the Crusades Christendom was said to be surrounded by and shot through with unbelief. Indeed the fear that infidels were on the verge of triumph over the one true faith accounts directly for the Bethlehemite mission to England. A "New Beethlem" was needed at the westernmost edge of Christian influence in order to solicit funds for the restoration of ground zero after the fall of the old Bethlehem to Khwarazmian Turks.[31] Although it was possible at the time for Christians to see the most recent monotheists to appear on the scene as members of a kindred faith—"we who believe in and confess the one God," as Pope Gregory VII (1073–1085) wrote to a North African Muslim ruler—it was equally common to condemn the infidels' lack of connection to anything sacred.[32] Theirs was either a posture of belief designed to mask secular self-interest or an unwitting acceptance of degrading, worldly things in place of divinity. To the extent that the Turks then occupying Bethlehem were in fact members of a faith intimately related to Christianity, Christians found themselves subject to their own strategy of forced disenchantment. What Muslims did not "disfigure," "overturn completely," or permanently "defile"—according to the English Benedictine and contemporary chronicler, Matthew Paris—they "desecrated [*polluerunt*]" through removal, transferring sculpted columns, for example, "to the sepulcher of wicked Mohammed out of contempt for Christians and as a token of victory."[33] In response to the latest defeat in the Holy Land, Innocent IV dispatched the bishop of Bethlehem, Goffredo de Prefetti, to the British isles with an encyclical granting indulgences to anyone who gave money to repair the "considerable loss of

---

30. Lagenissière, *Histoire*, 86, 88, respectively; the latter quote is from a thirteenth-century bishop; see also Vincent, "Goffredo de Prefetti," 224.
31. *Calendar of Patent Rolls Preserved in the Public Record Office, Henry III: 1247–1258* (London: Mackie and Co. for His Majesty's Stationery Office, 1908), 555.
32. Quoted in James Muldoon, *Popes, Lawyers, and Infidels* (Philadelphia: University of Pennsylvania Press, 1979), 39.
33. *Matthaei Parisiensis, Monachi Sancti Albani, Chronica Majora*, ed. Henry Richards Luard (London, 1877), 4:340. See also Denys Pringle, *The Churches of the Crusader Kingdom of Jerusalem: A Corpus* (Cambridge: Cambridge University Press, 1993), 1:139; Vincent, "Goffredo de Prefetti," 23.

property in the general Eastern calamity at the hands of the enemies of faith [*inimicos fidei*]."[34] On October 23, 1247, Goffredo got the deed from fitzMary that would lay the foundation for the institution now called Bedlam.

The financial success of the English Bethlehemites contributed directly to the priory's secularization. In 1308 their license to solicit funds on behalf of the Virgin was revoked by Bishop Wulfram "because they, and in particular a questor named Thomas, had abused their privileges, presumably by collecting money for their own private profit."[35] Sixty years later the king apprehended the master of the order and a proctor on the charge of collecting alms with the help of forged indulgences. The impression at court seems to have been that the priory had all too happily given itself over to the profane world and should therefore be converted to a more beneficial use. In 1373, the king made a sinecure of Bethlem's mastership to reward loyal servants with whatever money they could reap from fitzMary's land, its buildings, and, by the late fourteenth century—when the priory's conversion into an asylum was all but complete—those buildings' inmates.[36] Well in advance of being officially "ruinated" by the Protestant Reformation, the priory had already been "thoroughly secularized" in the sense that lay people were placed in positions of management by royal fiat.[37] We do not know exactly when but at some point the keepers began to charge admission so that visitors, according to Thomas More, might "see one laugh at the knocking of his head against a post."[38] The commercial theaters that arose on monastic estates and in secularized friaries later in the sixteenth century would operate on the same financial model. For the first time in theater history, you had to pay for admission to a gated building.

Soon after the priory's conversion into an asylum, talk arose of its containing inmates "so possessed of unclean spirits that they must be restrained with chains and fetters."[39] When released, these unfortunate souls created the "proof and precedent" for Edgar's imitation of the

---

34. *Les registres d'Innocent IV*, ed. Élie Berger (Paris, 1884), 1:158 (no. 980).
35. Vincent, "Goffredo de Prefetti," 230.
36. Patricia Allderidge, "Management and Mismanagement at Bedlam, 1547–1633," in *Health, Medicine and Mortality in the Sixteenth Century*, ed. Charles Webster (Cambridge: Cambridge University Press, 1979), 141–64, esp. 144.
37. [Richard Johnson], *The pleasant walkes of Moore-fields* [etc.] (London, 1607), B2r, and Andrews et al., *History of Bethlem*, 85, respectively.
38. Quoted and discussed in Ken Jackson, *Separate Theaters: Bethlem ("Bedlam") Hospital and the Shakespearean Stage* (Newark: University of Delaware Press, 2005), 15, 164–65.
39. *The Register of Thomas Bekynton, Bishop of Bath and Wells 1443–1465*, ed. H. C. Maxwell-Lyte and M. C. B. Dawes, Part I ([London]: n. p., 1934), 59; discussed in Martha Carlin, "Medieval English Hospitals," in *The Hospital in History*, ed. Lindsay Granshaw and Roy Porter (London: Routledge, 1989), 21–39, esp. 34.

> Bedlam beggars, who with roaring voices
> Strike in their numbed and mortified bare arms
> Pins, wooden pricks, nails, sprigs of rosemary.
> (KL 2.2.185–87, Qc/Q2)

What made "this horrible object" so difficult to contemplate, besides the mental anguish to which it bore witness, was the fear that such behavior might be an effect of bewitchment. Any time a case of this sort appeared in a village there was a danger that the possessed might trigger a legal inquiry by naming the witch who was responsible. Such inquiries demanded, above all, "proof" of possession, which was established in large measure by ruling out alternative, nondemonic causes of the same symptoms. Consultation with a secular physician was the first, indispensable step whenever a person lost their wits in circumstances that suggested a case of witchcraft. The physician gathered a history from associates of the afflicted and observed the patient, taking careful notes "to satisfy . . . remembrance the more strongly" (*Macbeth* 5.1.33–34). You knew you were in the presence of a preternatural phenomenon beyond the known range of material causes only when you found a doctor willing to declare, "this disease is beyond my practice" (*Macbeth* 5.1.59). At the start of the seventeenth century, such willingness was in shorter supply than ever before.

The two most common nondemonic, nonmagical causes of symptoms virtually identical to those of bewitchment and possession were either a humoral imbalance (as we see in Lear) or some kind of fraud (as we see in Edgar). At the time of the play's first performance, the traumatic loss of magic that according to the chroniclers had preceded Leir's historical reign—to say nothing of the great weakening of demons by Christ that had intervened between the reigns of Leir and King James—was being forcibly reimposed on the mentally disturbed. When the Anglican Church turned against miracles and faith healing, in particular exorcism, it drew a direct parallel between the illicit theater practiced by dissident Christians and the preternatural effects accomplished by the King's Men in service of the crown. Neither involved miracles or magic, but only one was allowed (barely), because only one rested on the explicit premise that it operated without any superhuman agency and was subject to oversight by the temporal and ecclesiastical authorities. If we want to say that *King Lear* results from a process of disenchantment or that it makes a "drastic swerve from the sacred to the secular," we should bear in mind that the English Church actively endorsed such developments and that it could do so only because the groundwork had been laid in previous millennia.⁴⁰ Shakespeare's theater was a new and highly innovative institution, but the secularized sphere on which it rested was inherited from ancient and medieval intellectuals.

Hippocratic Medicine and the Madness of Jesus

Before our modern secular age, Charles Taylor argues, every case of madness was considered either an affliction sent by the gods or a form of demonic possession. The first century Palestinians to whom Jesus ministered, for example, "were too immediately at grips with the real suffering of this condition, in a neighbor, or a loved one, to be able to entertain the idea that . . . there were other, possibly more reliable aetiologies for this condition."⁴¹ And yet the writers of the New Testament already lived in a Hellenized world where other, possibly more reliable etiologies were available to learned physicians and to common theatergoers alike: Menander's *Aspis* features a character driven to "such distraction [*ekstasin*]" by his brother's scheming that he devises a plot to stage his own death from madness on the model of Greek tragedy.⁴² Tragic insanity was frequently inflicted on humans by the gods, but the New Comedy took great delight in discrediting this sacred etiology with the language of medicine.⁴³ Drama thus helped to spread medicine's particular brand of disenchantment across the Greek-speaking world. If Paul could quote Menander, so could other Christians.⁴⁴ And other Christians understood that the mentally afflicted were *"diversely* taken with diseases" (Mt 4:24, DR, emphasis added). Some were "possessed" by demons, others were "lunatics," and still others were "sick with the palsey" (Mt 4:24, DR). Demonic causation was only one possibility among several.

A key text for the strictly physiological interpretation of madness was *The Sacred Disease*, an ancient treatise, long attributed to Hippocrates, that attacks supernatural, daimonical, and magical explanations.⁴⁵ Madness here is "no more divine than the rest . . . but results from a natural cause"—namely, an imbalance

---

40. Stephen Greenblatt, *Shakespearean Negotiations: The Circulation of Social Energy in Renaissance England* (Berkeley: University of California Press, 1988), 126; cf. Greenblatt, *The Swerve: How the World Became Modern* (New York: W. W. Norton, 2011).
41. Taylor, *Secular Age*, 11.
42. *Aspis* 309 (LCL); Glenn M. Most, "The Madness of Tragedy," in *Mental Disorders in the Classical World*, ed. W. V. Harris (Leiden: Brill, 2013), 395–412, esp. 395–97 on Menander.
43. See Menander, *Samia*, ed. Alan H. Sommerstein (Cambridge: Cambridge University Press, 2013), 229n416 for multiple parallels with the Hippocratic corpus. See also J.-M. Jacques, "La bile noire dans l'antiquité grecque: médicine et littérature," *Revue des Études Anciennes* 100 (1998): 217–34.
44. 1 Cor 15:33; see Michael Benjamin Cover, "The Divine Comedy at Corinth: Paul, Menander and the Rhetoric of Resurrection," *New Testament Studies* 64, no. 4 (2018): 532–50.
45. Julie Leskaris, *The Art Is Long: On the Sacred Disease and the Scientific Tradition* (Leiden: Brill, 2002).

in "the brain."⁴⁶ The people who attributed an otherworldly cause to human mania were magicians (*magoi*), beggars (*agurtai*), and charlatans (*alazones*)—the sort of "men who claim great piety and superior knowledge" but find themselves at a loss to explain, much less cure, the insane (*Sacred Disease* 2, LCL). They therefore "cloak themselves and hide behind superstition, and call this illness sacred, in order to prevent their ignorance from being exposed" (*Sacred Disease* 2, LCL). They treat the mad as if they "had been bewitched [*pepharmakeumenous*] or had committed some unholy act" (*Sacred Disease* 4, LCL) and were now at the mercy of a higher power—Hecate, for example. Quacks of this type fabricate a superhuman cause together with a superhuman cure, performing "purifications and incantations" to ward off "avenging spirits" (*Sacred Disease* 4, LCL).

Faith healers adept at handling demonic possession were legion in first-century Palestine and had a well-won reputation for fraud. Recommendations are found in scripture and in the writings of the Fathers to avoid them and seek out competent physicians instead.⁴⁷ Mainstream medical opinion, together with the Bible, made it entirely possible to think of exorcists as charlatans preying on the mentally infirm. In fact it was possible to argue that the healers themselves, on account of a humoral imbalance, were suffering from delusions of grandeur. That is why the mother and siblings of Jesus rush to lay hands on him, fearing that "he was become mad."⁴⁸ He is said to be mad, not possessed, because his intimates insist on a secular diagnosis. They are being charitable. Christ's enemies, by contrast, are the ones who believe his behavior is demonic: "He hath Beelzebub and . . . in the prince of devils he casteth out devils" (Mk 3:22, DR). The reason he has such a dramatic effect on people afflicted by demonic possession, according to critics, is that he himself is possessed: "He hath a devil and is mad."⁴⁹

---

46. Hippocrates, *The Sacred Disease* 5 and 6 (LCL). This text was translated into Arabic by 1000 and seems to have been known to some Latins by the thirteenth century. See Laskaris, *Art Is Long*, 60; David C. Lindberg, *The Beginnings of Western Science: The European Scientific Tradition in Philosophical, Religious, and Institutional Context, Prehistory to A.D. 1450*, 2nd ed. (Chicago: University of Chicago Press, 2007), 172; Luke E. Demaitre, *Doctor Bernard de Gordon, Professor and Practitioner* (Toronto: Pontifical Institute of Mediaeval Studies, 1980), 160; Jacques Jouanna, "The Typology and Aetiology of Madness in Ancient Greek Medical and Philosophical Writing," in Harris, *Mental Disorders in the Classical World*, 97–118, and Vivian Nutton, "Galenic Madness," in Harris, *Mental Disorders in the Classical World*, 119–27, esp. 123: "As far as Galen is concerned, all mental disorders are the result of some lesion, some damage to the brain."
47. See e.g. Sirach 38 and John Chrysostom, *Fifth Homily Against the Jews*—both are appended, probably by Matthew Parker, to *The disclosing of a late counterfeyted possession by the deuyl in two maydens within the Citie of London* (London, n.d. [1574?]); see also Morton Smith, *Jesus the Magician* (San Francisco: Harper & Row, 1972).
48. Mk 3:21 (DR): *"furorem verens,"* translating the Greek, *exestē*. Anne Rebeca Solevåg, *Negotiating the Disabled Body: Representations of Disability in Early Christian Texts* (Atlanta, GA: SBL Press, 2018), esp. 95–116; cf. Justin J. Meggitt, "The Madness of King Jesus: Why Was Jesus Put to Death, but His Followers Were Not?" *Journal for the Study of the New Testament* 29, no. 4 (2007): 379–413.
49. Jn 10:20 (DR): *"daemonium habet et insanit,"* translating the Greek, *"Daimonion exei kai mainetai."*

From Christianity's earliest origins we see competing causal explanations for the maladies that sanctified healers might overcome, and it was supposed to be a testimony to their sanctity that they could handle the full range of possibilities, whether demonic or strictly physical. That supposition is at the root of what Julie Orlemanski calls the "etiological imagination" of the later Middle Ages, "an era broadly fascinated with explanatory invention and the tasks of envisioning, arbitrating among, and emplotting intricate causal chains."[50] Already in the late fourth or early fifth century, saint Macedonius could confirm that a mentally aberrant individual was possessed as a result of bewitchment by soliciting from her in court the name of the witch, along with "the whole plot of the tragedy."[51] By the same token Macedonius could also entertain a nondemonic explanation when the wife of a wealthy man "fell into a gluttonous frenzy" and consumed thirty chickens at a time but remained unsated: "some considered it the work of a demon, others a physical illness [sōmatos arrōstian]."[52] In both cases the victims were successfully cured by the saint, whose authority was increased by virtue of his ability to remedy aberrations of diverse origin, just as Jesus had been able both to exorcise demons and to staunch a naturally occurring hemorrhage that had frustrated "many physicians" (Mk 5:26).

"The claim that demoniacs were 'really' suffering from a medical condition that had 'natural' causes—from an organic disease or a mental illness—has been the most consistent secular, rational analysis of demonic possession since the period of Christian antiquity," writes Brian Levack.[53] Demon-free accounts of mental illness appear throughout the Middle Ages alongside the usual hagiographic narratives of saintly exorcism, which depend heavily on the counter-explanation provided by natural causation to show that the saint's miracles have surpassed the power of doctors—not to mention the power of witches.[54]

---

50. Julie Orlemanski, *Symptomatic Subjects: Bodies, Medicine, and Causation in the Literature of Late Medieval England* (Philadelphia: University of Pennsylvania Press, 2019), 2–3.
51. Theodoret, *Religiosa Historia* 13 (PG 82:1405D): "πᾶσαν τοῦ δράματος τὴν τραγῳδίαν"; German translation in *Des Bischofs Theodoret von Cyrus Mönchsgeschichte aus dem griechischen übersetzt*, trans. Konstantin Gutberlet (Munich: Jos. Kösel & Friedr. Pustet, 1926), 100.
52. PG 82:1405A. For similar stories see Sophie Lunn-Rockliffe, "Over-Eating Demoniacs in Late Antique Hagiography," in *Demons and Illness from Antiquity to the Early-Modern Period*, ed. Siam Bhayro and Catherine Rider (Leiden: Brill, 2017), 215–31.
53. Brian P. Levack, *The Devil Within: Possession and Exorcism in the Christian West* (New Haven, CT: Yale University Press, 2013), 111.
54. See Wendy J. Turner, *Care and Custody of the Mentally Ill, Incompetent, and Disabled in Medieval England* (Turnhout: Brepols, 2013); Carole Rawcliffe, *Medicine and Society in Later Medieval England* (Stroud, UK: Alan Sutton, 1995), esp. 10; Penelope B. R. Doob, *Nebuchadnezzar's Children: Conventions of Madness in Middle English Literature* (New Haven, CT: Yale University Press, 1974), esp. 10–32; Anne E. Bailey, "Miracles and Madness: Dispelling Demons in Twelfth-Century Hagiography," in Bhayro and Rider, *Demons and Illness from Antiquity to the Early-Modern Period*, 236–55.

The whole problem with witches, soothsayers, astrologers, would-be saints, and the like was their claim to transcend the *saeculum* through miraculous means when in fact their actions rested on poorly understood mechanisms of natural causation. The demons with whom they sometimes interacted, however capable of godlike feats, were entirely unable to perform genuine miracles and in fact relied more often than not on mere theater, according to an Augustinian-Thomistic framework that was essential to the *Malleus Maleficarum* and remained operative until the eighteenth century.[55] In fact Augustine made common cause with secular medicine against false belief: "To this category," he writes of superstition, "belong all the amulets and remedies which the medical profession also condemns, whether these consist of incantations, or certain marks which their exponents call 'characters.'"[56] People who made use of such magical salves were putting their faith in an "inane remedy" that would likely require a follow-up visit with a "real doctor [*verum medicum*]" (*De doct. Christ.* 2.31.76, ibid.). Use of amulets and other quasi-magical therapies continued to thrive despite this dubiety and were sometimes at one with it, as when physicians—from Avicenna to Edward Jorden—argued that amulets took on a "magical" power insofar as a mysterious efficacy was attributed to them by the imagination of a patient. These fetishistic remedies were what we have come to call a placebo and proved especially important to premodern doctors whenever the patient's condition was otherwise past hope.

Cunning men and women, pseudo-saints, and witches who used amulets without formal medical training—often in conjunction with various types of incantation—were increasingly targeted after the twelfth century by continental inquisitors. In England, concomitant with the adoption of the notorious statute *de haeretico comburendo* in 1401, practitioners of illicit magic were subject to burning along with religious dissidents of all sorts. Those charged with witchcraft or heresy (or both) were usually given a chance to abjure and survive; if they relapsed, they were "left to the secular court," which alone had the power of capital punishment and applied it without much hesitation whenever the criminal activity could be construed as a form of treason.[57]

---

55. See Augustine, *De divinatione daemonum*; Aquinas, *Summa theol.* I^a q. 114; *Malleus Maleficarum*, ed. Mackay, 36C–D; Stuart Clark, *Thinking with Demons: The Idea of Witchcraft in Early Modern Europe* (Oxford: Oxford University Press, 1997).
56. Augustine, *De doctrina Christ.* 2.30.75; Latin and English in *De doctrina Christiana*, ed. and trans. R. P. H. Green (Oxford: Clarendon, 1995), 90–93.
57. *De haeretico comburendo*; text in *Codex Juris Ecclesiastici Anglicani* [etc.], ed. Edmund Gibson (Oxford, 1761), 330 and 332 (for its repeal by Henry VIII and reinstatement by Mary); *Rotuli Parliamentorum; ut et Petitiones, et Placita in Parliamento* (London, n.d.), 3:459; F. Donald Logan, *Excommunication and the Secular Arm in Medieval England: A Study in Legal Procedure from the Thirteenth to the Sixteenth Century* (Toronto: Pontifical Institute of Mediaeval Studies, 1968), 68–71.

Madness, however, was a potentially exonerating condition that allowed for the medieval equivalent of an insanity defense: "What shall we say of the madman [*de furioso*] bereft of reason?" asks Bracton in the thirteenth century. The answer includes no mention of magic, demons, or exorcism. The insane, like other mentally compromised people—whether deranged (*mente capto*), delirious (*frenetico*), or developmentally delayed (*infantulo*)—"can no more commit an *injuria* or felony than a brute animal, since they are not far removed from brutes."[58] They needed treatment, not capital punishment. By 1403, if treatment failed, it was possible to confine them in Bedlam.

The York cycle contains five plays dramatizing the conflict between the secular power and "a begger of Bedlem" (York 32.106) accused by the "busshoppis" (York 30.481) of witchcraft, heresy, and treason but who may be merely insane and therefore innocent of the charges against him. English speakers before and after the Reformation were well aware of the combined power of church and crown to root out—or barring that, to manufacture—these types of threatening deviance. If "all theater is relentlessly and inevitably contemporary," as Sarah Beckwith argues, audiences of the plays over the course of the fifteenth century would have been increasingly hard pressed to avoid drawing parallels between the trial of Jesus for "heretical sorcery" and the trials of contemporary witches and heretics who were said to have threatened the body politic by attacking the king with magic.[59] The overlap in the plays between witchcraft, heresy, and treason, writes R. H. Nicholson, helped render "the biblical history fully intelligible through local, English expectations and judicial experience."[60] We can see the contempo-

---

58. *Bracton on the Laws and Customs of England*, trans. Samuel E. Thorne (Buffalo, NY: William S. Hein, 1997), 2:424; quoted in Sara M. Butler, "Representing the Middle Ages: The Insanity Defense in Medieval England," in *The Treatment of Disabled Persons in Medieval Europe*, ed. Wendy J. Turner and Tory Vandeventer Pearman (Lewiston, NY: Edwin Mellen, 2010), 117–33 at 118; Owen Williams, "Exorcising Madness in Late Elizabethan England: The Seduction of Arthington and the Criminal Culpability of Demoniacs," *Journal of British Studies* 47, no. 1 (2008): 30–52; Leigh Ann Craig, "The History of Madness and Mental Illness in the Middle Ages: Directions and Questions," *History Compass* 12, no. 9 (2014): 729–44.
59. Sarah Beckwith, *Signifying God: Social Relation and Symbolic Act in the York Corpus Christi Plays* (Chicago: University of Chicago Press, 2001), xvii; W. R. Jones, "Political Uses of Sorcery in Medieval Europe," *The Historian* 34, no. 4 (1972): 670–87 at 670, respectively; see also H. A. Kelly, "English Kings and the Fear of Sorcery," *Medieval Studies* 39 (1977): 206–38; A. R. Myers, "The Captivity of a Royal Witch: The Household Accounts of Queen Joan of Navarre, 1419–21," in *Crown, Household, and Parliament in Fifteenth Century England*, ed. Cecil H. Clough (London: Hambledon Press, 1985), 93–133; for other attempts to bewitch the king, see David Wilkins, ed., *Concilia Magnae Britanniae et Hiberniae ab Anno MCCCL ad Annum MDXLV* (London, 1737), 3:393; *A Chronicle of London from 1089 to 1483; written in the fifteenth century, and for the first time printed from mss. in the British Museum* (London, 1827), 107–8.
60. R. H. Nicholson, "The Trial of Christ the Sorcerer in the York Cycle," *Journal of Medieval and Renaissance Studies* 16, no. 2 (1986): 125–69 at 129.

rary judicial terminology, for example, in the description of Christ by his priestly accusers in N-Town as "an eretyk and a tretour" who is also guilty of "nygramancye" and deserves, instead of being crucified, to "ben hangyn and drawe / And thanne his body in fyre [to] be brent."[61] The parallels between the trial of Jesus in all the extant mystery plays and contemporary political events would have become particularly pressing after Henry VI was targeted for death by sorcery. In 1441, Eleanor of Cobham ("a witche and an heretyke"), Roger Bolingbroke, John Home, Thomas Southwell, and Margery of Jourdayne were condemned for "fals tresoun, and sorcery and nigromauncy ayenst all holy Chirch."[62] For decades their dark conspiracy was "probably the most widely-discussed issue in the country," bruited about by ballads and codified as history by the chronicles.[63] The scandal was alive and well among Elizabethans, who knew Jourdayne as "old mother Madge," or "the witch of Eye," burnt at Smithfield after she had "wrought wonders . . . by heresy."[64]

When the case against Jesus is referred by Caiphas and Anna to the temporal powers (first Pilate, then Herod Antipater, then Pilate again), the struggle to convict him—and the authorities' hesitation to do so—centers on the difficulty of establishing the exact nature of the "wonders that this wight has wrought" (York 29.96). All attempts to solicit a confession or abjuration are met with silence—a known tactic of witches.[65] Demands that he produce one of his famous "gaudes" or tricks put him in an irresolvable bind. If he admits that he cannot or will not work a miracle, he's a treasonous faker and blasphemer, claiming to be both king and God without basis. But if he does work some kind of wonder, he's a witch and also deserves to be killed (York 33.157–59). To agents of the secular court, however, his silence suggests a third, exonerating possibility: "Naye, we gete noght o worde," says a soldier, "For he is wraiste of his witte or will of his wone [distraught]" (York 31.271–72). Jesus is repeatedly described as a "sotte" (York 29.260) or "fond foode" (York 31.250); he is "madde," "witless," "wode . . . or ellis his witte faylis hym" (York 31.300, 302).

---

61. N-Town 26.309, 319–20; N-Town 30.47 in *The N-Town Play: Cotton MS Vespasian D.8*, ed. Stephen Spector (Oxford: Published for the Early English Text Society by the Oxford University Press, 1991), 1:257–58, 307.
62. Cotton. Vitellius A XVI, fol. 102v, in "a hand of the late fifteenth century" but clearly drawing on earlier sources according to Charles Lethbridge Kingsford, ed., *Chronicles of London* (Oxford: Clarendon, 1905), xvi, 154; *The Brut or The Chronicles of England*, ed. Friedrich W. D. Brie, part II (London: Published for the EETS by Kegan Paul, Trench, Trübner & Co, 1908), 481.
63. Jessica Freeman, "Sorcery at Court and Manor: Margery Jourdemayne, the Witch of Eye Next Westminster," *Journal of Medieval History* 30, no. 4 (2004): 343–57 at 343; R. A. Griffiths, "The Trial of Eleanor Cobham: An Episode in the Fate of Duke Humphrey of Gloucester," *Bulletin of the John Rylands Library* 51 (1968): 381–99.
64. *Mirror for Magistrates*; quoted by Freeman, "Sorcery at Court and Manor," 344.
65. *Malleus Maleficarum*, ed. and trans. Mackay, 1:622–23; 2:505–6.

The only "wonder" associated with him comes from the length of time that the authorities have spent interrogating someone who is plainly not *compos mentis*: "To medill with a madman is mervaille to mene" (York 31.336).

None of these concerns suffices to exonerate him, but they are enough to inspire Pilate's famous desire to wash his hands of the whole affair:

> *Pilatus*: Kyng, in the devillis name? We! Fye on hym, dastard!
> What, wenys [intends] that woode warlowe overewyn [to conquer] us thus lightly?
> A begger of Bedlem, borne as a bastard?
>
> (York 32.104–6; ms. reading)

Pilate is dismayed to learn that a low-born nobody could be crazed or "wood" enough to imagine overthrowing the imperial regime through treachery or occult knowledge, but he does not take the accusations brought to him by the clergy at face value, and in fact foregrounds the difficulty of arriving at a just verdict: "Warlowe" covers a range of relevant meanings (traitor, felon, infidel, deceiver, sorcerer), and it is Pilate's burden in the trial to determine if any of these labels justly applies to Jesus or if a diagnosis of madness makes the accusations moot. During the earliest stagings, "begger of Bedlem, borne as a bastard" could have been taken as a glancing reference to the gathering of alms by English Bethlehemites, who were subject to the standard anticlerical complaint of producing bastards—and thus more beggars—wherever they went. But as the years wore on, Christ's appearance to Pilate as a "woode," "witless," "fond" Bedlamite wandering the countryside would have increasingly aligned him with the secularized asylum. Its inmates had become notorious for begging upon release, even as their terrifying exploits—whether from madness, bewitchment, or knowing fraudulence—forced "from low farms, / Poor pelting villages, sheepcotes and mills" whatever "charity" people could muster to make the beggars leave (KL 2.2.188–91, F).

Pilate is surprised, after inquiring where Jesus learned the "lare" of witchcraft, to hear that his father was a "wri[gh]te" or carpenter lacking all "sotelté" (York 30.500, 504–5). The king suspects that Jesus's wonders have been imagined or fabricated by the witnesses against him, and he tries to poke holes in the prosecution's case—demanding, in effect, that a demonic marvel must occur in front of his very eyes before he will condemn Jesus for witchcraft. When the marvel finally comes, it appears as a comical bit of stage business. Without Jesus having uttered a single word, much less casting one of his "spellis" (York 29.238), the royal banners held up by the soldier-knights on distinctly medieval "launces" all bow (York 33.182). No matter how hard the soldiers struggle to hold up the banners, no matter how many reinforcements arrive, they are subdued by an object that to all appearances weighs very little. The conclusion drawn by Anna is that Jesus has "enchaunted and charmed oure knyghtis" (York 33.287). "Be his sorcery," Caiphas agrees, "he charmes oure chyvalers and with mysheffe enchaunted" (York 33.288–89). Pilate remains unconvinced—what "harmes" has he done with this trivial trick? "I kenne to convyk hym no cause" (York 33.292–93). The scale is finally tipped by the argument of the clergy that witchcraft is worthy of death not because it is a spiritual offense but because it might legitimize Jesus's claim "to be kyng" (York 33.329). "Sir, trulye," admits Pilate at last, "that touched to tresoune" (York 33.333), and treason is a crime that cannot leave a king unmoved. Any secular ruler claiming for himself an absolute supremacy is entitled to eliminate such challenges, provided he has first resorted to a rigorous, inquisitorial process of verification. In the York trial plays, God must die so that the state can reign in his place.

The York cycle lasted until 1569, when it fell prey at last to Protestant iconoclasm.[66] Theatrical explorations of absolutism and its ongoing conflict with magical or mentally impaired deviants did not, however, end with biblical drama. Shakespeare's first history plays depict the fifteenth-century political landscape that had provided a backdrop for the cycles, at a time when professional players were serving the court as never before.[67] Margery Jourdayne and the others gave the Lord Chamberlain's Men a welcome opportunity to return to the contest between treasonous witchcraft and the secular power when the conspirators were shown conjuring a demon named Asmath in hope of overthrowing the king: "*Here do the ceremonies belonging, and make the circle; Bolingbroke or Southwell reads 'Conjuro te', etc. It thunders and lightens terribly; then the Spirit riseth*" (*2 Henry VI* 1.4.22 SD, F). The Latin tag was likely inspired by the *Flagellum daemonum*, where it appears more than once prominently offset by the sign of the cross to indicate to performers which words should be accompanied by that gesture.[68] Composed by the foremost

---

66. James Simpson, *Permanent Revolution: The Reformation and the Illiberal Roots of Liberalism* (Cambridge, MA: Belknap Press, 2019), 222–26; see also 216–19 for a different, thought-provoking take on the York trial plays.
67. On the cycles as a model for the history plays, see O. B. Hardison, Jr., *Christian Rite and Christian Drama in the Middle Ages: Essays in the Origin and Early History of Modern Drama* (Baltimore, MD: Johns Hopkins University Press, 1965), 290; Jeffrey Knapp, "Author, King, and Christ in Shakespeare's Histories," in *Shakespeare and Religious Change*, ed. Kenneth J. E. Graham and Philip D. Collington (New York: Palgrave Macmillan, 2009), 217–37; Daniel Zimmerman, *The Sacrament and the Stage: Eucharistic Representations in English Theater* (PhD diss., University of Virginia, 2022).
68. Girolamo Menghi, *Flagellum daemonum, seu exorcismi terribiles, potentissimi, & efficaces* (Bologna, 1578), 124–29; reprinted many times with additions and translated into Italian by 1595; translated into German by Manfred Probst, *Besessenheit, Zauberei und ihre Heilmittel: Dokumentation und Untersuchungen von Exorzismushandbüchern des Girolamo Menghi (1523–1609) und des Maximilian von Eynatten (1574/75–1631)* (Münster: Aschendorff, 2008); see also Lynn Thorndike, *A History of Magic and Experimental Science* (New York: Macmillan, 1923–41), 6:556; Clark, *Thinking with Demons*, 389.

Franciscan authority on demons, Girolamo Menghi, the book circulated widely among travelling exorcists as a how-to manual for producing the desired effect upon devils, victims of possession, and audiences alike—hence Bolingbroke's reference to their acts of conjuration as "exorcisms" (*2 Henry VI* 1.4.4, F). This was the manual used by the Jesuits at Denham in 1586, and it may have come within the company's orbit before Shakespeare read Harsnett (who owned two editions and noted with a sniff that the exorcists did not follow Menghi to the letter).[69] In 1704 it was placed on the Index, evidently because the rituals it prescribed had contributed as often as not to conjuring devils rather than driving them out.[70]

Well before the Denham controversy, the arts of producing fake miracles and of performing magic, whether on stage or off, were on a strict continuum according to demonologists. Even when the devil was involved and the conjured effects were thought to be superhuman, those effects could not be supernatural precisely *because* they were demonic. They had to have arisen in that case from the arts of illusion and other processes of natural causation, as supplemented by the imagination of a mentally vulnerable person—for example, the "bedlam brainsick Duchess" (*2 Henry VI* 3.1.51, F), Eleanor Cobham. In reality the devil could not be commanded to appear through incantations. Sometimes he obeyed anyway to fool conjurors into believing that they could acquire otherworldly abilities through him, but in the end those abilities were no more supernatural than the miraculous healing feigned by Simon Simpcox and his wife at the shrine of St. Alban (*2 Henry VI* 2.1, F). Gloucester proves that Simpcox is a con artist and that anyone who believes in the miraculous restoration of his vision, such as Henry VI, is likely suffering from "churchly humours" (*2 Henry VI* 1.1.244, F). Actors and a psychologically unguarded audience sufficed to produce faith in miracles among the feeble minded.

Medicine and the Process of Canonization

After years of suspicions that Henry VI was a "natural fool," "not steadfast of wit," or perhaps even a "lunatic," in late summer of 1453 he suffered an unmistakable mental collapse—"indisposed suddenly ... and smitten with a frenzy

---

69. F. W. Brownlow, *Shakespeare, Harsnett and the Devils of Denham* (Newark: University of Delaware Press, 1993), 209.
70. Owen Davies, *Grimoires: A History of Magic Books* (Oxford: Oxford University Press, 2009), 59; Daniel Bellingradt and Bernd-Christian Otto, *Magical Manuscripts in Early Modern Europe* [etc.] (Cham, Switzerland: Palgrave Macmillan, 2017), 99.

and his wit and reason withdrawn."[71] In the coming years he experienced intermittent paralysis, mental incapacitation, and trancelike states, together with periods of lucidity and the occasional flash of wit. His reported quip, upon momentarily regaining his senses, that his newborn son must have been sired by the Holy Spirit seems like a comical attempt to cope with amnesia.[72] A group of physicians regulated his diet and prescribed all manner of treatment in accordance with the current understanding of Hippocratic-Galenic theory: pharmacological compounds, bloodletting, baths, purgatives, and so forth, possibly including a surgical incision "to relieve pressure on the brain."[73] For eighteen months after his initial breakdown, nothing worked. When the various therapies began to show at last signs of success, he quickly relapsed. The rite of exorcism was the one remaining remedy that might have alleviated his symptoms, but not one person, evidently, thought to administer it. Here was an instance of madness from which demonic causation was excluded from the outset.

If there was a preternatural element to Henry's suffering that went beyond the explanatory power of medicine, it came from divinity, not demons. He was known for his extreme piety and confided to intimates that he heard voices and saw visions. At Mass, he witnessed Christ in the flesh between the hands of the celebrant. Such was Henry's sensitivity to the Eucharist that he could tell when passing a church whether or not it contained a consecrated wafer—thus whether or not to doff his cap. Inexplicable phenomena reminiscent of the miracles recorded in scripture attended his presence. When, at war, provisions were scarce, he multiplied bread: "A sufficiency and even a superfluity [*sufficientia cum superfluo*] was forthcoming for all of his who sought and asked for it."[74] After his burial, further miracles were reported

---

71. R. F. Hunnisett, "Treason by Words," *Sussex Notes and Queries* 14 (1954–57): 117–119; "Robert Bale's Chronicle" (MS Vitellius A. XVI), in *Six Town Chronicles of England*, ed. Ralph Flenley (Oxford: Clarendon, 1911), 140, respectively; see also Bertram Wolffe, *Henry VI* (New Haven, CT: Yale University Press, 2001), 17 and 267–317; Cory James Rushton, "The King's Stupor: Dealing with Royal Paralysis in Late Medieval England," in *Madness in Medieval Law and Custom*, ed. Wendy J. Turner (Leiden: Brill, 2010), 147–76; Ralph A. Griffiths, *The Reign of King Henry VI: The Exercise of Royal Authority, 1422–1461* (London: Ernst Benn, 1981), 715–18.

72. *Calendar of State Papers and Manuscripts Existing in the Archives and Collections of Milan*, ed. Allen B. Hinds (London: Pub. by H. M. Stationery Off., printed by the Hereford Times Limited, Hereford, 1912), 1:58; cited by Helen E. Maurer, *Margaret of Anjou: Queenship and Power in Late Medieval England* (Woodbridge, UK: Boydell Press, 2003), 48.

73. Vivian Green, *The Madness of Kings: Personal Trauma and the Fate of Nations* (Stroud, UK: Alan Sutton, 1993), 66. For a list of therapies that the Privy Council licensed the king's physicians and surgeons to administer see *Proceedings and Ordinances of the Privy Council of England*, ed. Harris Nicolas ([London], 1837), 6:167.

74. John Blacman, *Henry the Sixth: A Reprint of John Blacman's Memoir*, trans. M. R. James (Cambridge: Cambridge University Press, 1919), 43 (English), 23 (Latin). Cf. Roger Lovatt, "A Collector of Apocryphal Anecdotes: John Blacman Revisited," in *Property and Politics: Essays in Later Medieval English History*, ed. Tony Pollard (Gloucester: Alan Sutton, 1985), 172–97.

by pilgrims to his gravesite and by those who invoked his name in times of duress: resurrections, spontaneous healings, including the restoration of several lunatics to sanity.[75] Richard III had Henry's remains transferred to St. George's Chapel in Windsor castle, presumably with the hope that a less accessible locale might extinguish this lingering remnant of Lancastrian devotion—or, if all else failed, that he might better control it. After Henry VII assumed the throne with the help of Lancastrian armies, the new king appealed to Rome to have Henry VI sainted so that his "anti-Yorkist cult" might be formally recognized.[76]

The Roman process of canonization presupposed a deep mistrust of parochial enthusiasms of this sort. Locals were well known to venerate madmen, witches, and heretics—often for the sake of political expediency. Toward the end of Alexander III's pontificate (1159–1181), the papacy reserved to itself the right to determine whether or not any given candidate for sainthood was worthy after a systematic attempt to discredit, if possible, his or her reported sanctity. In the process of canonization, that is, "church authorities aimed to identify false miracles, not true ones, because it was false miracles that justified their role."[77] The provincials who appealed to Rome *already* believed (or, at any rate, claimed to believe) that their candidate was a saint, and indeed countless people throughout Christendom were venerated without the blessing of the papacy. The centralization of authority created intense competition among devotees of unrecognized cults to produce legal evidence that might survive Roman vetting. Before their candidate could be considered for formal evaluation, extensive documentation had to be submitted. The first step for local acolytes, if they wanted Rome's attention, was to show that they had done a preliminary inquiry. This so-called *processus informativus* consisted mainly of gathering depositions in the native vernacu-

---

75. *Henrici VI Angliae Regis miracula postuma: ex codice Musei Britannici Regio 13. c. viii*, ed. Paul Grosjean (Brussels: Société des Bollandistes, 1935); *The Miracles of King Henry VI: Being an Account and Translation of Twenty-Three Miracles Taken from the Manuscript in the British Museum (Royal 13 c. viii)*, trans. Ronald Knox and Shane Leslie (Cambridge: Cambridge University Press, 1923).

76. John W. McKenna, "Piety and Propaganda: The Cult of Henry VI," in *Chaucer and Middle English Studies in Honour of Rossell Hope Robbins*, ed. Beryl Rowland (London: Allen & Unwin, 1974), 72–88 at 74.

77. Paolo Parigi, *The Rationalization of Miracles* (Cambridge: Cambridge University Press, 2012), 110; Eric Waldram Kemp, *Canonization and Authority in the Western Church* (Oxford: Oxford University Press, 1948), 82–106, esp. 99–102 (on Alexander III); André Vauchez, *Sainthood in the Later Middle Ages*, trans. Jean Birrell (Cambridge: Cambridge University Press, 1997), 22–112: "By instituting the process of canonization, it [the Roman Church] sought also to strengthen a control which was intended to offer models of unimpeachable orthodoxy for the imitation of the faithful" (110); Aviad M. Kleinberg, "Proving Sanctity: Selection and Authentication of Saints in the Later Middle Ages," *Viator* 20 (1989): 183–205.

lar to bear witness to any supposed miracles, providing the names of the witnesses who might later be called to testify, and composing a vita of the putative saint.[78] The vernacular accounts then had to be translated into Latin and submitted, along with a fee, to Rome for evaluation.[79] These documents, together with everything subsequently added to the file by papal investigators, formed the evidentiary foundation for the formal trial of the proposed saint—a process that developed more or less in tandem with the *inquisitio* of heretics and witches.[80] In every investigation of sainthood, "there was thus a quadruple question to be solved by the Inquisition," writes Henry Charles Lea—"whether the manifestations which excited popular reverence were really from God, whether they were honestly believed by the devotee while in reality the work of Satan, whether they were known to be demonic, or whether, in fine, they were simply fraudulent speculations on popular superstition."[81] The status of any would-be saint, suspected witch, or apparent demoniac was fundamentally ambiguous until their preternatural feats were subjected to meticulous documentation and rational scrutiny.[82] The *Miracle Book* that came into the hands of Harsnett and Bancroft around 1599, prompting them to investigate a series of Catholic exorcisms on recusant estates more than a decade earlier, was likely a record of this sort—one intended, that is, to catalogue the posthumous miracles that attended the relics of martyred priests such as Edmund Campion. The exorcists took the position that the miraculous healings they had witnessed when demoniacs came into contact with the martyrs' relics were entirely real. Harsnett and Bancroft played the role of medical examiners, making the counterargument

---

78. Christian Krötzl, "Prokuratoren, Notare und Dolmetscher: Zu Gestaltung und Ablauf der Zeugeneinvernahmen bei spätmittelalterlichen Kanonisationsprozessen," *Hagiographica* 5 (1998): 119–40.
79. Aviad M. Kleinberg, "Canonisation Without a Canon," in *Procès de canonisation au Moyen Âge: aspects juridiques et religieux = Medieval Canonization Processes: Legal and Religious Aspects*, ed. Gábor Klaniczay (Rome: École française de Rome, 2004), 7–18.
80. Thomas Wetzstein, *Heilige vor Gericht: Das Kanonisationsverfahren im Europäischen Spätmittelalter* (Cologne: Böhlau, 2004), 157–74; Bengt Ankarloo, "Postface: Saints and Witches," in *Procès de canonisation au Moyen Âge*, ed. Klaniczay, 365–70; Gábor Klaniczay, "The Inquisition of Miracles in Medieval Canonization Processes," in *Miracles in Medieval Canonization Processes: Structures, Functions, and Methodologies*, ed. Sari Katajala-Peltomaa (Turnhout: Brepols, 2018), 43–73; Sari Katajala-Peltomaa, *Demonic Possession and Lived Religion in Later Medieval Europe* (Oxford: Oxford University Press, 2020), 9.
81. Henry Charles Lea, *Chapters from the Religious History of Spain Connected with the Inquisition* (Philadelphia, 1890), 329–30.
82. See Catherine Rider, "Demons and Mental Disorder in Late Medieval Medicine," in *Mental (Dis)Order in Later Medieval Europe*, ed. Sari Katajala-Peltomaa and Susanna Niiranen (Leiden: Brill, 2014), 47–69; Nancy Caciola, *Discerning Spirits: Divine and Demonic Possession in the Middle Ages* (Ithaca, NY: Cornell University Press, 2003); Dyan Elliott, *Proving Woman: Female Spirituality and Inquisitional Culture in the Later Middle Ages* (Princeton, NJ: Princeton University Press, 2004).

that not one cure went beyond natural causes. They brought the Inquisition to Protestant England.

Roman inquisitors had to explore above all the possibility that reported miracles were the product of delusion, wishful thinking, melancholia, hysteria, or full-blown insanity. A mentally unstable visionary on the model of Henry VI, who "was wont almost at every moment to raise his eyes heavenward . . . like one rapt, being for the time not conscious of himself or of those about him, as if he were a man in a trance," raised questions that could only be answered through reasoned debate, after much consulting of evidence.[83] Demonologists for the most part agreed that seemingly divine hallucinations, if they did not in fact come from God, could be fabricated by the devil or produced through a variety of mental afflictions. There was reason to think, however, that the devil's fabrications could not come anywhere close to the appearance of a genuinely divine vision without an underlying, physical pathology in the brain of the witness; and there was no doubt at all that a depraved imagination could produce such revelations without any demonic intervention whatsoever. Joan of Arc—whom Shakespeare would depict in 1 Henry VI as a saint, whore, witch, *and* heretic—was a notoriously ambiguous case that inspired one of her defenders to write a careful treatise on the theological distinctions between true and false revelations.[84] But because these distinctions were so fine, inquisitors more often than not relied on the expertise of secular physicians to draw the line between supernatural and natural phenomena, even as doctors were further tasked with telling the difference, within natural phenomena, between demonic and nondemonic manifestations of mental illness.[85]

Just as it fell to Henry's doctors to rule out categorically the possibility of demonic possession and to prescribe natural remedies for his mental collapse, the same class of medical experts would have been called to answer at his trial for sainthood whether each of his alleged, posthumous healings went beyond the possibilities afforded by nature.[86] Doctors were tasked, that is, with saying

---

83. Blacman, *Henry the Sixth*, trans. James, 38.
84. Jean Gerson, *De distinctione verarum visionum a falsis* (1496); printed in *Opera*, ed. Peter Alliaco et al. (Paris, 1606), 575–93; English in Paschal Boland, *The Concept of "discretio spirituum" in John Gerson's "De probatione spirituum" and "De distinctione verarum visionum a falsis"* (Washington, DC: Catholic University of America Press, 1959); Dyan Elliott, "Seeing Double: John Gerson, the Discernment of Spirits, and Joan of Arc," *American Historical Review* 107, no. 1 (2002): 26–54; on Joan in *1 Henry VI*, see Emma Maggie Solberg, *Virgin Whore* (Ithaca, NY: Cornell University Press, 2018), 156–65.
85. Joseph Ziegler, "Practitioners and Saints: Medical Men in Canonization Processes in the Thirteenth to Fifteenth Centuries," *Social History of Medicine* 12, no. 2 (1999): 191–225; Sari Katajala-Peltomaa, "Demonic Possession as Physical and Mental Disturbance in the Later Medieval Canonization Processes," in Turner, *Madness in Medieval Law*, 108–27.
86. Lee Ann Craig, "The Spirit of Madness: Uncertainty, Diagnosis and the Restoration of Sanity in the Miracles of Henry VI," *Journal of Medieval Religious Cultures* 39, no. 1 (2013): 60–93.

MEDICINE AND THE SECULARIZATION OF MIRACLES 251

if any given recovery failed to meet the threshold of divine intervention, and they were amply rewarded for negative testimony. "The records of a papal commission of inquiry in 1318–19 into the sanctity and miracles attributed to Chiara of Montefalco (d. 1308) incidentally reveal the extensive availability and use of paid secular medical care in Spoleto and the surrounding region."[87] The church encouraged the flourishing of secular medicine and actively employed those whose training in "Olde Ypocras . . . and Galyen" made them predisposed to equate the wonder inspired by preternatural phenomena with an ignorance of natural causation.[88] The triumph of Henry VI's sanctity over these doubters would have required a substantial investment of time, hope, and money.

Time, hope, and money all ran out when Henry VIII broke with Rome, dissolved the monasteries, and banned pilgrimages to sites of feigned miracles.[89] As radical as this rupture must have felt to devotees of the old religion, its intellectual foundations had been laid by the tendency of medieval thinkers like Albert the Great, Thomas Aquinas, Roger Bacon, and William of Ockham to dissolve the realm of the preternatural and its associated wonders into secular components—a tendency, in the words of Lorraine Daston and Katherine Park, that "was ultimately to prevail in the early modern period."[90] The same type of *increduli* who, according to the vita of Henry VI, "did not want in any way to believe" in his miraculous powers carried the day not only for this individual case but for every future report of supernatural intervention in England.[91] "Nothing almost sees miracles / But misery" (KL 2.2.163–64, F) is the dictum of an age that had come to interpret any alleged suspension of natural law as a phantom born of desperation, poverty, or illness. If demonic intervention still counted for many observers among the possible explanations, that did not necessarily mark the degree to which examiners remained in a state of credulity but rather the degree to which they had ruled out supernatural causation.

By the late sixteenth century, observers within the Anglican hierarchy also wanted to exclude demonic agency. For them, every supposed possession—along with any miraculous restoration—was best interpreted through categories supplied by secular medicine, provided that the possession and exor-

---

87. Nancy G. Siraisi, *Medieval and Early Renaissance Medicine: An Introduction to Knowledge and Practice* (Chicago: University of Chicago Press, 1990), 39.
88. *The Riverside Chaucer*, ed. Larry Benson, 3rd ed. (Boston: Houghton Mifflin, 1987), 30.
89. Leigh Ann Craig, "Royalty, Virtue, and Adversity: The Cult of King Henry VI," *Albion: A Quarterly Journal Concerned with British Studies* 35, no. 2 (2003): 187–209.
90. Lorraine Daston and Katherine Park, *Wonders and the Order of Nature, 1150–1750* (Cambridge, MA: Zone Books, Distributed by the MIT Press, 1998), 127.
91. Blacman, *Henry the Sixth*, trans. James, 21 (Latin), 43 (English).

cism could not be discredited as acts of imposture. Many things far stranger than bewitchment occurred in the theater or by virtue of "natural diseases. Namely, from melancholy, mania, epilepsy, lunacy, lycanthropy, convulsions, the mother, menstrual obstruction and sundry other outrageous infirmities."[92] When Harsnett argued that supposed demoniacs were aided in their performances by "a little help of the Mother, epilepsy, or cramp," he was speaking a secular medical language to which the Anglican establishment had come to show overwhelming deference. Some doctors of course continued to sanction the view that a troubled patient was indeed possessed by the devil and cured by exorcism, but in that case, according to Harsnett, the doctors themselves were inviting their own mental diagnosis: "What a deliration [i.e., delirium] is this in our grave, learned, and famous college of ancient renowned physicians, to undertake a long, costly, and painful course of study in those excellent worthies of learned times—Galen, Hippocrates, and the rest—and to spend their money, strength, and spirits, in searching the treasury of nature," Harsnett writes, apropos of any doctor still willing to countenance superhuman explanations of human illness. "Let them cashier those old monuments of ethnick profane learning, and turn wizard, seer, exorcist, juggler, or witch: Let them turn over but one new leaf in Sprenger . . . and see how to discover a devil in the epilepsy, Mother, cramp, convulsion, sciatica, or gout, and then learn a spell, an amulet, a periapt of a priest, and they shall get them more fame, and money in one week, then they do now by all their painful travail in a year" (*A declaration* 27–28). Doctors worthy of their ancient and medieval lineage, by contrast, had to proceed with the thankless task of treating mental illness without recourse to witchcraft. They were the true custodians of "the old monuments of ethnick profane learning" and consequently the most forceful advocates for a process of disenchantment that, according to Weber, had begun with the Hebrew prophets and combined early on with "Hellenistic scientific thought" to repudiate "all magical means to salvation."[93] Arguably the Hellenistic science of greatest consequence was medicine.

Hysteria and the Madness of Kings

"The matrix or womb [*hystera*]," according to Plato's *Timaeus*, grows restive from prolonged chastity and, "by wandering through the body," interferes

---

92. John Deacon and John Walker, *Dialogicall discourses of spirits and divels* (London, 1601), 206; cf. Weyer, *De praestigiis daemonum* 5.28, in *Witches, Devils and Doctors in the Renaissance*, 446–47.
93. MWG 1/18:280; English in *The Protestant Ethic and the Spirit of Capitalism*, trans. Talcott Parsons (New York: Routledge, 1992), 105.

with the process of breathing so as to cause, along with the experience of suffocation, "all kinds of maladies" (*Timaeus* 91c, LCL). That description was omitted from Calcidius's Latin translation but still circulated widely in the Middle Ages thanks to the neo-Hippocratic understanding of *hysterica*. The various disorders going by that name included *hysterikē pnix*, which Latin physicians came to call *hysterica suffocatio, uteri suffocatio, suffocatio matricis* (or *matris*), *strangulatio uteri, hysterica strangulatio, hysterica passio,* and *uteri praefocatio*.[94] The condition caused suffers to be so breathless and immobilized they were sometimes pronounced dead. In the twelfth century, Johannes Platearius recommended placing a glass bowl on their chests to look for signs of life before burial.[95] The same remedy appears in *Lear* when the mad king, already afraid that his own shortness of breath and mental decline are the result of *hysterica passio*, hopes against hope that his daughter's strangulation might turn out to be not death, but something closer to a hysterical fit: "Lend me a looking-glass; / If that her breath will mist or stain the stone, / Why then she lives" (KL 5.3.259–61). Lear's dying hope, the hope that kills him, is that his daughter might be suffering from a family illness.

As the king's mental faculties begin to falter—"O, let me not be mad, sweet heaven, I would not be mad" (KL 1.5.44–45, Q)—he gives himself a profane diagnosis whose lineage stretches back through the Middle Ages to ancient Greek medicine:

O, how this mother swells up toward my heart!
Hysterica passio, down, thou climbing sorrow,
Thy element's below![96]

---

94. *Opera Ysaac* (Lyon, 1515), fol. clxv: "De suffocatione matricis" (printing the eleventh-century *Viaticum* of Constantine the African); Nicholas de La Roche, *De morbis mulierum curandis* (Paris, 1542), 61; reprinted in the popular *Gynaeciorum hoc est de mulierum tum aliis, tum gravidarum, parientium & puerperarium affectibus & morbis* [etc.], ed. Caspar Wolf (Basil, 1566), 394[sic]–385; Girolamo Mercuriale, *De morbis muliebribus praelectiones* (Venice, 1591), 222–36; for further medieval instances see *The "Trotula": An English Translation of the Medieval Compendium of Women's Medicine*, ed. and trans. Monica H. Green (Philadelphia: University of Pennsylvania Press, 2001), 23–34; Danielle Jacquart and Claude Thomasset, *Sexuality and Medicine in the Middle Ages*, trans. Matthew Adamson (Princeton, NJ: Princeton University Press, 1988), 173–77; on the Greek originals, their translation and transmission, see Ann Ellis Hanson and Monica H. Green, "Soranus of Ephesus: *Methodicorum princeps*," in *Aufstieg und Niedergang der römischen Welt* II, vol. 37, part 2, ed. Wolfgang Haase and Hildegard Temporini (Berlin: de Grutyer, 1994), 986–1075; Soranus of Ephesus, *Soranus' Gynecology*, trans. Owsei Temkin (Baltimore, MD: Johns Hopkins University Press, 1991), 149; *Claudii Galeni opera omnia*, ed. Carolus Gottlob Kühn (Leipzig, 1829), 17.2:824.
95. Green, *The "Trotula,"* 26–29; Monica H. Green, "The Transmission of Ancient Theories of Female Physiology and Disease Through the Early Middle Ages" (PhD diss., Princeton University, 1985), 263–68; Tony Hunt, *Anglo-Norman Medicine* (Cambridge: D. S. Brewer, 1995), 1:243–44.
96. KL 2.2.246–48, F4. Q and F print "Historica."

Lear understands enough about the Hippocratic-Galenic tradition to know that the "mother" arises when the womb wanders or, at any rate, releases upward-tending vapors that occasion both a loss of reason and difficulty breathing. The ambiguities of the one-sex model—according to which the scrotum and glans are an external equivalent of the uterus—were probably responsible for the application of this traditionally female ailment to men, as when the fraudulent demoniac Richard Mainy confessed to Harsnett that "a spice of the Mother," rather than any demon, "did there take hold of me."[97] Harsnett supplies the same technical Latin term, *"hysterica passio,"* that appeared four years earlier in a French medical treatise debunking the possession of Martha Brossier.[98] (This had been translated into English by Archbishop Whitgift's chaplain, Abraham Hartwell, who dedicated the work to Bancroft and initiated a print war between the bishops and exorcists.)[99] The diagnosis had also been offered in a more recent English case, of which Shakespeare and Harsnett were both well aware. In 1602 a London teenager named Mary Glover came to suffer terrifying fits after a tense exchange with an old neighbor, Elizabeth Jackson, and seemed to have been bewitched. Speaking in an inhuman voice, Glover called repeatedly for Jackson's hanging. In response, the authorities transformed the Glovers' house into a "kind of theatre" wherein to test the strength of Mary's accusation.[100] They staged confrontations between Mary and a stranger disguised as Jackson, then between Mary and Jackson disguised as someone else, so as to determine whether Jackson's actual presence, or merely its perception by Mary, could cause the fits. The opinion of Edward Jorden was solicited and published in 1603. He argued that Glover's symptoms were entirely compatible with *"Passio Hysterica . . . in English the Mother,"* no witches or demons necessary.[101] "We are not ourselves," as Lear tells Gloucester, "when nature, being oppressed, com-

---

97. Harsnett, *A declaration*, 263; Thomas Laqueur, *Making Sex: Body and Gender from the Greeks to Freud* (Cambridge, MA: Harvard University Press, 1992), 33–35.

98. Harsnett, *A declaration*, 25; [Marescot], *A true discourse, vpon the matter of Martha Brossier*, 14. *Hysterica passio* features prominently in the translation of Hippocrates by Louis Duret (physician to Charles IX), *Hippocratis magni coacae praenotiones: opus admirabile* (Paris, 1588), index under *hysterica passio*; Duret's son, Jean, was present at the examination of Brossier, whence "Hysterica or Suffocation of the Matrix" enters English.

99. See Marion Gibson, *Possession, Puritanism and Print: Darrell, Harsnett, Shakespeare and the Elizabethan Exorcism Controversy* (London: Pickering & Chatto, 2006); Brendan C. Walsh, *The English Exorcist: John Darrell and the Shaping of Early Modern English Protestant Demonology* (New York: Routledge, 2020).

100. Michel MacDonald, ed., *Witchcraft and Hysteria in Elizabethan England: Edward Jorden and the Mary Glover Case* (New York: Routledge, 1991), xiii.

101. Jorden, *A briefe discourse*, 5.

mands the mind / To suffer with the body" (KL 2.2.296–98, Q2, F). Madness was a physical condition forced on the mind by natural corruption.

When *Lear* was first performed, *hysterica passio* was the go-to diagnosis for madness in cases that might otherwise be attributed to magic, and it was being actively disseminated in print by Whitgift, Bancroft, Harsnett, and Jorden, plus the lesser known Deacon and Walker, in order to counteract what they took to be the feigned healings and staged miracles of Catholic and Puritan exorcists. In London, the conflict over demonic possession had become a proxy battle between the Anglican authorities who held "that miracles are ceased, and thereupon will have it that none can be possessed now," and the exorcists who argued that a bewitched demoniac might be miraculously healed.[102] Harsnett spoke for the Anglican consensus when he condemned would-be miracle workers for performing an ineffectual, toxic stagecraft upon the mentally ill: "Let them with all their juggling drive out a melancholic spirit, out of any poor soul in Bedlam."[103] In cases where alleged demoniacs were not actively faking their symptoms, they needed either confinement or medical treatment, not self-serving acts of prestidigitation and pseudo-religious magic.

When James came to the English throne, neither the exorcists nor the Anglican hierarchy knew whose side he might take. On the one hand, as king of Scotland, he had personally overseen the execution of witches, at least one of whom had confessed to using "sorcery, witchcraft and devilish practices" to make a rival suitor fall "into a lunacy and madness."[104] James had written his *Daemonologie* against the skeptical position of Reginald Scot, whom the Anglican coalition had come to endorse in print—an awkward point of tension that advocates for exorcism tried to exploit. On the other hand, James was committed to the idea that, "since the coming of Christ in the flesh, and establishing of his church by the apostles, all miracles, visions, prophecies, and appearances of angels or good spirits are ceased."[105] His skepticism toward miracles extended, if not at first to exorcism, then to the faith healings routinely performed by royals: James was so concerned about the efficacy of the King's Touch—and so fearful that his continued perfor-

---

102. John Darrell, *An apologie, or defence of the possession of William Sommers* [etc.] (n.p, n.d. [Amsterdam, 1599?]), 12v.
103. Samuel Harsnett, *A discoverie of the fraudulent practices of Iohn Darrel* (London, 1599), A4r.
104. *Newes from Scotland, declaring the damnable life and death of Doctor Fian a notable sorcerer, who was burned at Edenbrough in Ianuary last, 1591* [etc.] (London, 1592), Ciii^v; text and commentary in Lawrence Normand and Gareth Roberts, eds., *Witchcraft in Early Modern Scotland: James VI's "Demonology" and the North Berwick Witches* (Exeter, UK: University of Exeter Press, 2000), 318.
105. *Daemonologie* 3.2; text in Normand and Roberts, *Witchcraft in Early Modern Scotland*, 411–12.

mance of the ritual might constitute an act of superstition or some form of magic—that he declined to make the sign of the cross over the sick and had the scriptural epigraph removed from the "golden stamp" that he hung about a patient's neck.[106] Conscience mollified, he carried on with the counterfeit miracle, and "let the world believe it, though he smiled at it, in his own reason, finding the strength of the imagination a more powerful agent in the cure, than the plasters his surgeons prescribed for the sore."[107] Not until the eighteenth century would a remedy of this sort come to be called a placebo (echoing a liturgical hymn from the Office of the Dead), but the mechanism was known to medieval and early modern physicians: "The confidence of the patient in the means used," writes Jorden, "is oftentimes more available to cure diseases then all other remedies whatsoever."[108] Galenic medicine had carved out an acceptable role for seemingly magical props by attributing their potency to the human imagination rather than a spell or an enchanted object.

As it turned out, James's assumption of the English throne greatly increased his suspicion that most demoniacs were either imposters or people suffering from mental incompetence and that the miracle cure of exorcism was a placebo effect. The change has been much puzzled over, but the most likely explanation is that he fell into line with the medico-Anglican establishment. In 1605 he consulted with Bancroft, Harsnett, and Jorden in the examination of Anne Gunter, a Berkshire woman whose sudden mental decline suggested to some that she had been bewitched. The king and his new advisors discovered otherwise: "We find by her confession," James wrote to the Earl of Salisbury, "that she holdeth herself perfectly cured from her former weakness by a potion given unto her by a physician and a tablet hanged about her neck [and] that she was never possessed with any devil, nor bewitched."[109] Presumably the tablet was included in her therapy as a stimulant to the imagination, so that the power of fantasy might join with the natural remedy inherent in the "potion" to heal her damaged mind. Under no circumstances, Jorden stressed,

---

106. *Macbeth* 4.3.175; D. P. Walker, "The Cessation of Miracles," in *Hermeticism and the Renaissance: Intellectual History and the Occult in Early Modern Europe*, ed. Ingrid Merkel and Allen G. Debus (Washington, DC: Folger Shakespeare Library, Associated University Presses, 1988), 111–24, esp. 121–22; see also Peter Dear, "Miracles, Experiments and the Ordinary Course of Nature," *Isis* 81, no. 4 (1990): 663–83.
107. Arthur Walker, *The History of Great Britain: Being the Life and Reign of King James the First* [etc.] (London, 1653), 289; see Deborah Willis, "The Monarch and the Sacred: Shakespeare and the Ceremony for the Healing of the King's Evil," in *True Rites and Maimed Rites: Ritual and Anti-Ritual in Shakespeare and his Age*, ed. Linda Woodbridge and Edward Berry (Urbana: University of Illinois Press, 1992), 147–68.
108. Jorden, *A briefe discourse*, 25r, quoting the Canon of Avicenna.
109. Quoted in MacDonald, *Hysteria and Witchcraft*, xlviii.

should extraordinary properties be attributed to such therapeutic theater or its attendant objects: "pissing through the wedding ring, and a hundred such like toys and gambols: which when they prevail in the cure of diseases, it is not for any supernatural virtue in them."[110] The supernatural virtue associated with magical and miraculous remedies lies entirely in the mind, which has the ability to heal itself, in some cases, through the power of suggestion.

Performing *hysterica passio* at court might have encouraged at least some members of the audience to see an unsettling parallel between Lear's mental state and a congenital frailty of the Stuarts.[111] Mary Queen of Scots was "much molested with vehement fits of the mother," and James found his normal functions "manifestly perverted a great deal by mental disturbances."[112] We owe our remarkably detailed portrait of the king's psychological state to Theodore Turquet de Mayerne, a French Huguenot doctor; as the former physician-in-ordinary to Henri IV, he had been a participant in discrediting Martha Brossier before visiting London in 1605 and then joining the English court permanently in 1611.[113] James confided in de Mayerne that a painful colic was inherited from his "mother's family," though the doctor also noted bouts of "depression, shortness of breath, paranoia and other melancholic symptoms."[114] James experienced palpitations and pain in his heart (*palpitatio, cardialgia*), which could cease to beat altogether for short periods (*pulsus intercidens*) as a result of the fainting spells (*defectio animi*) that followed from his frequent "difficulty breathing, dread, [and] incredible sadness" (ibid., 166–67). His body was tortured by anguish, "his mind tossed with most violent motion," subject to seasonal change and other meteorological conditions. He was, in short, "one minded like the weather, most unquietly" (KL 3.1.2). Non-royals who fell ill with any of these ailments were still subject to exorcism—and their neighbors to witchcraft accusations—but by the time of *Lear* they were more likely than ever to receive treatment from secular physicians, regardless of social station, given the "growing trend towards judicial skepticism" that commenced under James.[115] Perhaps on account of his own condition, he had been persuaded by the religious and medical authorities

---

110. Jorden, *A briefe discourse*, 24v–25r.
111. Margaret Hotine, "Lear's Fit of the Mother," *Notes and Queries* 226, no. 2 (1981): 138–41.
112. *Calendar of the State papers Relating to Scotland and Mary, Queen of Scots, 1547–1603*, vol. 3, *1569–1571*, ed. William Boyd (Edinburgh: H. M. General Register House, 1903), 441, and BM Sloane MS. 1679, printed in Norman Moore, *The History of the Study of Medicine in the British Isles* (Oxford: Clarendon, 1908), 163, respectively.
113. Hugh Trevor-Roper, *Europe's Physician: The Various Life of Sir Theodore de Mayerne* (New Haven, CT: Yale University Press, 2006), 4, 354–55, 384n27.
114. Moore, *History of the Study of Medicine*, 166.
115. MacDonald, *Witchcraft and Hysteria*, l.

of the day that melancholia, epilepsy, and *hysterica passio* made for better explanations than demonic witchcraft. "Prithee, nuncle, tell me whether a madman be a gentleman or a yeoman?" the fool asks Lear. The answer: "A king, a king" (KL 3.6.9–10).

Miracles and the Theater of Mind

Shakespeare borrowed more words and phrases from Harsnett's A *declaration of egregious popish impostures* than from any other known source—"words that he had never used before nor would again."[116] He found there the names of Edgar's devils, together with a highly learned account of the human ability to generate seemingly miraculous and demonic phenomena through purely natural processes. And yet Harsnett was hardly Shakespeare's first foray into contemporary debates about miracles and magic. Preternatural appearances, witchcraft, and the specter of demonic agency are a mainstay of his corpus, as they were of the London stage more generally. Professional acting companies frequently explored their dangerous alignment with saints, priests, magicians, witches, and demons insofar as all of them might cause a wide range of preternatural phenomena to happen by occult or theatrical means. Actors also raised tempests, conjured devils, transformed humans into animals, removed limbs, gouged out eyes, cut off heads, populated their playhouses with ghosts, and brought the dead back to life. They impersonated characters whose physiological predisposition for hysterics, melancholy, jealousy, and so forth left them especially susceptible to misperception and deceptive manipulation. The predicament of Gloucester—willfully blind before being blinded in fact, wanting to die, and then being told that he had miraculously survived a suicide attempt—raised questions that were simultaneously theatrical, demonological, theological, and medical. What did it mean that any such miracle could be readily explained as an illusion and the result of some agent capitalizing on a physiological frailty? Could a fake miracle have any positive or even spiritual benefit? Was simulating divine intervention invariably an immoral form of deceit or might it also have some power to heal? Didn't fakery itself have a long-standing, respected position within medical practice as a kind of placebo?

---

116. James Shapiro, *The Year of Lear: Shakespeare in 1606* (New York: Simon & Schuster, 2015), 81; Kenneth Muir, "Samuel Harsnett and *King Lear*," *Review of English Studies* n.s. 2 (1951): 11–21; Muir, *The Sources of Shakespeare's Plays* (New Haven, CT: Yale University Press, 1978), 202–6; Muir, ed., *King Lear* (London: Routledge, 1993) 239–42 (appendix 7); John L. Murphy, *Darkness and Devils: Exorcism and "King Lear"* (Athens: Ohio University Press, 1984); Brownlow, *Shakespeare, Harsnett*.

Shakespeare's interest in *A declaration* was evidently personal. Harsnett mentions his cousin, Edward Arden (executed for treason in 1583), as a member of the "saint-traitorly crew" invoked by the priests to effect the miracle of exorcism (*A declaration* 85). One of those priests, Robert Dibdale, was born in the parish of Stratford-upon-Avon about the same time as Anne Hathaway and grew up in her village. Both were the children of local farmers, and Dibdale's sister-in-law witnessed the will of Anne's father. The priests frequently applied to (or inserted in) the possessed person's body relics of an English martyr, Thomas Cottam, who was the brother of the Stratford schoolmaster.[117] Even if Shakespeare did not know these men directly, he knew people that did. In Dibdale and Cottam he would have recognized two contemporaries from his home parish who had gotten intimately involved in the business of producing miracles by highly artificial, ritualized means. According to Harsnett, Dibdale had become an actor and used Cottam as a stage prop. Both belonged to "a holy troupe" of "wandering players" that had regularly performed in "their principal theatre, Sir George Peckham's house at Denham" (*A declaration* 10).

The Denham Manor had once been owned by Westminster Abbey and was leased to various occupants until the dissolution, when its title passed to the Peckhams.[118] They also purchased land formerly belonging to the Holywell Priory just outside London, to which the family still laid claim, despite an apparent sale, when James Burbage constructed the Theatre on the same plot. In 1582, Burbage had to hire men to protect his investment from agents of Edmund Peckham—the company manager, according to Harsnett, of the miracle troupe at Denham: "This is the man that still furnished the camp with all kind of luggage and pleasing provision, that scours the coasts to see that all be clear, that looks to the trusses and fardels [baggage], that no juggling sticks be left out: the sacrist of these holy mysteries" (*A declaration* 12). Shakespeare almost certainly heard from Burbage of the earlier conflict with the Peckhams and, if he did not already know, would have learned from Harsnett of a deeper, structural parallel. The troupe at Denham and the London acting companies were both dedicated to generating seemingly miraculous phenomena on newly secularized ground. Both exorcists and players trafficked in the preternatural, but the players alone were supported by the temporal power on the understanding that they served a useful social function, free from witchcraft, hypocrisy, or fraud, so long as they adopted the livery

---

117. Brownlow, *Shakespeare, Harsnett*, 108–9.
118. *Victoria History of the County of Buckinghamshire*, ed. William Page (London: St. Catherine Press, 1925), 3:256–57; Brownlow, *Shakespeare, Harsnett*, 202n4.

of an aristocratic household and did not dare to represent the persons of the Trinity. Their magic was closer in practice to the investigations of a philosopher or scientist than to a witch or exorcist, despite their quasi-demonic commitment to exploiting the dangerous power of the senses and fantasy. In fact the state suppression of miracle workers—like the state suppression of the monasteries and of overly religious drama—worked more or less directly to incite a theater of radical experimentation, especially at court: in masques, for example, and in scientific demonstrations such as the wondrous discovery of perpetual motion that was exhibited in 1607 by Cornelius Drebbel, James's chief illusionist alongside Inigo Jones, Ben Jonson, and the King's Men.[119]

Harsnett loathed the theater but supported its function to the extent that players were subject to authority. Indeed he was among the licensers of books for the press and reviewed at least one script performed by the Lord Chamberlain's Men—Jonson's medically inflected *Every Man Out of His Humour*—as well as a satirical publication by the company shareholder and clown, Will Kemp.[120] The point of Harsnett's many comparisons between players and exorcists was to impeach the latter by stressing the abomination that occurred when they operated an unlicensed theater in secret using pseudo-religious props to prey on the mentally unwell. Players and priests both performed miracles "for money" (*A declaration* 14, 50, 189). Both knew that all miracles were feigned, but only the priests were involved in "hypocritical dissimulation" because only the priests tried to convince an audience that they themselves genuinely believed in their fake miracles, when in fact their faith was strategic, cynical, and self-interested.[121]

According to Harsnett, not one person at Denham successfully maintained any belief in demonic possession—or in the need for exorcism. Many of the participants, he says, never believed in the first place. But they nonetheless continued to perform their charades out of a self-reinforcing cycle of compulsory make-believe. Anne Smith, whom Harsnett calls "an affectionate proselyte to that mimic superstition," admitted that she was never possessed but rather "sick of a disease called the Mother" (*A declaration* 20, 237). The priests

---

119. *Wonder-vondt van de eeuwighe bewegingh, die den Alckmaersche Philosooph Cornelis Drebbel door een eeuwigh bewegende gheest in een Cloot besloten te weghe ghebrocht heest* [etc.] (Alkmaar, 1607). Descriptions of this rare text and the motion machine are in Frans A. Janssen, *Technique and Design in the History of Printing* (Houten, The Netherlands: Hes & De Graaf, 2004), 341–42; Rosalie L. Colie, "Some Thankfulnesse to Constantine": *A Study of English Influence upon the Early Works of Constantijn Huygens* (The Hague: Martinus Nijhoff, 1956), 98–99; Jennifer Speake, "The Wrong Kind of Wonder: Ben Jonson and Cornelis Drebbel," *Review of English Studies*, n.s. 66, no. 273 (2014): 60–70.
120. Brownlow, *Shakespeare, Harsnett*, 174.
121. Harsnett, *A declaration*, n.p., preface "To the Seduced Catholics."

urged her to accept that her condition was better explained by demons and, "being wholly addicted to popery, she did reverence them very much, and durst not contradict them" (*A declaration* 242). So she outwardly agreed to the cause of her illness, "thereby to see if she might be helped, although all the while has had a conceit in herself that she was not possessed" (*A declaration* 239). Likewise Sara Williams, whose confession produced nearly all of the demonic names that Edgar uses, claimed of her possession that "she herself did then pretend something of it to be true" (*A declaration* 182). Again and again she admits to performing the script that the priests supplied her, "confessing that she did very often tell them those things which were untrue, after she perceived how she could please them" (*A declaration* 177). Even as the priests were supposed to be treating her symptoms, she was doing her best to help them maintain what she took to be their faith in demons and miraculous healings. Once, when George Peckham insisted that a devil had caused her briefly to levitate, although she knew that no such thing had ever happened, "she herself to please them did confess as much" (*A declaration* 185).

Harsnett's star witness for the shared unbelief of all the would-be demoniacs was Richard Mainy, a former seminarian at Rheims and member the "Bonhommes, or fratres minimi"—an especially austere order (*A declaration* 260). He was in no way deluded about the cause of his pseudo-demonic symptoms: "I knew very well, whatsoever they said, that the Mother was the only disease wherewith I was vexed" (*A declaration* 269). As far as he was concerned his sickness arose from a natural cause, but his symptoms had given the priests all they needed to pretend the devil was in him despite their knowing "well enough that neither I nor any of the rest before mentioned were indeed possessed" (*A declaration* 264). If we judge from the confessions of the would-be demoniacs, belief in bewitchment and exorcism was not a heartfelt conviction but rather an opportune pretense. Mainy was convinced that Machiavellian priests collaborated with the naturally impaired to stage miracles in which no one believed but in which some nonetheless found certain benefits. Even if we decline to take the professions of unbelief at face value—surely everyone felt pressured to tell Harsnett whatever he wanted to hear—we are faced with a situation in which unbelief was mandatory. Anglican authorities demanded and received an account of demonic possession such that every participant—including the exorcist—shared their skepticism. And yet for all that, we're told, the participants produced the painful antics of possession and exorcism with the hope that mere playacting could sometimes produce beneficial effects in the absence of faith.

Edgar's impersonation of a demoniac and his attempt to stage a miracle share the same hope—namely, that the artificial fabrication of a preternatural event might have a therapeutic effect even when the participants either suspect or know that the act does not involve any superhuman force. The expectation behind Edgar's performance is that the deceptions of a pretend demoniac might be turned toward an effective, if ultimately homeopathic and at times perverse or even cruel form of therapy, not far removed from the torturous remedies prescribed by doctors and surgeons (emetics, purgatives, bloodlettings, incisions) but easier to stomach insofar as the entry of a fictive illusion into the body is no more invasive than everyday sense perception. Once Gloucester succumbs to the melancholy belief that suicide alone can offer him a remedy, Edgar decides to follow the standard medical advice for treating a depraved imagination: "If we cannot moderate these perturbations of the mind by reason and persuasions," Jorden writes, citing Constantine the African (an eleventh-century medical authority), "we may politicly confirm them in their fantasies, that we may the better fasten some cure upon them."[122] Edgar will do what demons were said to do—possess some, lead others to suicide, fake miracles—but he will do it in the absence of any possible possession or miracle toward a strictly medical end: "Why I do trifle thus with his despair / Is done to cure it" (KL 4.6.34–35). He means to restore Gloucester's health by collaborating with him in a suicide attempt and then staging a miraculous survival. Gloucester's recovery (if we can call it that) will of course be no more supernatural than Edgar's possession was demonic. As in the upper echelons of the Anglican church, where miracles and possession were said to have ceased, a convoluted and savage but nominally therapeutic regime operates in their place.

The King's Men went to great lengths to stage a parallel between the performance of their tragedy and the treatment of Gloucester. Actors that could raise demons, storms, and the dead were professional technicians of the preternatural with a keen interest in the dependence of their art on practices and mental habits easily pathologized as forms of witchcraft, delusion, or "too great credulity."[123] Indeed it has often been said that Edgar's therapeutic ruse plays on the tendency of his "credulous father" (KL 1.2.177) to countenance all manner of superstitious fiction. And yet the scene on the imaginary cliffs of Dover shows two mutually unconvinced parties in a joint act of make-believe. Gloucester suspects that his Bedlamite guide is either delusional or engaged in some kind of pretense, but this suspicion presents no impediment to playing along:

---

122. Jorden, *A briefe discourse*, 25v.
123. [Marescot], *A true discourse, upon the matter of Martha Brossier*, 1. For the rich afterlife of this term in the history of animal magnetism, mesmerism, and clairvoyance, see Emily Ogden, *Credulity: A Cultural History of US Mesmerism* (Chicago: University of Chicago Press, 2018).

Gloucester: When shall we come to the top of that same hill?
Edgar: You do climb it up now. Look, how we labour.
Gloucester: Methinks the ground is even.
Edgar: Horrible steep.
Hark, do you hear the sea?
Gloucester: No, truly.

(KL 4.6.1–4, Q)

Edgar incorporates the inaudibility of his imaginary sea into a description of the fictive abyss below their feet in order to fool Gloucester into accepting that they stand at the perfect place to jump—"the murmuring surge / That on th'unnumbered idle pebble chafes, / Cannot be heard" (KL 4.6.20–22, Q). Since Gloucester is standing either on a small step or flat ground, the fall itself is difficult to stage without a degree of grim comedy; in fact the whole shtick of misleading a blind man originates in a medieval street farce.[124] But farce, perhaps, is the point. Even in the absence of supernatural intervention, the worst returns to laughter, as a comical contrivance prepares the way for a small restoration.

"Thy life's a miracle" (KL 4.6.55), Edgar says after the fall, now impersonating a random passerby at the bottom of the cliff. Gloucester once more responds with incredulity: "But have I fallen, or no?" (KL 4.6.56, Q2, F). To firm up his faith Edgar again points to what cannot be perceived—because it is not there—as evidence that a miracle has occurred: "Look up a height: the shrill-gorged lark so far / Cannot be seen or heard" (KL 4.6.58–59). Then, because Gloucester has "no eyes" (KL 4.6.60), Edgar paints him a picture in words that amplifies his deliverance. A miracle has preserved him not only from a fatal fall but, Edgar claims, from the demon who orchestrated his death:

Edgar: This is above all strangeness.
Upon the crown o'the cliff what thing was that
Which parted from you?
Gloucester: A poor unfortunate beggar.
Edgar: As I stood here below methought his eyes
Were two full moons. He had a thousand noses,
Horns wealk'd and waved like the enraged sea.
It was some fiend. Therefore, thou happy father,
Think that the clearest gods, who make their honours
Of men's impossibilities, have preserved thee.

(KL 4.6.69–74, F)

---

124. Edward Wheatley, "Voices of Violence: Medieval French Farce and the Dover Cliff Scene in *King Lear*," *Comparative Drama* 43, no. 4 (2009): 455–71. I am grateful to Viola Cozzio for this reference.

From a traditional Christian perspective, Edgar and Gloucester are both trapped in a tragic irony. "The clearest gods" of the ancient world, for all their seeming ability to accomplish the impossible, were in fact just as demonic and devoid of miraculous power as the "fiend" that led Gloucester to his fake precipice. "Men's impossibilities" were within the realm of possibility for these demons on account of their superior strength, speed, perception, knowledge of natural philosophy, and expertise in the theatrical arts of legerdemain—not on account of any ability to suspend the laws of nature. Their subjection to basic physics was exposed by the miracles of Christ, which secularized the gods of antiquity and, according to Protestants, ceased altogether after the apostles. From the specific perspective of the medico-Anglican establishment, human actors sufficed to occasion supernatural appearances in the theater of the mind, and even the incredulous could be cajoled into playing along. And what, in that case, could be the value of pretending to have come into contact with the divine?

Gloucester clearly suspects that no miracle has happened. But Edgar's complicated feigning nonetheless works in him a psychological remedy for his suffering:

> Henceforth I'll bear
> Affliction till it do cry out itself
> "Enough, enough" and die. That thing you speak of,
> I took it for a man. Often t'would say
> "The fiend, the fiend": he led me to that place.
>
> (KL 4.6.75–79, F)

Gloucester never comes closer than this to being convinced that he has had a supernatural experience, and even here he can only bring himself to assert what he always thought was the case. The alleged fiend was "a man" who spoke incessantly of demons—just as Edgar is speaking now in his latest role as good Samaritan: "Bear free and patient thoughts" (KL 4.6.80, F). His benediction is predicated on the hope that performing a pseudomiracle through nothing more than the natural act of make-believe might be *close enough* to divine intercession to occasion a real healing. His treatment of Gloucester is something on the order of a medico-theatrical experiment, designed to gauge whether the performance of otherworldly intervention in a world devoid of miracles might have cathartic effects in the manner of a bitter but medicinal purgative.

Lear, for his part, comes to believe that the only medicine capable of curing his ills is to experience the full depth of human misery: "Take physic, pomp," he says on the heath just before meeting Edgar's Bedlamite:

Expose thyself to feel what wretches feel,
That thou mayst shake the superflux to them,
And show the heavens more just.

(KL 3.4.33–40)

Because Lear offers this critique of "the heavens" while attempting to "pray" (KL 3.4.27), the speech can seem like the beginnings of a familiar Christian realization. The gods of antiquity, having no existence, do not sympathize with the wretched. True spiritual regeneration can only arise from the virtues of humility, penance, and charity. The word "superflux" is a Shakespearean coinage but may translate, according to Deborah Shugar, "a technical term from medieval canon law" for the percentage of one's income or goods that is owed to the poor.[125] At the same time the word recalls a common medical term for the "superfluous humors" or "superfluities" that require purgation, and this way of discharging excess from the body royal does not originate in Christianity.[126] If Lear nonetheless comes close to envisioning a proto-Christian social program founded on a charitable concern for the poor, it is one that Jacobean audiences had conspicuously lost: "Thanks largely to the Reformation," writes Roy Porter, "early modern England was, by the standards of comparable nations, singularly ill endowed with civic and pious institutions for unfortunates."[127] One implication of Lear's prayer would have been that godless, pre-Christian Britain all too closely resembled the secularized present. Just as Leir's father had his magic broken in the age of disenchantment initiated by the prophets (according to Monmouth and Holinshed), so too had the most recent Yahwistic puritans desacralized whole swaths of the country, with results that were widely perceived as tragic.[128] "The ambition to use monastic property and charitable donations to solve the problem of poverty painlessly had failed," writes Paul Slack. "The problem remained wholly

---

125. Deborah Shuger, "Subversive Fathers and Suffering Subjects: Shakespeare and Christianity," in *Religion, Literature and Politics in Post-Reformation England 1540–1688*, ed. Richard Strier and Donna Hamilton (Cambridge: Cambridge University Press, 1996), 46–69 at 53.
126. Edward Topsell, *Historie of foure-footed beastes* [etc.] (London, 1607), 426; Jorden, *A briefe discourse*, 7r.
127. Roy Porter, *Mind-Forg'd Manacles: A History of Madness in England from the Restoration to the Regency* (Cambridge, MA: Harvard University Press, 1987), 121.
128. Eamon Duffy, *The Stripping of the Altars: Traditional Religion in England, c. 1400–c. 1580*, 2nd ed. (New Haven, CT: Yale University Press, 2005); J. J. Scarisbrick, *The Reformation and the English People* (Oxford: Blackwell, 1984).

exceptional in London, and it grew worse."[129] Lear is unable to address the social costs of extreme disenchantment unless an ad hoc regimen of "physic" can heal him—and perhaps also the state—without the succor of divine help. Any miraculous balm (not to mention any redistribution of wealth) would have to come through human compassion; given its obvious limitations, compassion would not be enough but, for all that, was not nothing.

Humility in *Lear* is not so much a virtue as the truth. It is humbling to live in a world that offers humans only momentary spells of respite. It is humbling in times of serious illness to place one's hope in the hands of secular professionals. "Kill thy physician, and the fee bestow / Upon the foul disease" is Kent's version of the ancient dictum that if sickness doesn't kill you, doctors will (KL 1.1.164–5, Q). It was a view any number of Shakespeare's contemporaries shared, including King James: "He laughs at medicine," de Mayerne notes. "He asserts that it is an art supported by mere conjectures, feeble because uncertain."[130] After Lear's failed course of self-medication results in his madly "singing aloud," Cordelia enters in the quarto accompanied by a "Doctor" to whom she offers the whole of her "outward worth" if he can restore her father's "bereaved sense" (KL 4.4.2, 4.4.SD, 4.4.8–10, Q). The prayers, the invocations, the hope for divine intervention—all give way momentarily before the authority of medicine. The doctor alone has "a means" to cure the insane—namely, "repose" and "simples operative, / Whose power will close the eye of anguish" (KL 4.4.11, 14–15). Medical knowledge, though occult in the sense of drawing on "the unpublished virtues of the earth," has dispensed with spirits, demons, and miracles in favor of "man's wisdom" (KL 4.4.8, 16). The stage clears for more plotting by Cordelia's sisters, followed by Edgar's faux miracle—during which time, we learn, Lear has fallen asleep and is now dressed in "fresh garments" (KL 4.7.22). Cordelia calls upon the "kind gods" to "cure this great breach in his abused nature," but the cure, if it is to come, falls to the physician. His confidence in natural ministrations is total: "I doubt not of his temperance" (KL 4.7.24, Q), he says of Lear. The doctor cues music—a Galenic stratagem, according to Jorden, for "moderat-

---

129. Paul Slack, "Social Policy and the Constraints of Government, 1547–58," in *The Mid-Tudor Polity c. 1540–1560*, ed. Jennifer Loach and Robert Tittler (London: Macmillan, 1980), 94–115 at 112–13. See also Robert Henke, *Poverty and Charity in Early Modern Theater and Performance* (Iowa City: University of Iowa Press, 2015); William C. Carroll, *Fat King, Lean Beggar: Representations of Poverty in the Age of Shakespeare* (Ithaca, NY: Cornell University Press, 1996); Paola Pugliatti, *Beggary and Theatre in Early Modern England* (Aldershot, UK: Ashgate, 2003), esp. 149.

130. Moore, *History of the Study of Medicine*, 170. Doctors themselves were great complainers about the medical profession: see Charles Webster, *From Paracelsus to Newton: Magic and the Making of Modern Science* (Cambridge: Cambridge University Press, 1982), esp. 80–84.

ing the perturbations of the mind by the example of Asclepius."[131] While it plays, as though to supplement the doctor's simples with a charm all her own, Cordelia awakens Lear with a kiss: "O my dear father, restoration hang / Thy medicine on my lips" (KL 4.7.26–27). Lear comes to in a dream state, at first mistaking his daughter for "a soul in bliss"—which is to say, for the equivalent of a heavenly saint who has managed to resurrect him through a miracle or, from the Protestant perspective, some type of necromancy: "You do me wrong to take me out o'the grave" (KL 4.7.45).[132] The initial signs of recovery are somewhat bleak: "I will not swear these are my hands," Lear frets, before administering to himself the test commonly given by doctors to those who were allegedly bewitched: "Let's see— / I feel this pinprick" (KL 4.7.55–56). Unlike the demoniacs whose "numbed and mortified bare arms" could not feel "pins, wooden pricks, nails, sprigs of rosemary" (KL 2.2.186–87, Qc), Lear at last finds his sensitivity restored, along with his wits. The doctor advises giving him time and space to waken fully and assures Cordelia that the cure has taken: "Be comforted, good madam, the great rage / You see is cured in him" (KL 4.7.78–79, Q). Lear exits with a newfound self-awareness—"I am old and foolish" (KL 4.7.84)—fully reconciled with the daughter whom his mania had wronged.

In the chronicles and their retellings in Spenser and the anonymous *King Leir*, Cordelia and her father live to vanquish their enemies. Anyone who had seen or read the earlier play would have fully expected father and daughter to perform the business about who should kneel down to whom for forgiveness, then to triumph over adversity. Cordelia's sudden strangulation in Shakespeare's version would have been difficult to stage without raising the expectation that the appearance of her death was going to be reversed through some type of *deus ex machina*—presumably, given Shakespeare's invention of the doctor, a miracle of medicine. There were a number of treatable ailments whose chief symptom was "the very image of death," but *hysterica passio* was perhaps the defining instance.[133] Jorden cites a host of ancient, medieval, and modern authorities in support of the recommendation that the corpse of a person who has suffered from this specific form of "*strangulatus*" should remain unburied for at least three days since during this interval (sometimes longer) there had been documented cases of revival. For example, one "Bottonus, a late professor of Physicke in Padua, reporteth of a woman that, being given over for dead in a fit of the Mother, was by such

---

131. Jorden, *A briefe discourse*, 24r.
132. For the popularity of saint plays on the commercial stage and their connection to magic, see Gina M. di Salvo, *The Renaissance of the Saints After Reform* (Oxford: Oxford University Press, 2023).
133. Jorden, *A briefe discourse*, 9r.

conclusions as he tried, discovered to be yet alive, and recovered her former health again by such remedies as he prescribed."[134] Any number of people in the audience—above all King James—would have had reason to imagine that the physician tasked by Cordelia to treat her father might again arrive on the scene to resurrect her from suffocation. It was one of the more familiar wonders of medicine, which doctors had been capable of performing for centuries without any need for supernatural or demonic intervention. "When I listen to them," John of Salisbury writes of twelfth-century physicians, "it seems to me they have the power to raise the dead."[135]

All the same, the audience would also have known that Cordelia's loss of breath was not the result of hysteria. Edmund confesses the plot to suborn a servant to stage her suicide (KL 5.3.250–57)—a horrid echo of the scene at Dover—and Lear himself, if we can believe him, has already described his attempt to save her: "I killed the slave that was a-hanging thee" (KL 5.3.272). Only by virtue of his *own* hysteria is Lear able to continue hoping that she might somehow remain alive—and to invite an audience to hope along with him. We know that he is a man overcome by confusion—from grief, dotage, the Mother. A mind thus afflicted could see all manner of things that were nonexistent—Cordelia's disloyalty, for example. And yet this same vulnerability to mental phantasms offers Lear a saving grace. According to his final lines as they appear in the folio, his affliction generates the delusional experience of a miracle to "redeem all sorrows" (KL 5.3.264) when Cordelia's breath is restored, if not in the theater where the audience sits, then in the theater of his mind:

> Do you see this? Look on her: look, her lips,
> Look there, look there! *He dies.*
>
> (KL 5.3.308–9, F)

Edgar at first holds out hope that Lear's final collapse is merely another fit of the Mother—"he faints: my lord, my lord!" (KL 5.3.310)—but it soon becomes clear that the king, like Cordelia, is past all saving. He should be allowed to pass, Kent says, if there is to be any respite from "the wrack of this tough world" (KL 5.3.313, F). In fact the very toughness of the *saeculum* provides its own approximation of a miracle: "The wonder is he hath endured so long" (KL 5.3.315). Unredeemed endurance on this earth is a marvel worth as much admiration as the Resurrection or a life without end.

---

134. Jorden, *A briefe discourse*, 11v.
135. John of Salisbury, *Policraticus* 2.29 (CCCM 118:170; trans. Pike, 150).

Epilogue
Secularization After Shakespeare

In 1802, the Franciscan friary standing in Munich since the late thirteenth century was razed to make room for the National Theater. Its manuscripts went to the state library, where they were joined the year after by a trove of other monastic witnesses to classical and medieval letters—among them the text we know today as the *Carmina Burana*. A brewery in the friary's basement required no further secularization and continued to operate under new management, but everything else detachable—furniture, copper gutters, lead and iron fittings, window frames, artwork, altars, the organ and tower clock—went to the highest bidder to pay for the theater's construction. When three workers raising the roof beam fell into a pit, critics divined the hand of God in retaliation for the friary's ruin. Other observers took the workers' survival as a positive omen—God's benediction, perhaps, on the Bavarian dissolution. If so, the blessing was short-lived. In 1823, the theater burned to the ground, while onlookers reported seeing in the smoke "the face of a monstrous Franciscan."[1]

---

1. Claudia Ulrich, *Das königliche Hof- und Nationaltheater unter Max I. Joseph von Bayern: Vorgeschichte, Entwicklung und Wirkung eines öffentlichen Theaters* (Munich: C. H. Beck, 2000), 86, quoting a contemporary account. See also 60–62 on the building of the theater. For details about the friary that preceded it, see Wilhelm Kücker, "Das alte Franziskanerkloster in München," *Oberbayerisches Archiv* 86 (1963): 4–158; on

EPILOGUE

The theater was rebuilt, but now the Middle Ages arose from within. On June 10, 1865, it hosted the premier of *Tristan und Isolde*, Richard Wagner's latest in a line of compositions inspired by the biblical conviction that secular values have the power to supplant religious devotion. *Die Meistersinger von Nürnberg*—the work immediately following *Tristan* and his next to debut on the old monastic grounds—opens in church with a sacred hymn before shifting to a competition between two profane singers who hope to win the hand of Eve, the goldsmith's daughter. The victor takes inspiration from "an old book" by Walter von der Vogelweide, the early thirteenth-century minnesinger who stars in *Tannhäuser* and who, according to a source for *Tristan*, was famously devoted to Venus.[2] Walter's struggle to forsake "Madame World" (*Frô Welt*) likely provided one of the original templates for Tannhäuser's return to the *saeculum* after a failed attempt to rejoin the church.[3] Wagner changed the ending to secure Tannhäuser's unambiguous redemption through a "miracle of mercy" (occasioned by the intercession of Saint Elizabeth and the Virgin), only to spend the rest of his life regretting that decision.[4] "I still owe the world [*Welt*] a Tannhäuser," he said to Cosima before dying.[5] Audience members who treasured Wagner's genius nonetheless found ways—some of them temporary—to forgive his lapses into piety. When he first began to raise money for a custom-built theater in Bayreuth, his then acolyte, Friedrich Nietzsche, imagined that with further inspiration from Wagner's expository writings on music—"a revelation of the spirit!"—there might congregate around this new liturgy a "monastic and artistic community" exclusively committed to salvation through art.[6]

---

its dissolution, Sabine Arndt-Baerend, *Die Klostersäkularisation in München, 1802/3* (Munich: UNI-Druck, 1986). A small portion of this epilogue first appeared in John Parker, "Valhalla is Burning: Theory, the Middle Ages and Secularization," *PMLA* 130, no. 3 (2015): 787–98.

2. Richard Wagner, *Sämtliche Werke*, vol. 9, part II: *Die Meistersinger von Nürnberg, Zweiter Aufzug*, ed. Egon Voss (Mainz: B. Schott's Söhne, 1983), 37; Gottfried von Strassburg, *Tristan*, trans. A. T. Hatto (New York: Penguin, 1967), 107.

3. *Die Gedichte Walthers von der Vogelweide*, ed. Karl Lachmann (Berlin, 1827), 100; J. W. Thomas, "Walther von der Vogelweide and the Tannhäuser Ballad," *Neuphilologische Mitteilungen* 74, no. 2 (1973): 340–47. Cf. Mary Magdalene in the Longer Passion: "Praises to you, world [*Welt*], for being so rich in joys!" (CB 16*.47–48).

4. Richard Wagner, *Sämtliche Werke*, vol. 6, part 3: *Tannhäuser und der Sängerkrieg auf Wartburg, Handlung in 3 Aufzügen (1861–1875; mit Varianten) WWV 70*, ed. Peter Jost, 3rd ed. (Mainz: Schott Musik International, 2003), 212–15.

5. Cosima Wagner, *Die Tagebücher*, vol. 2: *1878–1883*, ed. Martin Gregor-Dellin and Dietrich Mack (Munich: R. Piper, 1977), 1098.

6. Nietzsche, *Briefwechsel: Kritische Gesamtausgabe*, ed. Giorgio Colli and Mazzino Montinari (Berlin: de Gruyter, 1975), II/1:166.

The hope that Wagnerian theater might one day rise to the level of a secular religion was modeled in large measure on the Romantic exaltation of Shakespeare.[7] For much of the preceding two centuries his reputation had languished in comparison with the authors beloved by neoclassical critics. The anachronisms, the lousy geography, the fondness for stupid puns, the disregard of the unities, and—perhaps more than anything—the grotesque ending of *Lear* had made his work subject to no little criticism. We owe the sea change in opinion to A. W. Schlegel, a central figure of the intellectual circle in fin-de-siècle Jena that included his brother Friedrich, Novalis, F. W. J. Schelling, and G. W. F. Hegel. Schlegel's translation was the first in German to attempt to replicate Shakespeare's verse form, and the result was an instant hit: "The influence that this work has exerted, and will continue to exert, on our language, literature, and poetic art," writes Ludwig Tieck, "is immeasurable."[8] The impact stemmed as much from the translation as from a course of lectures that Schlegel gave in 1809–1811 defending Shakespeare against negative assessment. According to these, Shakespeare embodies like no other dramatist "the spirit of the romantic poetry," which is synonymous with "the peculiar spirit of modern art [*den eigenthümlichen Geist der modernen Kunst*]."[9] Critics who understand the course of human history over the *longue durée*—to say nothing of the history of drama—understand that classical antiquity is gone, and there is no going back; hence "the name *romantic*, in opposition to the classical," for the culture that arose between the fourth and sixth centuries CE: "The word is derived from *romance*—the name originally given to the languages which were formed from the mixture of the Latin and the old Teutonic dialects, in the same manner as modern civilization is the fruit of the heterogeneous union of the peculiarities of the northern nations and the fragments of antiquity."[10] The notorious mish-mash of dissimilar, contradictory ingredients in Shakespeare's plays—for example, the anachronistic mixing of the past with the present or of comedy with tragedy, as we see in *Lear*—cannot be fairly censured with reference to classical norms

---

7. Curt von Westernhagen, *Richard Wagners Dresdener Bibliothek 1842–1849* (Wiesbaden: Brockhaus, 1966), 61–64; *Shakespeare unter den Deutschen: Vorträge des Symposiums vom 15. bis 17. Mai 2014 in der Akademie der Wissenschaften und der Literatur, Mainz*, ed. Christa Jansohn (Mainz: Akademie der Wissenschaften und der Literatur, 2015).

8. *Shakspeare's dramatische Werke*, Uebersetzt von August Wilhelm von Schlegel, ergänzt und erläutert von Ludwig Tieck, Erster Theil (Berlin, 1825), iv–v.

9. August Wilhelm Schlegel, *Kritische Schriften und Briefe*, ed. Edgar Lohner (Stuttgart: W. Kohlhammer, 1966–67), 5:21; on Shakespeare and the romantic see 6:111; English in Schlegel, *Course of Lectures on Dramatic Art and Literature*, trans. John Black (New York: AMS, 1973), 21, 342.

10. A. W. Schlegel, *Kritische Schriften*, 5:21; trans. Black, 21–22.

because the mish-mash is an index of the innovations, even the advance, of "modern civilization" over antiquity.[11]

Shakespeare epitomizes modern art, from this perspective, because he is the finest flower of "the so-called Middle Ages"[12]—a new epoch in world history that for Schlegel, as for Jena Romanticism more generally, began with the reduction of Greco-Roman culture to ruins: "The Roman empire was outwardly destroyed by the invasion of barbarians," Schlegel writes. "The destruction occurred earlier, however, essentially and on the spiritual side, with classical culture overall, through the triumph of Christianity over the national and political religion of pagans" (ibid.). The Jena circle saw in this cataclysmic event the inauguration of a geopolitical order in which they still lived. The revolutionary spirit of Christianity had become a permanent feature of European life, particularly among the radically enlightened who were at that moment targeting Christianity itself. According to Hegel, "what Enlightenment declares to be an error and a fiction is the very same thing as Enlightenment itself is. Enlightenment that wants to teach faith the new wisdom does not tell it anything new."[13] When the forces unleashed by the Terror attempted to break from the past by imposing a universally binding, rational ethics on a backwards population, they repeated the founding iconoclastic gesture of Abrahamic monotheism: "Christianity depopulated Valhalla," writes Hegel, "felled the sacred groves, extirpated the national imagery as a shameful superstition, as a devilish poison."[14] By violence and evangelism, nature as such was disenchanted or, to use a term that Hegel borrows from Schiller, "shorn of gods [*entgöttert*]."[15] Post-classical history became in this way a testimony to the wreckage left by the introduction of Christianity, as "the Spirit grew certain of itself from the crushing of gods and men."[16] For the Jena Romantics—to say nothing of those they influenced, such as Nietzsche and

---

11. See Margreta de Grazia, *Four Shakespearean Period Pieces* (Chicago: University of Chicago Press, 2021), 23–59, 145–76.
12. A. W. Schlegel, "Über das Mittelalter," in *Kritische Schriften*, 4:83.
13. G. W. F. Hegel, *Werke*, ed. Eva Moldenhauer and Karl Markus Michel (Frankfurt am Main: Suhrkamp, 1969–71), 3:406; English in *Hegel's Phenomenology of Spirit*, trans. A. V. Miller (Oxford: Oxford University Press, 1977), 334; see also Rebecca Comay, *Mourning Sickness: Hegel and the French Revolution* (Stanford: Stanford University Press, 2011).
14. Hegel, *Werke*, 1:150; English in *Early Theological Writings*, trans. T. M. Knox (Philadelphia: University of Pennsylvania Press, 1971), 146 (modified).
15. Hegel, *Werke*, 14:137; English in *Hegel's Aesthetics: Lectures on Fine Art*, trans. T. M. Knox (Oxford: Clarendon, 1975), 1:524; Friedrich Schiller, "Die Götter Griechenlands," in *Gedichte*, ed. Georg Kurscheidt (Frankfurt am Main: Deutscher Klassiker, 1992), 285–91 (line 168).
16. Hegel, *Werke*, 3:547; English in *Hegel's Phenomenology*, 455.

Weber—Christianity's fundamentally negative, yet enormously creative conquest had made it "the paradigmatic modern religion."[17] Everything that had happened in Europe since late antiquity was to some extent an aftershock of "that particular period of the deepest transformation," in the words of Schelling (Hegel's friend and fellow graduate of the Tübingen seminary):

> The old gods lost their power, the oracles and celebrations fell silent, and a bottomless abyss full of a wild admixture of all the elements of the past world appeared to open itself up before humanity. Above this dark abyss the only sign of peace and of balance seemed to be the cross, a kind of rainbow of a second flood . . . and this at a time when there was no other choice but to believe in this sign.[18]

Belief in the cross—chosen out of desperation, if not external compulsion—gave rise to a host of dialectical contradictions that were still being worked out on a global scale and that entailed a thought even more ominous and difficult than the nonexistence of the old divinities: namely, "the incarnation and the death of God."[19]

The line from incarnation to death, as we've seen, was central to the most elaborate liturgical performances earlier in the millennium at Christmas and Easter. Christ is born, destroys the idols, then later dies and leaves behind an unprecedented emptiness: "Exceeding pain holds us," sing the Maries before the empty tomb in the *Carmina Burana*, "while he is absent" (CB 15*.106). In Hegel's view the chief historical significance of the Crusades—ongoing when this play was performed—was to show Christians "a second time" that the sepulcher held nothing, even while a simultaneous, intramural campaign against "secular [*weltlich*] extravagances of passion" caused the church itself "to become secular [*verweltlich*] in the process."[20] By insisting that a form of worldliness utterly opposed to divinity was rampant *among Christians*, the Inquisition set in motion "the internalization of the secular principle [*das Insichgehen des weltlichen Princips*]" (ibid., 441; trans. Sibree, 381). According to Hegel's friend and fellow seminarian, Friedrich Hölderlin, this process of secularization followed inevitably from Christ having been "the last" of the

---

17. Terry Pinkard, *Hegel: A Biography* (Cambridge: Cambridge University Press, 2000), 293.
18. *Friedrich Wilhelm Joseph von Schellings Sämmtliche Werke*, part I, vol. 5: *1802. 1803* (Stuttgart, 1859), 429; English in Schelling, *The Philosophy of Art*, trans. Douglas Scott (Minneapolis: University of Minnesota Press, 1989), 61.
19. Schelling, *Sämmtliche Werke*, I/5:454: "Menschwerdung und Tod Gottes"; trans. Scott, 80.
20. Hegel, *Werke*, 12:471, 441; *Lectures on the Philosophy of History*, trans. J. Sibree (London, 1861), 409 and 381, respectively.

gods, whose most spiritual devotees "must also be secular [*weltlich*]" given the disillusionment that he left in his wake:[21]

Wenn aber stirbt alsdenn	But when he dies,
An dem am meisten	To whom beauty
Die Schönheit hing, daß an der Gestalt	So adhered that his person
Ein Wunder war und die Himmlischen gedeutet	Was a miracle, designated
Auf ihn, und wenn, ein Rätsel ewig füreinander	By angelic beings, and when they forever become
Sie sich nicht fassen können	Enigmas to each other, and elude each
Einander, die zusammenlebten	Other's grasp, they who lived in common
Im Gedächtnis, und nicht den Sand nur oder	Memory of him, and when sand
Die Weiden es hinwegnimmt und die Tempel	And willows are blown away, and temples
Ergreifft, wenn die Ehre	Are destroyed, when the honor
Des Halbgotts und der Seinen	Of the demigod and his disciples
Verweht und selber sein Angesicht	Is scattered to the winds and even
Der Höchste wendet	The Almighty averts
Darob, daß nirgend ein	His face, leaving nothing
Unsterbliches mehr am Himmel zu sehn ist oder	Immortal to be seen in the sky,
Auf grüner Erde, was ist dies?	Or on green earth, what is this?[22]

For the circle at Tübingen, being a Christian was virtually synonymous with experiencing the force of a spirit so critical, so overpowering, it carried all

---

21. Friedrich Hölderlin, *Sämtliche Gedichte: Studienausgabe in Zwei Bänden*, ed. Detlev Lüders (Bad Homburg: Athenäum, 1970), 1:332, 334 ("Der Einzige," ll. 33, 105); English in *Hymns and Fragments*, trans. Richard Sieburth (Princeton, NJ: Princeton University Press, 1984), 85–86; for the relationship between Hölderlin and Schelling's lectures on the philosophy of art, see George S. Williamson, *The Longing for Myth in Germany: Religion and Aesthetic Culture from Romanticism to Nietzsche* (Chicago: University of Chicago Press, 2004), 63–65.
22. Hölderlin, *Sämtliche Gedichte*, 344 ("Patmos," ll. 136–51); *Hymns and Fragments*, trans. Sieburth, 96–97; modified.

before it and then turned on itself through a variety of crusades, inquisitions, reformations, and ongoing enlightenments. The next generation of seminarians produced David Strauss and Ludwig Feuerbach, whose militantly historicist examinations of the New Testament and reappraisal of Christianity as a whole would impinge deeply on Marx, Nietzsche, and the burgeoning discipline of New Testament Studies.

Already by 1796, Jean Paul, the son of a Lutheran pastor, had included in his novel, *Siebenkäs*, a "homily of the dead Christ" that was excerpted, translated, and published separately in 1829 under the title "Vision of a Godless World."[23] Set in a graveyard, the episode has the entombed ask Christ, "Is there a God?" to which he responds with the truncated words of the Psalmist: "There is no God" (Pss 14:1, 51:1).[24] Like the Tübingen seminarians, Jean Paul was well aware that the earliest Christians had been reputed atheists on account of their assertion that Jesus was the only real god and their simultaneous admission that he had been executed: "How can it be that God has died? How did God die? Can God die?" Augustine asks (rhetorically, given the cross): "It is more incredible that the eternal has died than that mortal creatures will live eternally. And yet the more incredible fact is that of which we have proof already" (*Exp. in ps.* 148.8 [CCSL 40:2171; WSA III/20:482]). The resurrection could be debated, but Christians knew for a fact that God had died. After the council of Chalcedon (431) denounced Nestorius for allegedly separating Christ's divinity from his humanity in order to avoid the implication that divinity itself had suffered crucifixion, it was the *denial* of God's death that became heretical. That at least is how Luther explained the ancient scandal and came to the customary Augustinian conclusion, if perhaps, as suited his taste for the negative, with more than customary force: "Christ died, and Christ is God, therefore God has died."[25] When a mid-seventeenth-century lyricist followed Luther's lead and composed a hymn bewailing Calvary as the place where "God himself lies dead," those words became a mainstay in the Lutheran church.[26] The hymn is how Jean Paul, Hölderlin, Schelling, and Hegel all first learned to proclaim out loud

---

23. "The Vision of a Godless World," in *The Atheneum and London Literary Chronicle*, no. 67, February 4, 1829.
24. Jean Paul, *Siebenkäs*, ed. Klaus Pauler (Munich: Text Kritik, 1991), 53.
25. Martin Luther, *Von den Konziliis und Kirchen*, in *D. Martin Luthers Werke: Kritische Gesamtausgabe* (Weimar: Hermann Böhlaus Nachfolger, 1914), 50:589.
26. Theodor Hansen, *Johann Rist und Seine Zeit* (Halle, 1872), 191; Frederiek Depoortere, "'God Himself is Dead': Luther, Hegel, and the Death of God," *Philosophy and Theology* 19, nos. 1–2 (2007): 171–95.

that "God himself is dead." This "hard saying" expressed their religion's hardest truth: namely, that "the finite, the fragile, the weak, the negative are themselves a moment of the divine."[27] Nietzsche, the son and grandson of Lutheran ministers on both sides, sang as a child the same hard saying in the same hard pews. After a lifetime of coming to terms with this heritage, he knew better than most whereof he spoke when he complained that "the Protestant parson is the grandfather of German philosophy. . . One need merely say 'Tübingen Seminary' to understand what German philosophy is at bottom—a deceitful theology."[28] The theology was particularly insidious because it anticipated in advance every attempt to contest it. Thanks to Christianity, desacralization was now wholly of a piece with the modern mindset, as confirmed by Nietzsche's intellectual development. The New Testament had become both ubiquitous and insufferable to would-be adherents: "The sense of truthfulness, developed highly by Christianity, is nauseated by the falseness and mendaciousness of all Christian interpretations of the world and of history."[29] Most nauseating of all was the nihilistic interpretation of "the world" as something null and void unless grounded in an ideal Being whose alleged transcendence was little more than a curse on reality. "What has been the greatest objection to existence so far?" Nietzsche asked in the months before his final collapse. By then, the answer for him was unambiguous: *"God."*[30]

From his earliest school days Nietzsche had been surrounded by testimonials to the long history of secularization, and his first inclination was to oppose it. He spent his boyhood studying ancient languages, scripture, and Christian theology at the eleventh-century cathedral school in Naumburg, where his classroom overlooked a defunct cloister. In 1858 he moved to Schulpforta, a boarding school housed in a dissolved Cistercian monastery from the twelfth century. The days began with a prayer and a tenth-century Latin hymn in honor of the Trinity, whose glory was "before all

---

27. Hegel, *Werke*, ed. Moldenhauer and Michel, 3:547 (cf. 572); *Hegel's Phenomenology*, 455 (cf. 476); *Lectures on the Philosophy of Religion: One Volume Edition of the Lectures of 1827*, ed. and trans. Peter C. Hodgson (Berkeley: University of California Press, 1988), 468.
28. *The Antichrist* 10 (NKGW VI/3:174); English in *The Portable Nietzsche*, trans. Walter Kaufmann (New York: Penguin, 1954), 576 (modified).
29. Nachlass 1885–1886, 2[127], NKGW VIII/1:123–24; English in *The Will to Power*, ed. Walter Kaufmann (New York: Vintage, 1968), §1. Cf. Karl Jaspers, *Nietzsche and Christianity*, trans. E. B. Ashton (Chicago: Henry Regnery, 1961), 15.
30. *Ecce Homo* 2.3 (NKGW VI/3:285); English in *"On The Genealogy of Morals" and "Ecce Homo,"* ed. Walter Kaufmann (New York: Vintage, 1989), 245.

time [*ante omne saeculum*]."³¹ He communicated in Latin, continued his study of Greek, and picked up some Hebrew and French in addition to reading Schiller and Goethe. Against the express advice of a teacher, he developed a passion Hölderlin. On December 3, 1860, he requested *Shakspeare's dramatische Werke* for Christmas—"with plates"—and soon received the translation by Schlegel and Tieck.³² While awaiting its arrival, he continued work on a Christmas oratorio for a literary-musical society that he had formed with two friends from Naumburg. One of them, Gustav Krug, was a devotee of Wagner intent on converting Nietzsche to the cause despite Nietzsche's vehement defense of sacred music against secular intrusions. A strictly aural dramatization of the Nativity, he wrote to Krug, would "excite no other sense but hearing" and eschew the spectacular, overwrought effects of Wagnerian theater.³³ Whoever believed that the oratorio "has the same place in spiritual music [*in der geistlichen Musik*] that opera has in the secular [*in der weltlichen*]"—as though the two genres offered comparable rewards in separate venues—was guilty of "belittling" the spiritual (ibid.). A sacred oratorio dealt with materials "infinitely simpler and more sublime" than the secular and had the distinct advantage of being "effortlessly understandable even to the uneducated" (ibid., 138). If the oratorio was less popular than opera, that was not the fault of the genre but of the degrading fad whereby "the music is so often sacrilegiously mixed with the secular" (ibid., 138). Most people could not hear the simple, sublime grandeur on account of the added theatrical profanity, which misled them into overvaluing the most garish, worldly features.

Against the present trend, Nietzsche composed a series of Nativity scenes to demonstrate the basic principle of Augustinian-Calcidian-Boethian musicology: namely, that "God has given us music so that we should first of all

---

31. NKGW I/2:105; for the history of this hymn, see Gunilla Björkvall and Andreas Haug, "Performing Latin Verse: Text and Music in Early Medieval Versified Offices," in *The Divine Office in the Latin Middle Ages: Methodology and Source Studies, Regional Developments, Hagiography—Written in Honor of Professor Ruth Steiner*, ed. Margot E. Fassler and Rebecca A. Baltzer (Oxford: Oxford University Press, 2000), 279–81.

32. Nietzsche, *Briefwechsel: Kritische Gesamtausgabe*, I/1:133 [197] (the request); Friedrich Nietzsche, *Frühe Schriften*, ed. Hans Joachim Mette (Munich: C. H. Beck, 1994), 1:250 (a catalogue of the contents of his library after 1861, which includes "Sheakspeare 9 Bände" [sic]); also recorded in a separate catalogue in NKGW I/2:443. This edition is almost certainly the same one that Nietzsche possessed at the end of his productive life, currently held by the Herzogin Anna Amalia Bibliothek in Weimar: *Shakspeare's dramatische Werke*, übersezt von. A. W. Schlegel und L. Tieck. Neue Ausgabe in neun Bänden (Berlin: G. Reimer, 1853–54).

33. Nietzsche, *Briefwechsel: Kritische Gesamtausgabe*, I/1:137.

be led upwards through it.... But if music is used solely for enjoyment or to make a public exhibition of itself, it is sinful and harmful. Yet one now finds this frequently, indeed, almost all of modern music [*moderne Musik*] bears traces of it" (NKGW I/1:305–6). To erase these traces of secularization required the composition of a Nativity markedly more pious than the Christmas play that we see in the *Carmina Burana* (first brought to press by Johannes Andreas Schmeller in 1847). "Scene I" of Nietzsche's oratorio has the Magi or "Kings" express doubt and confusion *before* the appearance of the star, toward the end of showing that the star of Bethlehem alleviated, rather than caused, their forlorn condition:

Ich hab nicht Rast, ich hab nicht Ruh;	I have no rest, I have no peace,
Ists Tag, ists Nacht? Ich darf's nicht fragen:	Is it day, is it night? I dare not ask:
Den Sternen schau ich immer zu;	I always look to the stars;
Wann wird die Wundersonne tagen?	When will the miraculous sun rise?

(NKGW I/2:216)

The new star appears, they rejoice; the Black Magus or "Moor" sings an aria begging to be relieved of doubt.[34] A procession of prophets anticipates the good news of the Crucifixion before all the kings gather together for a final death scene presumably meant to symbolize the demise of paganism.[35] Between the kings' conversion and dying intervenes the Annunciation, followed by a shepherds' chorus that recapitulates the emptiness expressed by the Magi. The shepherds too keep watch through their dark night of the soul, longing for God's goodness, "which has been far from the world" (NKGW I/2:215). Their hearts are in anguish until a heavenly choir announces the Messiah's arrival by singing a Germanized version of the *Gloria*.

Krug expressed a certain appreciation but thought that some of the compositional difficulties could be resolved by borrowing from Bach's Christmas Oratorio; he promised to bring the score to their next gathering.[36] At the

---

34. Friedrich Nietzsche, *Der Musikalische Nachlass*, ed. Curt Paul Janz on behalf of the Schweizerischen Musikforschenden Gesellschaft (Basel: Bärenreiter, 1976), 259.
35. Cornelis Witthoefft, "*Pagan World and Christianity*: Nietzsche's Projected Oratorio and Its Consequences," in *Nietzsche and Music: Philosophical Thoughts and Musical Experiments*, ed. Aysegul Durakoglu et al. (Newcastle upon Tyne: Cambridge Scholars Publishing, 2022), 257–288, esp. 270.
36. Nietzsche, *Briefwechsel: Kritische Gesamtausgabe*, I/1:344

meeting over Easter vacation, Krug lectured on *Rheingold*—the first of Wagner's operas based on Schlegel's cherished *Nibelungenlied*—and presented Nietzsche with the freshly printed score of *Tristan und Isolde* for piano. They sat side by side on the bench to work out the fingering, starting with the notoriously complex, almost atonal first chord. ("At the first note," Nietzsche later said, "all the strange qualities of Leonardo da Vinci are disenchanted [*entzaubern sich*]"—recalling perhaps Leonardo's unfinished *Adoration of the Magi* in Florence; each successive revelation in the intertwined histories of art, religion, and theater transforms the earlier highpoint into an idol.)[37] For a long while thereafter Nietzsche became a confirmed Wagnerian wholly given over to the promise of secular music. He retitled his oratorio *Pain Is the Root Note of Nature* and eliminated everything but the longing for salvation in a world without God: "O, that soon the promise of the star might be fulfilled in glorious light! / O, that soon the dark night might be covered in miraculous radiance!"[38] That the promise had been given but remained unfulfilled made the night seem darker and without end.

On September 18, 1863, as Nietzsche prepared to leave the monastic setting of Pforta for the university of Bonn—two years after the attempted oratorio on Christ's Nativity—he sat down with a journal that he had been keeping since 1856 to reflect on his life and character. How, he asks, do we form a distinct image of any person, much less ourselves? It is best to start with the surrounding environment: the geology, the shades of the sky, the flora and fauna. Inorganic materials are the least distinguishing since in many places the same geological features arise according to the same laws; organic matter is different, however, as it somehow learns to adapt itself—to grow—in response to minutely divergent circumstances. A person's life was the same: "I was born as a plant near a graveyard, as a human in a pastor's house" (NKGW I/3:190). The pastor had died when Nietzsche was four; his only brother followed a month later. He and his mother were forced to move and wound up in Naumburg, he recounts, after which came the scholarship at Pforta, where an array of new interests took hold and threatened to overwhelm him: "The wisdom of several lexicons was in me and awakened every possible inclination. I wrote poems and tragedies, full of chills and boring

---

37. *Ecce Homo* 2.6 (NKGW VI/3:287–78); trans. Kaufmann, 250 (modified). Cf. Giancarlo Maiorino, "Fractures of Faith in the *Adoration of the Magi*," in *Leonardo da Vinci: The Daedalian Mythmaker* (University Park: Pennsylvania State University Press, 1992).
38. Nietzsche, *Musikalische Nachlass*, 295: "O, daß doch bald die Sternverheissung in lichter Pract sich erfüllte; O, daß doch bald die düstre Nacht in wundervollen Glanz sich hülle." On the repurposing, see 350.

to the point of horror. I labored at composing orchestral music and got so involved with the idea of acquiring a universal knowledge, a universal ability that I was in danger of becoming scatterbrained and a dreamer" (NKGW I/3:192). As the time neared when a decision would have to be made between studying Christian theology and classical philology at Bonn, it was dawning on him—with a heavy dose of Lutheran skepticism toward free will—that he would become whatever he was going to have been without understanding the etiology of his choices, much less the incalculable range of exigencies that had carried him from decisive moment to decisive moment. He was questioning the name for whatever deep, structural processes govern human ontogeny and endow individuals with the power to say Yes or No. He knew he would continue to grow—like a plant provided water, soil, and sunlight, he was not free not to—but in what direction, under what determining influence, and how far might he go? How far could humanity get as a whole? "And so man outgrows everything that first entangled him; he does not have to break his shackles but, unexpectedly, when a god wills it, they fall away. Where is the ring that will finally still encompass him?" (NKGW I/3:192). Where is the unsurpassable horizon that sets the limit to any possible human achievement? For all of Nietzsche's career he believed there were only two possibilities. They were the same two possibilities on offer to every inhabitant of every cloister and to every university student going back more than a millennium, and, like the faculty of Paris in the thirteenth century, Nietzsche debated which would prove to be the higher power: "Is it the world?" he asks, or "is it God?" (NKGW I/3:192).

If it was the world, then the best course of study was *saeculares litterae*. At Bonn, Nietzsche went all in on classical philology, but the choice, like the choice to become a confirmed Wagnerian, only brought him into more intimate contact with medieval Christianity. The whole of one's reputation in the field depended on an ability to assess and edit manuscripts copied by clerics.[39] He arrived with a letter of introduction to Friedrich Ritschl, the leading scholar of Plautus who was roughly two years out from publishing the first definitive edition—which is to say, the first to include a comprehensive collation of extant manuscripts in its critical apparatus. Nietzsche

---

39. See Joachim Latacz, "On Nietzsche's Philological Beginnings," in *Nietzsche as a Scholar of Antiquity*, ed. Anthony K. Jensen and Helmut Heit (London: Bloomsbury, 2014), 3–26; James I. Porter, "Nietzsche's Radical Philology," in Jensen and Heit, *Nietzsche as a Scholar of Antiquity*, 37–50; Cf. Bruce Holsinger, *On Parchment: Animals, Archives, and the Making of Culture from Herodotus to the Digital Age* (New Haven, CT: Yale University Press, 2022).

followed Ritschl to Leipzig, and on January 24, 1866, was asked what he planned to do with his senior thesis (*Valediktionsarbeit*) from Pforta—a Latin account of the original setting and textual transmission of the Greek poet Theognis.⁴⁰ Ritschl told Nietzsche—twenty-two years old at the time—that he had never seen anything comparable from a student "for strictness of method and assurance in collation."⁴¹ Nietzsche published it the next year and, on Ritsch's recommendation, was made a professor at Basel the year after. He published one last classical edition, with what he hoped would be "henceforth the definitive critical apparatus," but his mind was moving irreversibly toward the philosophico-historical implications of his editorial training.⁴² An early investigation of the gospels had already "sown the first seed of a thought, linking the slave-morality of the early Christians to the hate-filled resentments of the French Jacobins of 1789—which, twenty-four years later, blossomed dramatically in *Beyond Good and Evil* and *The Genealogy of Morals*."⁴³ Like Hegel before him he came to think of "the French Revolution as the continuation of Christianity."⁴⁴ The growth of that thought would have been aided by Ritschl's edition of Plautus, whose earliest textual witness, the so-called Ambrosian Palimpsest (Ambrosianus G 82 sup.), had been copied in the fifth century but was then overwritten in the eighth with the Book of Kings, such that the desecration of temples, the burning of idols, the attacks on astrologers and magicians, the defiling of graves, the felling of sacred groves, and the slaughter of priests on their altars (2 Kgs 23:4–24) were all superimposed on plays celebrating the vengeful cunning of the enslaved. Judeo-Christian morals collaborated with the social acrimony occasioned by ancient aristocracies to refashion old materials to revolutionary ends.

According to Karl Löwith, Nietzsche's attempt to endorse a pagan view of the world as an eternally regenerating entity full of immanent meaning was bound to fail because he could not help but conceive of that world in Christian, rather than classical, terms. The Nietzschean *saeculum* has a future—and a possible redemption—toward which we must somehow orient ourselves

---

40. *Nietzsche on Theognis of Megara*, ed. Renato Cristi and Oscar Velásquez (Cardiff: University of Wales Press, 2015).
41. NKGW I/4:515; partially translated in R. J. Hollingdale, *Nietzsche: The Man and His Philosophy*, rev. ed. (Cambridge: Cambridge University Press, 1999), 34.
42. Friedrich Nietzsche, "Der Florentinische Tractat über Homer und Hesiod, ihr Geschlecht und ihren Wettkampf," *Rheinisches Museum für Philologie*, n. F., 28 (1873): 211–249 at 239.
43. Curtis Cate, *Friedrich Nietzsche* (Woodstock, NY: Overlook, 2002), 34.
44. Nachlass 1884, 25[178], NKGW VII/2:57; *Will to Power*, §94.

by means of an ethical imperative directed toward the will.⁴⁵ The irony was that Nietzsche did not realize he had borrowed his arguments in favor of this world—and against the Christian God—from the polemics of the Fathers against pagans, "with the viewpoints interchanged."⁴⁶ In a sense Löwith is right, but he underestimates the significance of Nietzsche's awareness that the Fathers modeled their hostility to the world on the Bible. The prophets were the first to fuse "'rich,' 'godless,' 'evil,' 'violent,' and 'sensual' into one and were the first to use the word 'world' as an opprobrium."⁴⁷ Löwith also underestimates the significance of a born Christian deliberately transvaluing this ancient moral stigma by encouraging his readers to "break the maxims of world-slanderers [*Welt-Verleumder*]."⁴⁸ No one has better understood the Judeo-Christian disdain for the *saeculum* or responded more favorably to the demonic proposal that the world is eternal and self-creating. No one has explored more radically what it would mean to embrace a cosmos whose only intention or will is to overcome resistance. No one has more delighted in art, fiction, and performance despite an ingrained, patristic antitheatricalism; no one has accepted more deeply the magical power of words or more vehemently refused to be disenchanted.⁴⁹

Ultimately Löwith borrows his critique of Nietzsche from Nietzsche's own concern about the inability of German intellectuals to free themselves from their Christian heritage: "Nearly every Romantic of this type," Nietzsche says of Wagner—while no doubt also thinking of Jena—"ends up under the cross."⁵⁰ Nietzsche understood that his own philosophy was far from immune to the same criticism. Indeed many of the quotations that Löwith adduces in favor of his alleged obliviousness (particularly from the "counter-gospel" of *Zarathustra*) are part of Nietzsche's lifelong habit of *Selbstkritik*. That he had done everything in his power to surpass the religion of his forbears but found

---

45. See e.g. NKGW VI/2:128–30; English in *Beyond Good and Evil: Prelude to a Philosophy of the Future*, trans. Walter Kaufmann (New York: Vintage, 1989), §203.
46. Karl Löwith, *Meaning in History: The Theological Implications of the Philosophy of History* (Chicago: University of Chicago Press, 1949), 220; for a critique of Löwith's reading on different grounds than I raise here, see Walter Kaufmann, *Nietzsche: Philosopher, Psychologist, Antichrist*, 4th ed. (Princeton, NJ: Princeton University Press, 1974), 319n10.
47. NKGW VI/2:119; *Beyond Good and Evil*, trans. Kaufmann, §195. Weber greatly refines this insight in his studies of the ethical structure of ancient Judaism.
48. NKGW VI/1:253; *Thus Spoke Zarathustra*, Book III, "On the Old and New Tablets" in *Portable Nietzsche*, 317.
49. See esp. NKGW V/2:109–10, 115–18, 140–41, 298–300; English in *The Gay Science: With a Prelude in German Rhymes and an Appendix of Songs*, ed. Bernard Williams (Cambridge: Cambridge University Press, 2001), §§78, 84, 107, 368.
50. Nachlass 1885, 34[205], NKGW VII/3:211.

himself repeatedly overshadowed by the force of scripture's intervention in history is evident throughout his corpus: "For since we are the outcome of earlier generations, we are also the outcome of their aberrations, passions and errors, and indeed of their crimes; it is not possible wholly to free oneself from this chain. If we condemn these aberrations and regard ourselves free of them, this does not alter the fact that we originate in them."[51] A baptized and confirmed Lutheran like Nietzsche could not change his lineage; if he came to despise the gospel that was because some part of the gospel required it of him: "In me, Christianity overcomes itself."[52]

Nietzsche's critique of Christianity is at its most consequential—if we judge by its impact on Weber—wherever he stresses that critique as he knows it is an ancient inheritance, transmitted by the Bible. Wanting to destroy the dominant religious, moral, and aesthetic codes in the name of eternal truths was an impulse developed independently by Greek philosophy and Judaism, then later combined in the New Testament. This impulse is the legacy of what Nietzsche calls "Alexandrine culture," and it follows from antiquity's Hellenization: "Socrates is the archetype of the theoretical optimist who, in his faith in the explicability of the nature of things, attributes the power of a panacea to knowledge and cognition, and sees error as the embodiment of evil. To penetrate into those grounds and to separate true knowledge from illusion and error seemed to Socratic man the noblest, or even the only, truly human calling."[53] Socrates and his "like-minded successors through to the present day" (ibid.) have taken the world to be nondivine, knowable, finite, and open to manipulation toward moral ends. There is nothing more in line with monotheism (whether pagan or Abrahamic) than to attack idols, errors, illusions, and other forms of delusion with the hammer of ascetic rationality.[54] For Nietzsche this hammer is a tool shared by religion, philosophy, scholarship, and science.

Is it at all possible, then, for the Occidental form of reason to disentangle itself from the history of monotheism? Hans Blumenberg famously counters

---

51. NKGW III/1:266; English in *Untimely Meditations*, ed. Daniel Breazeale, trans. R. J. Hollingdale (Cambridge: Cambridge University Press, 1997), 76.
52. Nachlass 1888, 24[I].6, NKGW VIII/3:434.
53. NKGW III/1:96; English in *The Birth of Tragedy out of the Spirit of Music*, trans. Shaun Whiteside, ed. Michael Tanner (New York: Penguin, 1993), §15 (modified). Cf. *On the Genealogy of Morals* 3.25, in NKGW VI/2:420–23; Kaufmann, *On the Genealogy of Morals*, 160–61.
54. *Genealogy* 3.27, in NKGW VI/2:427; Kaufmann, *On the Genealogy of Morals*, 160–61; Cf. James Simpson, *Under the Hammer: Iconoclasm in the Anglo-American Tradition* (Oxford: Oxford University Press, 2010), 57.

the viewpoints I have been describing in this epilogue by arguing for reason's successful detachment from theology at the time of the Reformation. His conviction is that the German philosophers who saw firsthand the dissolution (*Aufhebung*) and secularization (*Säkularisierung*) of the Bavarian monasteries were wrong to speculate that modern ideas had been "secularized" in an analogous manner—superimposed, with a fresh sense of entitlement, on the culture to which they owed their enlightened animus against false sanctity. He wants to crush the inference that modernity is forever indebted to a religious past whose inheritance it is supposed to have dissolved but has in fact "suspended and carried forward [*aufgehoben*]."[55] The seminarians at Tübingen, Nietzsche, Weber, Löwith, Friedrich Delekat, and Martin Stallmann were all wrong to contest modernity's break with monotheism; wrong to argue that "secular [*weltlichen*] reason's consciousness of its own authenticity is a misleading veil over a reality that otherwise could not overlook its continuous historical descent from that upon which it denies its dependence."[56] They were wrong to think that the modern "denial of historical dependence is motivated by an epochal self-interest" derived from "ideological" premises (ibid.); wrong above all to argue that the production of post-Enlightenment culture through the secularization of monasteries was "a comparatively unimportant differentiation" when compared to "the unique epochal break that in one stroke decided in favor of both the Middle Ages and the modern age: the turning away from the pagan cosmos of antiquity, with its cyclical structure of security, to the one-time temporal action of the biblical/Christian type" (ibid., 36; trans. Wallace, 28). Blumenberg's position, by contrast, is that reason's self-assertion and reoccupation (*Umbesetzung*) of sacred ideas did in fact break decisively from past mythologies without owing them anything substantial on account of reason's inherent freedom to provide genuinely new answers to old questions. He ignores Weber's proposal that rational disenchantment defines monotheism—the proposal, in other words, that breaking decisively with past mythologies toward the end of

---

55. Hans Blumenberg, *Säkularisierung und Selbstbehauptung: Erweiterte und überarbeitete Neuausgabe von "Die Legitimität der Neuzeit," erster und zweiter Teil* (Frankfurt am Main: Suhrkamp, 1974), 27. The word in brackets is the past participle of the verb *aufheben*, which is used in German for the secularization of a monastery. English in *The Legitimacy of the Modern Age*, trans. Robert M. Wallace (Cambridge, MA: MIT Press, 1985), 19. See Karl Löwith, "Hegels Aufhebung der christlichen Religion," in *Sämtliche Schriften*, vol. 5: *Hegel und die Aufhebung der Philosophie im 19. Jahrhundert—Max Weber* (Stuttgart: J. B. Metzler, 1988), 116–66. For Nietzsche's version of this terminology, see *On the Genealogy of Morals* 3.27: "All great things bring about their own destruction through an act of self-dissolution [*Selbstaufhebung*]" (NKGW VI/2:428; Kaufmann, *On the Genealogy of Morals*, 161).

56. Blumenberg, *Säkularisierung und Selbstbehauptung*, 33; trans. Wallace, 25 (modified).

ethical betterment is the signature ideal of both scripture and modernity. He has zero time for Nietzsche's contention that Christianity shares with the radical Enlightenment a nihilistic commitment to processes of rational inquiry so uncompromising, so relentlessly assertive, that they eventually turn on themselves and leave every possible value in ruins.

The ultimate turn for Nietzsche comes with the shattering realization that faith in reason's transhistorical objectivity is, by any reasonable standard, itself a mythology, "as if the right and normal thing were for one to be guided by reason—with the passions as abnormal, dangerous, semi-animal, and, moreover, so far as their aim is concerned, nothing other than desires for pleasure."[57] Champions of logic in the mold of Kant and Blumenberg, from this viewpoint, are fundamentally mistaken to treat the faculty of reason "as if it were an independent entity and not rather a system of relations between various passions and desires; and as if every passion did not contain its quantum of reason" (ibid.). In reality, all thought as such is only a belated coming-to-consciousness of sensory input and a way of coordinating our drives with one another.[58] Moralities amount to a collective form of self-governance among historically specific social orders; each morality is "a sign language of the affects" belonging to a given community. For every ethical construct, "reason is merely a tool" that allows people to *rationalize* their conduct—which is to say, an instrument for bringing allowed behaviors into line with a system of calculation and, at the same time, for coloring social regulations with a transhistorical, unconditioned, objective legitimacy.[59]

Scholars in contemporary secularity studies are merely reasserting Nietzsche's position whenever they express a suspicion that rational critique might belong as much to a religious as to a secular mindset, that "reason always tenders a particular order of rationality, and that critique is inherently situated and partial."[60] It has become something of a commonplace to reject Blumenberg's argument that reason operates as a sovereign force beyond religion, politics, and ideology, given how easily it can wind up serving, in the words of Kathleen Davis, "the sanctification of particular vested interests."[61] And yet, for all that, Blumenberg's anti-Nietzschean insistence on a decisive

---

57. Nachlass 1887–1888, 11[310], NKGW VIII/2:373; *Will to Power*, §387.
58. NKGW VI/2:11, 50; *Beyond Good and Evil*, trans. Kaufmann, §3, §36.
59. NKGW VI/2:115, 109; *Beyond Good and Evil*, trans. Kaufmann §191, §187 (modified).
60. *Is Critique Secular? Blasphemy, Injury, and Free Speech*, ed. Talal Asad et al. (New York: Fordham University Press, 2013), xix.
61. Kathleen Davis, "The Sense of an Epoch: Periodization, Sovereignty and the Limits of Secularization," in *The Legitimacy of the Middle Ages: On the Unwritten History of Theory*, ed. Andrew Cole and D. Vance Smith (Durham, NC: Duke University Press, 2010), 39–69 at 41.

break between secular modernity and everything that precedes it still holds sway across large swaths of contemporary scholarship. Entire academic disciplines, hiring lines, and economies of prestige are founded on what Margreta de Grazia calls "the massive value judgment" of the medieval/modern divide, whose only serious rival, she notes, is the split between BC and AD time.[62] Arguments in favor of the privileges accorded to modernity and Christianity, it would seem, are genetically related. Anything that happened before one or the other's onset is of no significance unless it in some way foreshadows their advent. Each defines itself as something new (*Neuzeit*, New Testament) and "the repudiation of what went before" (ibid., 454), yet each must preserve testimonials from the Before Time to bear witness to the "new age [*nova secula*]" (CB 227.27). Behold modernity, the "new covenant" that renders the old "obsolete" (Heb 8:13b). "Everything old has passed away; see, everything has become new!" (2 Cor 5:17).

I have tried to show in this book that the temptation to lead a secular life is ancient. Scripture presupposes and even strengthens this temptation by hurling ceaseless invective against "the children of incredulity" (Col 3:6, DR), who are said to find in the world a source of autonomous value. If placing one's faith in nature, art, and human flourishing is no faith at all but rather a form of *infidelitas*, *incredulitas*, and an atheist way of being "without God in this world" (Eph 2:12, DR), then Christians in every era are required to entertain the possibility that their faith has failed. And entertain it they have. If the material supports requisite for the functioning of rival belief systems can be exposed as secular theater, so can icons and the liturgy. By the tenth century, the intimate connection between *ludi* and secular pastimes—rather than producing a religious culture exclusively committed to solemn performances of unquestioned piety—helped inspire liturgical actors to inquire ever more deeply into the close relationship between divinity and fiction. The church itself provided a sanctuary for airing extreme doubts about the alleged truths of scripture and for expressing a certain, bittersweet appreciation for the ability of artificially staged miracles to offer momentary deliverance. An irrepressible, ludic impulse to sanctify the pleasures of pretending generated a parade of spectacles so extravagant even an unbeliever could be scandalized.[63] Across Europe, on high holidays especially, forms of radical theatrical experimentation took hold that would endure or be reawakened

---

62. Margreta de Grazia, "The Modern Divide: From Either Side," *Journal of Medieval and Early Modern Studies* 37, no. 3 (2007): 453–67 at 453.
63. Herrad of Landsberg in Young 2:413: "*incredulus scandalizatur*."

long after the monasteries were secularized and miracles were ridiculed. The zeal of English reformers for deconsecration only drew more attention to the extent that worldly play had come to rival or outright replace the divine. When professional playing houses first appeared in the London Liberties, they returned to former monastic estates what reformers claimed the Catholic Church had always been—a commercial theater—toward the end of once again offering to rapt onlookers the secular benefits of witnessing an awesome spectacle.

Acknowledgments

This project began among the scholars and artists at the American Academy in Rome. Carmela Franklin changed my planned trajectory when she organized a reading of the *Carmina Burana* and recommended the work of Peter Dronke. Deepest thanks to David Humphrey for beholding with me and for all the joyful improvisation; to Jennifer Coates, Maryann Kranis, Andrew Kranis, Clem Coleman, Dana Spiotta, Marie Lorenz, Jeff Williams, Tim Allen, and Kurt Rohde for the illumination, camaraderie, and music. Eric Bianchi offered invaluable help with Pythagorean-Platonic theory and Kepler's Latin.

My work has benefited over the years from a variety of colloquia, presentations, and readings. Special thanks to James Simpson, Nicholas Watson, Gordon Teskey, Stephen Greenblatt, Maura Nolan, Jonathan Sheehan, Ryan Perry, Spencer Straub, Larry Benson, Claire Waters, Seeta Chaganti, Carol Symes, Theresa Coletti, Bernardo Hinojosa, Heather Hirschfeld, Blair Hoxby, Kristen Poole, Sara Poor, Nigel Smith, Jeff Dolven, and Leonard Barkan. Russ Leo provided great, formative insights. Harry Cushman and Taylor Cowdery showed me a tremendous vision of scholarship and music. Maggie Solberg and Noah Guynn each breathed into my ear a special inspiration. Will West and Julie Orlemanski have been models of generosity and incisevness. Mahinder Kindra's suggestions and expert shepherding of the manuscript made all the difference.

At the University of Virginia, Sherri Brown's talent for locating hard-to-find materials saved me untold hours. I am lucky to have had over the years a host of gifted colleagues and students working in premodern and adjacent studies: Gordon Braden, Clare Kinney, Dan Kinney, Elizabeth Fowler, Stephen Hopkins, Deborah McGrady, Katharine Maus, Jerry McGann, Mark Edmundson, Anna Brickhouse, Jim Nohrnberg, Rebecca Rush, Emma Bradford, Jared Willden, Spencer Grayson, Jack Crouse, Caitlin Hamilton, Daniel Zimmerman, Zach Stone, Gretchen York, Will Rhodes, DeVan Ard, Casey Ireland, and Viola Cozzio. Andy Stauffer, Steve Arata, and Jim Seitz improved this book in countless ways. Bruce Holsinger, fellow *citharedus*, has been an exhilirating presence at work and play. My gratitude to Margreta de Grazia—flashing-eyed Athena, Μέντορ—is without limit.

Every solstice, each mid-quarter day and equinox, I thank the stars for Emily Ogden and our boys, Luther and Neil.

Index

Abelard, Peter, 131–32
absolutism, 208, 245
Abulafia, Anna Sapir, 130n105, 171
accommodation, 197–98
actors, 192, 208, 234, 246, 264, 286. See also histriones; King's Men; theatrum
Aelred of Rievaulx, 9, 117, 133–34
Aeschylus, 30, 53–54
aesthetics, 3–6, 15–16, 41–43, 47, 66–67, 79, 170; autonomy of, 125
Aethelwold of Winchester, 114–15
Albert the Great, 134, 251
Alhacen, 172
Alexander III, pope, 248
Amalarius of Metz, 111–12
Ambrose, 57, 65, 111, 113
Ambrosiaster, 56
Amyot, Jacques, 90
anachronism, 36, 271
Anaxagoras, 28
Andrewes, Lancelot, 147
Anglican Church, 211, 228, 230–33, 237, 251–52, 255–62
Annunciation. See Virgin Birth
Antichrist, 22, 77n135, 86–89, 134
antisemitism, 40–41, 50–51, 59–60. See also Archisynagogus
antitheatricalism, 4, 9, 56, 59, 199, 192–3, 282; in patristic musicology, 107–113, 129–30, 187; in the Middle Ages, 116–17, 122–25, 137–38
Antony, Mark, 89–93, 98–99
apocalypse, 58, 160–61, 189–93, 216–17, 222. See cosmos: destruction of
appetites, 1–4, 9–12, 40–43, 45, 61, 89, 91–93, 224–27, 285
Aquinas, Thomas, 4–5, 80n, 124–25, 134, 147n21, 152n41, 233, 241, 251
Archisynagogus, 8, 64, 102–3, 130–36, 139, 162–63, 170–71. See also antisemitism
Aretin, Johann Christoph von, 177–81
Aristophanes, 26–28, 31–32
Aristotle, 8, 80n, 82, 91, 132, 164, 173, 219

Asad, Talal, 285
asceticism, 9–19, 90, 109, 112, 123, 283
Asclepius, 267. See also medicine
Assmann, Aleida, 19, 44
Assmann, Jan, 19, 24n6, 34n45, 49, 52, 72n118, 143–44
astrolabe, 107, 152, 155, 162, 172, 176
art, 34, 88, 178, 226, 269–72, 279, 286. See also aesthetics; glass; idolatry; ludus; music; theatrum
astrology, 3, 18, 43, 143–47, 157–63, 182–88, 191–94, 217–1. See also astronomy; Magi
astronomy, 23, 29–30, 107, 148, 188–91, 207, 216. See also astrology; Magi
atheism, 2–3, 48, 66–67, 70–71, 132, 193, 217, 229–33; Christianity as, 52, 157, 235, 272–76; earliest appearance of, 21–39. See also unbelief
Athens, 27–31, 54
Augustine, 38n55, 63, 97, 105, 164, 219, 277; in drama, 64, 103, 130–35, 139, 170–71; on astrology, 146–49, 151–52; on God's death, 60–61, 275; on medicine, 241; on similitudes, 169; on the Sybil, 156; on unbelievers, 25, 40–44, 51, 183; relation to theater, 111–13, 117, 129–30, 137, 187. See also saeculum: Augustine on
Averroes, 42
Avicenna, 229, 241, 256n108
Axial Age, 19–21, 23, 33, 53

Babylonia, 23, 84, 86, 200
Bacon, Roger, 150–55, 171–73, 176, 251
Bacon, Francis, 196
Bainbridge, John, 190–91
Balaam, 133, 156
Baldwin, Archbishop of Canterbury, 94, 99
Bancroft, Richard, 230, 249, 254–55
Bate, Jonathan, 153, 182
Beckwith, Sarah, 223n114, 242
Bedlam, 221, 230, 233–38, 255
Bellah, Robert, 19, 33, 53
Benedictine Rule, 13

INDEX

Benediktbeuern Abbey, 7, 14, 77, 155, 162, 177–81
Benediktbeuern plays. *See* biblical drama; *Carmina Burana*
Bethlehem, 18, 22–23, 62–63, 76, 235. *See also* Bedlam; star of Bethlehem
Bevington, David, 77
Bible, 1–3, 16–18; AV, 11, 36, 106, 161, 168; Bishops, 92, 216; Douai–Rheims, 10, 17, 18, 38–39, 51, 64, 72, 99–100, 105–6, 109–11, 159, 184, 233, 238–39, 286; Hebrew, 11, 33, 38, 51, 63–65, 72, 143; LXX, 24, 33–34, 42, 52–55, 63, 72; Vetus Latina, 2, 142; Vulgate, 24, 66, 68, 86, 101, 114, 121, 135, 160, 185; Wycliffite, 22, 41, 59, 106, 109–10, 145, 160. *See also* biblical drama; New Testament
biblical drama, 5–10; Flight from Egypt, 45, 53–66; Flight to Egypt, 8, 42, 45, 62, 70, 75–89; John the Baptist, 194–95, 198; Nativity, 8–9, 62–64, 76–78, 103, 116–17, 127–42, 151, 153–64, 170–71, 198, 221, 273, 277–79; Passion, 8, 77; Resurrection, 114–21, 129, 154, 273; suppression of, 199, 221, 245. *See also* antitheatricalism; prophets: procession of
Bischoff, Bernhard, 76
black bile, 230–31, 238n42
Blackfriars theater, 227, 234
Blumenberg, Hans, 149, 151, 174n118, 283–85
Bodin, Jean, 231
Boethius, 73, 80n, 106–9, 117, 126, 137, 154, 158, 277
Bolingbroke, Roger, 186, 243, 245–46
Bonaparte, Napoleon, 180
Bonaventure, 5, 124–26, 134
Bracton, Henry de, 242
Brahe, Tycho, 176, 187–89, 191, 201–3, 206–7
Brokaw, Katherine Steele, 14–15
Brossier, Martha, 229, 254, 257, 262
Brown, Peter, 70
Browne, Thomas, 230
Bultmann, Rudolf, 3, 35
Burbage, James, 259
Burkert, Walter, 27

Calcidius, 107–8, 117, 137, 154, 253, 277
Calvin, John, 195, 217, 224
camera obscura, 203, 209
Camille, Michael, 70, 73, 75n128, 88
Campion, Edmund, 249
canonization, 248–51. *See also* saints
capitalism, 11–15

Caspar, Max, 207
Caviness, Madeline, 170
Carmina Burana, 7–8, 10, 69–70, 94–95, 177–79, 269–270n3, 273; dating of, 77n135. *See also* biblical drama; Johann Andreas Schmeller
Cassiodorus, 109n39, 158
Chambers, E. K., 8–10, 77, 96n6, 116, 123n79, 128, 145n11
Chiari, Sophie, 152
Christ, 22, 24, 38, 50–52, 60–71, 90–91, 181, 273–76; an idol, 43, 59, 70–71, 74–76, 78, 86, 93, 102–3, 111; date of birth, 150–52; madness of, 238–39; on the *saeculum*, 2, 11; slave of, 13. *See also* biblical drama; disenchantment: Christ's advent as; miracles: cessation of; star of Bethlehem
Christianization, 5–6, 42–45, 66–69, 100, 110–1, 164, 217
Christmas, 60–65, 106, 114, 145–46, 214–15; *see also* biblical drama: Nativity
chronology, 159, 184, 199, 216. *See also* computus
Chrysologos, Peter, 61–62
Chrysostom, John, 61, 84
Cicero, 13, 25, 118, 147n20
Cistercians, 13, 167, 276
Clark, Stuart, 91n164, 187n14, 196n39, 208n72, 210n78, 217, 222n112, 241n55, 245n68
Clement of Alexandria, 53, 72, 110
Cleopatra, 89–93, 99
Clopper, Lawrence, 108n37, 123n79, 124n80
Cole, Andrew, 6
computus, 148–51, 162, 186
conductus, 79, 129
Confucianism, 15, 19
Constantine, 66–67
Constantine the African, 229, 253, 262
Cooper, Helen, 140–41
Copernicus, Nicolaus, 46, 149, 158, 176, 182, 190–91, 214–15
Cottam, Thomas, 259
Courson, Robert, 137
cosmos, 106–7, 112–13, 137, 154, 158–59, 200; destruction of: 83, 146–8, 156, 176; determining influence of: 191, 206–7, 217–18]; eternity of: 16, 34, 43, 79–83, 284. *See also* creation
Crane, Mary Thomas, 153, 176n124, 182, 215
creation, 16, 43, 82–83, 197. *See also* cosmos
credulity, 22–23, 148, 180, 231, 251, 262. *See also* unbelief
Creizenach, Wilhelm, 7, 77

Crucifixion, 42, 61, 67, 149. *See also* biblical drama: Passion
Crusius, Martin, 198
Cummings, Brian, 5
Crusades, 4, 16, 45, 69–70, 82, 150–52, 235, 273–74. *See also* Muslims

Danby, John, 182
Darwinism, 6–10, 19
Daston, Lorraine, 251
David, 26, 111, 113
da Vinci, Leonardo, 279
Davis, Kathleen, 285
Deacon, John and John Walker, 252, 255
Dee, John, 186–87, 196–97, 201, 210, 213
Democritus, 28
demons, 36, 70–71, 74, 147, 210; in Kepler, 203–5; possession by, 193, 230, 234, 236–37; as secular agents, 186–87, 194, 228, 246, 264; and witches, 241, 257
del Río, Martín, 217
Denham controversy, 230, 246, 259–61
Devil, 10, 71–73, 91, 103; in drama, 135–39, 163; in magic, 161, 196, 207–8, 210, 219
deus ex machina, 42, 118, 121, 267
Diagoras of Melos, 28, 37
Dibdale, Robert, 259
Digges, Leonard and Thomas, 176
Dionysius Exiguous, 150, 160
Dionysus, 4, 53, 93, 129, 138–39
disenchantment, 38, 44, 51–52, 70, 138, 143–44, 235, 266; and *Lear*, 183–88, 219, 237–39, 252; Christ's advent as, 18, 153–56, 192, 216–17, 283–85; in Weber, 14–19, 146. *See also* iconoclasm; monotheism
dissolution, *see* secularization: as monastic dissolution
de Grazia, Margreta, 6n11, 17n42, 46n22, 90, 183, 222n110, 272n11, 286
de Mayerne, Theodore, 257–58, 266
de Prefetti, Goffredo, 235
desecularization, 3, 35
Donne, John, 191, 213
doubt, 4, 24, 37, 55–56, 63, 165–67, 286. *See also* unbelief
Drebbel, Cornelis, 209–10, 260
Dronke, Peter, 38n56, 73n120, 94n1, 98n8, 100–1, 104–5, 107n35, 120n, 139n, 154

Easter, 59–60, 100, 114–17, 149–50, 215, 279. *See also* biblical drama: Resurrection
Egypt, 17, 23, 42, 45, 47–70, 74–95, 98–99, 102, 200. *See also* biblical drama; Moses; Pharaoh
Eisler, Robert, 174

Eleanor of Cobham, 243, 246
Elijah, 18, 184, 216
Elizabeth I, 187, 201
Elton, William R., 82–83, 182–83, 205
Elze, Karl, 6–8
enlightenment, 19, 37–38, 81, 125, 161, 165, 177–81, 275, 285; and Christ's advent, 51, 65, 147, 217; in Hegel, 272; in Kant, 45–52
Epicurus, 36, 39, 75, 80, 87, 89–90, 164, 185, 193, 233
Erasmus, 94
Eriugena, John Scotus, 121, 154
Eucharist, 59, 93, 247
Euclid, 152
Euhemerism, 3, 28–29, 37, 44, 71
Euripides, 27–28, 53
Eusebius, 53, 66–67, 132, 146n15
ex nihilo. *See* creation
Exodus. *See* biblical drama: Flight from Egypt; Egypt; Moses; Pharaoh
exorcism, 161, 211, 228, 237–240, 246–47, 249, 254, 257
Ezekiel, the tragedian, 53–56

Fabricus, David, 198
faith, 2, 4, 21–22, 41, 114, 151, 232, 263, 272; Greek terms for, 26–27, 30–9, 54. *See also* atheism; unbelief
Faustus, Doctor, 185, 191, 198, 208–9, 211
Feast of Fools, 10, 24, 134
Febvre, Lucien, 22, 25, 36, 71, 233
Feuerbach, Ludwig, 275
fiction, 3–5, 42–43, 118–20, 130, 135–38, 142, 216, 286; as therapy, 260–64. *See also* art
Fiery Trigon, 189, 222
fitzMary, Simon, 234–35
Fortuna, 163, 168–69
Foucault, Michel, 152, 228, 231, 233
Fourth Lateran Council, 3, 56, 133
Frederick II, Holy Roman Emperor, 163
Frederick II, of Denmark and Norway, 187–88, 206
French Revolution, 5, 272, 281
Fraunhofer, Joseph von, 180
Funkenstein, Amos, 197

Galen, 229–30, 239n46, 251–54, 256, 266. *See also* Hippocrates; medicine
Galileo, 187
Gauchet, Marcel, 19
Geffcken, Johannes, 114
Geoffrey of Monmouth, 18, 184, 216, 265
Gesta Romanorum, 25
glass, 155, 165–72. *See also* lens; telescope

INDEX

Glover, Mary, 254
Gmirkin, Russell, 32–33
Gödelmann, Johann Georg, 212
Golden Calf, 10, 54, 56, 110, 134
Golden Legend, 65
goliards, 8, 76–79, 104, 128, 132, 140, 198
grace, 91, 224, 268
Grant, Edward, 83n145, 95n3, 121n73, 151–52, 189n21, 214n89
Greenblatt, Stephen, 24–25, 64, 142n134, 237–38
Gregory, Brad S., 23n4, 153n50
Gregory of Tours, 149
Gregory VII, pope, 235
Gresham, Richard, 227–28
Grosseteste, Robert, 172
Gunter, Anne, 256
Guynn, Noah, 10, 75n129
gypsies, 91

Hainault, Jean, 176–77
Hardison, O. B., jr., 10n21, 59–60, 245n67
Harriot, Thomas, 186, 201, 213
Harris, Max, 9
Harsnett, Samuel, 230, 246, 249, 252, 254–55, 258–62
Hartwell, Abraham, 229, 254
Harvey, Richard, 190
Hathaway, Anne, 259
Hecate, 217–19, 239
Hegel, G. W. F., 5–7, 46, 51, 55, 271–76, 281
Heinsius, Daniel, 42, 62
heliocentrism, 214–15. *See also* Copernicus, Nicolaus
Hellenization, 16, 33, 46, 53, 238, 283
Hengel, Martin, 34
Henri IV, 257
Henry VI, 243, 246–48, 250–51
Henry VII, 248
Henry VIII, 227n7, 251
heretics, 1, 11, 41–43, 55–56, 70, 79, 169, 217, 229, 248; execution of, 17, 241–46. *See also* unbelief
Hermann of Reichenau, 162
Hermes Trismegistus, 38
Herod Antipater, 243
Herod the Great, 61, 86, 90, 116, 134–36, 199
Herrad of Landsberg, 116–17, 286
Hippocrates, 228, 232, 238–240, 251–54. *See also* Galen; medicine
histriones, 56, 96, 111n51, 113, 123–28, 133–39. *See also* actors; *ludus*; *theatrum*
Holinshed, Raphael, 18, 183–84, 216, 265
Holsinger, Bruce, 87n156, 111n50, 280n

Hölderlin, Friedrich, 273–75, 277
Honorius Augustodunensis, 123
Horace, 96, 125, 127n96
Hugh of St. Victor, 121–23, 125
Huot, Sylvia, 102
hysterica passio, 229, 250, 252–58, 260–1, 267–68

icons, 15, 57–58, 69–71, 74–76, 85, 165–67, 173, 227, 286. *See also* iconoclasm; idolatry
iconoclasm, 15–16, 43–45, 52, 66–77, 79. *See also* icons; idolatry
idolatry, 3, 8, 15–19, 36, 46, 56–59, 121–22; Christianity as, 73–89, 102–3, 129, 135–46; music as, 109–113. *See also* iconoclasm; unbelief; *saeculum*
Ignatius of Antioch, 147
Ilardi, Vincent, 175
imagination, 210, 231, 234, 241, 256, 262. *See* placebo
immanence, 3, 41, 51–52, 56, 73, 82, 97, 102, 126, 140, 158, 185, 281
Incarnation, 24, 61, 75, 133, 136–37, 190, 273
Increduli. *See* unbelief
Infideles. *See* unbelief
Innocent IV, pope, 235
inquisition, 3–4, 178, 186–87, 229, 233, 241–45, 273–74
Isidore of Seville, 51n48, 122, 148n25, 159, 161n67, 164n80
Islam. *See* Muslims

Jackson, Elizabeth, 254
James VI and I, 147, 188, 206–13, 219, 222, 255, 266, 268
Jaspers, Karl, 19, 276n29
Jean Paul, 275
Jefferay, Richard, 89
Jesus. *See* Christ
Jews, 1, 37, 40–41, 48–52, 79, 163; in dialogues and drama, 53–64, 118–119, 130–35, 169–71. *See also* antisemitism; Bible: Hebrew; unbelief
Jerome, 62–64, 66, 125, 145n11, 147
Jesuits, 13, 178, 230, 246
Joan of Arc, 250
Joas, 18, 184, 216
John of Salisbury, 104, 161–62n70, 229, 268
Jones, Inigo, 260
Jonson, Ben, 91n163, 209–10, 212–13, 217, 260
Jorden, Edward, 229, 241, 254–57, 266–67
Josephus, 49n41, 99n10, 144n6, 199

Jove, 78–79; Zeus, 26, 29, 34
Judaism. *See* antisemitism; Bible: Hebrew; Jews

Karnes, Michelle, 14–15
Kahn, Charles, 33
Kant, Immanuel, 46–51, 285
Kemp, Will, 260
Kepler, Johannes, 107, 175, 177, 186–88, 192, 196, 217, 222–23; and King James, 200–1, 206–13; *De stella nova*, 188–91, 206, 212–13, 220; *Harmonice mundi*, 107, 200, 213; mother's witchcraft trial, 202–3, 213–14; *Somnium*, 202–6, 218; theatrical career, 198
Kingdom, the. *See* apocalypse
King Lear, 1, 16, 90, 153, 188, 212, 216, 271; Cordelia, 183, 216–19, 253, 266–68; Edgar, 218, 236–37, 258, 261–64, 268; Edmund, 182–86, 204–5, 215, 218–225, 232, 268; Gloucester, 205, 215, 222–23, 258, 262–64; Kent, 251, 266, 268; Lear, 217–19, 222, 232, 237, 253–55, 257, 264–68. *See also* Geoffrey of Monmouth; Holinshed, Raphael
King Leir, 267
King's Men, 187–88, 209–12, 215–16, 237, 258–60, 262
Klauck, Hans-Joseph, 93n167, 99–100, 156
Klocker, Karl, 14, 178
Knight, G. Wilson, 185
Kolve, V. A., 24–25
Koopmans, Jelle, 75–76
Krug, Gustav, 277–78

labor, 12–14
Lake, Kirsopp, 33
Laroque, François, 153, 182
Latour, Bruno, 19, 37, 46n22, 57, 70n112, 76, 171–72
Lea, Henry Charles, 162n70, 186, 249
lens, 14, 155, 171–3, 209. *See also* glass; telescope
Leo, Russ, 42, 52, 54n58
Leo the Great, 145
Levack, Brian, 240
liberal arts, 82, 121, 158, 161n68, 163–64, 174–75, 203
Liberties, 227, 287
Lindberg, David, 23, 171n106–173n116, 239n46
Lipphardt, Walther, 115–16
liturgy, 4–10, 15–16, 45, 59–60, 68, 77, 106; and astronomy, 146, 148–53, 183; as theater, 102–4, 107–8, 110–29

Lombard, Peter, 125, 134
Löwith, Karl, 5n9, 281–82, 284
Lucretius, 2, 75, 80n, 164
ludus, 2, 9–10, 57, 86, 98–99, 108, 116–18, 138, 286; defined by scholastics, 5, 121–30, 134, 204
Luther, Martin, 14, 46, 48, 51, 190, 197, 275, 280

MacDonald, Michael, 209n73, 231, 254, 256–57
Macedonius, saint, 240
Machiavellianism, 90, 182, 223
madness, 228–32, 242. *See also* black bile; *hysterica passio*
Magdalene, Mary, 8, 77, 115, 120, 270n3, 273
Magi, the three, 18, 23, 116, 136, 157–64, 176, 190, 234. *See also* star of Bethlehem
magic, 4, 15–19, 22, 44, 56, 74, 143–47, 160–61, 193, 217; and theater, 195, 200, 210, 258–60; at court, 187–8, 209–14; of Leir's father, 18, 183–84; natural, 196, 199–201, 203, 207–13. *See also* disenchantment; science
magic lantern, 209
Maimonides, 233
Mainy, Richard, 254, 261
Malleus Maleficarum, 228, 241, 243n65, 252
Margery of Jourdayne, 243, 245
Marlowe, Christopher, 64, 208, 211, 233
Martianus Cappella, 137n122, 214
Marx, Karl, 11, 51, 275
Mary, Queen of Scots, 257
Mary, the Virgin, 8, 76, 77, 105, 115–16, 199, 234, 270, 273; and rape, 105, 128–30, 139, 165–73. *See also* Virgin Birth
mathematics, 30, 47, 102, 106–7, 148–51, 176
Matthew Paris, 235
Maximus of Turin, 145
Mazzio, Carla, 152
mechanical arts, 121, 125–26, 202–3, 207–9
medicine, 195, 207, 227–32, 237–41, 247–58, 266–68
melancholia, 250, 258. *See also* black bile
Menander, 53, 238
Menghi, Girolamo, 245–46
Meyer, Eduard, 11
Middleton, Thomas, 195, 218
miracles, 22, 54–59, 65, 141, 166–71, 192, 222; benefits of faking, 261–64, 286; cessation of, 183, 193–94, 229–30, 232, 237, 255–56, 262, 264; differentiated from magic, 18–19, 208–9, 217, 241,

miracles (*continued*)
  246; in Kepler, 177, 196–98; process of authentication, 3–4, 233, 248–51; Protestant attacks on, 227–32
modernity, 33, 60, 95–96, 126, 162–63; and science, 152–54, 173–81, 231–32; as Christianization, 6–25, 36–38, 44–46, 83, 142, 157, 271–86
monasticism, 3, 10, 25, 78, 95–96, 121–26; and astronomy, 149–51; in Weber, 15; and Nietzsche, 276–80. See also *Regularis concordia*; secularization: as monastic dissolution
monotheism, 9–10, 23–24, 67, 99, 156, 232, 272; and monolatry, 72; in Paul, 36, 44–45; opposition to, 52, 87–89. See also disenchantment
Moore, R. I., 131
morality plays, 6
Morgan, Theresa, 36–37
More, Thomas, 236
Moses, 17, 45–48, 91, 103, 183
Moshenska, Joe, 45, 75n129
Mullaney, Steven, 227n3, 234
Munich National Theater, 269–70
music, 9, 94–99, 102–119, 123–30, 133–42; a capella, 4, 111; medical therapy, 266–7. See also magic
Muslims, 52, 58–59, 79, 83, 162–63, 169, 235. See also Crusades
mystery plays, 6, 8, 129, 221. See also N–Town plays; Towneley Second Shepherds' Play York plays
mythography, 73–75

Nash, Thomas, 91
natural philosophy, 3, 29, 132, 153–54, 163, 187, 208–13, 228–230. See also science; magic
nature, 5, 13, 34, 73, 78, 122, 154, 228, 232–33, 272. See also natural philosophy
Nebuchadnezzar, 133, 156
Nestorius, 275
New Testament, 22, 24, 30, 33, 37, 50, 55, 63, 90–3, 144, 276; novelty of, 27, 193–94. See also Bible
Nietzsche, Friedrich, 32, 83, 87–89, 129, 163, 270, 272, 275–85; Dionysian worldview, 4–5, 93, 268; influence on Weber, 9–10, 13n31, 15, 17, 283
Nilsson, Martin, 29
North, Thomas, 90
Norton, Michael, 117–18
nova, 21, 176–77, 220. See also star of Bethlehem

Novalis, 271
N–Town plays, 128n98, 243

Odo of Tournai, 132
optics, 171–77, 180–1, 201. See also lens and telescope
Origen, 147
Orlemanski, Julie, 119n68, 240
Otto of Bamberg, 68–69
Ovid, 109, 127, 163, 168, 218

Pacificus of Verona, 173–74
Page, Christopher, 111n57, 123n78–24n80, 126–27, 129n100, 139–40
Paracelsus, 230, 232
Park, Katherine, 251
Paul, 24, 34–38, 44, 50, 60, 135, 185, 238; on astrology, 191; on idolatry, 56, 66, 68, 71–72, 158–59; on resurrection, 99–100
Peckham, Edmund and George, 259, 261
penance, 91, 94, 217, 222–25
Perkins, William, 191–2, 212, 216, 219
persuasion, 30–32, 35
Peter of Blois, 94–105, 127, 137
Peter the Chanter, 123
Petrarch, 94, 104
Pharaoh, 17, 53–55, 57–60, 95, 103, 161
Philo, 34n46, 46, 49, 52, 144
Philodemus, 37
Pierre de Tarentaise (pope Innocent V), 124
Pilate, Pontius, 60, 119, 243–45
Piscator, Johann, 50
placebo, 241, 256
Platearius, Johannes, 253
Plato, 8, 25–32, 37, 43–44, 47, 82, 137, 164, 233; *Timaeus*, 107, 252–53
Plautus, 280
play, 5, 10, 194, 204, 261–64. See also *ludus*
Pliny, 161n67, 173
Plotinus, 38–39
Plutarch, 28n26, 37, 90, 99n12, 146n15, 218
Popelard, Mickaël, 152
Porter, Roy, 265
preternatural phenomena, 171, 188, 194–96, 222, 233–34; and medicine, 228–32, 247–53; in the theater, 188, 195, 209–12, 233–34, 237, 258–62. See also demons; saints
Prodicus, 28, 36
Prometheus, 104
proof, 22, 26, 30, 32, 35, 54, 137
prophets, 63, 137, 183, 232; and idolatry, 43–44, 68, 70, 79, 143–44; and music, 109–10, 137; in Monmouth, 18, 184, 216; in Nietzsche and Weber, 16–17, 252, 282; procession of, 64, 127, 130, 132–35, 162

INDEX

Pseudo-Matthew, 68, 85, 136
Ptolemy (the astronomer), 152, 157, 163–64, 172–73, 215
Pythagoras, 8, 47, 82, 106–7, 164

Quasten, Johannes, 110
Quadrivium. *See* liberal arts

Real Presence, 59, 197
reason, 83, 91, 118, 124, 132, 167–71, 207–8, 233–34; and music, 102, 106–110; in Blumenberg, 151, 283–84; in Kant, 46–49; in Hegel, 6; in Plato, 31–32; in Nietzsche, 285
Reeves, Eileen, 173
Reformation, 5–6, 11, 14–16, 21, 44–46, 182, 217, 236, 242, 275, 284
Regularis concordia, 114–15, 120–21
resurrection, 22, 100–1, 114–20, 136, 149, 248, 267–68, 275
rhetoric, 30–32, 35–36
Richard III, 248
Ritschl, Friedrich, 280–81
Robertson, D. W., 46, 78
Roeslin, Helisaeus, 190n24, 222
Rose, Paul Lawrence, 51
Rudolf II, 187, 189, 211

sacraments, 6, 14–15, 59, 91, 149, 212, 217, 223–24
saeculum, 8–9, 52, 89–90, 158, 171, 196, 225, 241, 268; in scripture, 1–4, 11, 145, 185, 200; in Augustine, 25, 38, 51n48, 73, 79–82, 112, 148, 164; in Nietzsche, 276–83; in Peter of Blois, 95–97, 102–6; in Wagner, 270. *See also* Egypt; biblical drama: Flight from Egypt; biblical drama: Flight to Egypt; idolatry; unbelief
saints, 71, 110, 227–28, 233, 240–41, 248, 258
Saladin, 70
Schelling, F. W. J., 271, 273–75
Schiller, Friedrich, 272, 277
Schlauch, Margaret, 130n105–131, 170
Schlegel, A. W., 271–72, 277, 279
Schlegel, Friedrich, 271
Schmeller, Johann Andreas, 7, 76, 278
Schopenhaur, Arthur, 47
science, 23, 46, 152–55, 180; and magic, 159–62, 187, 200–6, 219, 66n130; and theater, 204. *See also* natural philosophy
scripture. *See* Bible; biblical drama; New Testament
Scot, Michael, 163
Scot, Reginald, 193–96, 204, 206, 230n16, 255

secularization, 1, 26, 34, 43–45, 114, 145–46, 161; of Benediktbeuern, 155, 177–81; as monastic dissolution, 5, 14, 221, 226–28, 233–36, 259, 269, 276, 284; theories of, 5–20, 77–78, 96, 103–4, 151, 272–87
secular literature, 4, 8, 112, 121, 158, 280
Seneca, 42, 120
Sergius the Stylite, 71
Shakespeare, 1, 5–7, 42, 46, 82, 90, 96, 142, 152–53, 246, 254, 271–72, 277; and King James, 187–88, 207–12, 237, 255–60; *All's Well That Ends Well*, 184, 230; *Antony and Cleopatra*, 45, 89–93; *Hamlet*, 6, 135, 211–12; *Julius Caesar*, 93; *Macbeth*, 205, 209, 212, 218–19, 232, 237, 256; *Measure for Measure*, 224; *Midsummer Night's Dream*, 218; *1 Henry VI*, 250; *Othello*, 212; *Richard III*, 223; *Romeo and Juliet*, 224; *Tempest*, 218n101; *Twelfth Night*, 212; *2 Henry IV*, 215; *2 Henry VI*, 86, 245–46; *Troilus and Cressida*, 215. *See also King Lear*
Shapiro, James, 182–83, 258
Shepherds, 135–42, 221, 278
Shugar, Deborah, 265
Shylock, 64
Sidney, Philip, 223
Simon Magus, 18
Simpson, James, 70n112, 187n15, 283n54
Slaughter of the Innocents, 42, 61, 199
Slack, Paul, 265–66
slavery, 12–13, 56–57, 81, 281
Smith, Anne, 260
Socrates, 8, 25–29, 31, 36–37, 82, 164, 283
Solberg, Emma Maggie, 64, 128, 250n84
sophistry, 27, 29, 31, 33, 35–36
Southern, R. W., 94, 102, 104
Spalding, Johann Joachim, 50
Spenser, Edmund, 220, 267
star of Bethlehem, 146–47, 176, 234–35; in drama, 42, 133, 151–58; in Kepler, 177, 189–91, 196–99, 221–22; in Nietzsche, 278
Strauss, David, 275
Stubbes, Philip, 192–93, 220
Strabo, 173
Strier, Richard, 183, 219
superstition, 16, 37, 155, 159, 179–80, 227, 249, 256; in Augustine, 43, 241; in Francis Bacon, 196; in Hippocrates, 239; in Kant, 48; in Kepler, 200–1, 207, 212; in *Lear*, 217–19
Sybil, 133, 155–57, 176, 190
Symes, Carol, 96, 114n58, 122nn75–76
Syrophanes, 74

Taylor, Charles, 21–22, 25, 31n35, 71, 231–33, 238
Tegernsee Abbey, 178. See also Antichrist
telescope, 173–76, 209. See also lens
Tetragrammaton, 34
Terence, 127, 129
Tertullian, 3, 56, 83
Thales, 47
theatrum and *ars theatrica*, 4–5, 9, 103, 108, 111–30, 147, 187, 194
Theodore the Studite, 70
Theognis, 281
Thomas of Chobham, 123–24
Tieck, Ludwig, 271, 277
Towneley Second Shepherds' Play, 140–42
tragedy, 52–54, 74, 183–85, 240, 264–65
transcendence, 12, 41, 46–47, 58, 124, 126, 183; in Kant, 46–47; of music, 106–8, 111, 277–78; of the divine, 15–16, 19–21, 27, 34, 105, 232–33, 276
treason, 241–45
Tübingen, 198, 202, 273–76, 284

Ulrici, Hermann, 6, 8
unbelief and unbelievers, 1–4, 19, 65–82, 93, 96, 114–20, 150–54, 184–85, 286; and the Virgin Birth, 165–69. See also Archisynagogus; atheism; Augustine: on unbelievers; idolatry; Jews; Muslims; *saeculum*
universities, 3, 17, 78–80, 227, 280

Vattimo, Gianni, 87
Venantius Fortunatus, 166
Venus, 78, 80, 94, 98, 129, 139, 270; the planet, 154, 157, 214, 216
Virgil, 133, 156
Virgin Birth, 18, 42, 63–65, 86, 127–28, 132, 221, 278; as fiction, 135; as fantasy, 165. See also Mary, the Virgin

Wagner, Richard, 51, 270–71, 277, 279, 282
Walker, D. P., 204n60, 232
Walter von der Vogelweide, 77n135, 163, 270
Weber, Max, 9–19, 44n17, 146–47n17, 220, 252, 273, 282n47, 283–84
West, William, 2n1, 208n71
Westman, Robert, 149n28, 187n17–188n19, 197n41, 201n53, 204n, 213n84–214n89, 222n112
Whitehead, Alfred North, 153
Whitgift, John, 232, 254–55
William of Aulnay, 95–101, 104n24
William of Blois, 96
Williams, Sara, 261
Winter, Bruce, 35
witches, 55, 91, 184–86, 195–97, 201–6, 210, 216, 229, 233, 248; floating test, 212–13; and demonic possession, 237, 240
Wittreich, Joseph, 183
Wright, Stephen, 84
World. See *saeculum*
Wotten, Henry, 213

Yahweh, 16, 33–34, 72–73, 143
York plays, 57–59, 233, 242–45
Young, Karl, 77, 133n, 153–54
Young, R. V., 183

Zysk, Jay, 14–15

www.ingramcontent.com/pod-product-compliance
Lightning Source LLC
Chambersburg PA
CBHW030524230426
43665CB00010B/754